PROBLEMS IN FOCUS SERIES

Each volume in the 'Problems in Focus' series is designed to make available to students important new work on key historical problems and periods that they encounter in their courses. Each volume is devoted to a central topic or theme, and the most important aspects of this are dealt with by specially commissioned essays from scholars in the relevant field. The editorial Introduction reviews the problem or period as a whole, and each essay provides an assessment of the particular aspect, pointing out the areas of development and controversy, and indicating where conclusions can be drawn or where further work is necessary. An annotated bibliography serves as a guide for further reading.

TITLES IN PRINT

List continues overleaf

D0322482

Problems in Focus
Series Standing Order
ISBN 0–333–71704–X hardcover
ISBN 0–333–69348–5 paperback
(outside North America only)

You can receive future titles in this series as they are published. To place a standing order please contact your bookseller or, in the case of difficulty, write to us at the address below with your name and address, the title of the series and the ISBN quoted above.

Customer Services Department, Macmillan Distribution Ltd
Houndmills, Basingstoke, Hampshire RG21 6XS, England

The English Civil War

Conflict and Contexts, 1640–49

Edited by

JOHN ADAMSON

palgrave
macmillan

Selection, Introduction and editorial matter © John Adamson 2009;
Chapter 1 © David Scott 2009; Chapter 2 © Anthony Milton 2009;
Chapter 3 © Jason Peacey 2009; Chapter 4 © Jane Ohlmeyer 2009;
Chapter 5 © Allan I. Macinnes 2009; Chapter 6 © Clive Holmes 2009;
Chapter 7 © Ian Gentles 2009; Chapter 8 © Philip Baker 2009.

First published 2009 by
PALGRAVE MACMILLAN

Palgrave Macmillan in the UK is an imprint of Macmillan Publishers
Limited, registered in England, company number 785998, of
Houndmills, Basingstoke, Hampshire RG21 6XS.

Palgrave Macmillan in the US is a division of St Martin's Press LLC,
175 Fifth Avenue, New York, NY 10010.

Palgrave Macmillan is the global academic imprint of the above
companies and has companies and representatives throughout the
world.

Palgrave® and Macmillan® are registered trademarks in the United
States, the United Kingdom, Europe and other countries.

ISBN-13: 978–0–333–98655–4 hardback
ISBN-10: 0–333–98655–5   hardback
ISBN-13: 978–0–333–98656–1 paperback
ISBN-10: 0–333–98656–3   paperback

This book is printed on paper suitable for recycling and made from
fully managed and sustained forest sources. Logging, pulping and
manufacturing processes are expected to conform to the
environmental regulations of the country of origin.

A catalogue record for this book is available from the British Library.

A catalog record for this book is available from the Library of Congress.

10   9   8   7   6   5   4   3   2   1
18 17 16 15 14 13 12 11 10 09

Printed and bound in China

Contents

Abbreviations

Abbott, *Cromwell*	Wilbur Cortez Abbott (ed.), *The Writings and Speeches of Oliver Cromwell*, 4 vols (1937–47; reprinted Oxford, 1988)
APS	T. Thomson and C. Innes (eds), *The Acts of Parliament of Scotland*, 12 vols (Edinburgh, 1814–75)
BL	British Library, London
Bodl. Lib.,	Bodleian Library, University of Oxford
CJ	*Commons Journals*
CSPD	*Calendar of State Papers, Domestic*
CSPI	*Calendar of State Papers, Ireland*
CSPV	*Calendar of State Papers, Venetian*
Gardiner, *Constitutional Documents*	Samuel Rawson Gardiner, *Constitutional Documents of the Puritan Revolution, 1625–60* (Oxford, 1906)
HMC	Historical Manuscripts Commission
LJ	*Lords Journals, England*
LJI	*Lords Journals, Ireland*
NA	National Archives, Kew
NAS	National Archives of Scotland
SP	State Papers
TCD	Trinity College, Dublin

Notes on the Contributors

John Adamson is Fellow in History, Peterhouse, University of Cambridge.

Philip Baker is Senior Research Officer at the Centre for Metropolitan History, Birkbeck College, University of London.

Ian Gentles is Professor of History, Glendon College, York University, Toronto and Visiting Professor of History at Tyndale University College.

Clive Holmes is Fellow and Tutor at Lady Margaret Hall, University of Oxford.

Allan I. Macinnes is Professor of Early Modern History at the University of Strathclyde.

Anthony Milton is Professor of History at the University of Sheffield.

Jane Ohlmeyer is Erasmus Smith's Professor of Modern History at Trinity College, Dublin.

Jason Peacey is Lecturer in History at University College, London.

David Scott is a Senior Research Fellow with the 1640–60 Section of the *History of Parliament*, London.

Introduction: High Roads and Blind Alleys – The English Civil War and its Historiography

JOHN ADAMSON

In Britain's long, supposedly stately progress from medieval monarchy to modern liberal state, the twenty years between 1640 and 1660 have always stood out as a singular and violent exception. For almost a decade from 1640, the usual points of reference by which the peoples of the Stuart realms used to orientate themselves – in religion, politics, and government – were thrown out of alignment by the storms of civil war. Some were destroyed altogether. In the great moment of climacteric, what Cromwell termed 'that memorable year 1648[–9]', the very foundations of the state seemed to have been dissolved. For some, it presaged nothing less than the end of the world, the moment when Christ would come again to earth and reign in glory with his Saints.[1]

Amid the *sturm und drang* of the Apocalyptic visionaries, however, there were less dramatic experiences which nevertheless imprinted themselves no less forcefully on collective memory. In all three kingdoms, the collapse of the old order permitted the empowerment of men who had never expected to hold the reins of government, or even to have a voice in the public realm.[2] In England and Wales, men of ability from relatively humble origins found their way onto the county committees – the instruments of the Parliament's administration of the localities – and even into the highest counsels of the state, and went about the tasks of governing, assessing, taxing, and fining their knightly and noble neighbours in a way that would have been unthinkable before the Civil Wars.[3] Nor could anyone any longer pretend, after the tumultuous 1640s, that 'there was a unified political culture to which everyone, deep down, subscribed'.[4] The effects of the 'troubles' were no less marked on the relations between the three kingdoms. Scots, accustomed for centuries to military domination by their bossy southern cousins, found themselves with the tables turned, and able to intervene militarily in both England and Ireland in a bid to recast both neighbour kingdoms in a distinctively Scottish mould.[5] Likewise, in Ireland, at least until the Cromwellian reconquest of 1649–51, large sections of the Gaelic Catholic majority experienced the exhilaration of freedom of worship, and even, for a time, the hope that they too might be the masters, under God, of their own destiny.[6]

Amid the maelstrom, men and women searched for points of reference that would give some measure of coherence and comprehensibility to this disordered and often frightening world. Some found it, with relative dispassion, in history – by seeking parallels between present and past. Others discerned it in the supernatural, in signs and portents that presaged yet further upheavals to come; still others in the millenarian conviction that the conflicts of the Stuart kingdoms were the outward manifestations of a far larger, but otherwise invisible, cosmic struggle – between the 'mystery of iniquity' and the angelic host – which presaged the Second Coming and the imminent rule of Christ and his Saints.[7] Almost all turned in some way, and at some point, to the Bible, finding in it – according to the reader's disposition – injunctions to acceptance of the Lord's providential judgements on the world; stern admonishments to action; or sometimes simply a sense of bafflement, in which the deity's intentions for the world seemed depressingly inscrutable and opaque.

No change, political or religious, was morally neutral. To the self-styled 'godly', the destruction of such adornments to churches as stained-glass windows and the statues of angels and saints was a necessary 'purging of the land' of the relics of Popery;[8] to others, with equal conviction, it was wanton destruction, an instance of the lawlessness and fanaticism that were certain to run unchecked, should the English Parliament ever prevail in its contest with the king. One man's idea of the New Jerusalem was his neighbour's idea of Bedlam. Nor were these divisions merely symptomatic of the polarization between 'Royalist' and 'Parliamentarian' – or, according to taste, between the 'king's party' and the 'rebels'. For the profundity and complexity of these fissures exerted a destabilizing influence on the political and religious structures of all three kingdoms well beyond the Restoration of 1660, when there was an attempt to impose on the Stuart realms a simulacrum of the political order that had existed *ante bellum*.[9] The longevity and exact political consequences of those divisions may be a matter of debate; what is not in dispute, however, is that from 1660 well into the mid-twentieth century, the crisis decades of 1640–60 became the prime historical reference-point for British politics and, with different emphases, for Irish politics as well.[10] The cry '1641 is come again', heard during the Exclusion Crisis of 1679–81, resounded into the eighteenth century, and was apprehended either as a dire warning of the imminence of social anarchy and civil war or as an exhilarating rallying-cry to a new generation of reformists, intent on resuming the struggle for 'liberty' begun in 1640–41.[11] Indeed, after 1660, it was difficult to refer to the events of the mid-century crisis without the very choice of words becoming an implicit declaration of Civil-War allegiance.[12] Some, of course, strove at anodyne neutrality by referring to the conflict as 'the late troubles'.[13] But to refer to the 'Great Rebellion' was, implicitly, to assign moral right to the Royalists; and, as late as the 1930s, even the seemingly even-handed term 'Civil War', when used as an alternative to 'the Great Rebellion', had partisan implications. By declining to cast the Parliamentarians as rebels, its user hinted at latter-day Roundhead sympathies. And the tradition of regarding the royalist and parliamentarian parties of the 1640s as the intellectual progenitors of the Tory–Whig divide remained a powerful influence in the formation of political identity in Britain well into the twentieth century.[14]

Even with the advent of professional, supposedly dispassionate, 'scientific history' at the end of the nineteenth century, these choices of language have rarely been uninfluenced by present-centred political assumptions and preoccupations. The Gladstonian Liberalism of S. R. Gardiner, for example – the pioneering Victorian historian whose work remains the standard narrative of the war years – profoundly influenced his view that 'the Puritan Revolution' was not only morally justified, but also laid the foundations for England's rise to greatness as a liberal, democratic power.[15] The advent of Marxist theories of revolution, from the late nineteenth century to their apogee in the 1950s and 1960s, provided yet another explanatory framework within which the choice of terms to describe the circumstances of the 1640s became a badge of partisan allegiance.[16] By the 1980s and 1990s, repudiation of the term 'revolution' to describe the events of the 1640s and 1650s almost invariably signalled a rejection of Marxist (and social-change) modes of historical interpretation more generally[17] – albeit that the anti-Marxists themselves constituted a relatively broad and politically heterogeneous coalition.

This element of political engagement doubtless accounts for much of the perennial vitality – and intermittent acerbity – of Civil-War historiography. As Blair Worden has argued, every generation re-fights the

English Civil War after its own fashion.[18] Viewed over the *longue durée*, however, these contests can present a slightly dispiriting spectacle. Competing schools of interpretation have tended to anathematize their competitors with an almost religious ferocity. And as the radical revisionism of one generation has been seen to become the orthodoxy of the next, only to be supplanted – in its turn – by the ideas and interpretations of yet another generation of Young Turks, there are moments when Civil-War historiography seems to be condemned to an endless dialectical to-and-fro, in which hopes of a heightened understanding of the past are raised, only to be dashed by the next incoming interpretative wave. As Sir Keith Thomas has observed, at the beginning of the twenty-first century – after a hundred years or more of the 'professional' study of the Civil War – the historiography of the 1640s and 1650s seems more fragmented and resistant to synthesis than ever.[19]

This chapter will attempt two related tasks. First, it will seek to offer some answers as to why the historiography of the Civil War, at the end of the past 100 years of modern research, should remain so disjointed. This entails going further back, and looking in rather greater detail at the intellectual foundations of the present-day edifice of interpretation than is perhaps usual in an introduction to a volume of new interpretative essays. It also requires us (within the strictly limited confines such an essay allows) not just to examine what has been written about the course of the war itself, but at times to broaden our focus and consider the changing theories about its causes as well; for it is often the underlying assumptions about the conflict's causation that have determined the interpretation of the war itself. Brisk and over-schematic as such an exercise necessarily must be, it is one that is worth attempting nevertheless; for – to adapt an over-familar dictum – those who cannot remember their historiography may well be condemned to repeat it.[20] And before introducing the essays in this present volume, it is as well to understand the route we have travelled to reach our present position. Only then can we begin to appreciate how, in many respects, key elements of the prevailing 'modern' accounts of the Civil Wars remain in interpretative thrall to an only partially acknowledged historiographical legacy of the past.

This, in turn, prompts my second question: if a new synthesis (assuming such to be possible) were to be offered, of what would its elements consist? This is the great riddle currently confronting historians of the mid-century crisis in the Stuart kingdoms; and neither this introduction, nor even this book, presumes to offer a single, definitive answer. But as the dust of almost a century of near-continuous controversy begins, if not quite to settle, then at least to become less opaque, some of the major components of that answer are starting to emerge – and many, if necessarily not all, will be discussed in the essays which follow.

Before turning to these, however, that unavoidable question: how did we reach the current apparent impasse?

I GARDINER AND HIS GHOST

The modern historiography of the 1640s crisis in the Stuart monarchies effectively begins in the 1880s, with the publication of Samuel Rawson Gardiner's *History of the Great Civil War, 1642–9*, in three volumes between 1886 and 1891.[21] Influenced by the new German philosophy of empirical, 'scientific history', Gardiner famously claimed that 'he who studies the history of the past will be of greater service to the society of the present in proportion as he leaves [contemporary preoccupations] out of account';[22] and after the hectoring partisanship of the generation that immediately preceded him (and especially the exclamation-filled pages of Carlyle), his writing does indeed seem coolly detached and even-handed by comparison. Though his sympathies were clearly with the Roundheads as the party of constitutional progress, he could nevertheless discern merit, even heroism, in some Royalists;[23] and, with his own penchant for Victorian High Church liturgy, he could look comprehendingly, if never quite sympathetically, on the reformist ambitions of Archbishop Laud.[24]

Gardiner also outlined an explanatory framework which seems, in twenty-first-century retrospect, enormously ambitious in range and no less prescient in having identified the 'great themes' that historians, during the ensuing century or more, would think it relevant to address. Of course, Gardiner's questions have gone in and out of fashion. At some points, often for extended periods, they have been forgotten entirely; at others, those same questions have been re-asked, and even held out as novel advances in scholarship, by enquirers seemingly oblivious to the fact that they have been posed before. But Gardiner's themes have never quite gone away; and, since they are arguably more influential on Civil-War historiography at the beginning of the twenty-first century than at any point since the 1890s, it is worth reminding ourselves of their *fons et origo*, and of just how perceptive they were.

The first of these themes is the interdependency of the English, Scottish, and Irish narratives of the 1640s. To Gardiner, it seemed self-evident that only through an integrated study of politics in each of the Stuart realms could 'irresponsible government in the three kingdoms' be understood.[25] A century before the 1990s, when the discovery (or rather rediscovery) of the 'British Problem' was being hailed as a major new insight into our understanding of the mid-century crisis,[26] Gardiner had long since been fully aware of the way in which developments in one of Charles I's kingdoms had knock-on effects in the other two. His accounts of the Covenanter revolt in Scotland in the late 1630s; of the origins of the Irish rebellion; and of the influence of the Scots in the English peace negotiations of the mid-1640s — to cite but a few instances — are all predicated on the assumption that the historian must be the master of all three national narratives, and alive to the points of interconnection and reciprocal influence between them. These were injunctions which, when dusted off and reissued, with only minor modification, in the 1990s, seemed the last word in cutting-edge 'Revisionism'.[27]

Nor is this quest for an integrated 'British' or 'three-kingdoms' history the only aspect of late Victorian historiography that anticipates the work of the post-1970s Revisionists. Partly because of this three-kingdoms approach, Gardiner placed heavy emphasis on religion as a common source of conflict between, and within, each of the three Stuart kingdoms. In a way that foreshadows more recent scholarly emphasis on the 'innovatory' quality of Laudianism as the principal source of conflict within the British polity[28] (and, to a lesser extent, in Ireland as well), Gardiner pointed to the emergence, in the reigns of James I and Charles I, of 'a new and rising school amongst the clergy [the Arminians, who] threw [themselves] back on the teaching of the more conservative reformers' and thus brought themselves into conflict with 'the country gentlemen [who] were Calvinists almost to a man'.[29] It was the 'impatient violence'[30] of Archbishop Laud, the new anti-Calvinists' chief backer, which made some form of conflict inevitable.[31]

Likewise, Gardiner saw the king's party during the 1640s as no less worthy of study than the Parliamentarians. True, he shone his torch on them as often to reveal their weaknesses of character, personal vices, and enthralment to the essentially regressive cause of 'personal monarchy'. But he was also aware that the king's party was never homogeneous in structure or belief, and he had a keen sense of the variety of 'royalisms' — plural — that were to be found within it.

How useful this Gardinerian agenda may be will be considered later in this introduction. In historiographical retrospect, however, perhaps the striking feature of the period between the publication of his multi-volume *Great Civil War* in the 1880s and the mid-1970s is how comprehensively so many, if by no means all, of Gardiner's insights and approaches disappeared from view (the multiple-kingdoms approach to British politics most thoroughly of all). This prompts an obvious question: why? – a query which acquires all the greater relevance when we consider, as shortly we will, how many of Gardiner's themes were to be reprised in the last decades of the twentieth century – indeed were to become the hits of the 'revisionist' 1970s and 1980s.

II WEBER AND THE PROBLEM OF THE DISAPPEARING ROYALISTS

Perhaps the obvious, certainly the most frequently proffered, explanation lies in the massive influence exerted on early and mid-twentieth-century academic life by Marxism.[32] Yet, there was another mode of historical explanation which made its mark on British historiography earlier, more subtly, and arguably more pervasively, and which also originated in the German-speaking academic world: the new sociological theories of Max Weber (1864–1920) and his circle. And here no aspect of his thought was more influential than his version of the theory, already widely current in late nineteenth-century Germany, that major historical events could be explained as the consequences of social change.[33] First advanced in a mature form in Weber's *The Protestant Ethic and the Spirit of Capitalism* (1904),[34] this work famously postulated a linkage between the middle classes' obvious commercial and political success, on the one hand, and the spirit of enterprise and achievement engendered by Protestantism, on the other. Such theories were not, of course, unique to Weber's thought. Well before the publication of Weber's *Protestant Ethic*, British Civil-War historians had already embraced the Weberian *zeitgeist* and were invoking it to explain a variety of problems in the study of mid seventeenth-century Britain: from the 'backwardness' of Ireland in the 1640s (attributable, in Weberian terms, to its lack of a Protestant middle class) to the success of the New Model Army (attributable to its repudiation of 'feudal' aristocratic control, and the zeal of Cromwell's 'russet-coated captains' – drawn from the 'middling sort').

Ironically, one of the reasons why such ideas took root with such swiftness in British (and, to a lesser extent, American) academic life after they were first popularized in the decade immediately after the First World War (1914–18) was that the ground for them had been partly prepared by Gardiner himself. German-speaking and well acquainted with the major trends in German sociological writing already by the 1880s, Gardiner had adopted a version of Weberian social-change theory – a sort of Weberianism *avant la lettre* – that profoundly influenced his own account of the causes and course of the Civil War: namely, the conviction that the Civil War was a conflict between a declining feudal order, represented by the monarchy and nobility, and a rising and increasingly confident gentry – energized and emancipated from its feudal habits of deference by Calvinist Protestantism. (Indeed, this was the one element of Gardiner's explanatory scheme that was to survive, virtually unchallenged, until the mid-twentieth century.)

Gardiner's belief in the 'progressive' power of Protestantism emerges perhaps most clearly in his attitude towards the Confederates in Ireland: the Catholics who supported the Rebellion of 1641 and sought to create an autonomous government, under the Stuart Crown. To Gardiner, this insurrection was a rebellion against the laws of History itself; for in seeking to create an independent Catholic state, the Irish were 'throwing themselves athwart that stream of European progress, of which the impelling force was Protestantism'.[35] Conversely, Scotland, the heartland of the initial revolt against Stuart rule, represented the antithesis of Ireland's anti-progressivism; for there, the 'impelling force' of radical Protestantism enabled the Scottish middle classes 'to throw off the yoke of the feudal nobles and ultimately to assert their own predominance'.[36] In England, this radical Protestantism took the form of Puritanism, and likewise found its strongest adherents among the middle class (in the form of the landed gentry). Puritanism, then, provided the assertive, energizing and 'progressive' force that would sweep away the English *ancien régime* during the 1640s and lay the foundations of the political liberties that were to be consolidated in the Glorious Revolution of 1688–9.

Such a conceptualization of the Civil War and its causes in terms of contrasted 'dynamic' (progressive) and 'static' (retrogressive) elements within the English polity inevitably made for a distinctly one-sided conflict, a one-sidedness for which Weberian sociological analysis seemed to provide a convincingly modern and 'scientific' rationale. One party, the Parliamentarians – predominantly the Puritan gentry – had Progress on their side; the other, the 'king's party' – the Royalists – were placing themselves 'athwart' the stream of 'European progress'. And the widespread acceptance of this analysis for much of the last century –

both in Britain and, with even greater enthusiasm, in triumphantly middle-class, largely Protestant, America – has had a profoundly skewing influence on the historical profession's estimation of what aspects of the Civil War were worthy of study, the consequences of which are only now beginning to be redressed.

For much of the period between 1870 and 1970, Civil-War historiography was concerned overwhelmingly with the struggle's long-term winners. This meant, in social terms, the gentry in general, and the puritan gentry in particular; in institutional terms, the House of Commons and the (necessarily puritan) leaders who marshalled these progressive forces and made them an effective political force.[37] The series of countervailing 'retrogressive elements' – historical groups that either impeded this progressive dynamic, or were ultimately vanquished by it – could therefore be consigned to the periphery of the historical profession's concerns. These constituted an extensive list: the nobility and its institutional embodiment, the House of Lords;[38] the royal court (except in so far as it exemplified extravagance and corruption); the Laudians of the 1630s; and the Royalists of the 1640s – among others.[39] These last, in particular, were consigned to a scholarly No Man's Land, whence they emerged – if at all – as heroic, lace-collared Cavaliers in the pages of Edwardian and later romantic novels.

At the time, these choices and emphases appeared to have been soundly made. For they seemed to be corroborated by developments in contemporary politics. Lloyd George's protracted struggle with the House of Lords, for instance, a contest which culminated in the crisis over the 'People's Budget' of 1910, provided Sir Charles Firth (Gardiner's friend and continuator) with the occasion for his opportunistically timed monograph on an earlier and equally progress-obstructing upper House. In his *The House of Lords during the Civil War* (1910),[40] Firth portrayed the 1640s parliamentarian lords as reactionary, obstructive, and the butt of ridicule; in other words, in almost exactly the same terms in which the pro-Lloyd George press was presenting the obstructive Tory peerage of 1910. And he also provided the contemporary Lords with an implicit warning as to the fate that awaited them – abolition (as in 1649) – should they, too, set themselves 'athwart' the High Road of constitutional advance. As Firth noted ominously in the book's preface, he set forth the 'opinions and arguments [of the 1640s Parliament-men] for the instruction of their descendants'.[41]

What influence Firth's book had on the crisis of 1910 is unclear. On historical scholarship, however, the judgement of the most esteemed

Civil-War historian of the day was definitive. The question of the nobility's role in the 1640s was all but closed down as a subject worthy of serious scholarly enquiry for the next fifty years.[42]

By the early twentieth century, then, a series of themes in Civil-War historiography was acquiring broad scholarly assent in Britain and on the other side of the Atlantic as well: the 'progressive' influence of radical Protestantism; the central importance of the gentry (and their political representatives, the Commons) as the promoters of this transformative creed; and the reactionary character of the king, the nobility, and the Royalists as opponents of social and political progress. These considerations defined historians' sense of who fought the war, and why. There was, of course, no shortage of debate about points of detail. But the essential lineaments of the broader interpretation were beginning to be clearly defined.

The first few decades of the twentieth century – when the influence of the 'new' German sociology became ever stronger on British academic life, and, with it, the quest for social causes of the Civil Wars of the 1640s – might well have been the moment for a phase of revisionist reaction. Yet, despite criticism of Gardiner's methods and conclusions, an effective assault was never made.[43] Paradoxically, the new Weber-inspired methodology seemed to corroborate so many of the key elements of Gardiner's account of England's experience in the early seventeenth century that its overall effect was not to subvert the older political–constitutional narrative but to endow it with a new vigour. And no one did more to introduce the English-speaking scholarly world to Weber's theories, and to apply them to the origins and course of the Civil War, than R. H. Tawney – the London-based historian and Christian socialist, whose ideas were to dominate the study of early-modern England into the 1960s.[44]

Tawney's study of *Religion and the Rise of Capitalism*, first published in 1926 and continuously in print ever since, assimilated the new Weberian theories about the linkage between Protestantism and the economic dynamism of the middle classes to the older Gardinerian tradition of the Civil War as a gentry-led, constitutionally progressive 'Puritan Revolution'.[45] This was not an uncritical adaptation of Weber's ideas, not least because Tawney believed that the rise of capitalism had been deeply destructive of a set of older, more benign social relations. But in Weber's understanding of Protestantism as the engine of bourgeois economic advancement he found a new and powerfully affirmative dimension to the Gardiner–Firth thesis that the gentry and the

Commons had been the forces of constitutional progress. The old nineteenth-century Whig–Protestant interpretation underwent a gleamingly modern twentieth-century makeover, and was reissued in Weberian sociological guise.

The effect of this was to refocus the explanatory spotlight, more sharply than ever before, on the most zealous sorts of Protestants – the Puritans – as the prime agents of political and economic change. The grand theme in Tawney's account, as in Gardiner's before him, was modernization: England's transition from a deferential, feudal, superstition-filled world to one which was individualist, capitalist, and (in comparison with the dark days of Popery) rational, even sceptical, as well. Tawney was unequivocal:

> The growth, triumph, and transformation of the Puritan spirit was the most fundamental movement of the seventeenth century. Puritanism . . . was the true English Reformation, and it is from its struggle against the old order that an England which is unmistakably modern emerges.[46]

The critically important aspect of this transformation was not so much its theological as its social dimension. For, of course, the men who embraced this modernizing 'Puritan spirit' were the middling ranks of English society:

> the chosen seat of the Puritan spirit seemed to be those classes in society which combined economic independence, education, and a certain decent pride in their status, revealed at once in a determination to live their own lives, without truckling to earthly superiors. . . . Such . . . were some of the gentry. Such, conspicuously, were the yeomen . . . especially in the freeholding counties of the east.[47]

During the 'formative period of Puritanism, before the Civil War', its adherents developed a consciousness of their separateness – so the argument ran – and this arose 'not merely by birth and breeding, but by [the Puritans'] social habits, their business discipline, the whole bracing atmosphere of their moral life, [and their apartness] from a Court which they believed to be godless and an aristocracy which they knew to be spendthrift'.[48] This inner sense of confidence, Tawney contended, made the Puritan 'a natural republican, for there is none on earth that he can own as master'.[49]

With its elegant synthesis of religious, economic and political analysis, Weberian thought (as popularized by Tawney) defined the agenda for Civil-War historiography for the next half-century. From the 1920s, Stuart politics and society could be regarded more than ever as a series of antitheses in which each progressive element in society – be it class, ideology, or institutions – had its retrogressive errant twin, destined, sooner or later, for the historical scrap-heap. Hence, contrasted with the industrious upwardly-mobile gentry (and, later, the 'middling sort', aspiring to be minor gentry) was the 'spendthrift', declining aristocracy. Liberating, gentry-empowering Puritanism confronted authoritarian, clericalist Laudianism; the virtuous 'Country' stood in opposition to the 'godless Court'; and so on. Every locus of virtue had its corresponding repository of vice; each forward-moving element of progress was opposed by its own laggardly agent of reaction. These were the polar opposites that eventually found violent and bloody expression in 1642 in the confrontation between Parliamentarian and Royalist.

Such tidy dualities almost invited parody, and it was not long before they received it. In 1930 – just four years after Tawney's *Religion and the Rise of Capitalism* – W. C. Sellar and R. J. Yeatman offered their justly famous summary of the Weber–Tawney thesis in *1066 and All That*: the two sides, quite simply, were

the Cavaliers (Wrong but Wromantic) and the Roundheads (Right but Repulsive).[50]

And it is perhaps not coincidental that Weber's *Protestant Ethic*, the work that had been Tawney's starting point, made its first appearance in English translation, with a foreword by Tawney himself, in the same year as *1066 and All That*.[51]

Inevitably, there were casualties. The new emphasis on the *social* contextualization of religion (Puritanism as the creed of the enterprising gentry and thrifty 'middling sort') opened up wide possibilities for various reductionist interpretations of religion: at their crudest, a discounting of spirituality and theological conviction as an authentic mover of human action, and its reduction to a series of convenience beliefs, largely adopted to advance the social and economic circumstances of the believer.[52] We were on the way to regarding religion as little more than an emotionalized version of economic self-interest – with even zealous Puritanism regarded as scarcely more than a means of 'social control'.[53]

As we shall see, many of the themes which were to emerge as dominant in the historiography of the 1980s and 1990s were a belated (and often eloquent) rebuttal of arguments that owed their currency to these early twentieth-century developments.[54]

But if religion were one casualty of the interwar emphasis on the social causation of great events,[55] so, too, was Gardiner's emphasis on the need for a 'British' – indeed, 'three-kingdoms' – context for the understanding of the political crisis of the 1640s. For if the causes of the breakdown of what Tawney termed the 'old order' were largely societal (and hence the explanatory focus was on which groups in society were rising, and at whose expense), it followed that the appropriate context for any explanation was unlikely to extend further than the nation-state – the entity that provided society with its territorial, institutional, and cultural boundaries. Moreover, as almost all historians agreed, the most important and influential nation-state within the Stuart realms was England. Their enquiries therefore turned inwards, from the 1920s, to the *intra*-societal tensions and conflicts that made for an emphatically *English* Civil War. To query whether Scotland or Ireland might have had a major role in the crisis of the 1640s – or to consider the wider European diplomatic networks in which all three Stuart kingdoms were enmeshed – was to ask a *question mal posée*.

And by the 1930s both these tendencies – a reductionist view of religion and an Anglocentrism that virtually ruled out of account the late Victorians' British and internationalist concerns – were about to be reinforced by the powerful, if rather belated, impact of Marxism on British intellectual life.

By the time of Marx's death in 1883, his reputation was principally as an economic writer 'who had predicted the collapse of capitalism through successively more severe crises of underconsumption'.[56] It took almost half a century for his writings to be translated into English and for their implications to make their mark on an ever more monoglot British intellectual culture; and, above all, for his predictions to be vindicated (or so it seemed) by recent events. The Russian Revolution of October 1917; the stock market crash of 1929; the Great Depression (which looked, to many, as though it were the collapse of capitalism that Marx had foretold): all these lent credibility to a Marxist view of contemporary events – and, in consequence, to events in the past as well.[57] From the 1930s, the English Civil War and the French Revolution became, in John Burrow's words, the

test cases for the Marxist conception of history. . . . If these
conformed to the Marxist category of 'bourgeois revolutions', sweeping up the debris of feudalism and paving the way for the advent of
capitalism (as the necessary preliminary to its own eventual collapse),
[then] there was all the more reason to expect that collapse – and thus
the final victory of the proletariat, apparently presaged by the
Bolshevik Revolution.[58]

The English Civil War and its causes thus became a sort of laboratory
in which, it was believed, the truth of Marx's historical theory could be
tested and demonstrated to the world. In Christopher Hill's short
polemic of 1940, timed for the tercentenary of what he pointedly
termed *The English Revolution, 1640*,[59] the experiment was pronounced a
success. The Civil War was declared to satisfy Marx's criteria for a
bourgeois revolution, with the rising 'progressive gentry' assailing, and
eventually sweeping away, the last remnants[60] of England's feudal *ancien
régime*.[61]

In practice, however, the concerns of the 'new' Marxist-influenced
history of the 1940s and 1950s – in particular, its preoccupations with
class-conflict between rising gentry and declining nobility, with the
House of Commons as the champion of bourgeois interests against
Lords and Crown, and with long-term economic analysis as the
explanation for political change – mapped closely onto the older
Weberian–Tawneyite agenda for analysing the causes and course of
the Civil War; so closely, in fact, that it was often difficult to determine
where Weber's influence (as mediated through Tawney) ended and
Marx's (as mediated through Hill and a dozen others)[62] began. The
two Germanic tributaries converged to form early-modern British
history's intellectual mainstream,[63] and over the following decades it
was a minority of historians who contended against its powerful
current.[64]

One of the immediate consequences of this alteration in Britain's
intellectual topography was a narrowing yet further, from the 1930s, of
the historical terrain thought relevant to the explanation of the crisis of
the 1640s. If Tawney had had little time for Gardiner's three-kingdoms
explanations, still less did Hill and his mid-twentieth-century
contemporaries. If what needed to be explained was an 'English revolution', then the obvious place to find that explanation, it seemed, lay
in the social and economic conditions of England's 'middle ranks',
and in their natural habitat: the English counties.

III THE QUEST FOR AN OPPOSITIONIST GENTRY

For the next fifty years, from the mid-1920s to the late 1970s, it was the gentry and the social units in which they were to be found, their partic- ular 'county communities', that provided the core subjects of research, and the chief topics of academic controversy, for historians seeking to elucidate the causes and true nature of the 'Puritan Revolution'.[65] Its starting point was the testing of the Tawneyite hypothesis that the gentry had been rising economically and gaining in power at the expense of a declining nobility (a case first stated explicitly in an article of 1941).[66] And testing quickly turned to attempted refutation, with the most power- ful challenge coming, in 1953, from Hugh Trevor-Roper, the twentieth- century's most able and agile historical controversialist.[67] But by the time the full-scale scholarly battle was joined, Tawney's original contention had acquired a new polemical significance. Against the back- ground of the Cold War, the matter of whether a *social* explanation could be found for the English Revolution became, at its extremes, a battle- ground for Marxist and anti-Marxist, in which colleague smote colleague, usually in the pages of the *Economic History Review*, with a vehemence rarely matched before or since.

Yet for all its asperity, one can question whether this debate was ever really a contest between two definitively different interpretations of the Civil War, still less (despite Trevor-Roper's idiosyncratic Conservatism) a simple Cold-War confrontation between Marxists and their Tory (and Liberal) opponents. While both sides argued over which *elements* within the gentry were responsible for the 'Revolution', and whether their financial fortunes impinged materially on their choice of allegiance, neither side questioned the fundamental assumption (which had stood uncontested since Gardiner) that it was the members of the gentry, and the Puritan gentry in particular, who were the agents of 'progressive' political change.[68] It was this social group which challenged the régime of Charles I: first politically, in the Parliaments of 1640; then militarily, in the war of 1642. And finally, in 1645, it was the gentry's most zealous and energetic element – the radical Puritans, Tawney's 'natural republicans' – who created the New Model Army, the radical force that eventually swept away the last vestiges of an already enfeebled monarchy and House of Lords in the Revolution of 1649.

Even Trevor-Roper, the scourge of the Tawneyite Left and their 'rising gentry', seems to have accepted with only occasional demur many of these canonical elements of the Gardinerian narrative.[69] The great 'storm over the gentry', for all its ferocity, was only marginally a clash between two comprehensively different accounts of the causes of the Civil War. Right until its vituperative end, it remained an essentially intra-denominational controversy between the enthusiastic Weberians of the socialist Left (Tawney, Lawrence Stone, and Christopher Hill) and the sceptical Weberians of the liberal Right (pre-eminently Trevor-Roper and the American historian J. H. Hexter).[70] Indeed, it may well have been because the combatants were actually in agreement over so many fundamental articles of historical faith that their disputes over questions of explanation acquired their almost theological asperity.[71]

Paradoxically, then, the impact of the twenty years of 'gentry controversy' – from Tawney's initial article of 1941 to J. H. Hexter's rejoinder of 1961[72] – was not to direct Civil-War historiography towards pastures new, but to redirect it back along the already well-trodden paths first defined by Tawney back in the 1920s. More than ever, the gentry occupied centre-stage, even if controversy still raged as to whether and which of its component groups were rising or falling, and what were the various 'factors' that disposed them towards, or against, Parliament in the 1640s.

But there seemed to be a solution. What would answer these questions once and for all, it appeared, was detailed case studies of individual counties and the particular gentry families within them. Methodologically, the new approach married a type of Namierism (historical analysis on the basis of intensive and multiple biographical research) with Weberian social theory.[73] Only by this mode of analysis, it was suggested, would historians be able to elucidate what correlations (if any) there were between the gentry's social and economic standing, on the one side, and its political and religious allegiances, on the other. Indeed the 'gentrification' of Civil-War historiography reached its apogee in the 1960s and 1970s, when it was proposed that English politics could best be understood in terms of a series of almost autonomous 'county communities', and the completion of a county study – *Anothershire and the English Civil War* – became an almost required rite of passage for any scholar aiming to be taken seriously as a historian of early-modern England.[74]

And if social forces were responsible for the 'revolution' – whether that were located chronologically in 1640–41 or in 1648–9 – there was an equally strong imperative to seek out the real 'revolutionaries', the men who drove on the radical reformist agenda of the 1640s and early 1650s, and to explain their conduct in similarly socially referenced terms. This quest motivated two of the most distinguished political analyses to emerge from the 1970s: David Underdown's meticulous study of the army's *coup d'état* of December 1648, *Pride's Purge*, and Austin Woolrych's monograph on the nominated ('Barebone's') Parliament[75] of 1653.[76] Both 'doubled as extended tests of a variety of social characterisations, and even explanations, of the Revolution'.[77]

Complementing this intensive search for a rising gentry was an equally Tawneyite desire to investigate the gentry's moral and class enemies: that 'Court which [Puritans] believed to be godless and . . . aristocracy which they knew to be spendthrift', of which Tawney had written back in 1926.[78] These were the two sides of the same coin, since one of the major reasons for the nobility's spendthrift ways, as for the economic and political decline that these habits helped hasten, was the malign allure of the royal court. From the early 1960s, Perez Zagorin argued for the alienation of the noble-dominated 'Court' from the gentry-dominated 'Country' – a word that many localist historians regarded by then as synonymous with the 'county community'[79] – in a way that was complemented, on a far more ambitious (indeed magnificent) scale, by Lawrence Stone's pioneering work on the political, military, and moral decline of the English nobility, *The Crisis of the Aristocracy, 1558–1641*, published three years later.[80] Not surprisingly, the timeframe of Stone's study of aristocratic decline paralleled almost to the year that of Tawney's 1941 essay on the gentry's rise (1558–1640), and reached a broadly supportive conclusion. Although the cracks in the 'rising gentry' hypothesis were already evident by the mid-1960s,[81] the reality of a declining nobility, Stone contended, was no longer in doubt. The abolition of the House of Lords in 1649 – one of the defining moments of the 'English Revolution' – thus had relatively little to do with the dynamics of war or the contingent circumstances to which these gave rise. Rather, it was 'the culmination of a crisis of confidence [within the political élite] which had been maturing for well over half a century'.[82]

Stone's 'crisis of the aristocracy' thus provided reassurance for the county-community historians in their ongoing quest to explain the sociology of gentry allegiance in 1642: whatever the looked-for correlations between economic status and political outlook within the gentry eventually turned out to be, that it *was* the gentry, and they alone, who provided the dynamic force behind the 'revolution' (whether this were located in 1641 or 1649)[83] now seemed no longer in doubt. Even the involvement of 'opposition peers' in what Stone termed 'the struggle of

1640–41' could be dismissed as an instance of a politically ingénue nobility 'merely being used by the lawyers and gentry as a battering ram and a shield' in their battles against the Stuart Crown.[84] Stone had provided an apparently well-documented case for why, when it came to politics, the nobility could be left almost wholly out of account – and also, by implication, why the English gentry and their English 'county communities' were so properly the objects of the historian's attention.

Few would deny that this massive investment of academic labour has profoundly enriched our understanding of early-Stuart English society.[85] In the broader context of post-war European historiography, the early seventeenth-century English gentry is perhaps the most thoroughly researched of all pre-modern social groupings. Yet, partly as a consequence of the excellence and intellectual candour of that scholarship, the great thirty-year quest to define the social characteristics of the revolutionary gentry failed comprehensively to realize the objectives that had moved the historical profession to undertake the task in the first place. Instead, this body of scholarship both transcended and eventually subverted the original historiographical assumptions on which it had been begun. The central article of Weberian faith which had originally inspired Tawney and his younger admirers Lawrence Stone[86] and Christopher Hill – that there was (or would eventually be found) a demonstrable linkage, on the one hand, between the economic status of the 'rising gentry' and Puritanism–Parliamentarianism, and, on the other, a matching correlation between the 'declining gentry' and Anglicanism–Royalism – was revealed to be a delusion. In almost every English county that was studied, the gentry was revealed to have split either broadly evenly in the great crisis of 1642, or in ways that made nonsense of the claim that clear linkages could be made between partisan allegiance (Parliamentarian or Royalist) and economic status (whether rising or falling). Thirty years of research had produced a finding of momentous significance; but it was essentially a negative one. Dozens of interesting byways had been opened up *en route*, and important new questions had been posed; but the great hunt to find an explanation of the 'English Revolution' in terms of long-term social or economic change – and through an almost exclusive focus on the gentry and their respective 'county communities' – had ended in a blind alley.[87]

If the early twentieth century had seen a Tawney-encouraged turning away from the three-kingdoms and internationalist concerns of the late Victorians towards the problems of the unitary nation-state, so the post-Second World War county historians had shifted their attention, with only rare exceptions, towards a still more confined, if more precisely focused, perspective: from the single country to the single county. In consequence, at least until the 1980s, interest in the 'centre' (in the world of the Privy Council and the central administration at Westminster) hardly registered in most historians' field of vision[88] – except, of course, for those relatively rare moments when the gentry engaged in politics as members of the House of Commons;[89] and if some diverted their gaze occasionally towards the court, it was usually to survey its endemic 'corruption'.[90] Such narrowness was justifiable, it was argued by some if by no means all the county-community historians, because it replicated authentically the horizons of seventeenth-century gentlemen themselves. For in reality, it was alleged, the gentry were 'surprisingly ill informed' about 'wider political issues' and 'simply not concerned with affairs of state'.[91] It followed, therefore, that when conflicts arose, 'local issues' and concerns (particularly over taxation and military charges) were their principal source, as an out-of-touch 'centre' at Whitehall imposed unacceptable burdens on these hard-pressed county communities – a thesis that received its most influential statement in John Morrill's *The Revolt of the Provinces* (1976).[92]

Dissentient voices, however, were beginning to be heard; and in a highly influential article published in 1980, Clive Holmes, himself the author of an important study of seventeenth-century Lincolnshire, questioned the utility of the entire enterprise of self-contained county studies. Challenging the fundamental assumptions of the 'county community school of local historians' (in particular their belief that 'local issues' were the principal source of political conflict), Holmes argued that the cockpit of political events remained the centre – the world of Whitehall and Westminster – and that the leading men of the counties, far from contenting themselves with rustic insularity, were keenly interested in, and generally well informed about, metropolitan political life.[93] Since then, Holmes's argument has been strongly corroborated by a sequence of more recent county and localist studies.[94] Nevertheless, as Dr Holmes's contribution to this volume makes clear, the existence of a metropolitan-centred national politics – which was also locally understood and engaged with – is still insufficiently acknowledged.[95] Any understanding of politics at the county level properly requires an 'integrationist approach', alert to the way in which men and women far from Westminster knew how to use and co-operate with 'agencies and individuals beyond the immediate locality'.[96]

This desire to re-engage with the politics of the 'centre' has nevertheless confronted historians with a major problem (and does so still): in the absence of any detailed narrative of the political 'centre' since the days of the late Victorians, with what account were these local narratives to be integrated? This omission is partly a consequence of methodology – of the tools that historians thought it appropriate to bring to their explanatory tasks. From the 1930s, all the prevailing schools of thought, whether Weberian, Tawneyite or Marxist, were agreed that *structural* analysis seemed an intellectually superior mode of historical exposition to 'mere' narrative (which had come to be regarded as barely one up from storytelling).[97] But it was also no less a consequence of historians' deliberate choice of focus. With most early-modern scholars devoting their research energies to particular counties, there was an almost inevitable neglect of the predominantly metropolitan institutions which had provided the focal points for the great Gardinerian narrative of 1603–49: court, Parliament, and Privy Council. As one astute commentator has noted, 'by taking the political narrative produced by Gardiner more or less as read', most of these historians of the period between the 1950s and 1970s sought 'to penetrate the surface of political history' to what they regarded as 'the real causal motors of historical change and conflict in the society and economy of the day'.[98] In consequence, apart from three volumes of narrative 'popular history' by Dame Cicely Wedgwood (widely regarded by the historical Establishment as old-fashioned *belles lettres*),[99] there was no continuous, extended scholarly narrative of the early seventeenth century – or even of the reign of Charles I – until the publication in 1991 of Conrad Russell's *Fall of the British Monarchies, 1637–42* (and even then most of the detailed narrative was confined to a single year, 1641).[100] In the meantime, county-gentry-focused historians who wanted to know how to relate their localist analysis to a narrative of national events were forced, *faute de mieux*, to recur to Gardiner's magisterial account – in the process, still further entrenching its canonical status. As late as the 1980s, even Anthony Fletcher, no Whig himself, could preface his account of *The Outbreak of the English Civil War* (1981) with the admiring observation:

> The authoritative account [of the origins and course of the Civil War], now almost one hundred years old, remains that of S. R. Gardiner. His was a staggering achievement. His narrative only needs correction on a few points of detail.[101]

Gardiner's was indeed a staggering achievement. But in some quarters, his fourteen volumes of narrative seem to have been more actively admired than closely read; and the perhaps too-ready assumption that there was nothing significant that could, or need, be added to his narrative may have acted as a powerful disincentive to anyone to scrutinize his account too closely – still less to try to replace it.

By the 1970s, then, the historiography of the origins and course of the Civil War was starting to look disconcertingly lop-sided. On one side of the ledger, the gentry-and-county studies account was massively in surplus. There was also, in the immediate aftermath of 1968 – the high-point of Left-wing student radicalism in Europe and the US – a newfound interest in the supposed 1640s precursors of the modern-day radicals: above all, in the Levellers, Diggers, and Ranters. For a moment, Flower Power peered into the murky waters of Civil-War sectarianism and, Narcissus-like, fell in love with its own reflection.[102]

At the same time, however, a younger generation of scholars was becoming increasingly exercised by the deficits on the other side of the ledger, which had become so many that they could no longer be ignored. Under a large number of headings (the significance of religious contro-versy, for example, or the interactions between England and her Scottish, Irish, and European neighbours, or the role of the Whitehall court, to name but a few), research had advanced relatively little in the previous half-century. The time for redress had finally come.

IV THE REVISIONISTS' REACTION: NEW WAYS AND PRESENT CONSEQUENCES

Premonitory rumblings of the reaction against this failing endeavour to explain the tumultuous 1640s in terms of long-term social change had been heard intermittently from the 1960s.[103] However, it was not until the 1970s that these took the form of a systematic undermining of the still standing, if now obviously creaking, edifice of historical orthodoxy. A new generation of scholars was insistent that a thorough-going revision of the long-term social-change explanations was imperative – Conrad Russell, Nicholas Tyacke, John Morrill, and Kevin Sharpe in Britain, Mark Kishlansky and Paul Christianson in North America. And it is they who have broadly defined the parameters of the historical argu-ment in the subsequent decades.

Far from their sharing a single outlook or methodology, the 'Revisionists' were united only by a 'series of negative propositions':[104] first, their rejection of the 'grand narratives', both the Marxist narrative of social change producing social conflict, and the older Whig narrative of constitutional 'progress', on which it had been superimposed; and secondly, their rejection of the teleology which these older accounts implied.[105] There were thus only ever Revision*ists*, never a creed that could be intelligibly described as Revision*ism*. It was a movement born, not of ideology, but of irritation.

Even so, certain interpretative traits were shared, if not universally, then sufficiently to be regarded – particularly in the eyes of the movement's critics – as the tell-tale marks of the early revisionist beast: a tendency to stress the general good order and relative stability of English society before 1640;[106] to downplay the role of secular ideological controversy before the Civil War; to imply, therefore, the largely accidental nature of that conflict.

Implicit in much of this work was a new chronology of modernization: recognizably modern 'adversary politics', it was argued, emerged only from the crucible of Civil War. This line of revisionist writing repudiated the old Weber–Tawney model – with its assumption that it was the 'progressive' (i.e. modernizing) forces such as the mercantile élites and the rising puritan gentry that caused the war. At least in politics, it was the Civil War that gave rise to modernization; not modernization that caused the Civil War.[107] This, in turn, had knock-on consequences for the periodization of the 1640s as a whole. Where earlier historians had tended to identify 1640–41 – the opening year of the 'Long Parliament' (of 1640–53) – as the decisive political break with the past (many actually referring to the 'revolution of 1641'), most of the Revisionists tended to downplay, or even deny, the 'revolutionary' character of that year, recasting it as a period of misunderstanding-fuelled conflict (and fuelled, above all, by misunderstandings about religion), producing a mostly accidental war in England in 1642. In this account, the conflict only really turned 'revolutionary' (if at all) after Pride's Purge in December 1648, the military coup that opened the way to the king's trial and execution.

The key objections to this first phase of revisionist writing – its apparent denial that the Civil War had any long-term causes, and over-dependence on contingency and mischance as explanations for war in 1642[108] – are well known and need no detailed repetition here. What concerns us now, when the dust of those early controversies has partially settled, is where that thirty-year-long process of assertion, criticism and reappraisal has left us. How are we to get the problem of the Civil Wars into clearer focus at the beginning of the new century?

Three principal ideas have come to enjoy a relatively broad consensus. Indeed, it was Russell himself who, in his Ford Lectures to the University of Oxford, *The Causes of the English Civil War* (published in 1990), defined what have since come to be broadly accepted as the decisive 'long-term causes of instability' within the Stuart kingdoms. All of these, Russell contended, were 'well established before Charles came to the throne': first, the 'problem of multiple kingdoms' (how the task of ruling England was complicated by ruling Ireland and Scotland as well); secondly, 'the problem of religious division'; and thirdly, the breakdown of a financial and political system in the face of inflation and the rising cost of war.[109] Contingency, nevertheless, retained a major role; for what made these combustible materials actually, as opposed to merely potentially, explosive was the 'fortuitous element' of the personality of the king: a man simultaneously of poor judgement, over-ambition, and fatal indecision.[110]

Russell illuminated these themes with a subtlety of exposition and a range of archival knowledge that few scholars of seventeenth-century politics have ever matched. But as a summary of the underlying problems that resulted in the Civil War, there is nothing here that would have startled an Oxford audience in the 1880s. These were the great topics that had galvanized the historical profession in the days of Gladstone: the problems (and benefits) that accrued from multiple states; the destabilizing force of religion; and the decisive influence of individual leaders' 'character' in the outcome of affairs.[111] It is testimony to how thoroughly the early Stuart historical landscape had been reconfigured after the First World War, largely in response to the ideas of Weber and Tawney, that the re-engagement with these late Victorian historical concerns should have come to seem, by the 1990s, quite so novel. The days when a very similar series of concerns had first been current, in the 1880s and 1890s, were sufficiently distant for this movement to become known, without irony, as the '*New* British History'.[112] Religion was 'back in fashion as an explanation for the English Civil War'.[113] And after almost half a century of narrow focus on the English nation-state, or on the even smaller unit of the English county, the three-kingdoms concerns of the 'New British Historians' did indeed seem to open up horizons of startling breadth and expansiveness.[114]

Of course, simply because similar questions have been posed before – and similar answers given – this invalidates neither the questions nor the answers; it may simply suggest that both questions and answers are the right ones. Lest this imply, however, that we are living, historiographically, in some sort of 'neo-Victorian moment', it is worth considering some of the broader, and genuinely novel, implications of the revisionist movement, as it is these which form the starting point for most of the essays in this volume.

Perhaps the most striking has been the emancipation of politics as, once again, a proper subject of historical enquiry.[115] Here, at least, there seems the chance to move out from under Gardiner's shadow. As Peter Lake has observed, nearly all the twentieth century's grand 'modernization narratives' were to some extent 'predicated upon, or at least conceived as being entirely compatible with, Gardiner's political narrative'. In fact, none of the major exponents of the social-change theories – R. H. Tawney, Christopher Hill, Lawrence Stone – saw themselves as 'in the business of writing, or even thinking, about political narrative'. But, as Kevin Sharpe pointed out as early as 1978, there was a logical fallacy in seeking the origins (in particular the social, economic or cultural origins) of particular events, when the nature of those political events was itself unclear – and long overdue for re-examination.[116] We needed, in Lake's words, 'to return to the construction and construal of the political narrative itself if any sense were to be made of the causes either of the English Civil War or of the revolution that followed it'.[117]

In the event, that task has proven easier to commend than to undertake. More than three decades on from the advent of the Revisionists, a sustained account of the 1640s that has anything approaching Gardiner's narrative detail and chronological sweep has yet to appear.[118] Not that there has been a shortage of single-volume narratives of the Civil War: since 2000 there has been a new one, on average, every two years.[119] Yet, despite the vast research efforts of the last half-century, even the most recent has curiously resulted, in the words of one distinguished critic, 'in a narrative of the period with which Christopher Hill, writing fifty years ago, would have found little to quarrel'.[120] What, then, might be the way forward?

V   TOWARDS A NEW SYNTHESIS

This series of essays cannot begin to supply that new narrative; but it can point to at least some of the elements, thematic and methodological, out of which it will eventually arise. Two of the essays – those by David Scott and Anthony Milton – ultimately derive from perhaps the most important, if least acknowledged, of the Revisionists' 'negative propositions': their rejection of what might be termed the 'implicit moralism' of the old

Whig and Weberian–Marxist grand theories; the division of the past into 'right' and 'wrong' sides according to whether they advanced or opposed the forces of modernity. In consequence, since the 1980s, whole areas of the past which had hitherto been regarded almost as no-go areas – the Laudians,[121] the Royalists,[122] the defenders of absolutism,[123] the long-neglected urban élites[124] – have gradually been opened up as subjects for respectable historical enquiry.

Perhaps the most extensive of these areas is what contemporaries termed the 'king's party', the Royalists – almost every aspect of whose experience has suffered from relative neglect as compared with their parliamentarian opponents.[125] The king's adherents, accordingly, figure prominently within this collection of essays. David Scott (Chapter 1) offers a broad overview of royalist factional 'high politics' during the Civil War, carefully relating the shifting patterns of influence (at the royalist capital, Oxford, and in the king's inner entourage) to the ideological divisions, within the royalist cause, over what sort of monarchy (and monarch-centred Church) they were fighting to restore.

'Faction', here, is not some arcane and dry-as-dust explanatory alternative to 'ideology' – a simple matter of freeze-framing the giddy gyrations of courtly 'ins' and 'outs'. Far from being the low-minded, even seedy, antithesis to virtuous, high-minded 'ideology' (as a number of the Revisionists' early critics implied),[126] faction emerges here as ideology's partner and twin. For the organization of factions, however loose and friable these may have been at their peripheries, was no less than the means by which contemporaries gave practical expression to divergent political ideals and principles (both high and low), and vied with each other to bring about their realization – whether on the battlefield,[127] in Parliament, or in the pages of the London and Oxford newsbooks. To object that, simply because 'many people moved between different factions at various times', this renders those factions only doubtfully worthy of study merely reveals a questionable grasp of the realities of seventeenth-century politics.[128] What Scott provides is the outline of a genuinely new account of how the leaders of the long-ignored Other Side engaged in the war, of the divergent motives which inspired their efforts to attain a royalist victory, and their equally divergent responses to the question of what that victory should and could involve.

The king's adherents also form the subject of Anthony Milton's essay, examining religion. This challenges the familiar characterization of Civil-War 'Anglicanism' as an essentially moderate, rational, and 'erastian' creed – 'in a sense the [religious] counterpart of the "constitutional

Royalism" described by other historians' in the political sphere;[129] a
war-time Church sharply contrasted with the innovatory ritualism and
rampant clericalism that had characterized the Church of the 1630s
Laudians. As Milton demonstrates, royalist religion, 'like Royalism itself,
was a more shifting, dynamic and complex phenomenon than is often
suggested'. Unsurprisingly, it too had its religious factions, and their
interplay had a decisive effect on attitudes towards negotiations with the
Westminster Parliament. Indeed, one of the most striking developments
of the early 1640s, Milton argues, was the return to prominence at court,
after the collapse of the king's hopes of a French military alliance in the
summer of 1643, of many of the figures who had been members of
Laud's circle – or, more importantly, had assimilated its language and
values – during the 'Laudian moment' of the 1630s.

Milton's chapter challenges the prevalent use of the term 'religion' as
a catch-all characterization of motive or allegiance into which most
things that have *any* tangentially religious or clerical association can be
collapsed. Hence, while it is frequently argued that the defence of episcopacy – the system of church-government by bishops – was one of the
Royalists' prime motives for siding with the king, Milton demonstrates
that from early in the 1640s, relations between the royalist laity and
royalist clergy were often acutely strained. During the successive peace
negotiations with the Parliament, for example, leading Royalists proved
all too willing to trade away the privileges of the Church (including its
system of government by bishops) in return for a permanent deal with
the Parliament. The rebuke offered by Henry Hammond, the royal
chaplain, to these high-ranking backsliders is a case in point: they
thought episcopacy to be 'so unconsiderable a thing, and so extrinsecall
to Christianity' that it could be surrendered 'merely out of intuition of
our own secular advantages'; and this is one of numerous instances that
call into question the extent to which the king's party was uncomplicat-
edly the 'episcopal party', and, by implication, whether the English Civil
War can in any direct and straightforward sense be described as a 'war
of religion'.[130] No sensible historian would deny that religion was *one* of
the things for which both sides were fighting. But the relationship
between an individual's personal piety and his or her actions in the
sphere of public affairs was often far from straightforwardly linear and
causative. As Alan Cromartie has argued, for Charles I – as for his
contemporaries – the 'problem was that the "constitutional" and "religious" spheres were not, in fact, entirely separate, and that the leakage
ran in both directions'.[131]

Here, one of the decisive influences which has shaped – and complicated – our understanding of such relationships has been the post-revisionist emphasis on political culture and mentalities: the study of how contemporaries conceptualized their place in the world and the communities – *inter alia* of status, religion, profession and locality – to which they belonged. Among the most fruitful of these new fields of study, explored in this book by Jane Ohlmeyer (Chapter 4), has been the concept of 'honour' as an influence on political and even military action.[132] Though notoriously difficult to define, this 'honour' culture was simultaneously the code of virtuous behaviour expected by the political élite of its members, and the system of collective reward (public esteem) and collective sanction (dishonour) for those who fulfilled, or failed, those expectations. Moreover, historians are only now beginning to explore the often fraught relationship between the imperatives of such honour codes and the competing claims of religious allegiance and an individual's preferred political principles. And the more diversified becomes the range of influences which affected choices of allegiance, the less likely it becomes that 'religion' – or, for that matter, any other single factor – can stand as the all-purpose explanation of the initial crisis of 1640–41 or for the side-taking in the Civil Wars that followed.

As Roger Manning has pointed out, one of the practical implications of this honour culture, in all three Stuart kingdoms, was the prominence of the titular nobility in directing the actual conduct of the various wars throughout the 1640s. With a prevailing expectation that the highest – indeed, most 'honourable' – form of public service for the peerage was command of armies in the field, well over two-thirds of the nobilities of England and Scotland had actual experience of military service by 1640; indeed, the proportion of the mid-Stuart nobilities that had seen military service was significantly higher than it had been in the reign of Elizabeth I.[133] And one might add that this background makes the English Parliament's decision, over the winter of 1644–5, to purge all noblemen from positions of naval and military command (analysed in this volume by Ian Gentles), all the more startling and exceptional, not less.[134]

The intensiveness with which the Irish nobility[135] involved itself with the command of armies and in the conduct of war between the insurrection of 1641 and the Cromwellian conquest prompts Professor Ohlmeyer to conclude that there was a 'baronial context' to the Civil War in Ireland, no less (and arguably even more so) than there was in England.[136] Of course, this is not to imply, in Ireland any more than in England, that these armed conflicts were simply re-runs of the barons' wars of the medieval past. However frequently contemporaries evoked medieval precedent to justify noble resistance to, or (less frequently) defence of, the Crown, this baronial context was never more than that: one of a series of contextual and imaginative points of reference – legal, religious, Classical humanist – whereby contemporaries justified and tried to make sense of their experience.[137]

We are also in the midst of an ongoing redefinition of the *dramatis personae*, the historical actors, of the 1640s. Reputations are being reassessed in the light of new archival discoveries and new research; and even 'King Pym', once *the* dominant figure of the 1640s Parliaments, has assumed a more modest if nevertheless important place on the political stage.[138] Here, too, one of the influences driving this process has been the newfound awareness of the extent to which interactions between the three kingdoms – and the policies pursued by Scottish and Irish grandees – helped shape the outcome of policy and events in England and else-where.[139] Largely as a result of the work by Jane Ohlmeyer and Micheál Ó Siochrú in Ireland, and Keith Brown, John Scally and Allan Macinnes in Scotland, there is a much keener awareness of how great aristocratic magnates – Ormond[140] in Ireland, Argyll[141] and Hamilton[142] in Scotland, to name only the most prominent – exercised a degree of influence within their native kingdoms that made them, at various moments, major figures within English politics as well. As Allan Macinnes argues in his chapter delineating the impact of Scottish inter-ventions in English politics, events in the 'southern kingdom' are not fully explicable without reference to the aspirations and actions of such over-mighty subjects as Hamilton and Argyll in the years between the Covenanter Revolt in 1638 and the departure of the Scottish army from England at the end of 1646 – what he terms England's 'Scottish moment'.[143] In fact, one might argue that the 'Scottish moment' extended significantly beyond the withdrawal of the Scottish army from England at the end of 1646. For so long as the Scots had an undefeated army, as they did until the summer of 1648, they had the capacity to intervene yet again in the internal affairs of their southern neighbour, and, as a consequence, the Covenanter grandees continued to exercise a powerful – and profoundly destabilizing – influence on English politics in the aftermath of the Civil War of 1642–6. Likewise, it now appears that such key events as the trial and execution of the king, in the winter of 1648–9, long accustomed to being considered within an exclusively English context, has an important Irish dimension – not least the politicking of the Marquess of Ormond, the king's Lord Lieutenant in the kingdom. Without that wider, multiple-kingdoms dimension, at least during the 1640s and 1650s, any purely 'English' explanation is incomplete and necessarily flawed.[144]

Yet, if this post-1980s research has brought a new awareness of the importance of magnate politics in Scotland and Ireland and of its intermittent capacity to influence the course of events in England, it has also served to highlight the very different social relations which pertained within the English élite. One of the reasons for this, of course, is that England had a gentry community which, in size and wealth, found no direct equivalent in either Scotland on Ireland. To this extent, Stone was right: by the 1640s, old-fashioned magnate politics, premised on extensive military retaining, were probably not a practical option for English noblemen – not that this stopped the Earl of Essex from behaving in the mid-1640s as though it still were.[145] These social realities made for power-relations within the aristocracy* that were more complex, more extensively negotiated, and perhaps more collegial as well. Indeed, if there were any institutional innovation that was the hallmark of central politics of the 1640s, it was the advent of the parliamentary standing committee of both Houses, in which peers and Commons-men sat together, toiled together (often for years at a stretch), and formed working relationships in the management of areas of government – among others, the army, the navy, the royal estates, the public revenues, the conduct of war and peace. These collaborations seem to have relied far more on co-operation and alliance-making across and between the social orders than they ever did on the pulling of rank.[146] Similar relationships and behaviours have been discerned within the king's party (not least in Dr Scott's contribution to the present volume), though, as Ann Hughes has long argued, successful alliance-making within the royalist aristocracy was further complicated, and often wholly subverted, by the caprices and inconsistencies of royal favour.[147]

This research by a new generation of historians is in the midst of a wholesale reconfiguring of 'high politics', both parliamentarian and

---

* I use this term in its contemporary sense (as, for instance, employed by the Civil-War polemicist Henry Parker) to mean the nation's élite considered as a ruling order that encompassed not only the titular nobility, but the politically active knightage and gentry as well. One of the blights on Civil-War historiography is that the two terms 'nobility' (the body of the titular peerage) and 'aristocracy' (meaning literally, the governing cadre of the 'best men', and which in the seventeenth century included Commons-men as well) are all too often used interchangeably. As John Morrill has pointed out, this is the very first ambiguity encountered in Lawrence Stone's *Crisis of the Aristocracy*; see his *Seventeenth-Century Britain, 1603–1714: A Critical Bibliography* (Folkestone, 1980), *s.v.*

royalist, during the 1640s; and it is not yet entirely clear what the final outcome will be. What is emerging, however, is not a simple inversion of the old Commons-dominated historiography, and its replacement by a model in which ermine-clad noblemen are calling all the shots; still less is it an Anglicized version of the clannish and manifestly noble-dominated politics recounted in more recent work on Scotland and Ireland.[148] Instead, a more nuanced picture is developing, in which there are several important forces at work. One, already noticed, is the rediscovery of just how bicameral and 'aristocratic' even parliamentarian politics remained, well into the late 1640s – a point which emerges strongly in Ian Gentles's essay in this volume, on the politics of the New Model Army.[149] Another is the realization that politics became far more adversarial, and far earlier in the 1640s, than the pioneer Revisionists of the 1970s and early 1980s supposed. To many of the first Revisionists, rightly anxious to unchain the Civil War from its great boulder of Tawneyite inevitability, the conflict in England was something that began only in the late summer of 1642 – and then as the largely accidental, generally unexpected, and only reluctantly accepted outcome of the political misunderstandings of the previous two years.[150] However, recent work by David Cressy, Quentin Skinner, and Alan Cromartie, among others, has emphasized how fundamental questions about the future government of the Stuart realms – and of the subject's liberties under that government – provoked an acrimonious public debate in the first two years of the November 1640 Parliament.[151] Others, linking the political debates to political action, have gone further, arguing that the extent of these divisions was such that parties willing and able to use force against one another were present in England as early as the late summer of 1640.[152] This, in turn, has major implications for the basic chronology of the conflict: can we speak of a state of war existing in England, not just in 1642, but perhaps earlier, in 1641 or even the late summer of 1640?

At least one contemporary had an unambiguous answer to that question. Writing at the end of the 1640s, Thomas Hobbes, perhaps the seventeenth century's greatest political theorist, argued that

> war consisteth not in battle only, or the act of fighting, but in a tract of time wherein the will to contend by battle is sufficiently known. . . . For as the nature of foul weather lieth not in a shower or two of rain, but in an inclination thereto of many days together, so the nature of war consisteth not in actual fighting, but in the known disposition thereto during all the time there is no assurance to the contrary.[153]

To Hobbes's contemporaries – and, increasingly, to present-day historians – this aptly described the state of England in 1640–2, and, still more obviously, its state in 1646–7, as the post-war settlement was negotiated against a background of a threatened new war between Fairfax's army (the English Parliament's 'New Model Army') and the English Presbyterians and their Scottish allies. Perhaps unsurprisingly, a number of recent historians (represented in this volume by Ian Gentles and Jason Peacey) have also argued the need to bring forward the date at which 'adversary politics' – a politics of fundamental, even irreconcilable, ideological division – first emerged: from the second half of the 1640s (as suggested by some of the 1970s Revisionists)[154] to much earlier in the decade, if not to the late 1630s.

No less important, however, to the reconfiguration of 1640s politics has been the impact of the new research into 'the king's party' in its manifold guises. Only now are we beginning to understand how factional ascendancies at Oxford were affected by changes in power at Westminster, and *vice versa* – to a point where the traditional treatment of 'royalist politics' or 'parliamentarian politics' as the activities of two almost self-contained worlds is no longer tenable.

Likewise, the restoration of the three-kingdoms perspective to our view of the mid-century crisis has revealed the extent to which considerations of race, ethnicity, and national identity – and the energies and hostilities that accompanied them – figured in the political experience of the period.[155] Once the Stuarts' imperfectly glued triple monarchy had fallen apart by 1642, England's dominant position within that trinity suddenly seemed challengeable, and with it the whole complex of relations between the three kingdoms (and the Principality of Wales). And if this was a prospect which brought heady delight to Confederate Catholics in Ireland and Covenanter Presbyterians in Scotland, it provoked commensurate alarm among the 'English supremacists' in parliamentarian London and royalist Oxford, insistent that the proper relation of Ireland and Scotland to England was one of subordination. Here, too, the addition of the royalist dimension has been revelatory, disclosing how hostilities provoked partly by ethnicity and partly by a sense of wronged nationhood could cut across, and even transcend, the royalist–parliamentarian divide.[156]

Nor does this new understanding of 1640s politics derive exclusively from the study of political élites. The extensive recent interest in print culture and the 'public sphere' of the 1640s (greatly facilitated by the online availability of almost every work published in England during the

period) is also transforming, often in unexpected ways, our understanding of the political world.[157] To some, the sheer bulk of what is now
available – the thousands of books, pamphlets, broadsides, and handbills
that poured from the presses after the overthrow of Charles's régime and
the plurality of experience and opinion to which they bear witness – is
almost overwhelming. Before the rising flood, the historian has little
alternative but to retreat into a Tower of Babel where every discordant
voice has equal force and the role of the historian is merely to note, with
a resigned post-modernist shrug, how 'plural, ambiguous, divided and
contrasting' it all is.[158]

Other approaches have, perhaps, been more discriminating – and
more illuminating. Recent work on the culture of print within the Stuart
kingdoms[159] has revealed the extensiveness with which political information and argument circulated (certainly after 1640) beyond the
metropolis. Moreover, by disclosing just how wide was the market for
(and, still wider, the readership of) such material, it has pointed up how
well-informed many of the 'localities' were about politics at the 'centre'.
Exemplifying this point, Clive Holmes's essay in this collection (Chapter
6) explores in detail how local communities applied a relatively sophisticated understanding of power-structures in London to the remedying of
local problems, and played rival metropolitan interests to their local
advantage. Here, too, recent research on what Hobbes called those
'many lesser Common-wealths' – the incorporated cities and towns
which accounted for almost 10 per cent of England's population by 1650
– has challenged the older assumptions about country-dwellers' insularity and political disinterestedness, and, in consequence, the sharp
distinction between 'centre' and 'locality'.[160] As Phil Withington has
argued, 'in certain key respects, the [London] metropolis and provincial
towns should be regarded as similar . . . entities that were linked culturally and institutionally within an expanding urban system'.[161]

Given that the theory of the 'public sphere' originated in an essentially determinist sociological theory (of yet another German, Jürgen
Habermas), the concept, as translated to the Anglo-American historical
world, has produced some highly paradoxical conclusions.[162] For historians of the Stuart-era 'public sphere' have thrown the spotlight back
again onto the importance of human agency and individual choice, and
at levels in society well below the élite. This is not to say that every street
urchin or agricultural labourer took a keen interest in court gossip or
parliamentary debates; but recent research has pointed up the extensiveness of the market for news, and the relative freedom with which

non-élite audiences – whether Midlands miners or the 'Colchester plunderers'[163] – could inform themselves of political and religious issues, and, within a complex web of economic and social constraints, make choices of commitment and action. Of course, this freedom to choose was never absolute; but the import of most recent work has been to expand the number of individuals and the width of the social strata to whom it was open to make informed – and, in many cases, relatively free – decisions about political and religious allegiance. And perhaps nowhere is the influence of print more evident during the 1640s than in the popular perception of the Westminster Parliament, the prestige of which declined steadily in the 1640s as its print-fostered reputation for faction and venality rose. As Jason Peacey observes, 'the ideas, conclusions, and even [the] terminology of [political] writers filtered down into the wider world of print and political comment, and influenced the views of gentry and even sub-gentry figures who are known to have been their readers'.[164]

Moreover, this newfound interest in political polemic, perhaps the most accessible component of the Stuart-era public sphere, has refocused attention on the relationships between the actual producers of print – the authors, publishers and printers – and the political context of the major cities – principally London and, from 1643, Oxford – in which they worked. Attention to the 'public sphere' has thus been another route by which historians have returned to the long-neglected political centre. Indeed, as Michael Mendle, Jason Peacey and David Como have revealed, opinion-forming through the medium of print became a highly organized and unashamedly partisan enterprise in the London of the 1640s and 1650s.[165] And while this research has highlighted, once again, the absence of a sustained decade-long account to replace Gardiner's, it has also begun to provide a number of the pieces of what will eventually be a much larger, if perhaps never wholly completable, jigsaw.

With new perspectives, of course, have come new puzzles. If Westminster politics remained essentially 'aristocratic' well into the 1640s, how do we account for the sudden collapse of the 'noble' element in that system during 1648–9 (or, arguably, much earlier) – a collapse, moreover, that seems to have had no parallel in the other Stuart kingdoms? To this extent, far from downplaying the revolutionary character of the events of that 1648–9 winter – the king's trial, the regicide, the abolition of the House of Lords – the developing picture of 1640s politics makes those outcomes all the more shocking, indeed all the more revolutionary, for the fact that none was in any sense inevitable; each was a deliberate and conscious, if sometimes reluctant, choice.[166]

And if the story of the 1640s has a republican end, in the declaration that England was a kingless 'commonwealth or free state', how early does republicanism figure as a major force in the politics at Westminster? Here, too, we are back with the chronology of radicalization, and at least part of the answer necessarily hinges on definitions. Does a republican state only come into being with the formal, legislative renunciation of monarchy (as happened, indubitably, in 1649)?[167] Or could the transition from monarchy to republic (and *vice versa*) be an incremental process, as Peter Heylyn had argued in the mid-1630s, in which the carapace of monarchy could be retained (as in that most famous of monarchical republics, Venice) while power, for all practical purposes, came to rest in an oligarchy, which merely paid lip-service to the people for the derivation of its power.[168] Many contemporaries (including Charles I) believed that, in this sense, a republic – a free 'commonwealth' – had been achieved in England by the end of 1641, and in Scotland even earlier. Indeed, the conviction that Charles had been in a sense 'un-kinged' by the English Parliament's constitutional innovations of 1641 provoked a powerful pro-royalist reaction in all three kingdoms.[169] In such circumstances, may we not speak of republicanism – or, if one prefers, the creation in 1641 of an English republic *de facto* – as being actually a cause as well as being, in its later *de jure* form, a consequence of civil war in England?

Part of the difficulty in answering such questions lies in the nature of seventeenth-century language itself, not least in the notorious slipperiness of the term 'commonwealth' (or its Latin equivalent, *res publica*). This, to take but one example, could either signify (among a large range of potential meanings) a kingless state such as Venice or Holland, or, far more neutrally, be the generic term for any well-ordered and virtuous polity – with only context (itself often imperfectly evidenced or construable) to guide us as to intention and meaning. An even greater difficulty, perhaps, has lain in the way the professional history of political thought and the professional history of politics have taken widely divergent trajectories over the last two decades. Much of the most important work in the area of political thought during this period has been devoted to theories of liberty – in particular, republican liberty – and England's intellectual engagement with classical Rome; its emphases, in consequence, have been primarily secular. Yet as the revisionist political historians developed their 'new' narrative of the crisis of 1637–42 – particularly in the versions written by Conrad Russell and proposed by John Morrill – their emphasis on religion as the principal (in some versions, almost the only) motive for going to war in 1642 has offered a view of Stuart England which bears only scant relation to that proposed by the historians of political thought such as Skinner, Cromartie and Johann Sommerville.[170]

In the final essay in this volume, Philip Baker – venturing where angels fear to tread – proposes a possible route whereby the two markedly divergent approaches might be made to reconverge. Contemporary public discourse, he argues, tended to be syncretistic, drawing 'not only [on] biblical references to England as suffering Israel, but also [on] appeals to Roman republican example', as well as 'usages drawn from medieval precedent and the nation's Gothic past'.[171] A fuller exploration of these two great sources of ideas and inspiration, the Biblical and the Classical, and how they qualified, compounded, and engaged with each other, is one of the major desiderata of seventeenth-century scholarship.

To represent the full conspectus of current work on the Civil War is an impossible task within the compass of a single volume; and so, inevitably, there are omissions in this one. In a world without word- or page-limits, this book would also have included chapters on such themes as the actual conduct of war, on its economic and social dimensions, on popular allegiance and side-taking, on the role of London, the various quests for settlement – on all of which there has been impressive new work in recent years – and a dozen more subjects besides. But it would have been a book of unmanageable size and would have long since incurred its publisher's veto on the grounds of cost alone.

To some, of course, this prevailing diversity of historical interests in and approaches to the Civil War is evidence of its fatal 'Balkanization' as a subject, and its imminent descent into incomprehensibility. In their various ways, the contributors to this volume prefer to regard the current absence of a single 'master explanation' rather differently; not just as a sign of the subject's vitality and enduring power to fascinate; but also as evidence that the unwritten constitution of history's Republic of Letters may be on its way to attaining a new maturity and sophistication. The discrediting of the old Whig and Marxist 'grand narratives' has, of course, left a scepticism not only about catch-all, all-encompassing theory in general. It has left, too, a distrust of mono-causal explanations in particular: the idea that political conflicts (and hence the Civil Wars of the 1640s) can be explained in terms of 'One Thing', whether that be (according to taste) class, social change, political principle or religious zeal.

1. Rethinking Royalist Politics, 1642–9

DAVID SCOTT

The Royalists are the Cinderella of mid-seventeenth century history. They are largely overlooked by the exponents of the 'New British History', and look like being bypassed once again in the current rush of interest in the Civil-War 'public sphere'. True, the Royalists remain one of the few groups in the Civil War that most of the public have actually heard of, if only as one half of the double-act of 'Cavaliers and Roundheads'. But among historians 'the king's party' is unfashionable, and royalist politics – particularly at the top end of the social scale – even more so. There have been several recent studies of royalist literature and propaganda (though few convincingly bridge the gap between political theory and practice);[1] David Underdown and Mark Stoyle have injected new life into the study of popular Royalism;[2] and the Sealed Knot and other battle re-enactment societies sustain a small but lively market in royalist military history.[3] But virtually all we have in the way of recent published work on royalist high politics is a few articles by Ronald Hutton and James Daly in the 1970s and 1980s, occasional, though illuminating, pieces by Ian Roy, and a ten-year-old monograph by David Smith.[4] One recent miscellany of essays devoted to 'Royalism' actually derides the study of court politics during the 1640.[5] No historian has focused specifically on the king, his supporters, his court, and his camp during the period from the collapse of the Personal Rule to the regicide. Analysis of royalist factions is in a similarly primitive state. As yet, no attempt has been made to trace the connections between the 'ultras', 'moderates', 'swordsmen' or any of the other royalist factions that have been identified in the early 1640s with David Underdown's 'Louvre party' and 'Old Royalists' of the 1650s.[6] Our picture of the three Stuart kingdoms during the 1640s cannot but be flawed while one whole section of the tableau remains virtually blank.

Why this neglect of the Royalists? Is it because, as Hutton and others have suggested, so much royalist documentation was burned by its owners at the end of the war as to make it very difficult to say anything

definitive about the structure of the king's party?[7] There is certainly
something in this. Clearly we lack the mass of material on the workings
of the central and local government under the king that we possess for
the Parliamentarians. On the other hand, we have more private correspondence for the royalist grandees (that is, the most influential men
around the king and queen),[8] particularly after 1644 when they scattered
to the four winds, than for their parliamentarian counterparts, who were
mostly living cheek by jowl in London and rarely needed to communicate by paper. But perhaps the main reason for the dearth of research
on the Royalists is simply the fact that they lost – and not just the first
Civil War but the second as well. The Royalists were two-time losers,
and their defeats gave force to the arguments of S. R. Gardiner and
other Whig historians that England's advance to constitutional maturity
under Victoria was a legacy of the parliamentarian victory. From this
teleological perspective, the Royalists were not just on the wrong side of
the war, they were on the wrong side of History. Until recently, most
studies of the 1640s were premised on the need to explain the English
Revolution, in which the Royalists' role was merely that of obstacles in
the path of the juggernaut. To explain why the Parliamentarians won
was at one and the same time to explain why the Royalists lost.

This teleological approach to the 1640s may have lost much of its force,
but it lingers on in the tendency to regard the Royalists as (in the words of
1066 and All That) 'Wrong but Wromantic'.[9] The effect is to lend a
distinctly Whiggish feel to the way we look at Royalism. There is a preoccupation with personality, as if the Royalists failed partly through want of
'character';[10] and a corresponding neglect of royalist wartime institutions
– from the royal court to the Parliament that the king summoned to meet
at Oxford in 1644.[11] Intrigue and factionalism at court are often attributed
to short-sighted and selfish motives, rather than a desire for power in order
to shape and implement policy. Above all, there is the continuing predilec-
tion when discussing Royalism for historians to employ curiously nineteenth-century terms like 'Constitutional Royalism'.

I   FALSE TAXONOMIES: THE MIRAGE OF 'CONSTITUTIONAL ROYALISM'

In the writing on Civil War loyalties since the 1640s, 'Constitutional
Royalism' is actually a recent invention. The great Whig historian
Thomas Babington Macaulay coined the phrase 'constitutional royalist',

but he applied it sparingly, and it did not catch on with his successors. Brian Wormald in his 1951 case-study of Sir Edward Hyde, Earl of Clarendon, referred to the 'so-called Constitutional Royalists'.[12] However, as this construction suggests, he found the term unsatisfactory, and particularly so with reference to Hyde himself. The historian who identified Constitutional Royalism as a distinct political theory, and constructed a royalist faction around it, is David L. Smith. In Smith's account, the Constitutional Royalists were those leading figures within the king's party whose support for a negotiated settlement amounted to a 'knee-jerk reflex'; its leading figures were the Duke of Richmond, the Marquess of Hertford, the Earls of Southampton, Lindsey, and Dorset, Viscount Falkland, Sir John Culpeper, Sir Edward Hyde, and a few others.[13] Smith sums up their credo as a belief 'that royal powers should be guided and limited by the rule of law . . . a respect for Parliament's place in the constitution . . . a defence of the existing Church of England and Protestant religion "by law established" . . . [and] a wish to preserve . . . royal discretionary powers'.[14]

Perhaps the most obvious problem with this formulation is its vagueness – not to say its potential for internal contradiction, as the king's discretionary powers could (and had) been exercised in ways that many considered at variance with the rule of law. To conceive of the 'ancient constitution',[15] and by extension royalist constitutionalism, in such broad terms is to render it virtually useless as a reference point for factional alignments within the king's party; for one would be hard-pushed to find Royalists who did *not* believe in the 'rule of law' or respect 'Parliament's place in the constitution'. This is what George Lord Digby, often portrayed as the most unconstitutionalist of the royalist grandees, had to say on such matters:

> The truth is . . . the Kings of England are never in their glory, in their splendor, in their Majestique Soveraignty, but in Parliaments. Where is the power of imposing Taxes? Where is the power of restoring from incapacites [*sic*]? Where is the legislative Authority? Marry in the King. . . . But how? in the King circled in, fortified and evirtuated [*sic*] by his Parliament. The King out of Parliament hath a limited, a circumscribed Jurisdiction. But wayted on by his Parliament, no Monarch of the East is so absolute in dispelling Grievances.[16]

We face a conundrum. If even Digby – the most politique of the royalist grandees – recognized the fundamentals of the ancient constitution, it is hard to see how a 'constitutionalist' outlook has any use as a factional label. And yet to employ a tighter definition of the ancient constitution may be equally self-defeating. As Glen Burgess has recently argued, early Stuart England had no constitution in the sense of a blueprint, or set of first principles, for governing. The 'constitution' was 'the complete set of laws, prerogatives and rights, and the polity they defined. The constitution had no existence, no formulation, apart from its specifics.'[17] Consequently, no two Royalists (or Parliamentarians for that matter) ordered and interpreted this mass of specifics in exactly the same way.[18] The ancient constitution was therefore at once too broad, and too narrow, a platform for factional organization.

This lack of consensus on constitutional details even afflicted the three men generally regarded as the 'leading theorists' of Constitutional Royalism – Viscount Falkland, Sir John Culpeper, and Sir Edward Hyde.[19] Their disagreement over the king's answer to the Nineteen Propositions (Parliament's eve-of-war ultimatum of 1642), and whether Charles was one of or superior to the three estates of the realm, is well known.[20] But they also disagreed on another supposed tenet of Constitutional Royalism – the maintenance of 'the Church by law established' as an integral part of the government of England.[21] Hyde, in his own words, 'did really believe the church of England the most exactly formed and framed for the encouragement and advancement of learning and piety, and for the preservation of peace, of any church in the world'.[22] He reverenced the Church of England not only as a necessary part of the political establishment, and an instrument of good government, but also because 'its politics encouraged the virtues, the good order, learning, and decency, that God intended for man'.[23]

But contrast his position with that of his friend Viscount Falkland. Falkland had 'a better opinion of the church of England, and the religion of it, than of any other church and religion. . . . But he had in his own judgement such a latitude in opinion, that he did not believe any part of the order of government of it to be so essentially necessary to religion, but that it might be parted with, and altered, for a notable public benefit or convenience.'[24] In other words, he thought that episcopacy – government of the church by bishops – should be retained, but not at the expense of achieving a lasting peace. Sir John Culpeper (appointed Master of the Rolls at Oxford early in 1643) took an even more pragmatic line, being 'very indifferent' in matters of religion, 'but more inclined to what was established, to avoid the accidents which commonly attended a change'.[25] Culpeper, a 'true *politique*', favoured episcopacy on grounds of political expediency, and once it had become inexpedient to do so (as it had by 1646) he was willing to endorse Presbyterianism for much the same reason.[26] Culpeper had spent some of his youth in military service abroad, and 'like a tall sword-man' he was quick to take and give offence.[27] True to his irascible nature, he put his faith in force or the threat of force, not in laws and constitutions;[28] and it is perhaps not surprising therefore that one of the most serious rivalries at Oxford was between him and the pompous, lawyerly Hyde.[29] During 1643, Culpeper made several attempts to block Hyde's preferment at court and, with John Ashburnham (Treasurer of the King's Army and a Groom of the Bedchamber), to encroach on his office as Chancellor of the Exchequer.[30] The resulting 'jealousy or coldness' between the two men poisoned their relationship for years.[31] Moreover, what is often cited as evidence of Culpeper's irenic disposition – his call for peace negotiations at the opening of the Oxford Parliament in January 1644[32] – looks on closer inspection more like that time-honoured courtier tactic of using Parliament as a platform from which to attack his rivals. Thus he made purging the court and camp of Catholics and those, such as Digby, who had been declared traitors by Westminster the crux of his 'peace initiative'.[33] As he probably predicted, his demand for the removal of highly-placed Catholics was taken up by the lower House, although ultimately to little effect.

And if Culpeper's 'constitutionalist' credentials are suspect, then those of the Duke of Richmond are non-existent. A cousin of the king and the highest-ranking figure at court after princes Rupert and Maurice, Richmond 'was of a great and haughty spirit, and so punctual in point of honour that he never swerved a tittle'.[34] He was apparently hostile to the Long Parliament's attack on the Personal Rule – with which 'Constitutionalists' were supposed to have been broadly in sympathy.[35] More to the point, he and another alleged 'Constitutionalist', the Earl of Lindsey, were devoted supporters of the figure widely regarded as the most hard-line royalist opponent of peace talks during the early years of the war, Prince Rupert, which is hard to reconcile with enthusiasm for a negotiated settlement.[36]

The argument for the existence of a coherent constitutionalist party is questionable in other ways. For example, there seems to have been no necessary connection between reverence for the ancient constitution and the advocacy of peace negotiations with the Parliamentarians, based on a genuine desire for compromise. As the case of Hyde demonstrates only too clearly, adherence to the ancient constitution and the common law as the touchstones of political action – rather than helping to bridge the distance between Royalists and Parliamentarians – could actually militate against the king offering the kind of generous concessions that would have been necessary if an irresistible momentum towards peace were ever to be created at Westminster.[37] Hyde's refusal to compromise on what he saw as 'the essential props and supports of the old Government' – which included the king's prerogative powers as well as the pre-war episcopal church – may explain why he came to be regarded by many Parliamentarians 'as a man who more industriously opposed peace than any other of the King's Council'.[38] Sir Edward Nicholas, one of Charles's two Secretaries of State and a close friend of Hyde's, shared the latter's resolve to maintain the full panoply of 'the auntient government of England'.[39] Indeed, it was precisely Nicholas's attachment to 'the best composed & equallest Gov[er]nem[en]t that ev[er] was Constituted under any Monarch in the world' that made him one of the more hawkish of the royalist grandees.[40]

However, supposing that Constitutional Royalism can be reified, then if it is to be anything more than a synonym for Royalism in general there must be a group to which the term cannot apply. In other words, there must be a faction that subscribed to a creed of Unconstitutional Royalism; and indeed just such a group has been identified, led by the queen, together with Prince Rupert, Lords Jermyn, Digby, Percy, and Wilmot, and the Groom of the Bedchamber, John Ashburnham.[41] The hallmark of these 'ultra-Royalists', by general consent, was a determination to eschew a negotiated settlement with Parliament in favour of an outright military victory, such as would allow Charles to rule as an 'absolutist' king – that is, without reference to Parliament or the laws of the realm.[42] Yet just as one struggles to find 'Constitutionalists' who were consistently and unequivocally in favour of negotiating in good faith with Parliament, it is equally hard to find 'ultras' who were consistently and unequivocally against doing so. Even some of the Army Plotters of 1641 (who had attempted to bring about the legislature's dissolution by force) – the figures at court allegedly most hostile to peace talks – ended up advocating negotiations with Parliament. Of Wilmot, Sir Philip Warwick remarked, 'he that marks [his] whole progress thro' this warr, shall find him much affected to be an umpire of peace'.[43] Lord Percy, another Army Plotter, was effectively sent into exile early in 1645 for his immoderate support for peace.[44] Likewise, Prince Rupert was weighing the benefits of a negotiated settlement well before the king's cause had become militarily hopeless.[45] Even Digby, the figure who conforms most nearly to the Whig stereotype of the brilliant yet weak-charactered Cavalier, was at times interested in negotiating with Parliament – though as I have already argued, support for negotiations did not necessarily equate with a desire for real compromise.[46]

The notion of an 'absolutist' faction at Oxford is even more problematic – not least because of our uncertainty as to what Caroline 'absolutism' might or should look like. According to Glenn Burgess and other revisionist historians, it is only those who held the view that the king could make and break laws at will, without recourse to any formal legal channels, who can properly be termed absolutists.[47] On this definition, very few besides Thomas Hobbes and (possibly) Sir Robert Filmer qualify, and it is not clear how much impact they had on royalist counsels during the Civil War.[48] To Johann Sommerville, however, this definition of absolutism is far too narrow, not to say anachronistic. He argues that the term 'absolutist' can be applied to anyone who maintained that royal power derived directly from God, and that the law therefore took its authority from the king (rather than vice versa), who was justified in overriding it in cases of necessity (of which he was the sole judge), and that subjects were obliged to obey even illegal royal commands provided that these did not contradict divine law.[49] On this definition, certainly, many royalist writers *were* absolutists; indeed, the difficulty lies in finding one who was not. It is also likely, though impossible to prove, that most of the royalist grandees embraced something resembling this view of the king's powers and the subjects' duties; although at least one of their number – Digby's father, the first Earl of Bristol – allowed for passive resistance to royal commands that subverted the law.[50] To complicate matters still further, Royalists did not equate absolute monarchy with arbitrary government (tyranny) in the way that parliamentarian polemicists did. Most Royalists could happily conceive of a limited, yet absolute, monarchy.[51] Hyde, for example, believed that the king was bound to rule according to law, but that this obligation was ultimately moral in nature and that there were no enforceable limitations upon his authority: 'His Majesty is not the first (and I hope will not be the last) King of England, that hath not held Himself Accomptable to any Earthly Power.'[52]

Militant and authoritarian strands of royalist thought were by no means confined to the fringes of the king's party. But to locate them within the context of a struggle between 'absolutism' and 'constitutionalism', still less to construct parties around these positions, cannot be sustained by the evidence. There were undoubtedly prominent Royalists whose ideas called into question the 1641–2 constitutional and ecclesiastical settlement and the re-establishment of 'known ways' in government should the king triumph. A number of senior royalist officers were impatient of civilian counsels and their powerbases such as the Privy Council; and it was feared that if Charles prevailed by force of arms then this impatience would translate into arbitrary government.[53] As we shall see, however, except during the opening months of the war, the swordsmen never formed a united bloc or possessed a coherent agenda.[54]

A more considered and sustained bid to build upon the achievements of the Personal Rule was made by leading clergymen at Oxford. As Anthony Milton's contribution to this volume reveals, many royalist clergymen repudiated the 1641–2 ecclesiastical settlement – and particularly the removal of bishops from the House of Lords.[55] There were also royalist divines, Calvinists as well as Laudians, who articulated exalted notions of divine-right kingship and the role of the clerical estate in government; and on this latter score at least they made enemies not only of the 'moderate' Falkland, but also the 'politique' Culpeper, and the 'extremist' Digby.[56] But the most serious challenge to the restoration of the ancient constitution came from the queen and several of her Civil-War circle, notably William Cavendish first Earl of Newcastle, Lord Jermyn, and Sir John Culpeper. These men had absorbed the key lesson of the Personal Rule (and of Strafford's lieutenancy of Ireland in particular)[57] and of the Civil War itself for the governing of the three kingdoms, and that was the indispensability of a standing, centrally-paid army to the effective exercise of power.[58] Newcastle is a particularly interesting member of this group. A patron of Hobbes and a close friend of Strafford's, he was implicated in the Army Plots of 1641; consistently opposed moves towards a negotiated settlement during the Civil War; and, by 1648, favoured a military alliance with the Scots to restore the king.[59] Like Hobbes, he maintained that 'theye thatt have the Armes have the Purse, & they thatt have the Purse hath obedience, So Thatt Armes Is all'.[60] This line of argument challenged some contemporaries' perception of how a law-abiding monarchy should function, just as Strafford's doctrine of 'Thorough' had in the 1630s.

But the queen and her circle were interested primarily in ways of enabling Charles to get things done, not in advancing theories of his legal and constitutional position. Their main concern, therefore, was how he would regain power and then enforce his will *between* the meetings of Parliament – which, they assumed, would remain occasional events rather than making for a semi-permanent executive. If they did make a philosophical case for their ideas it was couched not in terms of 'absolutism' versus 'constitutionalism', but in the more traditional form of whether royal authority should rest ultimately on 'force' or 'love'.[61]

If the attempt to explain the structure of royalist politics in terms of a constitutionalist–unconstitutionalist dichotomy is unconvincing, then how are we to interpret the divisions among the king's leading supporters? Ronald Hutton's ill-defined classification of 'ultras' and 'moderates' is simply a variation on the constitutionalist–unconstitutionalist theme, and has rightly been criticized for assuming more than it elucidates.[62] Ian Roy's structuralist model of court factionalism – implied in his taxonomy of 'swordsmen', 'courtiers', and 'civilians' – is more useful in that it acknowledges how different kinds of office and sources of power might lead to divergent political perspectives and expectations.[63] Nevertheless, it leaves unanswered the question of what religious and political differences, if any, underlay these divisions. However, one thing seems clear – the *parti pris* dualism of 'Constitutionalists' and 'absolutists', 'moderates' and 'ultras' will not answer. A new model of royalist high politics is needed, and the remainder of this essay will attempt to provide one, if only in outline.

II   THE EMERGENCE OF ROYALIST PARTIES, 1642–5

Royalist high politics presents a very confusing picture at the start of the English Civil War. There were clearly many tensions within the king's newly constituted party, notably between some of his more gung-ho military men and 'the Lords at Court' – the civilian nobles who occupied the senior posts in the royalist administration.[64] Broadly speaking, however, political divisions at Oxford (the king's headquarters) during the first year of the Civil War were analogous to those at Westminster. There were a number of courtiers who formed what might be called a 'peace interest', notably the Earls of Dorset and Bath, Viscount Falkland, and Lords Spencer and Savile.[65] Their conception of what constituted an acceptable settlement was evidently close enough to that of moderate Parliamentarians to make them willing to countenance major royal concessions. Indeed, to read Lord Spencer bemoaning the influence of 'Papists' and 'evil counsellors' at court, one might be forgiven for thinking that he *was* a Parliamentarian.[66] All were firm Protestants, and at least one – Falkland – was prepared to countenance limited godly reform of the Church of England. The unexpected success of the king's army during the Edgehill campaign of October–November 1642 undoubtedly weakened the influence of the doves at court, just as it strengthened that of the peace party at Westminster. Nevertheless, the peace lords maintained a foothold at court during 1643, and particularly it seems on the Privy Council and the 'sitting council' for the defence of Oxford.[67] Thus, in April 1643, Sir Edward Nicholas referred darkly to 'diverse [men]' about the king 'that would have an acc[o]m[m]odation att any rate [i.e. price]'.[68] And there was talk at Oxford, well into that summer, of 'hollow-hearted Counsellors who affect too much the Parliamentary way'.[69] But while the war went the king's way (as it did throughout the spring and summer of 1643), those at court who advocated genuine compromise were generally sidelined when it came to shaping policy and managing the war-effort.[70]

At the other end of the political spectrum were the true 'Cavaliers' – leading Royalists who were eager to settle the war solely by the sword. This 'war interest' included Prince Rupert, Prince Maurice, Lord Wilmot, and their hangers-on – for example, Daniel O'Neill and the 'bold and peremptory' Tom Elyott – and several men closely associated with the queen, notably Lord Digby and Sir John Berkeley.[71] Again, all the heads of this faction were Protestants, and in the case of Rupert a firm Calvinist. At the war interest's core were two overlapping groups: senior army officers, and men who had been implicated in the 1641 Army Plots or had otherwise incurred charges of treason against them at Westminster. For those in this second category, *any* kind of treaty with Parliament was dangerous, and therefore a military solution seemed their best option, at least for the first year of the war. Their position mirrored that of the leading 'fiery spirits' at Westminster – Viscount Saye and Sele, John Pym and their friends – who, having conspired to bring in the Scots in 1640, needed either an outright victory or the most stringent of settlements to preserve them from the king's future vengeance. Conversely, the fear of parliamentarian vengeance was never strong enough to hold the royalist war interest together, and by late 1643 its leaders were jealous of each other's influence and moving in different political directions.[72]

For much of the war, however, most of the royalist grandees, including men associated with either the war or peace interests at court, were willing at one time or other to pursue a third option between the extremes of 'an acc[o]m[m]odation att any rate' on the one side and a 'perfect [i.e. complete and absolute] victory' on the other. One of the leading exponents of this *via media* in royalist politics was Sir Edward

Hyde. It is revealing that during the Oxford peace treaty of March–April 1643, the 'hawkish' Digby warmly supported the promotion of the 'irenic' Hyde as Chancellor of the Exchequer.[73] What may seem like an act of political folly (or at least inconsistency) on Digby's part becomes readily comprehensible, however, once we realize that Hyde's role in the Oxford negotiations was not that of Wormald's compromising peacemaker, but that of a royalist *engagé*. Hyde utterly rejected any idea of a settlement on Parliament's official peace terms.[74] Instead, he favoured the secret and far more lenient propositions being put to the king covertly by the leader of the parliamentary delegation at Oxford, the Earl of Northumberland – and this, only as a means of dividing the parliamentarian peace and war parties so completely that he hoped further resistance to the king would collapse.[75]

Oxford politicians like Hyde had the latitude and the connections with disaffected elements among the parliamentarian leadership to explore the possibility of a political coup against the fiery spirits. On several occasions before the end of the war, especially when peace talks were in the offing, there was a group at court eager for the king to make enough concessions as would allow the peace party at Westminster to bring him in 'honour and safety' to London, where he might (in Hyde's telling phrase) be 'repossessed of his . . . power'.[76] For most of the war the commitment of supposed moderates like Hyde to a negotiated settlement was therefore qualified. They used negotiations not so much to forge a genuine accommodation as to force what would amount to a parliamentarian capitulation – and to a some extent therefore they shared the same ends as those courtiers who favoured a military solution.

The most revealing demonstration of this middle way in royalist politics occurred during the summer of 1643, and grew out of the rivalry in court and camp between the king's commander in the west, the Marquess of Hertford, and his adversaries Princes Rupert and Maurice.[77] The Earl of Newcastle's victories in the north of England in the first half of 1643, and Rupert's capture of Bristol (26 July), threatened to bring a 'perfect victory' within the king's grasp, with the expected result that the swordsmen would reap the rewards in terms of offices and power in the post-restoration court at the expense of landed magnates like Hertford. Moreover, by the summer of 1643, Rupert had alienated not only the 'lords at Oxford' but also several of his erstwhile supporters, notably Digby and Wilmot.[78] To forestall a military victory, Rupert's enemies at court hatched a scheme to bring the war to a swift and politically-engineered conclusion by closing the middle ground in

English politics, excluding both the royalist swordsmen and the fiery spirits at Westminster. The evidence for this design is fragmentary, but compelling.[79] With the connivance of Rupert's enemies at court, the Earl of Northumberland and other peace party grandees at Westminster drew up a series of vaguely worded peace propositions during the summer, which they presented to the Commons early in August. At the same time, they succeeded in winning over the commander of Parliament's main – indeed, by the end of July, only – field army, the Earl of Essex, who was Hertford's brother-in-law and friend.[80] It seems that the Westminster grandees and their allies at court hoped to use Essex's, and possibly Hertford's, army to underwrite the August peace propositions, and if necessary to quash opposition to them by force. With the hawks at Oxford and Westminster neutralized, it was thought that the king would be able to return to London and be restored to power on the very softest of terms. It is not surprising that Hyde, who was a close ally of Hertford's, was apparently involved in this design, for it was essentially a more ambitious version of what he and other leading politicians on both sides had been attempting during the Oxford treaty.[81] In the event, the August peace initiative collapsed after the king, at Rupert's insistence, removed Hertford from command, and the Commons rejected the Lords' propositions (the City militants having rallied in support of the fiery spirits in the House), whereupon Essex withdrew his support from the parliamentary peace party.[82] Significantly, one of the reasons plausibly advanced for Essex's defection from the peace camp at Westminster was because he believed that Hertford's services 'were not enough valued by the King'.[83]

Victory for the hawks in the summer of 1643 ended any prospect of an exclusively English settlement of the war, and ushered in a new phase in the conflict. Until the second half of 1643 the wars and unrest in all three Stuart kingdoms had consisted of a series of largely discrete, if causally interlinked, conflicts. But all this began to change in September with the king's endorsement of a temporary 'cessation' with the Irish Confederates – or Catholic 'rebels' as most people in England preferred to regard them – thereby allowing him to import some of the English troops that had been sent to Ireland following the Irish Rising in 1641. The king had approved the cessation in response to Parliament's efforts to negotiate a military alliance with the Scottish Covenanters, which culminated later that same month in the signing of the Solemn League and Covenant. Under the impact of the cessation and the Covenant, England became the main theatre in something not far short of a single 'archipelagic' war. And as the nature of the war in England changed, so too did factional alignments at Oxford (and Westminster).[84]

From the very emergence of the Royalist party there had been a major fault-line among the grandees over the propriety of bringing in foreign Catholic troops. Digby and several other members of the queen's circle were contemplating pitting Irish 'rebels' against English 'rebels' well before the outbreak of hostilities in England.[85] It was reported from London in January 1642 that the 'ill-affected party, which are those that follow the Court, do now speak very favourably of the Irish as those whose grievances were great, their demands moderate, and may stand the King in much stead'.[86] However, the mere suggestion a few months later that Charles intended to go to Ireland – ostensibly to suppress the rebellion, but (as the queen revealed) to 'join the army of the Catholics' – caused a ripple of anxiety among some of Hyde's royalist friends.[87] So long as victory by English force of arms, either on the battlefield or in support of a political coup, remained within Charles's grasp there was no imperative to press for foreign intervention, and therefore disagreement among the grandees on this issue was held in check. But the Covenanters' entry into the English Civil War on the side of Parliament at the beginning of 1644 required Charles to bring in troops from Ireland if he were to redress the military balance. Few, if any, of the grandees objected to the king importing Protestant troops from Ireland – and between October 1643 and April 1644 about 10,000 or so were shipped over piecemeal to English ports up and down the west coast.[88] The king's problem, however, was that these troops could not possibly offset the military advantage that Parliament gained from the 21,000 strong Covenanter army that marched across the Tweed – the Anglo-Scottish border – in January 1644. If he were to defeat both the English Parliamentarians and the Scottish Covenanters, Charles realized that he would have to import *Catholic* troops from Ireland as well, and this meant negotiating a peace treaty with the Confederates that allowed them freedom of worship and greater political autonomy. Some of the royalist grandees thought this an acceptable price to secure victory in England.[89] Others, however, including several figures committed to the vigorous prosecution of the war, found it extremely hard to stomach. Not only would a treaty with the Confederates threaten the Protestant ascendancy and English interest in Ireland, but it would also involve Catholic troops invading English soil.

The Royalists' defeat at Marston Moor in July 1644 forced the grandees to confront this foreign-intervention question head on. After

Marston Moor, victory for the king became, if not wholly unattainable, then difficult to achieve without foreign intervention – most obviously in the form of a Confederate army. Marston Moor – and, still more emphatically, the king's defeat at Naseby in June 1645 – left the Oxford grandees with only two real choices: either they too must bring in foreign troops, or they must seek a genuine accommodation with the Westminster Parliament. And during 1644 rival factions began to form around these stark alternatives.

The potential for this 'foreign intervention issue' to split the royalist grandees was already clear from the debates at Oxford in April–May 1644 over the king's Irish policy. Misgivings at court at the prospect of a treaty with the Confederates were so great 'that some of the Lords desired to avoid sitting in counsell when the businesse of Ireland was debated'.[90] In this atmosphere of apprehension and mistrust, the capture of the king's Irish policy by the mercurial Lord Digby did not help matters. Within a few months of his appointment as Secretary of State in September 1643 (in succession to Falkland), Digby had taken charge of the procuring of troops, both Protestant and even Catholic, from Ireland.[91] To Digby and his Irish royalist collaborators, the Earl of Antrim and Daniel O'Neill, bringing over Catholic troops from Ireland seemed both a logical and a necessary response to Parliament's military alliance with the Covenanters. But Sir Edward Nicholas (Digby's fellow Secretary of State), Hyde, and many others at court had no faith in 'popish undertakers' such as Antrim, and were deeply unhappy at the idea of employing Irish Catholic troops against British Protestants.[92] It seems likely that the proposal to set up a Council under the Prince of Wales in the west of England, which was presented to the Privy Council by Digby in May 1644, was intended partly as a way of removing those courtiers who were 'something rigide in the busines of the Irish'.[93] However, most of the grandees earmarked for banishment refused to co-operate, and so the proposal was shelved.[94] As a result, the king was forced to hand back negotiations with the Confederates to the king's Lord Lieutenant of Ireland, the Marquess of Ormond, who was no happier at the prospect of making concessions to Papists than were Nicholas and Hyde. The scheme for the Prince's Council would be revived immediately after the collapse of the Uxbridge treaty in early 1645 – in other words, when the king's need for Irish troops had become critical, and the 'cautious councillors' at court were once again an obstacle to achieving this objective.

Digby's involvement in Irish policy was also unfortunate in that it added a political dimension to his feud with Prince Rupert – the personal antipathy which of all the rivalries in the king's party was the most damaging. One of the few issues on which Rupert's thinking seems to have moved beyond personal interest and pique was that of making significant concessions to the Confederates in return for Catholic troops to win the English Civil War. He, too, was distrustful of Antrim and O'Neill, and the only political reason he gave for urging an accommodation after Naseby was the conviction that the Confederates would cheat the king.[95] Yet Rupert's dislike of Digby and his political machinations might have been contained but for another unfortunate development – the queen's departure from Oxford in April 1644.

Although Henriette Marie's arrival at Oxford in July 1643 is generally seen as a major blow to the royalist 'moderates', her departure ten months later, accompanied by her closest adviser, Jermyn, was actually far more damaging to court unity. Over the winter of 1643–4 the queen's circle had made great efforts to reach an understanding with Rupert. Digby failed in this enterprise, and was covertly returning Rupert's hostility with interest by early 1644.[96] But Jermyn, with the help of Ormond's client and Rupert's court intelligencer, Arthur Trevor, was spectacularly successful.[97] Jermyn, the consummate courtier, might almost have been fashioned just to smooth Rupert's easily ruffled feathers. Besides soliciting the queen and the Oxford Parliament on Rupert's behalf, Jermyn kept a 'particular watche' on Digby and the prince's other court rivals.[98] According to Trevor, neither 'Rupert nor all the numbers in arithmeticke have any efficacy, but are cyphers, without lord Jermine'.[99]

Jermyn's departure from Oxford destroyed this promising new alliance. More than that, it deprived Rupert of his link to the queen, and to the influence and resources she commanded, just weeks after his brilliant victory at Newark on 22 March 1644 had raised the jealousy of his rivals to new heights. With both Rupert and Jermyn absent from court during the summer, the prince's great enemies – Digby, Culpeper, Percy, and Wilmot – openly professed indifference whether he or Parliament prevailed in the north.[100] Rupert, the exiled soldier-of-fortune, had no political power-base independent of the personal favour his success as a general brought him from the king.[101] Once his luck on the battlefield deserted him, his rivals realized it would be an easy matter to complete his estrangement from the king. Rupert's humiliating defeat at Marston Moor, in July 1644, offered them their chance.

In the wake of Marston Moor, Rupert vacillated between anger and despair, and spent much of September and October 1644 sulking at Bristol.[102] Indeed, on several occasions that autumn he declared that if his enemies at court were not suppressed he would abandon the royal cause.[103] Although he was made nominal commander-in-chief of the royal army in November 1644, this appointment, as he quickly discovered, was merely a precursor to the creation of a rival command – under the general of the king's western army, George Lord Goring – to 'counterpoise' (and neutralize) his own.[104] By mid-December, Richmond's secretary, Thomas Webb, was reporting that 'our soldiers are most for peace, Prince Rupert first of all'.[105] Rupert's great ally, Richmond, was also becoming disillusioned with court politics by December 1644. His efforts to advance the forthcoming peace talks with Parliament at Uxbridge were seen by the king as backsliding on the duke's part.[106] Within a few months of the collapse of the treaty in February 1645 – which the pro-accommodation faction blamed on Digby[107] – Richmond and Webb were involved in secret negotiations with the Independent grandees to surrender Oxford to the New Model Army.[108]

By the late summer of 1645 the factional battle-lines among the grandees were beginning to harden. The heads of the foreign alliance faction were Digby, Jermyn, Culpeper, and possibly the crypto-Catholic Lord Cottington; shortly to be joined by Ashburnham. In the pro-accommodation camp were Rupert, Richmond, Rupert's old enemy the Marquess of Hertford, and a majority of the 'Oxford lords', including the Earls of Dorset, Lindsey, Southampton, and Portland.[109] The Prince of Wales's councillors were too busy fighting their own battles in the West Country to engage fully with the deepening conflict among their former colleagues in Oxford and Paris.[110] The exception was Culpeper, whose willingness to consider 'expedients' had brought him closer to Digby from mid-1644;[111] and by the summer of 1645 his letters were echoing the views of the foreign alliance faction.[112]

III WHICH ALLIANCE? RIVAL ROYALIST STRATEGIES, 1645–7

Even after the crushing royalist defeats in England (at Naseby in June 1645) and in Scotland (at Philiphaugh that September), Digby, Jermyn, and Culpeper – the leaders of what might be termed the 'foreign intervention faction' – did not abandon hope of a Confederate army coming to the king's rescue. However, with Ormond seemingly taking forever to negotiate a treaty with the Irish, the English advocates of a foreign intervention began to consider an even more controversial course – a military alliance with their ostensible enemies, the Scottish Covenanters.[113] In this, their task was made easier by developments at Westminster. There, the growing power of the anti-Scottish, Independent faction was placing ever increasing strain on the Parliamentarian–Covenanter alliance; and by the autumn of 1645 the Scots were beginning to question whether their interests might not be better served in alliance with a defeated and, they hoped, chastened king rather than with the English Parliament.

The willingness of some Royalists to continue the war by allying with the Scots destroyed any prospect of the king's party uniting in the face of defeat. To the opponents of such an intervention – Richmond, Hertford and their circle – the idea of a restoration by means of a Covenanter army represented a far greater betrayal of the king's cause, and a more flagrant foreign encroachment on English sovereignty, than the importing of Irish Catholic troops. Hence, from the autumn of 1645, the Richmond–Hertford group was defined largely by its conviction that a negotiated settlement with Parliament was preferable to a rapprochement with the Scots. Consequently, in seeking an accommodation with Parliament it looked naturally to the Independents, who were themselves resolutely opposed to continuing Scottish intervention in English affairs.

To the dismay of the Richmond–Hertford group and their Independent allies, the conjunction of king and Covenanters became a reality in May 1646, when at the instigation of the queen and the French government, Charles surrendered to the Scottish army at Newark. Anxious to avoid a confrontation with the New Model Army, the Scots hurriedly decamped with their royal prize to the Covenanter garrison of Newcastle, out of reach of any parliamentarian bid to recapture the monarch. This was the opportunity the advocates of a foreign intervention, the Jermyn–Culpeper faction, had been waiting (and almost certainly planning) for – the king was in Scottish hands; the French were on side; and the Scots' allies at Westminster, the Presbyterians, were poised to lend political and military assistance if Charles and the Covenanters could reach an agreement. Only one contingency, it seemed, could undermine this projected alliance: if the Independents could seize the Prince of Wales and, should the king refuse their terms, set him on the throne in his father's stead.

The Channel Island of Jersey thus became the focus of the Jermyn–Culpeper faction's anxieties. The prince and his Council had taken refuge there in April 1646 after the collapse of the royalist war-effort in England, and although they were relatively safe in this island redoubt, rumours nevertheless abounded that the Independents were intent on the prince's capture.[114] Moreover, the queen and her circle had doubts as to the political reliability of the Prince's Council. They suspected, and with good reason, that some of the Councillors had tried to use the prince as a means of brokering a settlement with the Independents.[115] In June 1646, therefore, Jermyn, Digby, and Culpeper arrived on Jersey with explicit orders from the queen to remove the prince to France. This was the first time that the queen's circle and the prince's Councillors had rubbed shoulders in over a year, and it was only now that Jermyn, Digby, and Culpeper publicly made clear their support for a military alliance with Covenanters, backed by the French.

The arrival of Jermyn and his colleagues on Jersey precipitated a bitter quarrel among the assembled royalist grandees. When the prince's Councillors discovered what Jermyn, Culpeper, and Digby were advocating, most of them were appalled – in particular Hyde, the Earl of Berkshire, Capel, Hopton, and the king's veteran Lord General, the Earl of Brentford. Their hostility to a royalist–Scottish alliance was emphatic. Better, thought Hyde, that the king had been captured at Oxford by the New Model Army, than to seek restitution of his throne at the hands of the Scots.[116] The ensuing debate over how to respond to the queen's orders for the removal of the Prince of Wales to France (orders by now confirmed by the king) split the royalist grandees on Jersey down the middle. Predictably, the supporters of the royalist–Scottish alliance, Jermyn, Digby, and Culpeper, urged the Prince of Wales's immediate removal, arguing that their greatest hope of restoring the king lay with the French, 'not only for the assistance they were to receave from them in men or money, but for what the Scotts should doe for the Kinge; and that ... without the Prince's goinge into France, they would doe nothinge'.[117] Hyde and his friends responded that the king's best policy lay in fomenting the divisions between Independents and Presbyterians at Westminster. They argued that placing the Prince of Wales in the custody of a foreign (and Catholic) power, whose interests they regarded as antithetical to those of England, would only serve to re-unite the parties at Westminster, undermine the prospect of a negotiated settlement, and alienate the affections of the English people.[118] But the prince, eager to sample the delights of Paris, was quickly won over by Jermyn, and this 'great combustion' among the grandees ended rancorously, with a 'visible strangeness' growing between the two sides.[119] When the prince left for Paris – accompanied by Jermyn, Digby, and Culpeper – Hyde and his friends disdained to follow, remaining defiantly on Jersey. From then on, Hyde's circle was broadly aligned with their fellow opponents of the alliance with the Scots (and French), the Richmond–Hertford faction, back in England.[120]

The strategic and political choices that the pro-foreign intervention-ists had outlined on Jersey dictated the kind of royal concessions they thought were necessary in matters of religion. With the king and the Prince of Wales safely beyond the Independents' clutches, Jermyn, Culpeper, and Ashburnham wrote a series of letters to Charles begging him to abandon episcopacy in England and to take the Covenant (committing himself to a Presbyterian settlement throughout all three kingdoms). The Scots would not engage on his behalf, they assured him, unless he accepted a Presbyterian Church settlement in England.[121] But, they told the king, these would not have to be concessions made in good faith. They calculated that the king's engagement with the Scots would provoke a new civil war, and that a restoration of monarchy by means of an Anglo-Scottish Presbyterian army,[122] backed by the French, would give Charles the power, somewhere down the line, to restore his Crown and Church to their pre-war glory.

Theirs, however, was not the only royalist counsel the king was receiving during his Scottish captivity. In September 1646, while the Jermyn–Culpeper faction tried desperately to get Charles to do a deal with the Scots, Richmond and Hertford collaborated with leading oppo-nents of the Scots at Westminster – Sir Henry Vane junior, Oliver Cromwell, and other Independent grandees – to prevent such a conjunc-tion.[123] Communication between this anti-Scottish, Independent–royalist coalition and the king was difficult. From the moment of Charles's flight from Oxford in May 1646, the Scottish Covenanters had barred Richmond and his circle from attending the king,[124] and there-fore the Independent–royalist coalition conveyed its terms to Charles in secret, via the Clerk of the Closet (the cleric who controlled the king's private chapel, or 'closet'), Dr Richard Steward – a man who, it was noted, was 'animated in the highest degree against the Scotch and Presbyterians'.[125] The terms offered by the coalition were calculated to appeal to the king. If Charles would allow limited religious toleration, and wash his hands of the Covenant and Presbyterianism, Richmond and his Independent allies offered to restore him to 'the full execution of his regal authority', and to establish a 'moderated Episcopacy'.[126] In the event, the king – confident that he could do better than either set of

terms – rejected them both, and for a brief period over the winter of
1646–7, it looked as if the Scots had turned their back on Charles and
the fate of his English kingdom. The Scots agreed to withdraw their
army from England, and early in 1647 collected the first instalment of
the £400,000 they had been voted at Westminster to quit the kingdom,
and handed Charles over to the English Parliament. The strategy of
restoring the king's fortunes by seeking a foreign alliance, which had
already failed in the Irish context, now failed comprehensively again in
the Scottish; and the political standing of its leading advocates – Jermyn,
Culpeper, and the queen – declined accordingly.

The final reshuffle among the royalist 'gamesters' occurred in
response to the Scots' handover of the king to the English Parliament in
January 1647 – a readily justifiable and yet seemingly unsavoury trans-
action. Even men who had striven to remain above the factional fray, or
who had backed the idea of foreign military intervention, now looked
favourably on doing some kind of deal with Parliament's Independent
(and anti-Scottish) faction. To Ashburnham, Cottington, and Nicholas,
for example, the surrender of the king represented one betrayal too
many by the Scots, and they made common cause with the long-estab-
lished opponents of the Scots, the Richmond–Hertford faction.

IV   ROYALIST ENDGAMES, 1647–51

In the context of 1647, the first full year of peace in England since 1641,
it looked as though they had backed the winning side. Indeed, the internal contest between the royalist factions was all but decided, or so it
seemed, by the New Model Army's seizure of the king in June 1647. The
army's professed determination to restore the king to his 'Honour,
Crowne, & Dignity' gave the Richmond–Hertford faction and the
Independent grandees the perfect opportunity to resurrect their peace
initiative of September 1646.[127] Moreover, although the queen generally
favoured the Presbyterian interest, the Scots' 'betrayal' of Charles at the
beginning of 1647 had apparently dampened her enthusiasm for a
Scottish-brokered settlement. All that Jermyn and Culpeper could do, to
ensure they had at least some input in the anticipated settlement, was to
send one of their own circle, Sir John Berkeley, to mediate with the king's
captors.[128] Berkeley was joined on this mission by Ashburnham, who by
now was 'an implacable enemy to the Scots, and no friend to the other
[i.e. English] Presbyterians'.[129] Although Ashburnham co-operated with

Berkeley, in practice he seems to have answered principally to the Richmond–Hertford grandees, and their Independent allies.[130] The two men were assisted by 'the counsels and pressing persuasions of three persons permitted by the army at that time about him [the king], and in great credit with him' – apparently Richmond, Hertford, and Hyde's close friend, Lord Capel.[131] And the peace propositions that emerged from the army's consultations with the Independent and Richmond–Hertford grandees in the summer of 1647 – the Heads of Proposals – were probably an extended version of the terms they had offered the king the previous autumn.[132]

Whatever their origins, however, the Heads represent the fullest expression of the convergence between the anti-Scots Royalists and Independents within the English Parliament. Their alliance was based on a number of shared convictions. First, there was an appreciation that there could be no viable settlement that ignored the strength of feeling in England for episcopacy and the Book of Common Prayer, or that failed to extend liberty of conscience to the godly.[133] Secondly, there was a chauvinistic tendency to see the relationship between the two British kingdoms in terms of England's 'ancient superioritie' over Scotland;[134] and in both camps this English chauvinism shaded into a xenophobic dislike of the Scottish people themselves – 'the Off-Scum[m]e of the world' as one Royalist called them;[135] 'that beggarly nation', in the words of the Independent grandee the Earl of Northumberland.[136] Thirdly, there was a shared desire to demarcate and preserve an English frame of government, and an apprehension of the threat to national sovereignty and honour posed by foreign intervention – particularly in the form of Covenanting 'confederalism', as Allan Macinnes has termed it (Scottish desires for a 'joint interest' in governing all three Stuart kingdoms). Figures as seemingly poles apart as Oliver Cromwell and the Duke of Richmond's secretary, Thomas Webb, interpreted the Scots' political ambitions in almost identical fashion – as an attempt to 'vassalise' the English people.[137] Finally, the anti-Scots Royalists and the Independent Parliamentarians were united, too, by a deep distrust of the French Crown and its perceived ambition to keep England weak and divided.[138] It is revealing that most of the leading figures in the pro-Spanish (and therefore, of course, anti-French) clique at court during the 1630s aligned with the Richmond–Hertford faction in the 1640s.[139] Several of the Jermyn–Culpeper faction, by contrast, were pensioners of the French Crown.[140] And whereas the Richmond–Hertford faction at the very least acquiesced in the Independents' programme to re-assert

English hegemony in the three kingdoms, the pro-Scottish (and pro-French) Jermyn–Culpeper faction apparently envisaged a state of pragmatic collaboration among the British and Irish Protestant élites, possibly involving the creation of an Anglo-Scottish court of the kind that was to be outlined in the Engagement – the treaty that Charles signed late in 1647 with the Covenanter faction led by the Duke of Hamilton.[141]

Charles's rejection of the Heads and signing of the Engagement revived the political fortunes of the Jermyn–Culpeper faction, which had been scheming in favour of Scottish military intervention since 1645. At the same time, however, the Engagement served to widen the breach in royalist ranks. The Richmond–Hertford grandees would have nothing to do with a royalist campaign based upon another Scottish invasion; while Hyde denounced the Engagement as a thing 'most scandalous and derogatory to the honour and interest of the English nation'.[142] The Richmond–Hertford faction and the Independent and army grandees continued to pursue their goal of an exclusively English monarchical settlement to within a few days of king's execution in January 1649.[143] After the regicide a distraught Richmond, Hertford, and their circle withdrew from political life. But although the king's grisly demise was a consequence, if not an inevitable one, of the failure of the royalist–Scottish alliance, Jermyn and Culpeper continued to insist 'that the condition of his [Charles II's] affayres doth enact noething in the world soe pressingly of him as that he goe to the utmost length he can possibly for suche a satisfaction of Scotland as may beget an unanimous engagement of the nation for his interests'.[144] The power-struggle between the rival royalist factions had fatally undermined the king's cause during the Second Civil War (summer 1648), and was to have a significant negative impact both on Ormond's royalist coalition in Ireland in 1648 and 1649, and on the Scottish invasion of England in 1651.[145] Only the Scots' defeat at the battle of Worcester in September 1651 finally gave victory in this struggle to Hyde and other anti-foreign-intervention grandees – the group that was to dominate royal counsels through to the Restoration and beyond.

V THE ROYALISTS, THE CONSTITUTION, AND THE PEOPLE

Here then are the outlines of a new model of royalist politics, highlighting the 'British' and European context of divisions in the king's party.

Despite fears in the Richmond–Hertford camp that their rivals' policy of allying with the Scots would subvert the integrity of English government, there is no evidence that the warring royalist factions had come to embrace radically different ideas about the constitution in the sense of the rules and laws defining the scope of royal authority. Their quarrel was more political and tactical than ideological. Two rival royalist networks had emerged by 1647 – one in Paris around the queen and the Jermyn–Culpeper grandees, the other centred upon Richmond and Hertford – and both were determined to exclude the other from any honour or advantage entailed in restoring the king.

The rival royalist camps were sharply at odds not only over the means by which the king should be restored but also about how he was to re-affirm and exercise his authority in the post-restoration order. The Richmond–Hertford group attached great importance to the re-estab-lishment of episcopacy in some form or other – partly no doubt because they knew the king would settle for nothing less; but also because, like Charles, they regarded it as integral to the proper exercise of royal authority. Not that Richmond and his allies were all devout sons of the Church of England, or that the Jermyn–Culpeper group were closet Catholics or irreligious pragmatists. The most notorious Catholics or crypto-Catholics at court – 'Don' Cottington and Endymion Porter – aligned with the Richmond–Hertford faction.[146] And although Digby would convert to Catholicism in the 1650s, during the 1640s the queen's circle were all avowed Protestants (with the possible exception of Jermyn, whose confessional allegiance was and remains a complete mystery).[147]

Unfortunately, we know so little about the political calculations of the Richmond–Hertford grandees that we have to rely instead on the writ-ings of Hyde, Nicholas, and their correspondents, who were clearly in sympathy with the grandees' objectives but not necessarily privy to their counsels. But if we can take Hyde and Nicholas as broadly representa-tive of the Richmond–Hertford group, their desire for an episcopal Church settlement was linked closely to their conviction that much of the king's power was located in the affections of the English people, 'without which he hath no hope of reigning'.[148] Royal authority, to their mind, was not an exclusively political phenomenon, derived from specific rights and powers; it was also a moral force, rooted in a recipro-cal relationship of trust and loyalty between monarch and people, and indivisible from the honour of the English nation.[149] This view of the monarchy shaped their political priorities. The king, they believed, was obliged to regain power, but only in a manner consistent with retaining the affection of his subjects; which, in turn, meant respecting their attachment to traditional worship according to the Book of Common Prayer. One of the most effective instruments for governing the people's affections, thought Hyde and Nicholas, was the episcopate: the group of 'lords spiritual' whose nomination and promotion was entirely in the king's power. As Hyde explained: 'There is no question the Clergy will always have an extraordinary influence upon the people; and therefore . . . there must be a way to govern the Clergy absolutely, and keep it subject to the rules, and orders of State; which never was, nor ever can be, without Bishops; so that in truth civil prudence would make unanswerable arguments for that order, if piety did not.'[150] The 'right and reverence of the Crown' were thus inseparable from episcopal government of the church.[151]

The pro-Scottish group of courtiers – and, in particular, Jermyn and Culpeper – took a very different view. They perceived the monarchy in more narrowly political terms, as one among several competing interests. And just as the forging of a strong military party was the 'only engine' to restore the king, so the sword, as embodied in the militia, was necessary to maintain 'the power and dignity of [the] . . . Crowne' thereafter.[152] Without 'the power of the sword', wrote Jermyn and Culpeper, '. . . the Kingly office signefyes very litle'.[153] Even before the Civil War, Culpeper had feared the 'dreadful consequences which would attend the yielding in the point of the militia'.[154] He and Jermyn had little faith that the English people's loyalty to the king could be harnessed for political or military purposes. Popular approval, or disapproval, therefore figured little in their calculations, and could be set aside altogether for the sake of obtaining foreign military assistance. 'All that they [the Scottish Covenanters] can ask' (including, of course, the abolition of bishops from the English Church), argued Culpeper, 'or the King part with, is a trifle in respect of the price of a Crown.'[155] All, that is, except military resources. Control of an army was the key to power, not control of the pulpits. Jermyn and Culpeper, like another key figure in the pro-Scottish alliance faction, the Earl of Newcastle,[156] subscribed to Hobbes's dictum 'that he that is Master of the Militia, is Master of the Kingdom, and consequently is in possession of a most absolute Sovereignty'.[157]

Obviously, the manner and terms of the king's restoration would have huge implications for the constitutional arrangements in and between the three Stuart kingdoms. But to portray royalist factionalism as essentially a struggle for or over the constitution is a distortion. None of the royalist grandees wanted to grub up the foundations of English government and restore the king as an arbitrary ruler. Their quarrel was not about whether Charles should govern with or without Parliament, through or above the law. It was rooted in deeper tensions – conflicting ideas about the foundations of royal authority (were they essentially moral or political?); the relationship between the Crown and the people (should it rest upon force or love?); and even the nature of English nationhood itself (could another nation, like the Scots, be allowed a voice in deciding the future of its Church?). Inviting Irish Catholics and Scottish Covenanters to restore the English monarchy challenged royalist thinking on all these issues, and it is here that any investigation into the structure of the king's party during the 1640s must begin.

2. Anglicanism and Royalism in the 1640s

ANTHONY MILTON

Royalist religion has generally received little attention from historians compared with the care that they have lavished on the religious concerns of Parliamentarians. Nevertheless, a number of important studies have emphasized the importance of religious conservatism in generating support for Royalism. Particularly important here has been the pioneering work of John Morrill, who in a celebrated article traced the significant evidence of Anglican survivalism and liturgical conservatism in the 1640s, which suggested that the Book of Common Prayer had dug deep roots into popular, parochial culture. The work of David Underdown and Mark Stoyle has connected these forms of religious conservatism explicitly with popular Royalism, linking popular attachment to parochial religious traditions with a broader attachment to festive culture and hatred of puritans in securing royalist allegiance.[1] In this work, 'Anglicanism' can thus be seen as providing a critical ideological cement for Royalism, providing a focus for cultural conservatism that could unite élites, middling sorts and poorer groups alike. It would become a rallying call for anti-puritan opinion and, as such, a crucial spiritual and social resource for those opposed to the political and social developments of the 1640s and 1650s.

This picture provides a notable contrast to historians' work on the pre-war Church of England, which has often emphasized the degree of hostility that the Church had generated in the 1630s. Under Archbishop Laud, the clergy and their officials had stirred up bitter controversy, their doctrinal and ceremonial innovations and their clericalist agenda serving to alienate the laity, so that when the Long Parliament met in November 1640 it was besieged by complaints against the Church and clergy. How, then, did the Church regain lay support? Partly, it is implied, this was because the destruction of Laudianism allowed people's natural allegiance to the structures of the Church of England to re-assert itself. It was also because the clergy themselves adopted a more low-key and circumspect demeanour, far removed from the clerical excesses of the 1630s Laudians. The 'Anglican' ideology of the 1640s and 1650s has thus often tended to be described in terms of moderation, rationality and 'erastianism' (in the broad sense that 'Anglican' divines accepted that the Church should be subordinate in its affairs to the wishes of the secular authorities).[2] Historians have written of the 'transformation' of 'Anglicanism' in this period, and the growth of 'moralism'. Shorn of abrasive Laudianism, it emerged instead as a religion which was 'theologically prudent, socially deferential and liturgically restrained' – ready to become the understated, syncretic and quintessentially moderate 'Anglicanism' more readily recognizable to modern eyes than that of the Calvinist prelates of Elizabeth I or the rampant Laudianism of Charles I.[3] It is in a sense the counterpart of the 'constitutional Royalism' described by other historians.[4]

A general picture has thus emerged of a chastened Church of England, rediscovering the people's devotion only as it loses control of events after the excesses of Laudianism. Essentially, it has regained its appeal for the laity because it has assumed again its role as supporter of the forces of social conservatism. This is a union encapsulated most vividly in the pages of the royalist newsbook *Mercurius Rusticus*, where accounts of outrages suffered by gentry and noble families merge imperceptibly into narratives of attacks on churches and clergymen.[5] The alliance of church and aristocracy is further manifested in the famous images of suffering clergymen taking refuge in gentry households, writing improving works of practical divinity, and ministering to the needs of a local congregation devoted to the simple non-controversial rhythms of the Prayer Book. It is Jeremy Taylor at the Earl of Carbery's Carmarthenshire countryseat, Golden Grove; Henry Hammond in the Pakington household; Gilbert Sheldon making his home with the Okeover and Shirley families.[6]

In contrast to the clericalism of the 1630s, then, this is a de-Laudianized clergy and a de-Laudianized religion. It is essentially erastian in outlook, deferential to lay (and especially gentry) interests and attentive to lay concerns. Most of all, it is attentive to the Crown: it is churchmen who oversee the process whereby the executed king is turned into an Anglican martyr. And with the developing cult of the royal martyr, the union of Anglicanism and Royalism seems complete.

There is much evidence to support this picture. But this evidence often tends to come from the 1650s. It is less clear that Anglicanism was playing the same erastian, conservative, moderating role in the 1640s. Moreover, this is a picture that tends to conflate certain developments in Anglicanism and Royalism, and to assume the triumph of shared interests.

In this essay I wish to focus on the relationship between Anglicanism and Royalism, and particularly the apparent reconciliation of the clergy and the laity. Had the Church of England and its clergy truly turned into the de-Laudianized, moderate, deferential and erastian divines who could endorse the social and cultural conservatism that was so central to the royalist message? As I hope to demonstrate, the relationship between Anglicanism and Royalism was not straightforward, and the interests of Stuart Royalism and of the Church of England need not necessarily have run in the same direction. There were important potential tensions and divisions. And the 'Anglicanism' of the 1640s was not necessarily as reflective or quietist, or indeed as erastian, as has often been implied. Doctrinal innovation and radically new modes of thought can be found among 'Anglican' royalist divines as well as among the Parliamentarians. It will be suggested that royalist religion, like Royalism itself, was a more shifting, dynamic and complex phenomenon than is often implied.

I ROYALISM AND THE RETREAT FROM LAUDIANISM

We should begin with the fact that, if we study the emergence of Royalism in the early 1640s, it does seem marked by a determined effort to turn its back on the Laudian past. Future Royalists seem to have been prepared to contemplate significant reforms of episcopacy and of the Prayer Book, and if a settlement had been reached in either 1641 or 1643 it might have seen some significant changes in the English Church.

Royal policy in the early 1640s seemed to turn itself resolutely against Laudianism. Laud himself was abruptly and unceremoniously abandoned by the king. Just as significantly, Laud's *bêtes noires* John Williams (the Bishop of Lincoln) and James Ussher (the Archbishop of Armagh) were welcomed back into the king's counsels.[7] A series of new appointments to bishoprics in the years 1641–3 included a number of Calvinist divines who had either been in trouble with Laud or had mustered little obvious enthusiasm for his reforms.[8] Among them, John Prideaux had been an outspoken enemy of Laud and his allies since the 1620s, and Thomas Westfield had opposed the '*et cetera* oath' and the sitting of Convocation after the dissolution of the Short Parliament in May 1640. Ralph Brownrigg, another newly appointed bishop, was married to John Pym's niece and had already played a notable role in opposing

Laudianism in Cambridge University in the 1630s and in the Short Parliament Convocation of 1640.[9]

Many of these appointments to bishoprics might appear to be attempts to buy off the opposition in 1641 – even at the time Charles had urged them as evidence that he had altered his former views 'to satisfye the times'.[10] But with the need to appeal to the middle ground in 1642, the initial mustering of the royalist party was carried out with the tone of the religious revolution of 1640–41. Of the list of Lenten preachers at court in 1642, more than one-third had been either unenthusiastic or positively hostile towards the Laudian reforms of the 1630s.[11]

The court struck a determinedly anti-Laudian note in other ways. Charles repeatedly promised in the early 1640s to maintain the Church of England in 'the established and true reformed Protestant religion as it stood in its beauty in the happy days of Queen Elizabeth, without any connivance of popery'. This undertaking was most notably made, perhaps, in 1643 as a formal public oath before receiving communion from (significantly) Archbishop Ussher. Charles's words were shot through with ambiguity, of course: the same words had been used in the preface to the Laudian canons of 1640. But as John Adamson has recently noted, more important than Charles's actual words was the presence of the famously anti-Laudian and unimpeachably Calvinist Ussher when he spoke them.[12]

It was Ussher, too, who (along with Richard Holdsworth and Ralph Brownrigg) had presented Charles with a plan for 'reduced episcopacy' in 1641.[13] And it was plans for a 'moderate' or 'regulated episcopacy' that often seem to have been the Royalists' chosen stance in their negotiations with Parliament during the Civil War.[14] Various royalist divines wrote in support of it. The removal of the coercive elements of episcopacy, and perhaps also the abolition of clerical JPs, appears to have been a price that most Royalists considered worth paying in peace negotiations, even if they were still insistent that episcopacy must be retained in some form. With the Royalists in a weaker position in later negotiations, royalist divines seem to have been ready to contemplate various forms of religious toleration, as well as further limitations on bishops' freedom of action.[15]

In ideological terms, too, it is clear that at various points the royalist position was expressed in directly anti-Laudian terms. In royal declarations, the king distanced himself from the extremes of the 1630s – indeed, the final royal declaration issued on 12 August 1642 before the outbreak of war made precisely this point, condemning the excesses of the Court of High Commission in particular.[16] In that other fundamental (if posthumous) statement of the Caroline position, the *Eikon Basilike*, Charles stated that on the calling of the Long Parliament he resolved to expiate, by laws, the odium and offences 'which some mens Rigor and Remisness in Church and State had contracted upon my Government'.[17]

This concern to distance themselves from the excesses of Laudianism was not merely felt by lay Royalists. A series of royalist divines such as George Morley and Robert Sanderson also explicitly condemned the policies of the 1630s. In a visitation sermon at Grantham in 1641, Sanderson specifically distinguished the Church of England's position from those who had busied themselves and troubled others with putting forward new rites and ceremonies with scandal and without law, using the Church's name to serve their own purposes. In his *Modest Advertisement* of 1641, George Morley defined himself very specifically at the end of the work against those who would not accept changes to episcopacy. He stated unequivocally that it would be a sin not to harken to the people's complaints. It was the Church's deafness to such complaints that was the cause of God's current chastisement. In particular, Morley appealed for a more rigorous observance of the Sabbath, urged 'that pietie and godlinesse (the substance of Religion) be more attended than rites and ceremonies', and argued against arbitrary church government, and clergymen 'hunting after secular imploiment'.[18]

Several historians have noted that these developments all seemed to promise a very 'low church' form of Anglicanism. Conrad Russell has suggested that if peace had come in 1641, a revitalized Church under Williams would have been closer to the Church of James I than to that of the 1630s.[19] Similarly, John Adamson has recently argued that, had the Royalists secured a victory in 1643, the prominence of Ussher and Williams in Charles's counsels suggests that it would have resulted in a very 'Low Church' settlement indeed.[20]

II THE RETURN OF LAUDIANISM?

The anti-Laudian and erastian tone of the early years of Civil-War Royalism are, then, unmistakable. What is less clear, however, is whether this represented the emergence of a more supine clergy, ready to accept erastian tutelage. It is understandable that historians should sometimes have made this assumption. The clerical leadership, as we shall see, seems to have been happy to comply with their less assertive, essentially supporting role, and to recognize the need for religious compromises in peace negotiations. After all, the concessions drawn up by the Oxford clergy before the Uxbridge negotiations in January 1645 allowed for religious toleration and a curbing of the powers of bishops, and in 1647 a number of prominent clergymen similarly advised Charles that he could allow the toleration of another religion if necessity required it.[21] Rather than the assertive Laudian clergy, we seem to have a craven one happy to support whatever seems in the changing interest of the Crown. There also seems to be a new generation, a new set of names, promoting this newly discreet 'Anglicanism' – headed by the likes of Richard Steward, Gilbert Sheldon, Jeremy Taylor and Henry Hammond.

Nevertheless, as I hope to demonstrate, there are problems in this view of a discreet, erastian and fundamentally supine royalist clergy. One basic problem with this account (and indeed with the view of the 1650s with which we began) relates to the role of Laudianism – there seems to be an assumption in this model that it has simply disappeared, or has been surgically removed. It cannot be denied that some famous Laudians were indeed out of the way – William Laud and Matthew Wren were in the Tower; Richard Montagu, Francis White, Richard Neile and John Pocklington were dead. But there *were* still Laudians in the public domain, and they were not inactive. Most notable in this respect are the editors of the royalist newsletter *Mercurius Aulicus*: Peter Heylyn and John Berkenhead were both men of impeccable Laudian credentials.[22]

Moreover, men like Heylyn and Berkenhead were not simply muttering resentfully on the sidelines. If a study is made of the lists of Lenten preachers at court for 1644 rather than 1642, it is clear the Laudian clergy seem to have regained the driving seat. Over two-thirds of the listed preachers had clear Laudian credentials, and only two had records of being unenthusiastic towards the Laudian reforms.[23] If there were an anti-Laudian swing in the highest royalist circles in the early 1640s, it would seem to have been reversed by 1644. Indeed, if Ussher and Williams are taken as the leading anti-Laudian religious figures, it would seem that they had both been effectively marginalized by 1644, with Williams away in Wales and Ussher alienated by the court's increasing recourse to Irish Catholics for military support. The new, more Calvinist episcopal appointments of 1641–3 do not appear to have played any significant role in the king's counsels thereafter. It was veterans of the

Laudian 1630s such as Duppa and Juxon to whom the king appealed for instruction of his conscience in 1646.[24]

Moreover, the suggestion that is sometimes made that the 1640s were marked by the emergence of a new moderate clerical generation, with no links to the past, is arguably based on something of an optical illusion. Many of those clergymen gaining greater prominence in Charles's counsels in the 1640s had enjoyed good relations with Laud in the 1630s. For example, if Jeremy Taylor was not a Laudian in 1642, then it is difficult to see who was. Taylor had been briefly Laud's chaplain and was unquestionably the archbishop's protégé: Laud had secured him his Oxford fellowship, was the dedicatee of Taylor's first published work, and would have been of his second, if he had not been imprisoned in the Tower in the meantime.[25] Newly prominent figures such as Richard Steward and Gilbert Sheldon also appear to have been unquestioned allies of Laud in the 1630s.[26]

Nevertheless, there is no need for us to become involved in a pointless parlour game of who in the 1640s should be taken to 'count' as a 'Laudian'. I have argued elsewhere that it might be more helpful to think of the 1630s, not as the triumph of a Laudian 'party', but rather as a 'Laudian moment', which embraced clergymen from a very diverse range of backgrounds and temperaments. In this sense 'Laudianism' was more a dominant discourse in Church and state, a set of associations and a language that people learned to speak. Many clergymen were swept up by this increasingly dominant discourse, an additional attraction being that it was an obvious route to preferment.[27] It was a 'moment' that for many was over in 1640, with the fall of Laud himself, and some clerics concentrated on then distancing themselves from 'Laudianism'. These included the saintly Robert Sanderson, who enthusiastically dedicated sermons to Laud in 1637 – 'preached by appointment of your grace' – and then (as we have seen) self-righteously condemned Laudian excesses in 1641.[28] Even Laud himself hastily rejected the 1640 canons, and condemned the implementation of the Scottish Prayer Book.[29] By 1641, 'Laudianism' had become the phenomenon that people distanced themselves from – a useful 'other' which could be condemned in order to vindicate the orthodoxy of one's own position. What was happening in the early 1640s, then, was not the mere disappearance of a party, but rather a process whereby different former participants in the 'Laudian moment' embarked upon a new range of different political and ideological trajectories. We cannot therefore attempt to write the 1640s as if we are starting afresh with a new collection of clergymen and a new consensualist 'Anglicanism'. The reality is a good deal messier and murkier, and marked by complex continuities and discontinuities. 'Laudianism' emerged in the specific context of the 1630s – there was no single obvious route that a 'Laudian' should tread in the 1640s. After all, William Juxon was Laud's friend and ally and the overseer of his will, yet he managed to remain in good odour with most of the Parliamentarians throughout the 1640s.[30] There is a danger, too, that when historians note clergymen like Richard Steward or Brian Duppa being prepared to support religious concessions as part of peace treaties, they are tempted to take this as evidence of their lack of Laudian concerns, rather than as evidence that those of documented Laudian convictions might be prepared under duress to contemplate such concessions.

But even as we note the value of anti-Laudianism to future Royalists in the early 1640s, it is perhaps worth raising a caveat against the temptation to see this as a dominant discourse within Royalism. Even the 1641–2 petitions in favour of episcopacy and the Prayer Book fail to distance themselves from any specific Laudian errors. Eleven of the petitions collected by Dr Maltby make no allusion whatsoever to any religious problems of the 1630s, while the remainder make only the briefest and vaguest references to the errors of 'some particular persons', 'late innovations' and 'exorbitancies'.[31] Even vague allusions to the ecclesiastical 'excesses' of the 1630s are quite rare in the religious writings of royalist clergy, and became all the more infrequent as the 1640s continued. It is notable that the author of *A Vindication of Episcopacie*, published in 1644, felt no need to concede that there had been any Laudian excesses when he confuted the charges that bishops had recently entrenched upon the subjects' liberties and had been guilty of popish innovations.[32] The author rebuffed the charges by having recourse to anti-Puritanism – an increasingly prominent discourse in Royalism that would only have been weakened by specific anti-Laudian allusions.[33] Historians may sometimes need to pay more attention to what royalist divines were *not* saying, and how far they were really prepared to associate themselves with the ecclesiastical reforms of 1641.[34]

III   CLERGY AND LAITY

In fact, if the evidence of the 1640s is studied without an assumption of the pre-existence of a sanitized, reasonable, moderate and normative

'Anglicanism' that would consolidate in the 1650s and ultimately triumph at the Restoration, then a more complex picture of the clergy, and of royalist religion in general, tends to emerge. A key issue here is the apparently natural alliance of lay and clerical interest in Civil-War Royalism. We are so used to the image of Royalists collectively swooning at the death of the noble Lord Falkland that it is worth observing that *Mercurius Aulicus* was notably perfunctory in describing his death, while Heylyn noted in his diary: 'this day died Lord Falkland, in whom the Church lost no great friend – I am sure I did not'.[35] Falkland had been happy to launch a systematic attack on Laudian clericalism as the price for impeding the Root-and-Branch petition against bishops. The Laudian bishops and their adherents were, he proclaimed, guilty 'of the destruction of unitie under pretence of uniformity: to have brought in superstition, and scandall, under the titles of reverence, and decency; to have defil'd our Church by adorning our Churches'. Obsessed with preaching 'the sacrednesse of the clergie' and working to create 'a blind dependance of the people upon the clergie', Falkland depicted the Laudian clergy as ultimately being of popish beliefs: some were 'so absolutely directly and cordially Papist, that it is all that fifteene hundred pounds a yeare can doe to keep them from confessing it [Popery]'.[36]

Small wonder, then, that Falkland was happy to support the bill to exclude bishops from the House of Lords. But he was not the only prominent Royalist to have supported the bill, and it was on the advice of Sir John Culpeper – the Chancellor of the Exchequer – that Charles had given his assent to the Bishops' Exclusion Act in 1642, ejecting the entire episcopate from the House of Lords. And even when the peers had initially refused to exclude bishops from the House in June 1641, they had happily agreed (royalist peers among them) to the exclusion of clergy from the Court of Star Chamber, the Privy Council, temporal courts, and from being Justices of the Peace. Lord Digby and Sir John Culpeper had also presented grievances against Laudianism to Parliament; indeed, Digby had proposed to the Commons that evidence should be gathered against all those ministers responsible for the policies of recent years.[37]

The years 1640–2 had then seen a systematic attack on the Church of England, with bishops imprisoned and ministers deprived of their livings and freehold by Parliament; the Court of High Commission abolished; iconoclasm; attacks on cathedrals and their chapters; countless clergymen petitioned against and summoned before Parliament; church courts stifled; the licensing of religious literature taken over by

Parliament; and bishops excluded from the Lords.[38] Not only had some future Royalists been complicit with this – and in some cases they had been in the vanguard of the attack – but also the bishops' removal from Parliament was in a sense enshrined in one of the most important but also problematic of royalist documents, the *Answer to the Nineteen Propositions* of June 1642.[39] The *Answer* rendered the three estates of Parliament as king, Lords and Commons, rather than as Lords Spiritual, Lords Temporal and Commons, thus treating the bishops as no longer one of the estates. This fundamental royalist text could therefore be construed as supporting the Bishops' Exclusion Act of February 1642 – a contentious piece of legislation that was physically re-enacted every day that the Oxford Parliament (convened in January 1644, the royalist rival to the Parliament at Westminster) met with no bishops present.

It is important for historians to consider how these sorts of attacks could have left real scars and resentments among the clergy. In the face of such assaults, the royalist clergy were understandably on the defensive. But they were not simply acquiescent, and their resentment can sometimes be observed seeping out. Most notable in this respect are the writings of Bishop Griffith Williams. Incidentally, as Williams is sometimes described as 'the Irish bishop', with the implication that he was marginal to the English political and religious scene, it must be stressed that he had spent many years at the Caroline court as domestic chaplain to the Lord Chamberlain, the fourth Earl of Pembroke; he was only appointed Bishop of Ossory in 1641 at the age of 52, and fled back to England within a month of his consecration (although he did return to Ireland on subsequent occasions).[40] Williams was forthright in his denunciation of the behaviour of lay Royalists towards the Church. He stated bluntly in his *Discoverie of Mysteries* published in 1643 (despite Falkland's attempts to block it)[41] that he now feared the secret enemies of Church and state who lurked at the king's court more than those enemies who lay in the Earl of Essex's camp.[42] Williams traced a plot against Church and state dating back to the beginning of the Long Parliament, but saw the plot still at work in the *royalist* camp, especially among those around Charles who supported an attack on the government and patrimony of the Church, who 'pretending great loyalty unto him . . . either to raise or to secure their owne fortunes, would perswade S. Paul to part with S. Peters keyes, so he may still hold the sword in his hand; or to speake more plainly, to purchase the peace of the Commonwealth with the ruine of Gods Church'.[43]

There were other writers expressing alarm, even if they were less outspoken. John Bramhall in his *Serpent Salve* of 1643 was clearly writing through gritted teeth when he remarked that he assumed that there was a good reason for removing the bishops' votes in the Lords, but he did not doubt that there would be other good reasons for restoring them again.[44] When Heylyn and Williams complained that slavery had been imposed on the clergy by depriving them of their parliamentary representatives, they were not necessarily alone in their thinking.[45] The omission of the bishops from the three estates in the *Answer to the Nineteen Propositions* was attacked directly in a work by Heylyn that was stopped at the Oxford press, and another by Griffith Williams that got through.[46] But it was also rejected by implication in works by Bramhall, John Doughty and Henry Ferne – indeed, it is difficult to find any clerical authors agreeing with it.[47]

Moreover, Heylyn and Williams were not alone in distrusting the devotion of the royalist high command when it came to upholding episcopacy. Some of the most important defences of episcopacy were in fact written in order to prevent fellow-Royalists from sacrificing it in peace agreements. Henry Ferne wrote a whole tract specifically against those who felt that episcopacy might be abandoned without prejudicing their religion and their devotion to the king's cause.[48] Similarly, Henry Hammond's *Considerations of Present Use concerning the Danger resulting from the Change of our Church Government* (1645) was specifically aimed at those who believed that episcopal government was lawful but yet thought that to sacrifice it was not a change of religion; he criticized the 'sonnes of this Church' who thought Church government 'so unconsiderable a thing, and so extrinsecall to Christianity' that it could be surrendered 'merely out of intuition of our own secular advantages'.[49] It is notable that Hammond set himself to oppose the charge that those who insisted on the need to preserve episcopacy simply preferred 'the interests of some inconsiderable men before the inconveniences and common wishes of all', and that it was only clergymen whose interests were concerned in the business – this was presumably the complaint being made in lay royalist circles.[50]

In this context, historians might profitably reconsider some of the strident attacks made on royalist immorality from Oxford pulpits in the 1640s, where the debauchery and irreligion of royalist soldiers was condemned as inviting God's retribution. Preachers such as William Chillingworth frankly expressed the wish that the Royalists believed in God as much as they believed in the king.[51] These could simply represent early manifestations of that preoccupation with personal and collective morality which, it has been argued, would come to characterize Interregnum Anglicanism.[52] But these assaults were being made by a clergy anxious at being sidelined. In the hands of one writer, at least, the political potential of such jeremiads was laid out specifically. Griffith Williams noted sourly how young lords spent their time dicing and whoring, in order to bolster his argument that bishops were much more fit than such debauched aristocrats to advise the king on political affairs at court and in Parliament.[53]

That these disputes and tensions between laity and clergy existed on the royalist as well as the parliamentarian side should not come as a surprise. The work of Andrew Foster has amply demonstrated how strong the resurgent clericalism of the early seventeenth century was, and just how violent a lay reaction it provoked (even if this was sometimes disproportionate to the ground that the clergy had in fact regained).[54] Attacks on clerical JPs, and on the secular powers of bishops, were the latest stage of a very long-running battle that transcended the divisions of Royalist and Parliamentarian. For all of the apparent reconciliation of gentry and clergy in the 1650s, that incorrigible royalist the Earl of Newcastle was presumably not alone among royalist aristocrats in his emphasis that lay support would be forthcoming only on the condition of 'the Clergye not medleing in Laye Busines . . . and the Church not being proude, And Haughty, over the Layety, but Gentle & Curtious to them'. For Newcastle, this meant (among other things) no bishops being made Lord Keeper or Lord Treasurer, and no clergyman being made a Justice of the Peace.[55]

Given these tensions, it should be clear that clergymen's constant emphasis in royalist propaganda on the interdependence of Church and state, and on the secular utility of episcopacy and the established Church, was not just a parroting of a staple *topos* of Royalism. It also in part reflected an ongoing struggle by the clergy to defend their own position against lay hostility and indifference, and the charge that they were obstructing a political settlement. In this context, newsbooks such as *Mercurius Rusticus* – edited by the royal chaplain, Bruno Ryves – did not simply attempt to stir up royalist outrage and fear with their tales of outrages against gentlefolk and clergymen. They also sought systematically, by their wealth of horror stories, to prime the reader to assume a natural and fundamental connection between the fortunes of the clergy and of the gentry, between anti-clericalism and sacrilege on the one hand and the assaults and indignities suffered by social élites on the other. This makes it all the more significant that those royalist newsbooks that were not the work of clergymen may have displayed much less concern with the fate of the Church and clergy.[56] Clergymen's constant emphasis on the interconnection of the fate of the Church and of social hierarchies, and the more general phenomenon of the Anglican clergy's apparent erastianism in the 1640s and 1650s, can be explained in part by simple practicalities: the Church was no longer there to provide defence, patronage and support to clergymen. These resources could only be obtained from the king and from social élites. The systematic attempts by Sheldon and Hammond in the 1650s to place displaced royalist clergymen in gentry households were not simply motivated by the need to provide for clerics in need, but also were a means of ensuring that the royalist gentry were kept firmly on the Church's side.[57] In this sense, the erastianism of those divines of the king's party was a practical response to the reality of the weakness of the Church as a source of power and patronage, but did not necessarily represent an ideological shift on the clergy's part.

These practical concerns of the royalist clergy are important to bear in mind when we consider their backing for some of the peace negotiations during the Civil War and afterwards. As we have noted, they drew up a series of major concessions before the Uxbridge negotiations that seemed to comply with a more erastian agenda. Similarly, prominent bishops assured Charles in 1646 that it would be legitimate for him to allow Presbyterianism for (an experimental) three years. In 1647, a number of prominent royalist clergymen similarly advised him that he could allow the toleration of another religion if necessity required it. And in 1648, at Newport, it was even reported that bishops Juxon and Duppa begged the king to agree to the alienation of bishops' lands to save his throne.[58] But how far should these responses be read as simple evidence of moderation and peaceableness on the part of the clergy concerned? There is a danger that some essentialist 'moderation' on their part is being assumed, when the clergy concerned may rather have simply displayed a readiness to contemplate a series of disagreeable expedients when the very survival of the Church and bishops was at stake.[59] Forms of reduced episcopacy might be suggested, and theoretically endorsed, but no real theological or historical justifications for such a reduced episcopacy found their way into print. Ussher's scheme was not published until after his death in 1656, and Civil-War authors such as Hammond, Taylor and Ferne wrote no sustained justifications for such a scheme.[60] Nevertheless, 'reduced episcopacy' was always the best that the royalist clergy could possibly hope for, and after September 1643, when

Parliament had entered the Solemn League and Covenant with Scotland, there seemed little hope even of that.

But when the question raised was not that of temporary concessions on points of detail but of the actual abolition of episcopacy, the same royalist divines who were ready to yield on some points of episcopal power in negotiations took up a much more rigid stance. Henry Ferne stressed that the abandonment of episcopacy would be against religion, and Henry Hammond declared in 1645 that the abandonment of episcopacy would be a work of 'practicall Atheisme'.[61] At other times, too, the same divines could suggest that what was needed was an *enhanced* rather than a reduced episcopacy. Ferne even claimed that, in appointments to livings, it would be better if *more* freedom were given to the episcopal power, and less to patrons of livings to overrule them.[62] There was never any compromise offered on Presbyterianism, which continued to be condemned unequivocally by all royalist writers. Duppa declared emphatically that Presbyterians were worse than Jesuits.[63] Similarly, the institution of lay elders was always implacably opposed. Even those who voiced their support for 'reduced episcopacy' were emphatically against the institution of lay elders, one of the cornerstones of the Presbyterian system (indeed, plans for 'reduced episcopacy' seem to have been specifically intended to prevent the intrusion of the laity in this fashion).[64]

The offer of religious toleration made by the Oxford clergy before the Uxbridge negotiations needs, then, to be set in context. The Uxbridge negotiations began on 29 January 1645 at the end of the month which had seen Laud executed and the Book of Common Prayer abolished – the royalist clergy involved in the Uxbridge offer are unlikely to have been transported with irenical enthusiasm towards the parliamentary delegates, although they may well have been fearful of the results if they were not as flexible as possible. In the following year, with the war lost, and the Prayer Book already abolished by the victorious Parliamentarians, expediency dictated that arguments for religious toleration should suddenly become *de rigueur* on the royalist side, prompting Jeremy Taylor's *Liberty of Prophesying* (among other works in print and manuscript), as Royalists sought toleration for the exercise of Prayer Book worship.[65]

The Heads of the Proposals of 1647 offered the final chance for reduced episcopacy, with bishops preserved and the use of the Prayer Book permitted, even if bishops were to be shorn of 'all coercive power, authority and jurisdiction' and Prayer Book usage was to be voluntary.[66] There is clear evidence of orchestration among prominent royalist clergy in their seeking to ensure that, when the king asked them for their advice in the matter, he would receive a unified positive assurance that 'in case of such exigence and concernment of Church and State as that they cannot in humane reason probably be preserved otherwise', the king could legitimately tolerate the exercise of other religions in the country 'besides the Religion established'.[67] It is notable that Laudian bishops as well as Calvinist ones agreed, but also significant that several entered caveats – one bishop specifiying that of course the king should not bind himself to a toleration forever, but only 'untill he may regaine the Powers given him by God, whereby to reduce them . . . to one right and well grounded Religion'.[68] Another bishop insisted that toleration of other religions that 'consist of Principles destructive to the State politiq[e]', and which practise toleration of all other religions even if they undermine fundamental doctrines of faith, was unjustifiable.[69] In the late autumn of 1648, with the 'second Civil War' already lost, the readiness of Juxon, Duppa and Taylor to allow the king to sacrifice almost all of the Church of England in the last frantic weeks of the Newport negotiations can be read as evidence of just how dire they considered the Church's predicament to be – rather than of their moderate temperament.[70]

That being said, it should not be suggested that responding flexibly to the exigencies of the 1640s was simply a matter of cynical manoeuvring on the part of the clergy. Rather, their responses to the demands of changing contingencies generated remarkably fertile improvisation and striking new ideas. It is to the radical potential and the dynamism of royalist religion that we will now turn.

IV   RADICAL ROYALISM

David Loewenstein and John Morrill have recently appealed for a recognition that on *all* sides of the religious polemical exchanges of the period 1640–60 (including the Anglican royalist) there was 'an exhilarating freedom, a high dependence on contingency, a rugged individualism, [and] extraordinary improvisation'.[71] Royalist religion has often seemed staid and uninspiring compared with the religious excesses and enthusiasms of the Parliamentarians, with their doctrinal innovation, political daring, vivid Old Testament imagery, apocalyptic eschatology and fervent Providentialism. Yet many of these phenomena are also evident on the royalist side. Just as the chimera of 'constitutional Royalism' has given us a seriously attenuated and simplistic sense of royalist political behaviour and ideology, so its religious counterpart – the image of a low-key, rational, quietist and moderate Anglicanism – has obscured the extent to which Royalism shared in the radicalizing religious landscape of the 1640s.

Doctrinal innovation was certainly not limited to the parliamentary side. In many areas of Anglican thought, far more emphatic and extreme 'high church' ideas can be observed than are visible in the 1630s. Jeremy Taylor's *Of the Sacred Order and Offices of Episcopacy* is a much more extreme defence of episcopacy as crucial to the very being of a church than any of the Laudians of the 1630s (including Heylyn) had ever managed, and is possibly the first work in defence of the Church of England's episcopal order to deny categorically the validity of the clerical orders of the foreign Reformed Churches.[72] Many other ideas that have to be teased out of pre-1640 works are stated much more bluntly in the 1640s. The denial that the Pope is Antichrist is made much more emphatically in the work of Henry Hammond, who was the first English writer seriously to adopt the interpretation of the late sixteenth-century Spanish Jesuit Luis de Alcasar, which limited the historical content of the Book of Revelation entirely to the period before Constantine.[73] That the English Reformation had proceeded on principles fundamentally distinct from those of the foreign Reformed Churches, based in part on the historical autonomy of the Church of England, was certainly implied by Laudian writers in the 1630s, but it was only in the Interregnum that writers such as John Bramhall and Peter Heylyn created a full historical account and reasoned defence to justify explicitly such claims.[74] Arminian and anti-Calvinist ideas are expressed more overtly and emphatically in the works of Thomas Pierce, Henry Hammond and Laurence Womock in the 1650s than they ever were among the so-called 'English Arminians' of the 1620s and 1630s.[75] The Calvinist Thomas Barlow identified the first corrupting of the doctrine of justification by faith alone by the introduction of the condition of 'obedience', not in the Laudianism of the 1630s, but in Henry Hammond's *Practicall Catechisme* of 1645.[76] Jeremy Taylor's *Unum Necessarium*, published in 1655, flatly denied the doctrine of original sin (thereby rejecting the ninth of the Thirty-Nine Articles, among other statements of Christian doctrine).[77]

On political matters, it is important that the more absolutist royalist voices are not relegated to a marginal 'unconstitutional royalist' position. Similarly, it should not be assumed that the most radical and absolutist clerical voices in Royalism were those of die-hard 'Laudians'. In fact, some of the most hard-line, 'unconstitutional' royalist writers were of a more Calvinist persuasion. The Calvinist Bishop Thomas Morton was more uncompromising than most Laudian bishops when he was consulted over the legitimacy of the king making concessions to the Independents during negotiations in 1647.[78] And another writer constantly invoked when historians seek for advocates of royal abso- lutism – Griffith Williams, Bishop of Ossory – hardly counted as a Laudian in the 1630s. In fact, Williams had irreproachably Calvinist credentials, albeit of a moderate kind.[79] It is exactly the doctrinal perspective that we would expect of someone who had enjoyed the patronage of Laud's *bête noire*, Archbishop Abbot, and who had been the domestic chaplain of Laud's opponent, the Lord Chamberlain and famous promoter of the 'Protestant cause', the fourth Earl of Pembroke. In fact, it might arguably be the case that it was Calvinists who migrated most easily towards absolutist and apocalyptic styles of argument. It was the Calvinist Williams, not the Laudian Heylyn, who erected an apoca- lyptic reading of the events of the Civil War and Interregnum on the basis of an identification of the Long Parliament with the Antichrist.[80]

But there are also radical *tolerationist* views to be found among royal- ist divines. Jeremy Taylor's *Liberty of Prophesying* was confessedly prompted by the need of Church of England clerics to appeal for toler- ation for themselves in the wake of the Royalists' defeat. But the logic of his argument takes him a great deal further, and produces a programme of religious toleration that is more comprehensive than most of those emerging on the parliamentarian side. The most radical and outspoken take on religious toleration is contained in another royalist work that has been completely ignored by historians of religious toleration, although historians of political thought have given it partial attention. This is *The Divine Right of Government* (1647) by Michael Hudson, the chaplain with whom Charles had fled Oxford in 1646. It is usually simply noted for its absolutist arguments on royal sovereignty, but Hudson's dedicatory epis- tle to the king makes it quite clear that he has written the book solely to make the case for the necessity of religious toleration, and to warn of the evil of trying to enforce particular forms of religious behaviour on Christians who do not wish to follow them. Hudson is emphatic that kings commit sacrilege if they impose conformity of evangelical worship and service on people who have scruples over the usage. On this basis, Hudson tells Charles unequivocally that the king has been guilty of sacri- lege, although with the reassurance that Charles has sinned innocently in the matter.[81] As usual, contingency can explain much – written from

the Tower in the summer of 1647 (completed on 9 September), it was
clearly an attempt to persuade Charles to agree to the religious aspects
(at least) of the Heads of the Proposals. But like Taylor's tract, it is in
many ways more audacious than most parliamentarian works. It may
well also be the only book written by a royal chaplain that begins by
accusing his master of committing sacrilege.

Bloodcurdling accusations of sacrilege are, of course, nothing new in
royalist writing. And it should be emphasized that, while royalist religious discourse could be rational, moralistic and moderate in tone, it
could also adopt more belligerent languages and images. Just like
Parliamentarians, Royalists saw England as Israel and applied biblical
texts to her fortunes. It is often forgotten that there were fast sermons
preached before the Oxford Parliament, as well as the ones in
Westminster.[82] And in royalist sermons the congregation could be
warned of the sin of 'formality' and condemned for failing to display a
zeal for reformation, in tones as emphatic as those used in the puritan
pulpit of Westminster.[83] Old Testament proof-texts and warnings could
be invoked by royalist preachers just as often as they were used by parliamentarian preachers.[84]

Other phenomena that are often taken to epitomize parliamentarian
religion can also be found in royalist religious writings. Eschatological
observations – citing biblical warnings of the emergence of false prophets
in the latter times – are a regular feature of royalist writings. When even
mainstream divines such as Jeremy Taylor write of the abolition of episcopacy as being the forerunner and 'preparatory for the Antichrist, and
grand Apostacy', such remarks should not necessarily be read as merely
empty rhetoric.[85] Apocalyptic interpretations of the civil conflict can be
found on the royalist as well as the parliamentarian side. The Book of
Revelation presented some very obvious readings of the current rebellion, and ingenious attempts to create the number '666' from the titles of
the Long Parliament, or the number of words in the Covenant, can be
found throughout the Civil War and Interregnum.[86]

Providentialism – in which events in the world are seen as reflecting
God's direct, personal intervention – also found a place in royalist as well
as parliamentarian texts. Even before the outbreak of war, one pamphlet
reported on the divine punishment meted out on a churchwarden of
Towcester, Northamptonshire, in 1641 who had removed a stained-
glass window and subsequently went mad and died, while his sister tore
the Book of Common Prayer out of her Bible and then found that the
hands that had committed the deed proceeded to rot away. It was

presumably a measure of the success of puritan providentialist pamphlets (and conceivably a reflection of initial royalist lack of confidence in embracing such a medium) that the account of these events in Towcester only alluded coyly to the precise content of the events on the title-page, perhaps intending to entice a puritan reader hoping to read of more providential judgements against papists or prelates.[87] But providentialist royalist pamphlets soon became a genre in their own right.[88] The search for vindications of the Prayer Book could take some peculiar turns. It was reported in a royalist newsletter of the early 1640s that in the haunted house of one Mrs Gibson at Limehouse, the 'ill Spirit' knocked three times to signal (when asked) that the Book of Common Prayer was lawful (although Mrs Gibson remained unconvinced 'because it was the Devill, who gave that testimony').[89] Stories of the providential deaths of opponents of the established Church in the war appealed to the authors (and presumably the readers) of royalist pamphlets and newsbooks. Of these, none was more relished than the death of parliamentarian firebrand Lord Brooke, the opponent of cathedrals who was killed by a shot fired from a cathedral, which entered his eye (he having said that he hoped to see the day when St Paul's in London was destroyed) and killed him instantly (he having condemned the litany for including a prayer against sudden death).[90]

The most extreme providentialist royalist pamphlets were of course those, post-1649, that related to the martyr king, and especially the miraculous cures effected by a handkerchief dipped in Charles I's blood. The story of Mary Bayly, the Maid of Deptford, who was cured of scrofula – the 'King's Evil' – by being touched with a cloth soaked in the blood of the executed King Charles – had a pamphlet all to itself.[91]

V   A NEW ROYALIST HISTORY

Royalist religion has emerged from this study as far removed from the staid, restrained, socially deferential and understated 'Anglicanism' that scholarship on this period has often represented. Rather than the simple antithesis of clericalist Laudianism, it appears instead to have retained its clericalist ambitions, although bowing to political necessity whenever it was prudent to do so. Royalist divines were also capable of daring theological radicalism, lively providentialism and war-mongering rhetoric. Royalist religion was an active participant in the religious upheavals of the Civil War period, rather than a detached and disapproving .

onlooker, waiting politely for the Restoration. And its fabled deference towards social hierarchy could barely hide a deep distrust of the laity, and even of the king himself.

It seems appropriate to end, in fact, with a few caveats about the ready association of the clergy with the cult of the martyr king and support for the Stuart dynasty. Not all of the clergy were enthusiastic about the cult. Heylyn has recently been described as 'the defender of cult orthodoxy', but he was anything but that. In fact, he had many critical things to say about both Charles I and James I. His objections to Charles went to the heart of the cult's rationale: he condemned the king for having divested himself 'of that Regall Majesty which might and would have kept him safe from affront and scorn, to relie wholly on the innocence of a virtuous life, which did expose him finally to calamitous ruine'.[92] Moreover, the events of the late 1640s and early 1650s were pushing some royalist clergy even closer to asserting the independence of Church and state. Even in the 1640s, Herbert Thorndike had been attacking the 'vulgar mistake' (of King James among others) that sovereign powers were called gods in scripture, and questioning the argument that Christian princes had the same rights in the Church as the kings of Judah had in the synagogue.[93] The abolition of episcopacy had already driven writers such as Thorndike to reason that, as the temporal powers of the state had opposed religion and created schism, therefore the people should separate themselves from the state Church and adhere instead to a state-less 'Society of the Church'. This growing sense of the independence of Church and state would only have been exacerbated by the execution of Charles I and the abolition of monarchy, and was heightened further by Charles II's betrayal of the episcopalian Church in 1650–1 with his alliance with the Presbyterian Scots and taking of the Covenant, which produced a crisis in clerical allegiance to the Stuart dynasty.[94]

An alternative strategy, of course, was to offer the Church of England's support to a potential new monarchical protector. And here we might note Peter Heylyn's *Ecclesia Vindicata*, published in 1657. It is a volume which includes a number of works written in royalist Oxford, but carries a remarkable preface in which the author denies categorically that James's famous dictum 'No bishop no King' can be reversed to imply 'that there can be no Bishop where there is no King'. On the contrary, Heylyn urges the examples of Naples, Venice and Florence to demonstrate that episcopacy could comply perfectly well with republican government. Heylyn's preface continually alludes to an intended reader 'advanced perhaps unto some eminent degree of Trust and Power in the present Government', and he declares that he lays the work 'with all humble reverence at the feet of those who are in Authority'.[95] A copy of the work in the Bodleian Library would seem to clarify Heylyn's intentions. It bears a manuscript dedication by Heylyn to Oliver Cromwell, urging him to restore the Church of England and suppress sectarianism as the best guarantee of the security of his régime. Heylyn was always emphatic that the Church needed a political sponsor, and as the momentum gathered to offer Cromwell the Crown (and Heylyn explicitly referred to his hope that 'our Affaires shall be reduced to a settled Government'), it made perfect sense for the Church of England to offer its services as a guarantor of order and loyalty to the potential new monarch.[96] It was also around this time that Griffith Williams delivered in the presence of Henry Cromwell, then Lord Deputy of Ireland, a sermon upholding the episcopal order and the liturgy and calendar of the Prayer Book.[97]

This was not, perhaps, what those Royalists emphasizing the secular utility of the Church of England had initially had in mind. It helps to remind us, however, that Anglican Royalism was a dynamic, shifting and potentially radical phenomenon. Even devotion to Charles I could not ultimately be guaranteed.

3. Perceptions of Parliament: Factions and 'The Public'

JASON PEACEY

Unlike the 'Tudor revolution in government', the transformation of Parliament in the 1640s has rarely provoked scholars to confront directly the historiographical problems which they face. Although a broad consensus exists that Parliament underwent dramatic change during the Civil Wars, in the dismantling of 'king-in-Parliament', the hijacking of the royal prerogative, and the exercise of executive authority, there is less agreement regarding the nature of factionalism – in terms of the timing of its emergence and the basis of 'party' formation and alignment – and regarding parliamentary management.[1] Such controversies result not just from the inscrutability of parliamentary politics and processes, in the absence of full parliamentary and political archives, but also from conflicting approaches to sources. While some scholars emphasize prosopography (the use of biographical studies to establish political networks) and ephemeral sources (such as warrants or estate papers) in order to re-create factional structures and patronage networks,[2] others challenge the interpretative weight that such sources are made to bear, and concentrate instead upon 'pure' parliamentary sources (journals), and upon 'formal methods, procedures, and functions'.[3] The aim of this chapter is to demonstrate the value of one particular kind of source, not merely for shedding light upon these controversies, but also for re-mapping scholarship on Parliament in the Civil Wars. My focus is upon contemporary perceptions of the parliamentary process, in private correspondence and the paperwork of organizations which encountered and interacted with Parliament. More importantly, evidence is drawn from contemporary pamphlets and newspapers, whether written by members of the Commons, their friends and associates, or observant commentators. The explosion in political news and comment in cheap and regular tracts and newsbooks was one of the most important developments of the 1640s, giving contemporary readers unprecedented information and insight into political life, in terms of both individuals and processes. In what follows, a few writers will figure particularly prominently, and the bulk of evidence cited will be drawn from the writings of leading journalists (such as Marchamont Nedham), members of Parliament (such as Clement Walker), and other polemicists closely attached to leading politicians (such as David Buchanan). The prominence of these writers in my account reflects the sophistication of their analyses, as well as the merits of their prose; but strenuous efforts have also been made to demonstrate that their ideas were echoed by other writers, as well as by their readers.

Historians have clearly not ignored such sources, but their interpretation and significance have been contested, and the full impact of their message has thus far not been fully appreciated.[4] This chapter employs them in three main contexts: first, as part of an exploration of what contemporaries knew about Parliament and of the sophistication of their analysis of structures, procedures, and politics at Westminster; secondly, to explore how far such analysis spread; and thirdly, to discern what historians can learn from their comments, as a source for parliamentary history and Civil-War politics, not least by comparing their conclusions with the findings of modern scholarship. In addition to utilizing the *rhetoric* of Parliament in order to enhance our understanding of the reality of parliamentary power, politics, and procedures, it also argues that such sources provide a means of exploring the dynamic of public politics. Contemporary reflections upon Parliament fostered concerns within the political élite regarding 'popular perceptions', and resulted in attempts to increase public awareness of Parliament's business and internal affairs. The growth of such knowledge contributed to a profound re-evaluation of the role of Parliament and its members, and of the relationship between representatives and represented. As we shall see, viewing parliamentary business in this light, in turn, permits a re-evaluation of Civil-War 'radicalism'. What will emerge is that it was the experience of parliamentary practices during the 1640s which promoted, or at least crystallized, an idealized vision of the way in which Parliament operated, or ought to operate. It was the emergence of this parliamentary ideal which provided a framework within which to judge the behaviour of political factions during the Civil Wars, and to propose a variety of measures to cure its corruption.

I CONTEMPORARY PERCEPTIONS

Contemporary complaints – and the use of near-apocalyptic language to voice them – regarding parliamentarian rule are well known. Allegations that Parliament was riven with illegality, oppression, arbitrariness, and corruption, and that liberties had been usurped, were regularly rehearsed.[5] This is generally discussed, however, in terms of the response to county committees, martial law, and the excise, and little recognition has been given to the extent to which contemporary disillusionment reflected analysis of factions.[6] Yet, such factions were suspected of enabling small groups to exert excessive influence: to abuse, corrupt, and over-awe Parliament, and to ensure that public welfare was sacrificed to private interests.[7] This factionalism became associated with MPs abusing their privileges, indemnifying themselves, and failing to pay personal debts, thereby bringing hardship to merchants and creditors, removing the benefit of justice, and replacing liberty with slavery.[8]

Before 1642, contemporaries detected merely the influence of 'the faction' of 'fiery spirits', who were most eager for 'further reformation', and who spearheaded the assault upon the royal prerogative.[9] Soon after the outbreak of war, however, contemporaries detected the existence of two more or less fluid groups, which approximate to our notions of 'war' and 'peace' parties, and there is certainly little hint in contemporary comment regarding a 'middle group' of the kind famously postulated by the American historian J. H. Hexter, in the 1940s.[10] From early 1644, such groups were given more settled labels, and as contemporaries observed the 'realignment' of particular individuals and groups – not least the closing of the Earl of Essex's party with the Scots – the language of 'Presbyterians' and 'Independents' emerged in the winter of 1644–5.[11] Thereafter, this bifurcation and the variations thereon – such as Nedham's portrayal of the Presbyterians as 'the gang of Scottified jockies in the House' – became common currency in the press, and in the correspondence of interested observers.[12] Having identified such 'interests' and 'parties', contemporaries not only argued that factions sought to 'engross all power', but also plotted the shifting balance of power between such groups within Westminster.[13]

There was a broad consensus on the trajectories traced by the respective factions. In the autumn of 1643, therefore, it was clear that Essex's peace party had been 'undone' by the war party, and by the group of peers around Viscount Saye.[14] During 1645, observers noted the growing dominance of the Independents, just as the Presbyterians were regarded as having staged a political comeback in 1646. Despite being weakened by the death of the Earl of Essex that year, the Presbyterians – contemporary commentators agreed – had undermined the Independents by the spring of 1647, though their fortunes were to be reversed during the course of that year.[15] Even during the politically complex events of 1648, commentators felt able to map factional influences and follow their relative fortunes.[16] Moreover, although contemporary accounts do not always tally with the views of modern-day scholars, observers were also able to attribute specific policies to particular factions. Commentators analysed the instigation of specific committees, the formulation of peace proposals, and the pressure for 'recruiter' elections (the bye-elections held to fill vacancies in the Commons caused by the expulsion of Royalists), and they revealed the factional influence behind the enforcement of the Solemn League and Covenant, votes for 'no further addresses', the reform of the militia, and the appointment of commissioners to treat with the king.[17] By pigeonholing individual MPs, the most astute observers were able to understand the factional basis of particular initiatives, and the journalist Marchamont Nedham even employed such prosopography in order to dismiss the seriousness of the legal proceedings against Charles I in 1648.[18] Moreover, contemporaries also recognized important subtleties regarding factional policies, in ways that affect our understanding of their attachment to 'ideology'. They appreciated, for example, that parties practised dissimulation over particular issues as part of their factional struggles, and that the power politics of factional rivalries could influence substantive policy positions. Similarly, Nedham explained that the Independents' support for proceedings against Charles was motivated by the need to destroy the Presbyterians, rather than by animus towards the king.[19]

Contemporaries deepened such analysis by examining party structures, the relationships upon which they were based, and the goals of those involved. They recognized that factions were loose associations – that both Independents and Presbyterians were coalitions or 'confederacies' which suffered from more or less serious internal divisions – and that this could have a profound effect upon political developments, in so far as compromise proved necessary to maintain unity.[20] In early 1649, for example, Nedham stressed that the planned proceedings against the king reflected the Independents' need to retain the support of the 'fantastic John Leydons'* among the radicals.[21] Commentators were also aware that such interest groups were bicameral, and that divisions within Parliament tended to be vertical rather than horizontal.[22] Nevertheless,

---

* The extreme radicals, so named after John of Leiden, the self-styled King of Münster, who led a popular rebellion in the city in 1534, establishing a theocratic and polygamous state, forcibly suppressed the following year.

while individual peers were credited with significant power, the leadership of factions was not regarded as having rested solely in the upper House.[23] Thus, although it was suggested in December 1647 that the Independents sought 'a very great lord to be their head', and that Cromwell served a 'lordly interest', the relations between grandees in either House were generally portrayed in terms of collusion rather than clientage, and by mid-1648 Nedham even suggested, probably correctly, that peers' influence was more apparent than real, and that 'the lower is the upper House'.[24]

Indeed, it proved possible to identify small groups of leaders drawn from both Houses. This was true of the 'fiery spirits', such as Saye and John Pym, in the early phase of the Long Parliament, as well as of Independents such as Sir Henry Vane the younger, Oliver St John and Lord Wharton later in the decade.[25] Their rivals – at first known as the 'peace interest' or, later, the Presbyterians – were initially perceived as being led by the Earl of Essex, but by early 1644 commentators recognized the growing importance of Denzell Holles, Sir Philip Stapilton, and Sir John Clotworthy.[26] As factional divisions hardened, a broader range of observers was able to appreciate the oligarchic nature of such groups, to agree on the identity of their leaders, and to concur regarding the emergence of new power-brokers.[27] Most obviously, they were able to recognize the emergence, from the late spring of 1647, of Cromwell, who by May 1648 had even been labelled, mockingly, 'King Oliver'.[28] Indeed, as astute analysts realized, what mattered was not the number but the quality and zeal of these grandees – 'the prime men, active and diligent' – whose role in initiating policies and legislation came to be widely understood.[29] Thus, by the later 1640s, those factional leaders who had come to be dubbed 'grandees' were styled 'hocas-pocasses', the 'jugglers', 'the cabinet', and 'the junto-men', and such terminology quickly spread through the world of the pamphleteers.[30]

Contemporary observers also sought to analyse the internal dynamic of parliamentarian factions in terms of the relationships between grandees and their Westminster supporters. Such explanations went beyond describing Sir Thomas Wroth as the 'fool' or 'monkey' of Edmund Prideaux; John Swynfen as Prideaux's 'spaniel'; or Cornelius Holland as 'Sir Henry Vane's zanie'; and also went beyond identifying kinship ties between the likes of Anthony Nicoll and John Pym.[31] Nevertheless, while it was suggested that some MPs were 'servants and tenants' of peers, and while the aristocratic connections of members such as Michael Oldisworth and Robert Scawen were occasionally outlined, members were rarely characterized as being merely 'clients' or 'men of business' in the sense of having no political life independent of their employers.[32] Grandees were certainly regarded as being reliant upon the support of others, and writers recognized how MPs gravitated around them.[33]

In so far as contemporary analysis of the composition of Parliament was clear, however, it provides challenging interpretations for modern scholars. The bulk of members were categorized as 'politicks' and 'confederates', or as 'mechanicks' and 'creatures'.[34] Together they were 'the puppets', upon whom the grandees worked by 'gulling and deluding'.[35] The 'politicks' were the active and aligned portion among 'backbenchers' – the 'zanyes and jack-puddings . . . and agitators' – who were styled 'the common vote-drivers of the faction in the House', or the 'Parliament drivers'.[36] These 'bilbo-worthies', who existed in both Houses, were, in Nedham's words,

> the swordmen . . . that keep all the rest in awe, and . . . wind up their fellow members like Jacks to provide roast meat for their myrmidions, and what by striking terror into the old ones with their power, and working upon the litter by policy, they carry the votes which way they please, and set the House upon wheeles.[37]

Such 'tame patriots' – by which he seems to have meant the members who acted like modern-day 'whips' – ensured that no 'juggling' could be effected 'but by consent of the Hocus-Pocusses' (his term for the Parliament's leaders or 'grandees'). From 1647 onwards, private correspondence and public newspapers became filled with lists of their names, and with estimates of their numbers.[38]

The 'mechanicks', on the other hand, were a far larger group, and although their identity remained obscure, they probably included those whom Clement Walker called the 'vulgar Independents', who were 'but the props and properties to the grandees', and those whom Nedham called 'the Brazen heads', who were 'taught to speak Aye or No, which they deliver at certain hours by direction, just like Cheapside clock-strikers'.[39] They were, in other words, mere lobby fodder, and 'voting instruments', whom Nedham derided as 'those state-catamites, upon whom any votes whatsoever may be begotten'. They were thought to include the servants and tenants of the grandees, who were 'packed into this Parliament to carry and vote', and who rarely assumed positions of importance in the House.[40]

In analysing relations between such groups, moreover, contemporaries offer interpretations that historians have largely overlooked. The 'mechanicks' were regarded as those inactive or insignificant members whom the grandees were likely to find most malleable and reliable. The 'politicks' and 'vote-drivers', on the other hand, were more prominent in the Houses, and, though more obviously aligned, were rarely, if ever, described in ways we might describe as clientage; they were seen as being somewhat kept in the dark by the grandees on matters of intelligence and tactics, 'for fear it should spoil their barking'. Robert Baillie claimed that such men were 'not of their mysteries [privy to the grandees strategies], and of no great parts either for counsel or action'.[41] Moreover, such 'vote-drivers' were not only considered to have been motivated by political zeal, but were also regarded as being more ideological than the grandees, who were perceived to be more interested in power than in political principles or religious purity. Clement Walker, therefore, suggested that the 'politicks [i.e. politiques]' pursued factional goals 'with more seriousness than their leaders, as not perceiving anything of design therein', and as having 'studied the upholding of their parties with earnestness'. In other words, Walker claimed, grandees displayed far weaker attachment to particular policies and principles than those who were their most important allies and instruments.[42]

As a result, contemporaries suggested that factions were divided between 'pure' and 'mixed' strands, and between 'royal' and 'real [i.e. true]' wings.[43] The grandees, whether 'royal Presbyterians' or 'royal Independents', differed among themselves not over substantive issues, but rather over who should bring the king back to the throne, 'who shall be the princes of the people under him' and 'who shall sit nearest to the throne'; and the Independent grandees, in particular, were regarded as being profoundly oligarchic.[44] Radical commentators such as John Harris and John Wildman alleged that the grandees, who had succumbed to 'those cursed tares of court principles', had betrayed 'real' Independents.[45] This situation, moreover, was regarded as having forced the grandees to dissimulate, and to deceive and delude their supporters in order to 'seem as real in their reciprocal oppositions [i.e. the professed hostility between Presbyterians and Independents] as those silly ones who are in earnest', as well as to purchase their loyalty with financial rewards by conferring 'something of advantage upon those that are subservient to them, as five pounds a week, or some petty employment'.[46] Some commentators even suggested that there was greater unity *between* grandees than within factions. Clement Walker, whose loss

of office at the hands of parliamentarian factions made him a particularly and perhaps overly cynical observer, argued that the 'grandees of
each party in private close together for their own advancement, serving
one another's turn', and that they were prepared to put faction aside in
order to help each other, 'unless something of particular spleen or
competition come between, which causeth them to break the common
rule'.[47]

Contemporary analysis, therefore, demonstrates an awareness of the
nature of parliamentary factionalism, the complexity of factional structures, and their ideological nature, in ways which both complement and
contrast with modern scholarship. Few commentators joined
Marchamont Nedham in embracing a system of analysis that involved
the balancing of such conflicting 'interests' but many perceived something at odds with the picture painted by historians such as Mark
Kishlansky: that adversarial politics emerged in the early 1640s, far
earlier than Kishlansky suggests; and that 'ideological' divisions had
always been present, even if they never became all-encompassing,
because of the pervasive lure of power. The views of contemporary
commentators regarding the status and motivation of individual parliamentarians, and the types of relationship which existed between
grandees and 'backbenchers', are not necessarily at odds with the views
of historians such as John Adamson. Nevertheless, they provide a typology of members which is rarely discussed in recent scholarship.[48] While
modern historians are not obliged to privilege the views of Civil-War
commentators over conclusions based upon dispassionate analysis of all
the available evidence, the ideas of such journalists and pamphleteers
certainly require greater consideration.

II   THE EXPLOITATION OF PARLIAMENT

In addition to analysing the nature and structure of parliamentarian
factions, contemporaries also studied the means by which these factions
exploited the political process. They explored the ways in which
grandees, 'politicks', and 'mechanicks' operated through 'underhand
dealing' and 'artificial practices', and it was claimed that 'if one should
take in hand to set down in writing all the cunnings, devices, artifices,
deceits and crafts known to many . . . it would make a great volume'.[49]
Commentators detected, for example, a growing culture of secrecy,
whether in terms of surreptitious planning meetings, or in terms of

parliamentary proceedings and judicial hearings, and Buchanan complained that matters were transacted 'hugger-mugger, to the prejudice of the public service'.[50] Moreover, such tactics were perceived to extend beyond the House of Lords to the Commons, which came to be seen as being run like a committee rather than a court of judicature; closed and secretive rather than open to its constituents and receptive to their demands.[51] However, contemporary analysis also extended to a much more detailed appreciation of parliamentary processes and practices, examination of which enhances our appreciation of the nature and timing of what Kishlansky has described as the 'assault on parliamentary politics', namely the movement away from conventional practices and procedures.

Factions were perceived to have manipulated Parliament both by controlling its membership and by influencing its agenda and debates. In addition to noting how certain courtiers and monopolists had been permitted to remain in the House, commentators recognized the importance of electoral influence. As early as 1643 it was suggested that procedures for vetting elections were biased, and that elections proceeded 'underhand'. The Commons' Committee for Elections was dubbed the Committee of 'Affection', which ensured 'undue courses' in electoral cases, and electioneering was understood to involve organization, planning, and 'underhand letters'.[52] Later, the 'recruiter' elections were perceived to have been instigated and managed in order to bolster factions and protect their interests, not least through the return of kinsmen, servants, and tenants.[53] Having exerted influence over the electoral process, factions were alleged to be able to politicize the parliamentary process, as petitions, motions, and bills were blocked or promoted according to factional interests. In 1647, army propaganda accused the Presbyterians of being 'obstructers and prejudgers of several petitions to the Parliament for redress of public grievances', and they claimed that business was 'obstructed' and 'not suffered to come to a hearing', while another anti-Presbyterian pamphlet suggested that petitions were either 'admitted through favour, or rejected for want of friends'.[54] However, others were accused of similar tactics, and one Presbyterian petition was allegedly blocked because 'the Independents made their favourers snuff at it, and struggle to reject it'.[55]

Conversely, it was alleged that bills that were supported by, and reflected the interests of, Independent grandees were given preferential treatment.[56] What this attested to, contemporaries believed, was the planning of parliamentary business. Nedham, for instance, exposed particular meetings between grandees such as Lord Wharton and Nathaniel Fiennes; and Robert Chestlin suggested that 'by the Sunday's sermon, or a lecture, they could learn, not only what was done the week before, but also what was to be done in Parliament the week following'.[57] Such planning ensured that the timing of petitions was carefully arranged, and that speeches were 'elaborately composed' in advance, and 'read out of a hat perhaps, or behind a friend'.[58]

Parliamentary management was also conceived to have affected debates and voting, since 'men that have cunning wits will drive every vote to their own ends'.[59] As war thinned the Houses, it was recognized that the grandees found it easier to assess the likely voting behaviour of individual members, 'their daily sitting [having] made them expert in discerning the face of the House, to know their own strength, [and] how vote would be at that time'.[60] This enabled steps to be taken to guarantee the presence in the chambers of sufficient support to win divisions, and the 'politicks' or 'vote-drivers' were alleged to have mastered techniques for monitoring and manipulating attendance. From the early 1640s, grandees apparently ensured that 'emissaries' were 'constantly attending the door of the House of Commons, to call in members of this faction to vote what they pleased, to advance their design upon notice of a small appearance in the House'.[61] By 1647, this had become a highly sensitive political issue, as both Independents and Presbyterians were accused of exploiting such practices, not least during the controversy surrounding the 'Eleven Members' (the Presbyterian leaders impeached by the army in the summer of 1647).[62] Moreover, it was also suggested that factions delayed debates and votes when the composition of the House was unpropitious, particularly by means of influencing the Speaker, who was regarded as having been in the pocket of the Independents.[63]

Not content with influencing membership, proceedings, and attendance, factional leaders sometimes sought to stifle debate entirely – or so contemporary commentators alleged. By early 1643, it was recognized that grandees sought to proceed, not by 'reason and strength of argument, but by putting it to the question and carrying it by most voices'. Indeed, this was conceived to be integral to factional politics, 'where the greater number were so far from understanding ... the force of arguments ... but thought it was enough for them to vote with Master Pym or Master Hampden by an implicit faith'.[64] This was intimately linked to the exploitation of attendance, and commentators became aware that measures could be pushed through a 'thin' House, 'whilst those who should attend to hear and judge are in bed or at play, or some worse employment'.[65] Such tactics too were developed in the early 1640s, not least during debates over the abolition of episcopacy, when the House only considered the matter 'so late every day' that 'it was very thin':

> they only who prosecuted the bill with impatience remaining in the House, and the others who abhorred it, growing weary of so tiresome an attendance, left the House at dinner time, and afterwards followed their pleasures, so that the Lord Falkland was wont to say that they who hated bishops hated them worse than the devil, and that they who loved them did not love them so well as their dinner.[66]

Pamphleteers began to document incidents where poor attendance was exploited, not least in order to pass controversial resolutions such as the Declaration of Dislike (the Parliament's condemnation of the army's petitioning in March 1647) or the vote of 'no further addresses' to the king (in January 1648). It was even alleged that proceedings were deliberately extended long into the night in order to achieve a sufficiently empty chamber.[67]

On other occasions, however, techniques for stifling debate were perceived to be more forceful in nature. Prynne referred to 'menacing speeches', while other commentators outlined methods for silencing inconvenient speakers and instances where members were 'not suffered to speak', called to the bar, committed to the Tower, or even expelled from the House for unwelcome contributions.[68] Ultimately, force, or threats thereof, were regarded as having become a tactical device with which to terrify members into acquiescence or even absence, and in order to secure particular votes – whether over Strafford's attainder in the spring of 1641 or in tense debates over the army and London militia during 1647.[69] This formed part of the charge against the Eleven Members, but it was also suggested that the votes regarding the London militia on 22 July 1647 – which effectively precipitated the tumultuous 'forcing of the Houses', when a mob of apprentices stormed the palace of Westminster and prompted Independent members to flee to the safety of the army – resulted from the Commons 'being very thin and many members driven away by menaces'.[70] Subsequently, Royalists claimed that the younger Sir Henry Vane 'openly threatened the bringing up again the army' in response to a petition from London Presbyterians, and thereby caused their supporters in the House to withdraw, enabling the Independents to exploit their numerical advantage.[71]

Ultimately, it was possible to affect the balance of power permanently, either by means of the mob, or by impeachment, or 'purge'. The mob ensured the departure of Royalists from Westminster in 1641 and 1642, and the Solemn League and Covenant (with its commitment to a Presbyterian Church settlement in all three kingdoms) was enforced by opportunistic political Presbyterians later in the decade in order to prevent Independents from taking their seats.[72] More famously, of course, the army sought to 'sift and winnow' Parliament of Presbyterian members in June 1647, not least as an 'act of terror' to influence other members, 'to fright more Presbyterians from the Houses', and to strengthen the Independents' grip on Parliament.[73] Eventually, in the most dramatic example of the use of force to influence the composition of the House, the army purged Parliament in December 1648.[74]

Contemporary commentators, as well as pamphleteers of a variety of political persuasions, shed valuable light on recent historiographical debates by recognizing that parliamentary processes – in terms of membership, formal proceedings, and debates – were profoundly affected by factional divisions within Westminster. They perceived both the nature and extent of parliamentary management; the fact that this 'assault' on conventional parliamentary politics began in the earliest phase of the Long Parliament; and that it was spearheaded by grandees from both Presbyterian and Independent factions. As such, they began to appreciate not merely that parliamentarian politics was factional, and that factionalism involved the triumph of private or sectional interests over those of the 'public', but also the ways in which such interest groups sought to achieve their ends.

Equally stimulating is contemporary analysis of other developments in parliamentary politics during the 1640s, not least because of its recognition of the dynamic and innovatory role of the Independent grandees – and it is to this that we now turn.

III   THE INDEPENDENT 'CABAL'

The most astute contemporary observers quickly realized that grandees appreciated the advantages of sidelining Parliament entirely, rather than merely managing its proceedings effectively. As such, commentators recognized the importance of committees as an arena for factional politics, and that such bodies came to dominate all important business.[75] This explains why writers as diverse as John Lilburne and William

Prynne decried the 'tyranny' of 'illegal' committees, and why 'committee law' was conceived to be as oppressive as martial law.[76] In order to exploit committees, it was clearly necessary to dominate their membership, and contemporaries assessed how factions influenced the nomination process, and how they ensured that committees were 'packed' as a matter of course. David Buchanan, a Scot, suggested that Independents, 'by craft from the very beginning of this war', had 'screwed themselves in employment and got in to have a main hand in all businesses.'[77] Once again, planning, zeal, and influence over the Commons' Speaker, William Lenthall, were regarded as crucial. Clement Walker claimed that the 'active speaking men' named one another 'of every committee', and it was observed how 'friends' and factions ensured that members of committees were 'birds of a feather'.[78] Early in the decade, it was suggested that 'the Speaker diligently watches the eye of Pym', and that factions operated 'by planting in their instruments for chairmen of committees, and into all places of action'.[79] Journalists and pamphleteers analysed particular committees, demonstrating how individuals were intruded and cashiered, and how grandees sought to ensure that factional 'creatures' were nominated. They even recognized that factions created new committees in situations where they were unable to control existing ones, and that they established secretive sub-committees when their enemies secured nomination to particular bodies, thereby challenging their iron control.[80]

To the extent that factions dominated committee membership, they were able to control their operation.[81] The small size of such committees made their outcome more predictable, and it was alleged that these bodies themselves were pared down in size in order to effect business more easily.[82] By early 1643, observers recognized 'notable friending there [in committees] in causes [i.e. individual cases]', and observed of MPs that there was 'much siding and engaging one another in their committees in matters if civil justice'. Later years saw commentators outline cases of 'packed' committees proceeding in a blatantly biased fashion.[83] Likewise, committees provided a means by which to smother particular business and favour specific interests; one former MP suggested that

> no committee was so soon made as it was immediately converted to serve the revenge, envy, avarice, or the corrupt humours and passions of the authors, so that to commit a business signified no more, for the most part, but to give members advantages of working their own, or their friends business and designs with success.[84]

As a result, it was argued that 'the remaining part of the House are but cyphers to value and suffragans [deputies] to ratify what is forejudged by the said committees'.[85] Moreover, committee reports were liable to factional manipulation 'as they affect or distaste the parties', and the army certainly complained that 'untrue informations and reports' ensured that Parliament was 'abused and misled'.[86] Another common complaint centred upon the secrecy with which committee proceedings had been undertaken since the early 1640s, a trend which provoked outbursts by radicals such as Lilburne, neutrals such as Walker, and crypto-royalists such as [Sir] John Maynard.[87] On other occasions, however, committees considered it necessary to exploit publicity, and to allow a 'rabble' to attend their proceedings in order to harangue opponents.[88]

While all committees came to be regarded as being susceptible to factional manipulation, particular concern was expressed regarding 'standing' committees; those bodies which met regularly over extended periods. The Committee for Examinations, for example, came to be regarded as being susceptible to factional abuse, and its 'victims' likened it to the Star Chamber and the Inquisition.[89] Complaints were made that such bodies operated not merely secretively (behind closed doors) but also clandestinely (behind doors unknown). One observer explained that the Committee of Revenue 'meets but seldom, sometimes not full, and most times when they have met, full of great causes, and the time of their sitting being but from 8 in the morning till 9'.[90] The bodies that aroused most suspicion and opposition, however, were the major executive committees. The Committee of Safety (the parliamentarian executive from 1642 to 1643) was widely derided as a factional tool of those with the most aggressive policy towards the war, and became the model for complaints about 'close' committees.[91] The Committee of Both Kingdoms (the much smaller executive that replaced it from 1644 to 1646) was perceived to have been established by the Anglo-Scottish war party as a 'great bulwark' against the Earl of Essex, who opposed its creation and renewal. It came to be regarded as an Independent cabal, from which the Scots were increasingly excluded, as recent analysis has gone some way towards confirming.[92] Much more detailed criticisms were levelled at another Independent-dominated body, the Derby House Committee (the major executive committee of the period from October 1646 to 1648): the 'packed committee of juglers', as it was dubbed; or 'the fraternity of Hocus Pocus', which was home to the 'junto', the 'hocasses', and the 'states', for whom the two Houses acted as mere 'journeymen' (i.e. common labourers).[93]

Indeed, the 'cabinet at Derby House' was considered to epitomize the workings of a single faction, with a tiny core of Independents being privy to planning, strategy, and information, and knowing 'more of affairs abroad than the common vote-drivers of the faction in the House, from whom all bad news is concealed, for fear it should spoil their barking'.[94] As with all committees, the problems with such executive bodies related to both composition and process, and contemporaries appreciated factional struggle over the appointment of their membership, and subjected them to detailed prosopographical analysis.[95] They also recognized the tendency for grandees to create 'sub-committees' when they were unable to control even such select bodies, the most famous of which was devised in order to exclude the Scots from negotiations with Royalists in the summer of 1645.[96] Moreover, such executive committees were perceived to provide the supreme demonstration of the encroachment upon, and sidelining of, Parliament, the assumption of kingly authority, and the separation of power and interests between grandees and 'real Independents'.[97]

More serious than manipulation of the membership of, and manoeuvrings within, Parliament, according to contemporary analysis, were tactics and trends that hinted at the sidelining of the two Houses, in favour of standing and executive committees. This, in turn, tended to enhance the contemporary sense that factional politics promoted both secrecy and oligarchy. Moreover, observers and commentators tend to confirm the findings of those who suggest that the most powerful assault upon conventional parliamentary processes in the 1640s was led by the Independent grandees, motivated no doubt by the difficulty of maintaining a dominant position within both the Commons and the Lords. Once again, the views of contemporary commentators are borne out in the most important recent historiography.[98]

The strength of contemporary analysis of the assault upon parliamentary politics also lay in its appreciation of the hijacking of functions of both court and state, and this was another area where the Independents were perceived to have been the dominant and most deleterious force. Analysing such developments involved exploring the financial aspects of parliamentarian rule, and the seizure of the Exchequer. Contemporaries such as Clement Walker recognized that money represented the 'sinews of war' and a source of power; and, like all good investigators, they appreciated that to understand Civil-War politics it was necessary to 'follow the money'.[99] As such, they sought to understand 'the cunnings, devices, artifices, deceits and crafts' which were used 'to catch moneys'.[100] It was alleged, therefore, that Parliament had abandoned sound maxims of financial management, and by the end of the war had 'milked' over £40 million from the people. Such excessive taxation was thought to have caused confusion in the commonwealth, and bred apocalyptic language of 'locusts, caterpillars, and horse-leeches'.[101]

Having raised such money, the parliamentary factions were also understood to have controlled its management and distribution by creating new mechanisms and structures. Attempts were made, therefore, to identify the chief 'millers' of money, and during 1647 and 1648 Clement Walker (whose personal interest in the Exchequer, as a high-ranking official displaced by reforms of the 1640s, gave him a particular fascination with the novelties of the 1640s) provided a damning critique of the 'excoriating rabble of pestiferous vermine'.[102] He drew attention to 'the multiplicity of money committees' – 'where every man's profit and power is according to his cunning and conscience' – and particularly to the Committee of Revenue, study of whose membership revealed to him, as study of its operation has since confirmed to scholars such as John Adamson, that it was an Independent powerhouse.[103] The Scottish polemicist David Buchanan alleged that the Independents were 'the nimblest to harken after moneys', and noted how they 'thrust themselves' into positions 'where the fingering of money is'.[104] Moreover, as such critics recognized, 'he that commands the money commands the men'. As Walker claimed, 'these [financial] committee men are so powerful that they over-awe and over-power their fellow members'.[105] The Independents' withholding of money undermined opponents, and its distribution rewarded friends, built factions, and consolidated support. Of this, their enemies were only too keenly aware. Buchanan, for instance, claimed that the Independents 'pleasure some whom they do affect [were pleased with], and put nack [or block] upon others whom they do dislike', and that they 'distribute it for the most part among themselves'.[106]

Once again, the roots of such corruption were perceived to date from the earliest phase of the Civil War, not least in terms of the use of financial rewards in order to co-opt Speaker Lenthall. But such critics as Buchanan and Walker highlighted not merely payments to [Independent] grandees but also claims regarding the pecuniary rewards given to the humblest members.[107] The idea that money had been siphoned from the public treasury into private purses eventually became a commonplace in popular political literature, and precise details appeared frequently in the news press.[108] However, in addition to becoming animated about money, contemporaries also became troubled by the way in which offices and places of trust were bestowed upon kinsmen and allies.[109] Such claims emerged from the moment that war broke out, and in subsequent years writers explained in detail how such tactics helped to construct factions, and how the 1645 Self-Denying Ordinance (supposedly enacted to prevent all Parliament-men from profiting from war-time office) had been enforced only selectively.[110] Ideas regarding the manipulation of office-holding quickly spread from the substantial analyses of Buchanan and Walker into popular literature, not least into the weekly newsbooks.[111]

It was not merely members of the two Houses' financial remuneration or their acquisition of lucrative offices that proved controversial during the 1640s. Commentators also berated the absence of mechanisms by which to monitor places of trust and to account for public money. For the committees appointed to deal with such matters (the Commons' Committee for Accounts, and the extra-parliamentary audit commission, the 'Committee for Taking the Accounts of the Kingdom') came to be regarded simply as smokescreens to conceal, not reveal, malpractice: they attempted to 'blind the eyes of the world'.[112] The focal point for these criticisms was the Committee for Taking the Accounts of the Kingdom, chaired by William Prynne, which was perceived as being factional in its creation, biased in its operation, and ineffectual in its outcome.[113] Royalists suggested that it was 'a mere pageant to flourish among the people, for . . . 'tis madness to imagine the Parliament intends to give any account'. Even the Parliamentarian Clement Walker claimed that its orders pertaining to accounts were merely 'dilusory'.[114] Eventually, accusations regarding financial mismanagement came to form a central element of contemporary analysis of Parliament. Once again, it was Independents who were most commonly accused of failing to account for money that they controlled and distributed.[115] But they did not have a monopoly of financial vice. Prynne's committee was accused of Presbyterian bias, and during the summer of 1647 the Presbyterian grandees were accused of having 'swallowed down the money', and of having conspired with Prynne's committee to evade proper accounting procedures.[116]

Such evidence attests to the ability of contemporaries to recognize the extent to which the resources of court and state, in terms of patronage and the public purse, were seized and deployed by the parliamentarian authorities during the 1640s, and to appreciate, moreover, that such developments resulted from the manoeuvres of a junto of Independent grandees. Detailed recent research into the behaviour of the

Independent junto indicates, moreover, that the newsbooks and pamphlets which contemporaries read and absorbed in vast quantities in the 1640s were remarkably accurate in their analysis. Perhaps more contentious was their claim that control of offices and money had been sufficiently monopolized to provide a disincentive for factional leaders to seek a settlement with the king. It was claimed, for instance, that 'committee men love money and their friends' preferment better than peace', and that 'so long as Parliament men can get into their hands the riches and treasures of the kingdom, and live like kings and emperors and like lawless men . . . there will never be an end of this Parliament'.[117] *Mercurius Elencticus* concluded that 'peace would spoil their profit, and the king restrain their baseness . . . ergo . . . no such thing'.[118]

IV THE LITERATURE OF POLITICAL CRITICISM AND THE ACCOUNTABILITY OF PARLIAMENT

Contemporary comments indicate, therefore, the profound degree to which the traditional role and extent of parliamentary power was perceived to have been altered and abused in the 1640s. To the extent that a parliamentarian 'court' was considered to have emerged during this period, observers and critics echoed familiar hostility towards the 'corruption' of such cliques. However, in so far as actual parliamentary practice was affected, it is possible to detect evidence that, whether or not contemporaries possessed an idealized model of Parliament before the wars, they certainly began to develop one as they observed the practicalities of parliamentarian rule. Moreover, the existence of this critical response to factions and juntos at Westminster – and its highly public nature – highlights the need to explore the dynamic of contemporary perceptions of parliamentary politics. It is essential to examine, in other words, the growing interest in parliamentary affairs, the attitudes of grandees to the explosion in such information and analysis, and the implications for political life in the nation at large. It is obviously possible to question the accuracy, completeness, and rigour of contemporary analyses; and at times the clarity of their conceptualization of parliamentary politics is certainly wanting.[119] Nevertheless, it is important to recognize that it is only in recent years that scholars have subjected parliamentary factionalism to detailed scrutiny, and to stress that their research has demonstrated the extent to which at least some of the ideas of Civil-War commentators have been verified.

It is also valuable to recover the picture of the Long Parliament that was developed by men who participated in, and interacted with, its workings, since such views informed their actions and opinions.[120] This is particularly true given the contemporary penetration of such ideas, and it is not necessarily the case that contemporary polemical literature offered the views of merely a tiny group within 'Westminster village', that its readership was limited, and that the reaction that it engendered is irrecoverable. Walker's *History of Independency*, for example, was purchased by members of the gentry of various political persuasions, and Civil-War correspondence indicates not merely the enthusiasm with which contemporaries consumed newspapers and newsletters, but also the extent to which they relied upon them for analysis of parliamentary affairs.[121] The ideas, conclusions, and even terminology of such writers filtered down into the wider world of print and political comment, and influenced the views of gentry and even sub-gentry figures who are known to have been their readers.[122]

As such, the importance of contemporary analysis lies not so much in its accuracy, nor even in its potential for enhancing our knowledge of the emergence of factional and 'adversarial' politics, so much as in the way in which it underpinned the structures of political life in the 1640s. In part, this reflects the fact that public interest in parliamentary affairs, and the appearance of tracts and pamphlets analysing Parliament's proceedings, fostered concern with 'popular perceptions' within the parliamentarian élite. The Civil Wars bear witness to the willingness and ability of the grandees to exploit the print medium, and, since the mechanisms for exploiting the press clearly became more sophisticated during the 1640s, it is worth exploring political involvement in the forces influencing public discussion of the workings of Parliament. It seems likely that parliamentarian press strategy involved more than merely the enforcement of secrecy regarding parliamentary debates. Although particular policies were clearly 'spun' in the public domain, it is difficult to demonstrate with certainty that information regarding proceedings and tactics was deployed and leaked in order to foster positive public perceptions of the institution, and of specific factions. Nevertheless, secrecy was certainly regarded pragmatically, and was willingly abandoned in order to bolster the reputation of particular individuals – and occasionally to encourage participation in committee hearings and massed lobbying.[123]

Whether or not Nedham was fed information from within Westminster in order to inform (or, according to taste, mislead) the public regarding the Independents' intentions is unknown; but political exploitation of the press clearly involved discrediting factional rivals and making the public aware of their tactics and techniques of parliamentary management. Pro-Presbyterian works by David Buchanan and Thomas Edwards, therefore, were encouraged by the Scots' Commissioners, and benefited from information 'leaked' from within the Westminster system. Similarly, Prynne's pamphlets relating to financial administration and the Eleven Members deployed 'secret' information in order to fight factional battles and discredit opponents, and to shed light into corners of parliamentary practice which had hitherto remained shrouded in mystery.[124] Thus, while Civil-War pamphlets and newspapers enhanced public appreciation of the developments in Parliament in the 1640s, and constituted a profound challenge to the tradition of treating governmental matters as *arcana imperii*, this resulted not merely from royalist and radical muck-raking, but also from the willingness of parliamentarian grandees to undermine secrecy in order to win support and defeat factional rivals.

It is also possible to explore contemporary literary and journalistic responses to parliamentary affairs, and to demonstrate the importance of this literature for our understanding of political debate in the 1640s. The knowledge of the inner working of the institution that this literature opened up contributed to a re-evaluation of the role of Parliament and of its members, and of the relationship between representatives and represented.

What has largely been overlooked, however, is that this body of literature was also an important source for radical ideas; and, as such, prompts a re-evaluation of the emergence and nature of Civil-War 'radicalism' more generally. To the extent that factional politics encouraged new tactics, and to the extent that such tactics were exposed by those within the system, it is possible to argue that factional parliamentary management had significant unintended consequences. To the extent that such evidence emerged through public curiosity, it attests to important developments in the nature of representation and accountability in the early modern period. The historiography of the reaction to parliamentarian rule has been dominated by hostility to the 'tyranny' and 'illegality' of county committees, the burden of the army, and the excesses of taxation: Civil-War radicalism has generally been conceived as a response to parliamentarian policies and material grievances. By focusing, however, upon the response to what happened inside Westminster, rather than to what came out of the Commons and the Lords, it is possible to rethink civil war radicalism.[125]

The contemporary response to Parliament, printed and otherwise, appears in many ways to be 'conservative' in nature. Clement Walker damned factionalism and championed fellow 'neutrals' and, alongside William Prynne, advocated a return to traditional financial institutions, and government by the three estates of king, Lords and Commons.[126] However, the *modus operandi* of such authors conflicted with their determination that MPs ought not to be questioned or held to account for their 'demeanour within those walls', and their yearning for a return to the *arcana imperii*.[127] Their attempts to discredit Parliamentarians involved breaking down the very secrecy that they prized, and this paradox indicates the need to reconsider our appreciation of 'conservatives' in the 1640s.

Moreover, examination of the texts of 'radical' writers indicates the extent to which they too require re-evaluation, since their disillusionment can be shown to have been informed by observing parliamentary practice, rather than merely the substance of particular policies, whether religious, political or economic.[128] Although radicals naturally focused their criticism upon the upper House, they eventually extended their analysis to the lower as well in order to suggest, from as early as 1645, that 'subtle practices' entailed a betrayal of trust by members of the Commons, and required that they, too, be 'called to account'.[129] Financial impropriety by members of Parliament prompted John Wildman to ask 'to what purpose should the strength of the ploughman be spent in sowing the field, whose tender fruit is always blasted in the blossom', and to inquire 'wherefore should the people trifle away their precious time in tedious toilsome journeys to elections, to send the worthies of their country?'[130] Such disillusionment with members of the two Houses provoked the observation that 'every man's tongue is against them', and claims that members had 'alienated the minds of London from these present Parliament-men'.[131] The grandees were accused of having 'brought things to such a pass that not only did they lose their credit but they durst hardly appear in the streets . . . so odious were they become to the people'.[132] However, such 'radicalism' emerged from a number of different directions. It was the reformadoes from the brigade of the Presbyterian commander, Edward Massie, for example, who threatened tumults at Westminster in January 1647, having berated 'the liberal gifts of the Parliament to their own members', which were apparently 'much spoken of among the people, who say surely the Parliament is dying in that they distribute their legacies so fast'.[133] Likewise, it was a Presbyterian who claimed that 'the people . . . expect a more exact account and ample satisfaction than they have yet had, for their profuse expense of wealth and blood'.[134]

It was disillusionment with parliamentary procedures, rather than political theory, which prompted 'radical' solutions, and these can be shown to have emerged from across the political spectrum. Sir Cheney Culpeper, for example, supported 'the purging of our great committees', and George Wither and John Musgrave defended the right of the public to level accusations against offending members. Betrayal of trust was felt to justify proceedings against MPs, and the liberty to prosecute members was regarded by some as providing a bulwark against arbitrary government.[135] Army apologists annoyed Independent grandees by legitimizing the charge against the eleven Presbyterians on the grounds that men were 'experimentally conscious of some members [being] guilty of gross crimes', and of advancing their own ends and those of their faction.[136] However, it was not just radicals who advocated such dramatic action. One crypto-royalist tract from 1647 claimed that MPs who went beyond their trust could be held accountable, and that electors could 'recall them back again as often as they please and send others more honest, diligent, and better qualified', and that such malefactors ought to be punished by fines, imprisonment, and even death.[137] The Royalist Sir Roger Twysden looked to Holland as the model for ensuring that 'the elected are so strictly tied to the electors' instructions', and were 'subject to their censure'.[138] More importantly, from 1645 contemporaries began to call for the removal of MPs who neglected their duties, and for a wholesale purge, or even dissolution, of Parliament, in order to reclaim the power that had merely been entrusted to representatives.[139]

Similar ideas had been expressed in response to material grievances since before the war; but those who made such claims in the later 1640s tended to do so on the back of their analysis of parliamentary practice.[140] Once again, however, such language can be shown to have been deployed across the political spectrum, including by supporters of the Surrey petition for peace in May 1648, who warned that 'we will have a new Parliament . . ., we will have an account of all the monies that we have paid'.[141] More important still was the way in which disillusionment with parliamentary practice, rather than merely radical thought, fed into demands for reform of the representative system.[142] It led to demands for annual, or even biannual Parliaments, to prevent 'faction, oppression, partiality, and injustice', as well as for electoral reform, to prevent 'all court craft, and faction, avarice and ambition'.[143] Lilburne

demanded frequent elections in order to remove those whose performance in Parliament was found wanting; but such demands were also
echoed by quasi-royalist commentators, who demanded the enforcement of a sizeable quorum and called for greater publicity and openness
regarding parliamentary proceedings and individual members' contributions. They called for a public registry of members' votes, so that 'each
county, corporation or any particular man may see how they behave
themselves upon all occasions'.[144]

V CONCLUSION

Questions regarding the admissibility, reliability, provenance and significance of specific sources are (or ought to be) central to the historical
profession. Exploring the history of parliamentary politics by means of
contemporary commentators such as Nedham, Walker and Buchanan
proves particularly useful. This reveals that Westminster was recognized
as being riven by factions, which could be analysed in terms of their
internal structures and relationships. It also indicates that sophisticated
parliamentary tactics were conceived to be the tools of such interest
groups, and were intrinsically important to factional politics.
Commentators recognized the need to look behind the scenes and
beyond the two Houses, and to explore financial and administrative
management in order to appreciate the extent to which conventional
procedures had fallen prey to factional power, and to determine the
identity of those who bore most responsibility for such developments.
They clearly believed that the assault on conventional procedures could
be traced to the earliest phase of the Long Parliament, and that it had
grown apace thereafter.[145] As Sir William Waller later opined, the Long
Parliament was 'betrayed by the insidious practices of its own
members'.[146]

At the most basic level, contemporary comment and analysis
supplement our understanding of the timing and nature of key developments at Westminster: the intensification of adversary politics, the
assault on parliamentary procedures, and the character of factions and
parties. Such evidence will clearly be considered with a degree of scepticism in some quarters; but with Parliament and politics, sources
matter because of more than just their 'accuracy'. The explosion of
print and the growing interest in national affairs meant that parliamentary affairs became, to a degree unknown before, a question of

perception. Sources regarding the impact of factions and their tactics upon Parliament matter, therefore, because they reflected – and influenced – the ways in which contemporaries behaved, and because members of the political élite needed to engage with, and manipulate, public perceptions.

4. The Baronial Context of the Irish Civil Wars

JANE OHLMEYER

On 7 November 1651, Henry Ireton, general of the Cromwellian army of invasion who was stationed in Clare Castle, near Limerick, wrote to General Thomas Preston, Viscount Tara, Governor of Galway, ordering him to surrender the city. Preston took umbrage at his 'unsoldierly' demand and refused to yield Galway 'at such a distance' [i.e. 40 miles]. Ireton replied claiming that he was more concerned for the well being of the town's inhabitants 'who perhaps may not be so airy of the notion of soldierly honour'.[1] In a blatant attempt to divide the military and civic leaders, Ireton suggested to the Galway townsmen that they were 'under the power of a mercenary soldier who will perhaps pretend [a] point of honour' in order to further his own interests and self-glorification.[2] The townsmen avoided any discussion of 'points of honour' in their reply, but Preston reiterated his earlier censure, criticizing Ireton for breaking 'the rules of war'.[3] In the event, the exchange came to nothing. Ireton died suddenly of a fever three weeks later. As for Preston, with the surrender of Galway on 12 April 1652, he slipped off to France where he died three years later, aged 70.

However, the significance of this brief exchange between Preston and Ireton lies in what it reveals about 'soldierly honour' as perceived by two experienced commanders who hailed from very different social, religious and military traditions.[4] Ireton was an English Puritan, an ardent republican, Oliver Cromwell's son-in-law and a senior officer in the New Model Army. His background was that of a country gentleman who had received all of his military training and experience in the course of the English Civil Wars.[5] Ireton had his own clear sense of what 'soldierly honour' entailed. With the separation of military and political affairs that accompanied the creation of the New Model Army, Ireton became a professional soldier, whose principal job was to secure military objectives (that said, he nonetheless continued to be closely involved in politics). For his part, Preston stressed individualism and believed that the titled nobility achieved honour through service, loyalty, the exercise of arms and the attainment of glory on the battlefield.[6] As the second son of an Old English Catholic peer, Preston formed part of a community in which honour served as 'social glue'.[7] Years of service as a commander in the Spanish theatre of war had both reinforced these 'old-fashioned' views and exposed Preston to 'modern', Continental codes of honour and behaviour.[8]

Preston's elevation to the peerage as Viscount Tara in July 1650 underscores his position as a loyal servant rewarded by the king in what might be regarded as a 'baronial' civil war. In an influential article entitled 'The Baronial Context of the English Civil War', John Adamson analysed contemporary English preoccupations with medieval precedents and chivalric literature and argued that, prior to the creation of the New Model Army in 1645, key titled figures drew on these influences as they determined political and military affairs.[9] He suggested that 'the war was taking place within a tradition of aristocratic conflict – or, from the king's perspective, of aristocratic rebellion – a tradition which dictated the combatants' code of behaviour'.[10] He noted how during the 1640s a third of the English nobility led armies in the field, and how the war in its early stages was perceived as 'a series of localized aristocratic struggles for regional control'.[11] Finally, Adamson analysed the significance of the ascendancy of the Earl of Essex as captain-general of the parliamentary army and the extent to which his pre-eminent status precipitated 'an aristocratic reaction against the extent of his authority'.[12] The work of Barbara Donagan and Roger Manning has since sought to qualify some of Adamson's findings and to set them in a wider Continental context.[13] Donagan, for example, assesses the significance for Civil-War England of the experiences of those Englishmen who, during the early decades of the seventeenth century, had fought in the Continental conflicts or who had been exposed to the theory of war though military manuals and treatises. Manning, in a wide-ranging study of martial culture in the Stuart kingdoms, suggests that the proportion of English 'military peers' (i.e. career soldiers or those with direct experience of battle) increased significantly over the course of the early decades of the seventeenth century, rising from 45 per cent in 1605, to 69 per cent in 1640, to 71 per cent in 1645.[14] He attributes this remilitarization of the English peerage to large numbers of young men seeking active service either in Ireland or in one of the European armies, and argues that 'a rechivalrization of English aristocratic and gentry culture [occurred] as younger sons, heirs of peers, and peers themselves heeded the call . . . to validate their honour upon the field of battle'.[15]

Can the arguments advanced by Adamson, Donagan and Manning for England be applied to the neighbouring Stuart kingdom of Ireland? There was no equivalent to the Earl of Essex in Civil-War Ireland. Despite this and other obvious constitutional, religious and ethnic differences, the similarities are nevertheless striking. In fact, it could be argued that the context of the wars in Ireland (and for that matter Scotland as well) was more 'baronial' than in England. 'Baronial context' could be interpreted in a variety of ways and requires definition at the outset. At one level, it describes the involvement of individual Irish 'barons' in military and political affairs and includes the networks from which these lords often derived their military power. At another level, 'baronial context' evokes a culturally defined code of conduct and honour, which both drew on medieval precedents and 'ancient privileges' and was also shaped by contemporary Continental practices. This chapter will explore further these overlapping and intersecting contexts and suggest that while honour and 'honour politics' were not the exclusive preserve of the Irish élite, this shared code of conduct helped to define the peerage as a distinct and – even at the height of the Civil War – a relatively cohesive social group.

I 'FIGHTING WARRIORS'

General Thomas Preston personified what it meant to be Old English – as the descendants of the Norman settlers in Ireland were known – during the early decades of the seventeenth century. He represented, as Edward Hyde, Earl of Clarendon, put it, 'the more moderate party . . . whose main end was to obtain liberty for the exercise of their religion, without any thought of declining their subjection to the king, or of invading his prerogative'.[16] Equally important, Preston viewed himself, thanks to the good fortune of his birth and chivalric origins, as belonging to an honour community and enjoying a predisposition to honour. Many members of the ancient Irish nobility – the Butlers, Earls of Ormond, the Fitzgeralds, Earls of Kildare, the Burkes, Earls of Clanricard, the O'Briens, Earls of Thomond, and so on – shared Preston's well-established sense of honour and acknowledged how this prepared them for royal service both on the battlefield and off it.

Traditionally, these lineages had exercised considerable political and military power – especially during the sixteenth century, when baronial warfare had proved endemic and had escalated into major noble risings

(Silken Thomas's rebellion of the mid-1530s, the Earl of Desmond's of the 1570s and the Earl of Tyrone's of the 1590s). Each of these sixteenth-century rebellions had specific causes; but each one fed off the widespread lawlessness that afflicted Tudor Ireland.[17] This general disorder stemmed in large part from the fact that a small number of powerful Old English and native Gaelic-speaking Irish overlords not only controlled their own territories, but also collected tribute (in the form of military service, food, lodgings, and agricultural labour) and demanded submission from previously independent regions, thereby extending their political control and enhancing their standing within their own lordship. Since military might and robust baronial networks determined dynamic lordship, maintaining and sustaining an effective army became a priority for any sixteenth-century Irish lord. It also underpinned the social order, for a lord's followers were obliged not only to feed and house soldiers but also to offer military service themselves in return for his protection. This elaborate system of extortion, intimidation, and protection was known to the Old English as 'coign and livery' and enabled individual lords to field substantial private forces.[18] Since livestock, especially cows, constituted an important form of wealth, cattle raiding was also rife. A successful cattle-raid sometimes resulted in the submission of a territory, which enhanced the military and political standing of those who led the raids, and brought increased riches in the form of tribute. As a result, 'the chief inclination of these people', as one Spanish traveller noted in 1588–9, 'is to be robbers, and to plunder each other; so that no day passes without a call to arms among them'.[19]

During the early decades of the seventeenth century, the political, military, social and cultural landscape in which the Irish lords operated began to change rapidly thanks to a raft of 'civilizing' policies promoted by the Crown.[20] In addition, the king's brazen sale of Irish titles to the highest bidder – which resulted in the resident Irish peerage more than doubling, from 29 peers in 1603 to 69 in 1640 – threatened the very survival of the ancient lords as a distinct military and political class.[21] Unable to control entry into their ranks, it became critical for these peers to reinforce their individual (and collective) position in the social hierarchy: to consolidate their pre-eminence in the community of honour and to promote codes of behaviour that attempted to regulate relationships, especially those between the traditional leaders in Irish society and the *arrivistes*.[22] Many, though by no means all, of the newcomers were Protestants; and with these elevations the Crown created a 'service nobility', a new generation of ambitious and avaricious peers, who wanted either to consolidate their patrimonies and political influence or to make their fortunes in Ireland, and to secure public reward and social recognition. But they were also determined to establish themselves as men of honour and to create their own baronial networks.

Some later questioned the status of these new lords and the circumstances of their creation. In one particular exchange between the Lords and the Commons, the Commons-men refused to stand without their hats, as was the custom, prompting one peer to ask whether the Commons 'would all be lords'? In response, one quipped sarcastically that 'another rebellion may make us so, as well as former [rebellions] made your ancestors'.[23] And, of course, many of these 'ancestors' had been men of the sword from modest backgrounds, who had distinguished themselves on the battlefield during 'former rebellions' and especially the Nine Years War (1594–1603).[24] It thus became critical to demonstrate that the sense of honour of these newcomers was commensurate with their position in the early modern Irish social hierarchy. The language of honour associated with Sir Toby Caulfield's elevation to the rank of baron of Charlemont in 1620 highlights this. Particular mention was made of Sir Toby's defeat of 'the traitor', Hugh O'Neill, Earl of Tyrone. The letters patent extolled Sir Toby's worthy lineage, his military training in France and the Low Countries, and his soldierly triumphs in Ireland. He displayed 'true loyalty, unfailing constancy, and indefatigable labour, and the virtues of men devoted to their Prince'; which was in stark contrast to Tyrone, who was described as hateful, crafty, obstinate, perfidious and barbarous.[25] Since Sir Toby had never married, his letters patent provided for the transfer of his title to his nephew, Sir William, who was described as 'a man of distinguished talent and character, a strenuous imitator of his uncle's military and other virtues'.[26] In a similar vein, Lord Deputy Chichester's epitaph bears testimony to his military and civil achievements, which helped to consolidate his position as a man of honour:

> he did virtue and religion nourishe;
> & made this land late rude, with peace to flourish.
> The wildest rebel, He [by] power did tame
> & by true justice gained an honoured name . . .[27]

Whether the apparent peace that characterized Ireland during the first few decades of the seventeenth century can indeed be attributed to Chichester is debatable. However, during these years the Crown succeeded in establishing an effective monopoly over the exercise of violence and made considerable progress towards weakening the military power bases of the more considerable warlords.[28] On the eve of the 1641 rebellion, the Dublin government even boasted that 'the great Irish lords, who for so many ages so grievously infested this kingdom, are either taken away or so levelled with others in point of subjection as all now submit to the rule of law, and many of them live in good order'.[29] Yet, despite the rhetoric of over-optimistic officials, Ireland remained a militarized society, especially when compared with its neighbours. Manning has suggested that the number of 'military peers' in Ireland in 1605 was significantly higher (at 72 per cent) than either for England (45 per cent) or for Scotland (43 per cent). By 1625, the proportion of Irish 'military peers' remained the highest: at 68 per cent (the figure for England was 57 per cent, and for Scotland 55 per cent). It was 1640 before the numbers of 'military peers' in England (69 per cent) almost matched the figure for Ireland (71 per cent), while that for Scotland soared to 73 per cent.[30] Thanks to the exercise of martial law, which was in operation in Ireland for much of this period, and the maintenance of private forces, members of the Irish peerage, both the old and the new, exercised considerable military authority and seized moments of national crisis, especially during the 1620s, to consolidate and modernize their personal retinues.[31] Protestants dominated the military establishment and attempts in 1627 to appoint Catholic lords of the Pale as colonels of regiments, came to nothing.[32] Instead, Protestant peers commanded five (out of nine) troops of horse in 1630, and the non-resident Richard Burke, fourth Earl of Clanricard and step-father to the Earl of Essex, was the only ancient Catholic lord to serve as colonel of foot.[33]

Given the limited opportunities for Catholics to participate directly in war at home – at least before 1641 – and the continuing significance accorded to 'the exercise of arms' in noble culture, Irish lords looked to the Continental theatre of war as the most effective arena in which to secure military training. Exposure to warfare, often as part of a 'grand tour', in the various Continental conflicts, but especially the Eighty Years War (1568–1648) and the Thirty Years War (1618–48), offered young grandees the chance not only to gain practical military experience but also to garner military honour. During the early decades of the seventeenth century, the sons of Lord Louth and the Earls Roscommon and Antrim spent time living in France.[34] In the case of Antrim's eldest son, Randal, his French sojourn (1625–7) would have afforded him ample opportunity to make contact with his exiled O'Neill cousins serving in the army of Flanders, and with his four natural half-brothers, one of whom (Maurice) was an infantry captain in Flanders.[35] Antrim later claimed that he had 'no experience in war', but he nonetheless demonstrated during the 'Wars of the Three Kingdoms' in the 1640s a surprisingly clear idea of how an army should be organized and a knowledge of the basic principles of modern warfare.[36]

Similarly, the Protestant peerage proved anxious to secure experience of Continental warfare. During the 1620s and 1630s, Viscount Montgomery of the Ards dispatched his sons to France, Germany, Italy and Holland. His second son Hugh, later Earl of Mount Alexander, returned to Ireland 'accomplished in the French tongue', dancing, fencing, lute playing and riding and, more importantly, well versed in the intricacies of artillery fortification and modern warfare.[37] In 1635, Richard Boyle, first Earl of Cork, entrusted his two younger sons, Lord Broghill and Viscount Kinalmeaky, to a former Huguenot soldier who instructed them in mathematics, horsemanship, dancing and fencing, and showed them modern, new artillery fortifications as part of their grand tour of France, Switzerland and Italy.[38] On their return to the Stuart kingdoms, both youths saw active service: Kinalmeaky died (aged 23) of wounds received at the battle of Liscarroll (August 1642); and Broghill served first the Royalists and later the Parliamentarians; and during the Cromwellian conquest of Ireland he played a particularly brutal role in pursuing the war in Munster. Elevated to the earldom of Orrery at the Restoration, he published *The Art of War*, which recorded in considerable detail his military experiences during these years.[39]

Other young nobles took up arms on a more permanent basis and became professional soldiers in the service of the Swedes, the Dutch, the Spanish and Austrian Habsburgs, and the French, Russians and Poles. Many Irish Protestant peers had fought alongside members of the English expeditionary forces in the United Provinces, 'the Nurcery of Souldierie'.[40] Lords Caulfield, Chichester, Esmond, and Wilmot of Athlone were all veterans of the Dutch wars prior to their serving in Ireland during the Nine Years War. During the 1620s and 1630s, others followed their example.[41] In 1626 Sir Henry Blayney ran away to experience the wars in the Low Countries, returning to Ireland a few years later to succeed his father as Baron Blayney.[42] Edward, later Viscount Conway, together with many other Irishmen, volunteered for the Duke of Buckingham's disastrous 1627 expedition to the Isle of Rhé.[43] Those of Scottish provenance favoured Swedish service. For example, Hugh Hamilton, later Baron of Glenawley, left Ireland for Sweden as a private in 1624, later rising to the rank of lieutenant-colonel.[44] Similarly, from the 1590s their Catholic counterparts – Old English and native Irish alike – served as career soldiers in the Continental theatres of war and especially in Flanders, 'the only martial academy of Christendom', where they fitted into well-established kinship networks.[45] In the dedicatory epistle of *An Aphorismical Discovery of Treasonable Faction*, the anonymous chronicler evoked the mentality of these young men who were 'desirous of honor, [and] must trie theire fortune, in the recovery therof'. The virtues of Owen Roe O'Neill, to whom the book is dedicated, received particular praise: 'Owen Oneyll, cossen german to the late Tyron, residinge then colonell in Flanders, bred in that nurserie of armes at leaste 30 yeares, ever against the antigonists of religion. All the best sort of antiquarists and historiographers doe hould you for bloude noe lesse then royall, in behaviour a prince, in armes Mars, in bounty Alexander, in wisdome Salomon, in faithfullnesse David' and so on.[46] In a similar vein, a poem entitled 'Outburst of Sorrow and Dirge for the Lieutenant-General of Munster' by the poet-priest Pádraigín Haicéad, vividly recaptures the military achievements and virtues of another of these professional swordsmen, Captain Richard Butler, the third son of Richard, Viscount Mountgarret. The poet extolled Richard's virtues – his mastery of 'seven tongues', his desire to seek 'chivalry', and his acquisition of 'honour' – before relating his service to the Polish king and finishing with an account of his personal bravery during an encounter against the Russians at Smolensk, presumably in 1634.[47]

Whether on a temporary or a permanent basis, it is likely that a significant proportion of Irish peers had had an apprenticeship in arms and these military experiences exposed young Irishmen to Continental codes of honour and conduct. Those who did not travel could be instructed by reading military treatises, manuals on the exercise of arms, war memoirs, and translations of classical writers and historians which extolled battlefield valour and military virtue.[48] The influence of classical writers, usually read in translation, was particularly important and introduced Irish lords to Greek and Roman accounts of warfare and their associated language of honour.[49] For the anonymous author of the *Aphorismical Discovery of Treasonable Faction*, Greece was 'the nurse of science and chivalrie'. The Earl of Orrery's familiarity with Greek and Roman martial practices later attracted comment from his chaplain, who believed that 'there are things in this book [*Art of War*], which persons who have a military genius cannot but be pleased with'.[50] A generation earlier, Garret Barry, a veteran of the war in Spanish

Flanders, dedicated a drill manual – *Discourse of Military Discipline* (Brussels, 1634) – to Orrery's brother-in-law, the Earl of Barrymore. While the treatise was aimed at Barrymore's native countrymen who were 'not skil-ful in warres', the lengthy dedication focused on the earl and his 'incor-rupted virtues'. It reminded readers of the bravery and honour of Barrymore's ancestors, and urged the earl to revive 'theyre honour and parpetuall fame, as required and hoped of youre honourable birth and nobilitie, accordinge the great exspectationes of youre frendes, and well wisheres, to increase the honour of youre house'.[51]

After the outbreak of the Irish rebellion in October 1641, Garret Barry – like Richard Butler, Thomas Preston, and other Irishmen serv-ing in Germany, France, Flanders and Spain – returned to fight in Ireland, bringing with them Continental ideas of 'soldierly honour', as well as practical knowledge of every aspect of the early modern 'military revolution'.[52] These professional soldiers played a key role in training the native recruits, especially during the early years of the war. According to one hostile source these veterans, within a relatively short period of time, had 'reduced many of the natives to a more civil deport-ment, and to a pretty good understanding of military discipline'.[53] As Preston's textbook siege of Duncannon Fort (January–March 1645) highlights, his knowledge of fortifications and siege works – the staple of the wars in the Low Countries – was put to good effect.[54] The returning military migrants also introduced modern tactics, pioneered by Maurice of Nassau at the turn of the seventeenth century and continued during the Thirty Years War, whereby small tactical units fought in a linear formation 'in which the firepower of musketeers was co-ordinated with the shock strength of pikemen'.[55] The Irish victory at Benburb (June 1646) demonstrated the effectiveness of such linear formation fighting and how, on occasion, the Irish soldier appears to have been blessed with remarkable stamina, courage and endurance. By 1646, two leading Parliamentarians maintained that the Confederates 'have their men in a better order of war and better commanded by captains of experience and practice of war then ever they were since the Conquest'.[56]

II 'NOBLE AND VALIANT COMMANDERS': THE IRISH NOBILITY AND WAR

During the Irish Civil War of the 1640s, these career soldiers – many of whom enjoyed close kinship links with members of the resident Irish peerage – fought alongside recruits commanded by local lords. According to Manning, by 1645, 68 (out of 98) Irish peers had taken up arms and served with forces under the command of the Irish Confederates, the Crown or the English Parliament (and sometimes combinations of all three).[57] While only a number enjoyed senior commands, the majority fought at the provincial and county levels, defending their estates and neighbouring urban centres and capturing local places of military strength and strategic importance. Given the high levels of engagement, a significant number died in combat or sustained serious injuries over the course of the 1640s. Others were captured, imprisoned and then usually exchanged for enemy prisoners of a comparable rank.

As well as direct involvment in the conflict, there was also a wider perception of the war as a struggle dominated by the nobility. As in Civil-War England, popular pamphlets, especially those printed during the early years of the conflict, extolled the wartime exploits of titled commanders and recounted their regional skirmishes. There are numerous examples, including tracts with titles like *The Last and Best Newes from Ireland: declaring . . . the Entrance of some English and Scottish Companies into the North-Parts of Ireland under the Command of these Foure Noblemen; the Lord Grandison, the Lord Chichester, the Lord Conway, the Lord Cromwell . . .* (1641). Similarly, *A Renowned Victory obtained against the Rebels on the First Day of June, neere Burros the Duke of Buckinghams Castle, by the Valour of these Noble and Valiant Commanders. The Earle of Ormond. The Earl of Eastmeath. The Lord Don Luce, Earle of Antrim . . . Against the Lord Mountgarret. The Lord Dunsany. The Lord Plunket. The Lord Muskro. The Lord Dunhowin with 18000 rebels. Wherein is Manifested how the Lord Don-luce tooke the Lord Dunsany Prisoner, with Five of the Great Commanders, which are now Prisoners in the Castle at Dublin . . .* (1642) portrays the conflict as a struggle between rival noble warlords. More particularly, the author's representation of Antrim's personal combat with Dunsany, which is fully developed in the text, evokes chivalric warfare, with each combatant determined to authenticate his personal honour on the battlefield. A number of the pamphlets published during the 1640s also drew attention to rebellions and baronial revolts of the sixteenth century.[58] Equally interesting are the accounts of the war published after the Restoration.[59] For instance, in his manuscript history of the conflict, Richard Bellings, Caroline poet and confederate lawyer, argued that members of the titled nobility, and especially those of Old English provenance (whatever their religion), were Ireland's natural leaders, and his account dwells on the martial

conduct and wartime actions of these key figures.[60] Similarly, the Earl
of Castlehaven's memoirs portrayed the war as a noble struggle which
was defined by common codes of behaviour.[61]

Castlehaven and Bellings were, however, quick to remind their readers that Catholic lords had gone to war reluctantly. Even though Lord
Maguire had helped to orchestrate the rebellion which began on 22–23
October 1641, the majority of Catholic lords disassociated themselves
from the insurrection, which, according to Ulick, Earl of Clanricard, had
been hijacked by 'loose people, desperate in their fortunes'. The
Catholic Clanricard, writing in November 1641 to his half-brother and
the future commander of the English parliamentary army, the Earl of
Essex, maintained that the insurgents did not include 'any man of qualitie, either of English descent or antient Irish', or any 'nobleman in the
kingdom'.[62]

Indeed, most Irish lords professed their loyalty to the Crown in 1641,
asked for arms to defend their homes and did everything possible to
secure a political solution to the crisis.[63] The Dublin government
rejected their overtures and, to make matters worse, demanded that the
Irish Parliament, which had been adjourned in August that year, be
prorogued.[64] When Parliament finally reconvened, under an armed
guard, in mid-November, a committee from both Houses implored the
Lords Justices to reconsider their decision to abandon the session.[65]
They refused. Finally, in a last-ditch attempt to regain control over
events, the upper House instructed Viscount Dillon of Costello-Gallen to
travel to Scotland to persuade the king to continue the Parliament 'at
least till the rebels (then few in number) were reduced'.[66] After sitting for
two days, Parliament was prorogued, an act that Castlehaven later
claimed was the 'greatest discontent' of all. According to Castlehaven,
Parliament had become 'the only way the nation had to express their
loyalty and prevent their being misrepresented to their sovereign; which,
had it been permitted to sit for any reasonable time, would in all likeli-
hood, without any great charge or trouble, have brought the rebels to
justice'.[67] This abortive parliamentary session, combined with the
bungling and hyperbole of the Lords Justices, and the deteriorating
political climate in England, effectively undermined any negotiated and
honourable settlement to the crisis. Sir Charles Coote's military excesses
proved a particular source of contention amongst the peers and drove
many lords into the 'rebel' camp.[68] Clarendon in his *History* recaptured
the dilemma faced by 'many persons of honour and quality' during these
months when he noted how the course of events left them no alternative

but to engage 'themselves by degrees in it [i.e. the insurrection] for their own security'.[69]

As the rising gathered momentum and the 'comon sort of people of noe rancke or qualitie' seized the initiative, Catholic lords rallied behind the insurgents in order to regain control over their followers and to secure their estates.[70] Having done so, these peers – in order to ensure their own survival – pressured, cajoled and threatened their fellow Catholic lords to join them. Many, including Castlehaven, Antrim and Clanricard, initially refused. Others joined unwillingly and only when the spread of unrest to their respective localities had left them with no realistic alternative. For instance, news of the outbreak of the rebellion reached Viscount Muskerry, later Earl of Clancarthy, during a dinner party attended by the Earl of Cork, his sons 'and some other men of quality of the Irish nation, with whom they lived in an easy and familiar way'.[71] According to a later account, on hearing of the rebellion 'My Lord Muskerry, who was a facetious man and an excellent companion, employ'd all the wit he was master of to turn the whole story into ridicule'.[72] Of course, the insurrection proved to be no laughing matter, and in March 1642 Muskerry reluctantly threw in his lot with the insurgents, on the grounds that the rebellion had become the only means of preserving Catholicism, the king's prerogative and the 'antient privileges of the poore kingdome of Ireland established and allowed by the Common Law of England'.[73] Thus, from the outset, commitment amongst the Catholic lords to an armed rising as the best means of securing political, tenurial and constitutional objectives was fraught with contradictions.

Yet, despite this, the Catholic lords went on to make a major contribution to the confederate war effort: Muskerry and Taaffe, together with Antrim, Castlehaven and Westmeath, all held major commands. With the exception of Castlehaven, who during the late 1630s had spent some time observing the European theatre of war and later distinguished himself in French and Spanish service, none was a particularly gifted soldier. This hardly seemed to matter, since their military power stemmed from their extensive networks, which gave the confederate commanders access to large personal armies. For instance, during the early months of the rebellion, the aged Mountgarret called to arms the Kilkenny and Tipperary Butlers, together with the neighbouring Fitzpatricks, and led these troops deep into Munster before he retreated into politics as the first President of the confederate Supreme Council.[74]

Elsewhere, grandees summoned their followers, tenants and kinsmen to arms in a time-honoured fashion, reminiscent of earlier Irish
wars and of the 'barons' wars' of fifteenth-century England. The
contribution of the Earl of Fingal to the Catholic war-effort was typical. At a gathering at the Hill of Tara late in 1641, Fingal was
appointed general of the horse for County Meath with the power to
nominate 'so many captains as [he] though fitt out of the baronies'.[75]
The earl also raised provisions for the Irish forces and commanded a
troop of horse at the siege of Drogheda (November 1641–March
1642). Throughout the 1640s, he regularly attended the confederate
General Assemblies and fought at Dungan's Hill (August 1647) and at
Rathmines (August 1649), where he was captured (he died shortly
afterwards in Dublin Castle).

Those who had recently converted to Protestantism, including the
Earls of Barrymore and Kildare, were also invited to join the Catholic
cause. According to a government source, Barrymore 'hath been
tempted with promises, and threatened with menaces, to joyne with the
rebells in Munster'.[76] He refused and instead 'raised some 500 horse and
foot of his tenants and friends for the kings service and his own
defence'.[77] However, this did not prevent the capture and sack of his seat
at Castle Lyons by Muskerry, his erstwhile dinner partner (though significantly Muskerry allowed Barrymore to escape the onslaught
unharmed).[78] The outbreak of rebellion left the Earl of Kildare in a similar predicament. Despite repeated overtures from the insurgents to join
them, he declined.[79] In retaliation, they pillaged Kildare's livestock and
household goods, including 'divers bookes out of the earles studye',
before burning his 'new house at Maynooth'.[80] Despite speculations
about 'how he will proceed against his countrymen',[81] he quickly
became one of the 'strong pillars of the Protestant Army'.[82]

Elsewhere in Leinster individual Protestant lords bore the brunt of
insurgent attacks especially during the early years of the war.[83] Like their
Catholic counterparts, their baronial networks provided them with an
immediate pool of fighting men. When Viscount Moore of Drogheda,
learned of the rebellion he 'sent for all his tenants, and asked them, if
they would assist him in suppressing of the rebels; their answer was, they
would be ready at all times, to venture their lives, for their king, him and
their country'. In all he managed to raise nearly 1,000 men – 'all his
friends and tenants' (but only half of whom were armed) – before he died
in combat in the summer of 1643.[84] The viscount's younger brother,
Francis, became captain of a cavalry troop and, as observers noted,

conducted himself with great honour and bravery. In Ulster the Protestant peers – Lords Lecale, Montgomery, Clandeboy, Blayney and Caulfied of Charlemont – together with local grandees, raised 9,900 foot and 750 horse by 1643.

As in Ulster, Protestant baronial networks shaped the course of the war in Munster. It was the Earl of Cork who initially financed the Protestant war-effort. In addition to maintaining his own company at Lismore (at a weekly cost of £20, plus provisions) and funding the defence of Youghall (at a cost of £2,100), the army regularly siphoned off any spare cash he managed to accumulate, leaving Cork bankrupt by the time he died in 1643.[85] The most formidable military commander in Munster was Murrough O'Brien, Baron Inchiquin, a Protestant of Irish Catholic stock and related by marriage to neighbouring settler families.[86] Despite his relative youth (he was only 27 in 1641) and his limited experience of warfare (though he had spent some time in Spanish service in Italy during the late 1630s), he won early victories at Liscarroll (August 1642) and Bandonbridge (November that year). Inchiquin used his kin connections with the Irish to secure accurate intelligence of their plans and movements, and always led his men from the front. His leadership skills helped to overcome the perennial problems he encountered fighting in the Munster theatre of war: his forces constantly lacked seasoned reinforcements, sufficient money and adequate munitions; and his personal rivalry with the Boyles of Cork, especially Lord Broghill, left him vulnerable to politicking at Westminster. This helps to explain why he changed sides in 1644 (from the king to Parliament) and again in 1648 (when he returned to fight for the king). But whether fighting for king or Parliament, Inchiquin, it was reported, 'performed all the offices of a resolute man and a wise commander'; [87] and 'showed excellent demonstrations of his valour, and by his example encouraged all the army to acts of chivalry and honour'.[88] Yet, despite his reputation in the popular press as a man of 'chivalry and honour', Inchiquin committed numerous outrages, earning him the opprobrious nickname: 'Murrough of the burnings'.[89]

From a Protestant perspective, west of the Shannon was the most militarily vulnerable province – in part because the Protestant nobility did not enjoy a significant military presence there. The geographic isolation of the Earl of Thomond's estates ensured that he remained 'neutral' until 1646, when he handed Bunratty Castle over to a small parliamentary garrison and fled to England. In practice, as Bellings noted in his history of the war, Clanricard held much of Connacht for the Crown by virtue of 'the generall affection borne to his family, and the dependence upon him, by reason of his great estate'.[90] Because of the influence Clanricard wielded both at home and at the royal court, the Confederates repeatedly asked him to join their cause, appealing directly to his sense of honour.[91] In November 1642, a fellow peer evoked the memory of his ancestors and begged Clanricard 'not to expose the honour descended from so noble a father to so much obloquy, as that the world may see, when all the rest of the catholicks of this kingdom answer their father, your lordship should be the only branded member for denying to your own father, your king and country'.[92] Even though Clanricard refused these overtures, he nonetheless attempted to mediate a political settlement between the Crown and Confederates, and throughout the war he implored his fellow peers to act with 'honour' in their dealings with the enemy.[93] Interestingly, when Clanricard finally joined the Catholic Confederation (in 1647 and, significantly, after his half-brother Essex's death), he committed himself to their cause on 'the reputation and honour of a peere'.[94]

If Clanricard had joined the Confederation during the early 1640s, he might have brought to the Catholic cause the political leadership that it so desperately lacked. Peers played an active role in the confederate General Assemblies and served as members of the Supreme Council, its ruling executive. However, the bitter factionalism between the pro-clerical and pro-royalist groupings profoundly undermined the ability of the Confederates to wage war effectively; and this was further exacerbated by personal rivalries amongst the confederate lords.[95] For instance, the feud in 1644 between Antrim and Castlehaven over who should be given supreme command of all of the confederate armies ensured that the summer offensive against Ulster ended in a shambles. Contemporaries were acutely aware of this vacuum and Bellings noted 'the great scarsity and fatall barrenesse of abilityes among the then sett of noblemen'.[96] The deaths between 1642 and 1643 of three prominent lords – Westmeath, Slane and Gormanston – combined with the neutrality of key Catholics, like Clanricard, help to explain this 'fatall barrenesse of abilityes' amongst the confederate nobility. The first to die, in May 1642, was Westmeath, who had acted as a spokesman for the Old English grandees since the 1610s and had proved reluctant to join the insurrection.[97] It was not until the later 1640s that his teenage grandson and heir was in a position to provide comparable military and political leadership for the Catholic cause.[98] The other natural leaders lost at this time were William Fleming, Lord Slane, and Nicholas Preston, Viscount

Gormanston (Thomas Preston's nephew), who were regarded as being 'the two best peeres of Linster, for witt and loyalltie' and 'both yonge and reasonable'.[99] Slane and Gormanston were both succeeded by young sons. In short, the Catholic war-effort lacked an Earl of Essex who could provide decisive and over-arching political, as well as military, leadership. Instead, the confederate lords either politicked amongst themselves or allowed external forces – the Crown or the clergy – to divide and rule them.

But the Protestant cause in Civil-War Ireland had no equivalent to Essex either. While James Butler, twelfth Earl and later Duke of Ormond, as Lord Lieutenant and commander of the king's army, personified the royalist cause and used ceremonial and civic ritual to great effect to emphasize his pre-eminent status, he never posed the sort of political problem that Essex did, nor elicited an aristocratic coup against him (despite the Marquess of Antrim's best efforts).[100] However, Ormond's far-reaching kinship links, especially with the lesser Butler houses and with Muskerry, combined with the influence his clients (the 'Ormondists') enjoyed within the Confederate Association and his close personal relationship with Charles I, ensured that he exerted extensive political clout for most of the 1640s and beyond.[101] Despite the fact that Ormond had experienced only limited formal military training (Buckingham had refused to allow the teenager to join the expedition to the Isle of Rhé in 1627), in 1640 he assumed command of the Earl of Strafford's 'New Army' raised in Ireland, and from November 1641 he led the kingdom's Protestant standing army.[102] He won a number of victories, especially during the initial phases of the war (at Kilrush in April 1642 and at Old Ross in March 1643), but lacked the strategic vision of a great general. Despite this, Ormond was very keen to cultivate his image as a 'fighting warrior' and an 'illustrious cavalier' even if the court, rather than the camp, underpinned his prominence.[103] Whether on or off the battlefield, Ormond wanted to be represented as a man of public honour and private virtue whose conduct, especially during the 1640s, was beyond reproach. Later works by John Dryden reflected back on Ormond's conduct during this period and drew attention to his 'unblemish'd Loyalty', 'unwearied duty' and 'own Vertue'. In particular, Dryden's brief portrait of Ormond as Barzillai in *Absalom and Achitophel* (1681) reminded the London political elite of Ormond's sacrifice and suffering, his exile and undying loyalty to Charles I.[104] The emphasis was on his service, the basis of honour and noble status.

III 'SOLDIERLY HONOUR'

The experiences of Ormond highlight not only how Irish peers exercised military power, but also the extent to which they were involved
in, and committed to, culturally defined codes of honour. Despite the
brutal nature of the war in Ireland, especially in the months following
the outbreak of rebellion and during the later 1640s and early 1650s,
common codes of honour did influence, and even regulate, the
conduct of the war, especially between members of the titular nobility. Clanricard regularly wrote to his fellow peers – Catholic and
Protestant alike – and chastized them if troops under their command
committed outrages he considered inappropriate.[105] Others shared
Clanricard's views on how the war should be conducted. For instance,
when Catholic insurgents repeatedly attacked Lady Offaly's castle in
April 1642 she castigated their leader and her kinsman Viscount
Clanmalier, informing him that she would rather they batter her
castle down than surrender to men who have no sense 'either of
honesty or honour'.[106] Codes of conduct also regulated the exchange
of titled prisoners of war. Following his capture at the battle of
Benburb (June 1646), Viscount Montgomery languished in jail for
over a year until a confederate captive of equivalent rank – the Earl
of Westmeath, who had been taken prisoner after Dungan's Hill
(August 1647) – was identified and swapped.[107] So, despite the pressures that the onset of war inevitably brought, many continued to
adhere to a code of honour or, at the very least, believed that this code
should be adhered to.

When atrocities involving a lord (his tenant, servant or kinsman) did
occur, the honour of that individual was compromised, often resulting in
private distress and public humiliation.[108] Consider the response of
Viscount Mayo to a particularly brutal attack on a convoy of Protestants
travelling to Galway at Shrule Bridge, County Mayo, in February 1642.
Despite the fact that Mayo, the local power broker and a recent convert
both to Protestantism and to the peerage, had promised the refugees a
safe-conduct, Irish insurgents massacred them and robbed the bodies of
their clothing and other valuable items. According to one eye-witness
account, when Mayo heard this, he went into his 'chamber, and there
wept bitterly, pulling off his hair, and refusing to hear any word of
persuasion, and comfort . . . having no manner of means left him at that
time to be revenged for that inhuman and bloody massacre, and the
irreparable dishonour done unto himself'.[109] Mayo's genuine distress

about the nature of the atrocity and how it violated existing codes of conduct and honour is clearly evident.

Muskerry found himself in a similar position. During the early months of the war, he attempted (often unsuccessfully) to protect local Protestant refugees against the insurgents' onslaughts and organized safe convoys for them. Yet, a decade later, in December 1653, he stood trial before a Cromwellian court, charged with 'war crimes', allegedly committed during these early months of the insurrection. Interestingly, Muskerry had chosen to stand trial, returning to Ireland from exile in the Iberian Peninsula, to bear (as he put it) his 'crosses'. He offered a spirited defence and, after a three-day ordeal, was acquitted. In a moving speech he thanked the court, which, he believed, had acted 'with justice'. He continued: 'I consider that in this Court I come clear out of that blackness of blood . . . [which] is more to me than my estate. I can live without my estate, but not without my credit [i.e. honour and reputation].'[110]

Muskerry and Mayo – like Montgomery, Clanricard, Preston, Ormond, and Lady Offaly – belonged to a community of honour, where private virtues and public actions often transcended religious belief and ethnic origin. While religion and arguments over who should exercise political power did divide this community, the forging of a common code of honour was one of the key factors in facilitating the social and economic integration, the cultural cross-assimilation and the political co-operation within the Irish nobility, especially in the years before 1641 and after 1660.[111] Though contested, this honour code existed even at the height of the civil war of the 1640s. During the 1650s, the Cromwellians did everything possible to demilitarize Ireland and to dismantle the baronial networks that had underpinned the conflict there. And while the numbers of Irish 'military peers' decreased to 57 per cent by 1670 (in 1605 it had stood at 72 per cent), Irish lords continued to dominate the military establishment at home and sought military service and glory abroad. Royal service remained fundamental as the basis for honour. Chivalric values survived, as did the belief that peers needed to authenticate individual honour both off and on the battlefield.[112] Thus, during the 1660s and 1670s, writers lauded the martial exploits of Ormond's eldest son Thomas, Earl of Ossory, comparing him to Caesar or 'a Carthaginian prince' (he had trained at a Parisian military academy and fought in the Continental theatres of war before returning to serve as one of Charles II's leading commanders).[113] Ossory's was a world with which his father, Ormond, and Thomas Preston could have immediately identified and one where notions of 'soldierly honour' continued to determine, at least in part, military and political affairs. Yet it might also be argued that Ossory, like so many of his Irish contemporaries, now formed part of a 'military caste', itself linked to innovations associated with the 'Military Revolution' and to attempts – by the likes of Henry Ireton – to create a professional army.

5. The 'Scottish Moment', 1638–45

ALLAN I. MACINNES

In the spring of 1644, Hugh Mowatt, a Swede of Scottish extraction, was despatched as the Swedish kingdom's senior envoy to both Scotland and England. Like most diplomats from Scandinavia since the Bishops' Wars between England and Scotland of 1639–40, Mowatt chose to visit Scotland initially before moving south to England. This was not simply a demonstration of solidarity with his compatriots. It was also a clear recognition that the Covenanting movement had a position of leadership in shaping the political agenda throughout England and Ireland – and Scotland as well. In seeking to create a defensive and offensive alliance for Sweden against Denmark–Norway, Mowatt was concerned first to obtain Covenanting backing and then, through the auspices of their Scottish Commissioners in London, to secure the assent of both Scotland and England through the Committee of Both Kingdoms – the Anglo-Scottish executive that had been established after the Covenanters had come to the aid of the Parliamentarians in the English Civil War.[1] The international importance of Scottish participation on this emphatically *British* Committee is an understated feature of the historiography of the 'Wars for the Three Kingdoms'. Yet it was a feature immediately recognized by other diplomats. The Dutch jurist Hugo Grotius, then Swedish agent to France, viewed the Committee as a 'council of war' (*een crijsraidt opgerechd*) for Scottish Covenanters and English Parliamentarians; its members served as trustees for the implementation of the Solemn League and Covenant (the religious bond established by parliamentarian England and Covenanter Scotland in 1643), which had ratified military engagement in Ireland and justified armed intervention in England by Covenanting forces.[2] Émigrés resident in England also recognized the diplomatic standing of this committee. Indeed, Samuel Hartlib, pre-eminent as an educational reformer, intellectual and entrepreneur, thanked the Committee in January 1645, for sponsoring his endeavours to promote 'the Publicke Religion, Justice and Liberty of the Three Kingdoms' overseas.[3]

The institution of the Committee of Both Kingdoms in February 1644 was the culmination of an alternative Scottish agenda for the British Isles which had commenced confrontationally with Scotland's constitutional defiance of Charles I in 1638 and was subsumed gradually by the splits among English Parliamentarians into the factions known as the Presbyterians and Independents from 1645. The purpose of this chapter is not to argue that the Covenanting movement dictated the political agenda in the British Isles in the interim. Little purpose would be served in overstating the Scottish case as a counter to the insularity of Anglocentric historians, with their introspective concerns for the constitutional breakdown and civil wars between Royalists and Parliamentarians in England. Rather, it can be contended that the Covenanters offered a radical vision of Britain that was federative and constitutional, confessional but not sectarian. On the one hand, this Scottish perspective appears resolutely opposed to the authoritarian, monarchical view of empire by land and sea propagated by James I and his episcopate from 1603. This 'Britannic perspective' was made increasingly untenable through an over-reliance on prerogative powers under his son, Charles I. On the other hand, a federative Britain stood in uneasy alliance with the Gothic, historically-informed perspective that held sway among English Parliamentarians and which emphasized the primacy of parliamentary statute and the common law, with scant regard either to different legal traditions or to customary practices in Scotland and Ireland.

The 'Scottish moment', therefore, was neither an imperial nor a hegemonic construct that asserted a superior Caledonian identity or espoused territorial acquisitiveness. Rather it marked a British programme of confessional confederation (literally, a solemn league and covenant) to establish a godly monarchy in association with godly commonwealths in all three Stuart kingdoms. These seven years represented the only occasion in which a Scottish-led agenda prevailed in the British Isles during the early modern period.[4]

I   SCOTLAND'S EMERGENCE AS A MILITARY POWER

The National Covenant, first sworn in Scotland in February 1638, as Scotland rose in revolt against Charles I's absentee monarchy, was the public manifesto that formally marked the emergence of the Covenanting movement. It established a written constitution that was not concerned with the details of how power should be exercised or who should fill offices or places on councils and committees. Instead, priority was accorded to parliamentary supremacy within the fundamental context of a religious and constitutional compact between God, king and people. The National Covenant's clear distinction between the office of the monarch and the person of the king sustained loyalty to the House of Stuart, but not necessarily to Charles I. The signatories took an oath upholding the collective right of the people to resist a lawful king who threatened to become tyrannical. Such resistance was in fact undertaken by a centralized oligarchy of nobles, gentry (lairds), burgesses and clergy known collectively as the Tables. As the corporate embodiment of the national interest, the Tables (institutionalized as the 'Committee of Estates' from 1640) comprehensively controlled the coercive and persuasive agencies of government, which they used to exact unprecedented demands for ideological conformity, financial supply and military recruitment within Scotland on behalf of the Covenanting movement.

The National Covenant of 1638, then, was a revolutionary enterprise binding the Scottish people by social compact to justify and consolidate a revolt against the Stuarts' 'Britannic monarchy'. The most revolutionary component in British (not merely Scottish) terms was the Covenant's oath of allegiance and mutual association. Subscribers made only a conditional commitment to the monarch, for true loyalty was reserved only for a Covenanted king – that is, one who had himself accepted the contractual nature of his rule. In so far as the king would accept the religious and constitutional imperatives of the National Covenant, then he was to be defended. But, given the Covenant's clear distinction between the royal office and the person of the monarch, its subscribers found no necessary incompatibility in promising to defend royal authority in the abstract while simultaneously promoting policies contrary to the professed interests and intentions of the man, Charles I. Hence the paradox: resistance to Charles the man, the Covenanters held, was in the long-term interests of monarchy and people, a necessary curative if the kingdom were to be restored to godly rule.[5]

As well as equipping the Tables – revolutionary Scotland's new executive – with a rhetoric of defiance, the National Covenant provided the political will to effect what amounted to a revolution, a process which actually commenced at the General Assembly of the Kirk at Glasgow – a meeting of Covenanting-inclined ministers and elders drawn from all over Scotland – in November 1638. Though nominally summoned by Charles I, the Glasgow Assembly's composition, agenda and proceedings were in practice managed by the Tables. The two authors of the National Covenant, Alexander Henderson and Archibald Johnston of Wariston, were elected respectively as the Assembly's Moderator and Clerk. Unsurprisingly, on 28 November 1638, they led the Assembly to assert its right to try the Scottish bishops – an assertion which prompted a walkout by James Hamilton, third Marquess (and later first Duke) of Hamilton, the nobleman commissioned by the king to attend as his personal representative. Hamilton's command, in retaliation, to dissolve the Assembly was rendered meaningless by its own decision to continue to sit: the first open act of constitutional defiance of Charles's prerogative rule in the British Isles. What followed was no less assertive. The Assembly proceeded to sweep all vestiges of episcopacy, prerogative courts and liturgical innovations out of the Kirk before dissolving itself on 20 December, returning Scotland to the Presbyterian system of Church government it had adopted in the early Reformation – a system in which ecclesiastical authority was vested in ministers and elders, rather than in royally appointed bishops. The Assembly's final enactment claimed that henceforth the Kirk, not the monarch, should summon General Assemblies at least once a year. This constituted a second, blatant attack on the royal prerogative; and it was from this point that war became inevitable.[6]

The replacement of a system of Church government by bishops, with Presbyterianism, through an act of constitutional defiance lit the touchpaper for armed conflict between Charles I and the Covenanting movement: what came to be known as the two 'Bishops' Wars' of 1639 and 1640. The king's patent inability to defeat the Covenanting forces in these two successive campaigns obliged him to accept a constitutional settlement in Scotland which imposed permanent checks on the royal prerogative in both Kirk and state. In short, he was also obliged to recognize a new political order: adherence to the National Covenant, not acquiescence in the dictates of a Britannic monarch, was the vital prerequisite for the exercise of political power in Scotland.

Moreover, this Scottish resistance to Charles I had a European, not just a British significance. Whereas contemporaneous revolts in Portugal and Catalonia against a centralizing Spanish monarchy were essentially protests about the costs of Spain's continuing engagement in the Thirty Years War (1618–48), the Covenanting movement brought this European war to the British Isles: in essence, the Bishops' Wars constituted the British theatre of the Thirty Years War. Prior to that Scottish revolt, Charles I had been prepared to assist Spain against the Dutch

Republic, providing both Irish troops and English ships, ostensibly as a
diplomatic *quid pro quo* intended to secure the restoration of Charles's
Protestant nephew, Prince Charles Louis, to the Palatinate (his ancestral
territories in central Germany, from which his family had been ousted in
the opening phase of the Thirty Years War). In return for landing facil-
ities for Spanish troops in transit through the Channel, Spain became
Charles's best hope in his efforts to secure external assistance against the
Covenanters. This hope, however, was short-lived. The Dutch decisively
defeated the Spanish fleet in the Downs, off the Kent coast, in the
autumn of 1639, and the defeat – in which the English fleet failed to
intervene – demonstrated to Spain that Charles was of limited assistance
to the Habsburg cause. It also ensured that the Covenanters continued
to be supplied with men and munitions through the Dutch provinces of
Holland and Zeeland.[7] Indeed, the Covenanting movement drew on
diplomatic, military and material support from the reconstituted anti-
Habsburg alliance of France, Sweden and the Dutch Republic that had
continued the Thirty Years War in the aftermath of the 1635 Habsburg-
imposed Peace of Prague (the treaty that had been intended to end the
war in the Habsburgs' favour). The Covenanters had established their
own Dutch printing press even before the outbreak of the Bishops' Wars
in 1639, and, as part of this diplomatic realignment, the Covenanting
government in Edinburgh – rather than the court of Charles I – was the
first port of call for the embassies sent from Sweden and Denmark in
1639 and 1640. The Covenanter government also received covert diplomatic missions from France.[8] In turn, these international dealings
provide a wider context of Protestant anxiety for the ubiquitous fears of
'popish plotting' that had featured in the political life of all three kingdoms since the beginning of the century.[9]

Sweden, whose government gave unstinting diplomatic and military
support to the Covenanting cause, was the first foreign power to countenance external intervention in the Bishops' Wars. The Swedish
Chancellor, Axel Oxenstierna, deeply concerned that the growing
rapprochement between Charles I and the Habsburgs would inflame the
perennial antipathies between Sweden, Denmark–Norway and
Poland–Lithuania, was notably receptive to Covenanting pleas for assistance made by the Scottish general Alexander Leslie – a thirty-year
veteran of the Swedish service. General Leslie (later created Earl of
Leven) had returned discreetly to Scotland in 1638, equipped with arms
and ammunition as a retirement present, and ready to take charge of the
Covenanting army in advance of the Glasgow Assembly. Leslie was

undoubtedly the prime mover not only in securing his own release from employment in Sweden, but also the release of other leading Scottish officers in Swedish and Dutch service. By maintaining a regular correspondence with Oxenstierna, Leslie paved the way for still further releases of Scottish officers, who were rewarded with munitions on their departure in advance of the second Bishops' War in the summer of 1640. Diplomatic backing by the Swedes for a Scottish invasion of England was announced during the Covenanting embassy to Sweden in July–August 1640, undertaken by yet another military veteran, Colonel John Cochrane, when the Riksråd (the Swedish state council) authorized further supplies of munitions and copper to be sent to Scotland via Holland.[10]

Yet, Swedish sympathies for the Covenanting movement could not alone guarantee the passage of soldiers, arms and ammunition through the Baltic Sound and across the North Sea. This covert movement of men and materiel also involved the active collusion of the Scottish mercantile communities in Gothenburg, Danzig, Amsterdam and Campvere, as well as naval officers in both Danish and Swedish service. Diplomats from Covenanting Scotland also worked to counter the family ties to the Stuarts of King Christian IV of Denmark – Charles I's uncle, to whom he looked for military support. Instead, they urged the Danish king to mediate between Charles and his Scottish subjects during the Bishops' Wars, overtures that his nephew rejected in both 1639 and 1640.[11]

While the new Covenanting government sought diplomatic alliances abroad, at home it sought to restructure the movement's relations with the localities. Indeed, a blueprint for this had been drawn up as early as the Glasgow Assembly of 1638. As a result of these measures, Scotland was placed on a war footing: local Committees of War were established within the shires to liaise with, and carry out directives from, Edinburgh. These local Committees of War had extensive duties. Each had a permanent convener, and was instructed to levy, equip and train troops; to assess and exact a compulsory 'contribution' (a *de facto* tax) based on landed and commercial rents; and to encourage commitment to the cause in every presbytery and parish. War was their *raison d'être*. Indeed, the Covenanting leadership's immediate objective in re-orientating local government towards the needs of the centre was the mobilization and provisioning of a national army, a task in which they were greatly assisted by the influx of Scottish officers from abroad. Returning veterans from the Continental theatres of the Thirty Years War provided a readymade professional officer cadre. In fact, so numerous were these Scottish-born veterans that they filled every alternate position of command among commissioned and non-commissioned officers alike. Similarly, all artillery officers, gunners and engineers in the new army were veterans, as were the muster-masters recruited by the shire Committees of War to pass on the basic skills of drill and the use of musket and pike.[12]

This Covenanting military machine was soon put to the test. In 1639, during the first Bishops' War, the movement was faced with engagements on four fronts, though there was no major infantry battle – not least because the king was daunted by this array of Scottish military power – and the 'war' ended in a stalemate with a provisional truce, a 'Pacification', concluded at Berwick in June. Charles, however, remained determined to reconquer his northern kingdom and returned to the task the following year. Partly in response to the king's mobilization of a new English army in 1640, and partly as a result of encouragement from a group of disaffected English peers, who urged them to invade, the Covenanting government switched its strategy from defence to offence: that summer, a Covenanting army crossed the Tweed (the border between England and Scotland) and decisively routed part of the king's forces at Newburn (near Newcastle-upon-Tyne) on 28 August. As the commanders of the king's forces realized, the superiority of the Covenanting army was not merely numerical; it was second only to that of the Swedish Crown in that it was a standing army, conscripted for *national* service and sustained by a centralized government – a development that anticipated the emergence of the New Model Army in England by some six years and which was never achieved in Ireland by the Confederation of Catholics (whose government was based at Kilkenny) during the 1640s.[13]

II   SCOTLAND AND THE OVERTHROW OF CHARLES I'S RÉGIME IN ENGLAND

Central to this assertion of Scottish independence was a newly revitalized role for the kingdom's ancient representative bodies: the Parliament and Convention of Estates. Even before the Covenanting invasion of England in August 1640, the Scottish Parliament had ignored a royal order to suspend its sittings in June 1640 and continued to sit in defiance of the royal will. The actions it took had far-reaching implications.

Having validated the past proceedings of the Tables, the Estates proceeded to carry out what amounted to a constitutional revolution, amply demonstrating the institution's political vitality – particularly when viewed comparatively in a broader European context. There were four major reforms: first, the clerical estate in Parliament was abolished and the gentry, in recognition of their stalwart service on the Tables, had their voting powers effectively doubled; secondly, subscription (literally, the 'underwriting') of the National Covenant was made compulsory for all holding public office; and thirdly, a Triennial Act specified that Parliament should henceforth meet every three years, regardless of whether or not it received a royal summons. Finally, the powers of the executive were also radically redrawn. Ostensibly to meet the imminent threat of invasion by the king's English forces, a Committee of Estates was constituted formally with comprehensive powers to govern the whole kingdom during the absence of Parliament. The Committee, which consisted of 40 members drawn from the nobility, gentry and burgesses, was split into two sections, one sedentary and the other itinerant: equal numbers of each of the reconstituted three estates either remained in Edinburgh to sustain central government, or accompanied the army (whose movements were not restricted to Scotland). Finally, the Covenanters redefined the scope of treason so that all those who advised or assisted policies destructive of the Covenanting movement were deemed traitors. The waging of war on behalf of the Covenanting movement became a patriotic duty; waging war *against* it was henceforth treasonable.[14]

These military and administrative advances equipped the Covenanting leaders to export their revolution to England in the course of 1640. The Covenanting army followed up its rout of the king's English forces at Newburn by moving vigorously into the counties of Northumberland, Durham, and parts of Yorkshire. Covenanting control of the coal supply from Newcastle to London – and the refusal of the English peerage, which Charles had summoned to York in September 1640, to fund the continuation of the war – forced the king to begin negotiations for a peace. This English response was not entirely unexpected. From early in 1639 (if not before) the Covenanting leadership had proactively encouraged English support, not only from the dissident nobles and gentry (who hoped to bring about the summons of a Parliament in England), but also from the City of London (which was frequently the butt of criticism at court for its reluctance to finance the king's forces).[15] The Covenanting leadership promised that their army would observe strict military discipline in England, pending the conclusion of a settlement. To this end, the removal of the negotiations to London and the recall of the English Parliament were deemed indispensable by the Covenanters if they were to achieve their aims.[16]

The revolutionary significance of the Covenanting army's impact on the constitutional crisis then engulfing the 'Britannic monarchy' still tends to be underestimated, notwithstanding a growing appreciation of the trigger-effect that the Covenanting movement's emergence in Scotland had in provoking rebellion and civil war in Ireland and eventually England as well.[17] Of course, the Scottish revolt was not alone the cause of confrontation between Crown and Parliament in England, or, in Ireland, between Catholic Confederates, British planters and Charles I's Britannic monarchy. But only the presence of the Covenanting army in the north of England enabled Charles's English critics to put sufficient pressure on the king that he was obliged to summon a new Parliament wholly against his will. Similarly, once the new English Parliament convened in November 1640, it was only the security afforded by the Covenanting army that allowed the king's English critics to press with impunity for constitutional limitations on his powers – limitations that both safeguarded and revived the medieval, 'Gothic', tradition of parliamentary sovereignty.

Nor was the presence of the Covenanting army the only way in which Scotland's successful rebellion influenced the politics of her southern neighbour. The Covenanting movement also provided a constitutional model for revolt once the new English Parliament met in November 1640. In the course of 1641, an English Triennial Act – influenced by recent Scottish precedent – and an act preventing the dissolution of the current Parliament without its own consent enabled the new English Parliament – soon to be known as the 'Long Parliament' – to forestall dissolution by royal fiat and, in the longer term, to secure control over the apparatus of government in Church and state.

Developments in England also had a reciprocal influence on Scottish politics. The pressure to redress grievances generated by the Long Parliament in its first year meant that Charles was amenable to buying off the Scots in the autumn of 1641 – in the process, conceding most of the Covenanting leadership's demands for limitations on his powers as King of Scots – in order to concentrate on English problems and to neutralize the Scots' willingness to intervene on behalf of his English opponents. After the outbreak of a Catholic rebellion in Ireland in October 1641, the Confederates (as the rebels came to be known) partially justified their recourse to arms by citing the Scottish exemplar.[18]

Undoubtedly, the Long Parliament provided an opportunity for the airing of local and regional grievances on a national platform.[19] However, perhaps the most incisive petition presented to the Commons at the beginning of the Parliament was the Root-and-Branch Petition (so called because of its demand that bishops should be abolished 'root and branch'), presented by Isaac Penington on 11 December 1640 on behalf of (reportedly) 15,000 signatories, mostly drawn from London. This attacked not only Arminianism (the theological system promoted by Archbishop Laud, which was believed by its critics to smack of 'Popery') and the Laudian programme of innovations in the English Church; it also called for the wholesale abolition of episcopacy: the entire system of Church government by bishops. In this movement, the Scottish Commissioners – the Covenanter government's representatives in London – soon joined. In a highly provocative declaration issued on 24 February 1641 they reiterated the demand for 'Root-and-Branch' abolition of bishops, an essential element of the Covenanters' radical agenda.[20]

But if the Covenanting Scots had their allies and admirers in England, their interventions in English politics also created a powerful wave of hostility. This, in turn, contributed strongly to the creation of a royalist party in England in the course of 1641 and 1642.[21] Even among Parliamentarians (who were, in theory, the Covenanters' allies from the autumn of 1643), anti-Scottish sentiment – often underestimated by historians – continued to shape political alignments well after the Royalists were defeated in the first English Civil War (1642–6).[22] However, the issue of religion – and Scottish-style Presbyterianism, in particular – should not be seen as the sole cause of polarization in English politics. The pro-Scottish faction in the English Parliament, led in the Lords by Robert Rich, second Earl of Warwick, and in the Commons by John Pym, was concerned with a thorough reformation not only in the Church, but also in the state: as early as May 1641, the Covenanting leadership had designated them 'the Commonwealth's men'.[23]

The Scottish Commissioners in London strongly supported the treason charges against the Earl of Stafford, Charles's war-mongering Lord Lieutenant of Ireland, which led eventually to his execution on 12 May 1641. Nevertheless, the main thrust of their negotiating remit was to strengthen the bond of Union between both kingdoms, a cause that they had professed ever since their first sustained appeal to public opinion throughout the British Isles in the period before the Bishops' Wars of 1639–40. To the Covenanters, unity in religion and uniformity in Church government were secondary to a lasting alliance: a defensive and offensive league between Scotland and England. This was to be achieved by confederation, not by means of an incorporating union of the two kingdoms' Parliaments. However, the English negotiators were extremely wary of Scottish pressures to import Presbyterianism. They maintained the English Parliament would decide on the nature of the Church of England; and that it was not fitting for ambassadors of foreign princes, still less for Commissioners who were also subjects of Charles I, 'to insist upon anything distinctive to [the] government settled and established'. Indeed, the only institutional innovation agreed upon between the two parties was the appointment of parliamentary Commissioners from *both* kingdoms, charged with conserving the peace and redressing any breaches between the two nations in the intervals between their respective Parliaments. In ratifying the Treaty of London on 7 August 1641, the English Parliament conceded that, henceforth, the waging of war and the stopping of trade within the king's British dominions required parliamentary approval in both countries.[24]

Charles assented to the Treaty of London in August 1641 primarily in the hope of detaching the Covenanters from their alliance with the more radical English members of the Lords and Commons. Yet, this mission was forlorn. In Edinburgh, the Committee of Estates remained in close contact with the reformist group at Westminster. Despite its mandate having technically expired with the summoning of a Scottish Parliament (for 15 July 1641), the Committee continued to control proceedings in Edinburgh on behalf of the radical mainstream. To counteract this, Charles appeared in person in Edinburgh in August 1641 and he remained there until November. But his limited capacity to influence parliamentary proceedings in Scotland was critically undermined when he appeared to condone tumultuous – indeed lethally violent – lobbying of Parliament in October in what became known as 'the Incident'. In this, the rumoured assassination of the Earl of Argyll and the Marquess of Hamilton – the two noblemen grandees at the head of the Covenanting movement – was to be the prelude to a public rupture of the Scottish Estates by an armed force, and it was only forestalled by the flight of the intended victims from Edinburgh. The failure of the coup marked the nadir of royal authority in Scotland. Charles's misjudged insistence on a public investigation into 'the Incident' (hoping to embarrass the Covenanting leadership as well as Hamilton, his estranged favourite) hastened the creation of a political rapport between Covenanters and the king's more pragmatic supporters in Scotland, a rapport that obliged Charles to accept the constitutional dictates of the majority.[25] In the new constitutional settlement which emerged from this in the autumn of 1641, the Scottish Estates secured an effective veto over appointments to the executive and judiciary. It was a turning-point. These permanent restrictions on the royal prerogative fulfilled Charles's prophecy, in the spring of 1638, that the triumph of the Covenanting movement would leave him no more power than the Doge of Venice.[26]

III   TOWARDS A BRITISH WAR

Charles was further compromised in Covenanting eyes by his ambivalence towards the outbreak of rebellion in Ireland in October 1641, which provoked a distinctive response from the Covenanting leadership. In particular, from March 1642, there were Scottish troop mobilizations in Ireland under Major-General Robert Munro. Although Munro exercised overall command of the forces that had already been raised among the settlers in Ulster (who included Scottish as well as English officers), the published missives to the Commons from Ireland during the spring and summer of 1642 reported the providential success of this 'English' army. Ominously, no attempt was made by the English to talk about joint British – that is, Anglo-Scots – endeavours to secure redress for Protestant settlers in Ireland.[27] However, the descent towards civil war in England led to a growing realization among some Parliamentarians at Westminster of the pressing need to make an accommodation with the Scottish Covenanters over Ireland. Thus on 6 June 1642, the English Parliament specifically differentiated between the person of the king and the office of monarch, claiming that the latter could be exercised by Parliament as the supreme judiciary and Great Council of the realm. The trained bands and militia – it followed from this – were now at the disposal of the Parliament for its own defence, not just for the suppression of the Irish rebellion. Henry Parker, the most able and influential of the English Parliamentarian polemicists, claimed that Charles I, having deserted his capital, was now prepared by force of arms to invade his general council. Charles, claimed Parker in the summer of 1642, was reputedly more solicitous in regard to the interests of the Irish Confederates than to the many Protestants murdered daily by their hands. The king's 'illegal and vexatious' issuing of commissions of array to shire and borough constituencies served to depict those serving in the Lords and Commons as worse rebels, in the king's eyes, than the Irish. Parker saw the need for a British resolution. It was better that 'the State of Scotland were intreated to mediate and adjudicate' in this contest than that civil war should break out in England.[28]

Acutely conscious that a substantial majority of the Lords and a significant minority of the Commons had become Royalists once Charles had raised his standard at Nottingham on 22 August 1642, the pro-Scottish leadership at Westminster was instrumental in pushing for a military and religious alliance with the Scottish Covenanters, which opened up the prospect of still further confederal and confessional Union between the two kingdoms. Tripartite negotiations actually commenced in September 1642; however, they took almost eleven months to come to a resolution that favoured British confederation. Notwithstanding the enormous hostility in the English House of Lords to a treaty with the Covenanters, the main stumbling block to further Scottish military intervention in England came from within Scotland: the regrouping, under Hamilton, of the more pragmatic of the king's supporters within the Scottish Privy Council.[29]

However, this Council was not the only forum for the discussion of issues of war and peace in Scotland. As had clearly been demonstrated by the Covenanters earlier decision to intervene militarily in Ireland, the real source of initiative lay with the 'Conservators of the Peace' (the committee for conserving the Treaty of London), an exclusively radical body, dominated by the Marquess of Argyll and his associates – a group which retained contact with their English counterparts, and above all with the Warwick–Pym group. Simultaneously, the Scottish Parliament's main financial committee, the Committee for Common Burdens (which the radicals also controlled), managed the equipping and levying of the Covenanters' army already in Ireland. At a joint meeting of the Privy Council, the Conservators of the Peace and the Committee for Common Burdens on 12 May 1643, Argyll and his associates pressed successfully that a Convention of Estates (a new Parliament in all but name) be summoned as an effective substitute for the plenary Parliament that Charles I resolutely refused to call. As Hamilton regretfully informed the king's court in Oxford, the institutional dominance exercised by Argyll and his radical supporters had ensured that the Scottish Covenanters were now 'to be actors and no longer spectators in the English civil war'.[30] On 19 August 1643, the General Assembly, summoned to coincide with the Convention of

Estates, accepted an invitation from the English Parliament to observe, advise and direct discussions on the reformation of the Church of England. An Anglo-Scottish Assembly of Divines was summoned to meet at Westminster to advise the English Parliament on ecclesiastical reform. Suitably prepared and persuaded, on 26 August, the Convention of Estates cemented a formal alliance with commissioners from the English Parliament, led by Sir Henry Vane junior, for armed assistance to the Parliamentarians on the basis of this new alliance between the two kingdoms: the Solemn League and Covenant.[31]

III   THE EXPORT OF COVENANTING DOCTRINE

This Solemn League and Covenant, drawn up by Archibald Johnston of Wariston and Alexander Henderson (two prime figures in the Covenanter rebellion from its outset), confirmed that the Scottish Covenanters were in the driving seat in British revolutionary politics. True, Ireland had been included within the remit of the Solemn League and Covenant (not as a party to the negotiations, but as a territory that the treaty would affect), but only at the insistence of the English commissioners, the Scots being reluctant to accord equal standing to a satellite kingdom whose dominant confession was still Roman Catholicism. Notwithstanding the political incompatibilities – soon to be magnified – between the Scottish and English common-law perspectives, the Covenanting leadership was certainly determined at this point to implement a federative reconfiguration of the three kingdoms.* In effect, the Solemn League represented an extension of confessional confederation to

---

* The term 'federative' denotes a relationship that can be either confederal or federal. The specific term 'federalist', which relates to the division of power been a central British government and national governments in both kingdoms, has been erroneously applied to this relationship (D. Stevenson, 'The Early Covenanters and the Federal Union of Britain', in R. A. Mason (ed.), *Scotland and England, 1286–1815* (Edinburgh, 1987), pp. 163–81; K. M. Brown, *Kingdom or Province? Scotland and the Regal Union, 1603–1715* (1992), pp. 81–3; John Morrill, 'The Britishness of the English Revolution, 1640–60', in R. G. Asch (ed.), *Three Nations – A Common History? England, Scotland, Ireland and British History, c.1600–1920* (Bochum, 1993), pp. 83–115). Federalism did not feature in contemporary British political vocabulary until the early eighteenth century. Scotland and England were to remain independent kingdoms united by a common purpose rather than by a common parliament or even a common executive under the Solemn League and Covenant, that is, by a confederal arrangement. However, as the exact nature of this relationship was not worked out in detail in 1643 and the door was not closed to new consultative, advisory or even executive agencies, 'federative' is the most appropriate term to use at this juncture.

achieve common spiritual and material aims while maintaining distinctive national structures in Church and state. The right to resist the Crown was specifically exported from Scotland in clause three, which incorporated the covenanting oath of allegiance and mutual association.[32]

Although the export of Covenanting ideology from Scotland was to be characterized by the language of religious revelation, in 1643 the negotiations themselves had been founded primarily on political pragmatism and military necessity. The Scots had signalled their keenness to become involved in military affairs south of the border by re-occupying the garrison town of Berwick-upon-Tweed as early as 20 September 1643. However, another four months were to elapse before the Covenanting army began its advance into England – on 19 January 1644. The reformist clergy in London, who regarded the Presbyterian system, which the Covenanters had re-established in Scotland from 1638, as the obvious replacement for episcopacy in the Church of England, welcomed the prospect of Scottish military intervention. But it was also greeted enthusiastically by the so-called 'Independents' on the parliamentarian side: those who also supported a thorough reformation of the Church of England, but demanded freedom for particular congregations to form autonomous 'gathered churches' outside the national Presbyterian system. During the 1643 negotiations on the Solemn League and Covenant, the two parliamentarian clerics, Stephen Marshall and Philip Nye, acted as the respective representatives of these two interests, attending on the English parliamentary commissioners. Both saw the Solemn League and Covenant as 'the arm of the Lord' being extended to England. Thus, the new covenanting oath of allegiance was commended by Nye to his brethren in the Westminster Assembly as worthy to be adopted not only in all three Stuart kingdoms, but in 'all the Kingdoms of the world'. Similarly, his fellow Independent, Jeremiah Burroughs, asserted that Scotland – as a nation chosen by God – was 'united the most firmly under heaven: we may truly call it a Philadelphia [the Greek for 'Brotherly Love']'. England should rejoice to have the Scots 'in a near Union with us'.[33]

Religion, however, was only one facet of the new Covenant between the two British nations. At Westminster, Oliver St John, the Solicitor-General and one of the principal advocates of the new alliance, developed, from the autumn of 1643, the complementary theme of financial obligation. This was timely, as the English Parliament had failed to meet its obligations to supply the Scottish army in Ireland for the past fourteen months. Moreover, a significant portion of the 'Brotherly

Assistance' – the funds (£300,000) due to the Scots for the costs they had incurred in their invasion of 1640–41 and guaranteed under the terms of the Treaty of London – still remained unpaid. To many English Parliamentarians, the financial costs entailed in the new Anglo-Scottish Covenant of 1643 were more than justified: they were a means of purchasing the survival in England of the then beleaguered parliamentary cause.

The Covenanting government in Edinburgh was committed to sending an army of 18,000 foot and 2,100 horse into England – making it the largest army, at least on paper, then in parliamentarian service; moreover, around 300 Scottish officers were also integrated into other existing parliamentarian armies. This force was to be maintained at £30,000 per month from revenues raised by the sequestration of Papists and other 'malignants' (as Royalists and their sympathizers were known). However, the Covenanting leadership was also committed to negotiating a loan of £200,000, jointly with the English Parliamentarians, on the Continental money markets, with a view to providing immediate funding for the new army. The impending Covenanting intervention in England, therefore, opened up the twin prospects of ensuring a parliamentarian victory in the current civil war, and, no less importantly, extending the sequestration of royalist estates to meet the costs of the fighting.[34]

Religion was the professed justification for this undertaking. Confident that they were fighting a godly war, the Covenanters and their parliamentarian allies declared that they were intent on the preservation of the Church of Christ 'and this whole Island from utter ruine and devastation'. In January 1644, at the beginning of the Scots' intervention, public warning was given that neutrality and indifference would not be tolerated: there were only friends of the godly cause, and its enemies.[35] Although the Covenanters' intervention of 1644 did not enjoy the swift and spectacular success that had met their previous foray into England (in the second 'Bishops' War', in the summer of 1640), their army helped tilt the military balance in the war in the North of England in favour of the parliamentarian forces. In terms of set battles, the Covenanting army made a major contribution to the joint Scottish–Parliamentarian victory over the king's forces at Marston Moor in Yorkshire on 2 July 1644; but made little contribution to the parliamentarian war-effort thereafter. Their army was unable to take Newcastle-upon-Tyne until October 1644, and then only after a costly siege that had kept the army immobilized for almost three months.

This has left its mark on the historiography. The Covenanting inter-vention, as viewed in both English and Scottish writing, has tended to be written off as a naive and ultimately fruitless endeavour to shape the outcome of the English Civil War. The Scots demonstrated only a limited capacity to control events – so the argument runs – and tended to become the tools, if not the playthings, of rival parliamentary interests at Westminster.[36] Regarded as a military force, the Covenanting army has also tended to be viewed as secondary to the major English military narrative of the Civil War that culminated in the creation of the New Model Army in the spring of 1645, and that army's crushing victory over the Royalist forces at Naseby in Northamptonshire on 14 June 1645 – a battle in which no Scottish forces were involved.[37] Indeed, the three-year presence of the Covenanting army in the North of England has been regarded as counter-productive, in that it fostered anti-Scottish sentiment. Its presence even induced former Royalists in the localities to side with the Independents – the major anti-Scottish group at Westminster – to help effect its withdrawal from England by January 1647, without ever establishing Presbyterianism in the southern king-dom, the ostensible reason for the promulgation of the Solemn League and Covenant.[38]

However, the interests of the Covenanting movement need to be assessed within a broader British context, rather than in a focus that is narrowly English. They were maintained with an ideological consistency that was tempered by political pragmatism – a state of affairs that was recognized by diplomats from France, Sweden, the Dutch Republic, and from Denmark. During the mid-1640s, Scotland effectively expanded its territorial influence to an unprecedented extent through its armies of occupation: to the south, from the Tweed to the Tees and on to the Humber in England; and to the west, from the Solway Firth to Lough Neagh in Ireland. This military expansion, which was the greatest by any army prior to the Cromwellian occupations of Ireland and Scotland in 1650–1, provoked genuine, if unfounded, fears of Scottish imperial-ism in both England and Ireland throughout the 1640s.[39] It is to those fears, and the Scots' real intentions, that we now turn.

IV   COVENANTING OBJECTIVES: CONFEDERAL UNION

The key features of Covenanting policy during the period of English intervention were a demonstrable concern with confederal union; a pragmatic willingness to temper military force with peace negotiations; and an international commitment to Protestantism in Western Europe more generally, not just to Presbyterianism within the Stuart kingdoms. The new set of Scottish Commissioners, who arrived in London to liaise with the Lords and the Commons on 5 February 1644, were passionately committed to the pursuit of war against the Royalists. But they did not rule out the brokering of a negotiated peace between the king and the English Parliament that would be consistent with the Solemn League and Covenant and their Covenanting government's broader British aspirations.[40]

The Scottish position – which was consistently maintained by the commissioners in London, the Committee of Estates in Edinburgh, and the Scottish army in England – was to implement the Solemn League and Covenant as a written constitution for all three kingdoms in the same way as the National Covenant had served for Scotland. Again, the issue at stake was not the details of executive, legislative or judicial powers, but the prescription of 'covenanting' – the establishment of a formal compact between the peoples of the Stuart kingdoms and God – as fundamental to the exercise of power and the establishment of godly 'commonwealths' throughout the British Isles. The ideal was the permanent establishment of a Covenanted Stuart monarchy. Although Charles was not required in the end to covenant in person, the implication of the compact was that the peoples of all his three kingdoms had the right to resist his ungodly rule.

This was not a state of affairs that Charles was thought likely to embrace voluntarily. The Covenanters realized that the king had to be defeated militarily if ever there were to be meaningful negotiations. Thus, they differed – at least in the early phase of their intervention in 1644 – from the peace grouping led by Edward Montagu, second Earl of Manchester, and Robert Devereux, third Earl of Essex, in the Lords and by Denzell Holles, Bulstrode Whitelocke and, to a more equivocal extent, by Sir William Waller in the Commons; the Scots pursued war as an honourable means to bring Charles to the negotiating table without necessarily requiring outright victory. Initially – at least until talk came round to deposing Charles I – the Covenanters shared the desire to win the war conclusively that was held by the war grouping around Algernon Percy, tenth Earl of Northumberland, and William Fiennes, Viscount Saye and Sele, in the Lords and Vane junior, St John and Oliver Cromwell in the Commons – though relations with this group were to sour sharply towards the end of 1644.[41]

Notwithstanding the influential role played by Scottish clerics such as Henderson and his colleagues in the Westminster Assembly in promoting Presbyterianism, the Scottish Commissioners in London were not solely, or even primarily, concerned with effecting religious uniformity according to a Scottish prescription.[42] In order to secure a lasting peace between the king and the English Parliament, the Commissioners were instructed to negotiate 'with greater latitude'. The Scottish Covenanters, instead, had three principal concerns: the suppression of the Catholic Confederation in Ireland; meaningful British representation in both the royal household and the executive councils for all three kingdoms; and the opening up of colonial trade and mercantile adventuring to Scottish ships – as had been requested, but never actually conceded, during negotiations that culminated in the Treaty of London between England and Scotland in 1641.

In 1644, in order to prevent bickering in command between the Scottish and British armies in Ireland, they sought that overall command should be clearly vested in the Scottish Earl of Leven, as Lord General, and, under him, another Scot, Robert Munro. All the British in Ireland were to be obliged to subscribe the Solemn League and Covenant. At the same time, the Scottish Commissioners were insistent that Ireland was to be included 'under the name of England in all the articles'.[43]

Perhaps the key obstacle to the achievement of these ends was the king. Charles I remained adamantly opposed to a Covenanted monarchy – not least because it would clearly entail the abolition of episcopacy – and to the making of any concessions in England that would diminish his power to the point that had been secured by the Covenanters in Scotland by 1641. This posed the Covenanting Scots with a conundrum. Committed to the maintenance of monarchy – indeed, of the Stuart monarchy – they had no real alternative to Charles. They were therefore disconcerted to find, as the peace negotiations at Uxbridge for an English settlement broke up in acrimony in February 1645, that the parliamentary war grouping was increasingly drawn to the possibility of reducing Charles I from monarch to a royal cipher. These concerns were compounded by differences between Scots and English commanders over how hostilities were to be conducted and directed.[44]

For the Scots, the strategy of strengthening British unity entailed a convergence of public policy, not the merger of institutions in Church and state. However, the Committee of Both Kingdoms, the one British institution that did arise out of the Solemn League and Covenant, opened up the fault lines between the Parliamentarians and the Scots. Operating from February 1644 until October 1646, the Committee of Both Kingdoms had an extensive, if mutable, remit: keenly debated at its instigation; subject to periodic review as members and responsibilities were added; and the focus of rival antagonisms among the main players in the peace and war groupings. For Gerolamo Agostini, the Venetian Secretary in England, the Committee of Both Kingdoms, as a council of state, was a Scottish initiative that qualified the English Parliament's control over domestic affairs and took the initiative in international relations.[45]

In reality, outside domestic English issues, the Scottish commissioners enjoyed a disproportionate and moderating presence. Johnston of Wariston usually managed committee business that pertained to international relations where the Committee was projected as a *Concilium Amborum Magnae Britannia* (joint-council of Great Britain).[46] Viewed within diplomatic and political circles as an executive agency, the Committee, which met at Derby House in London, was empowered to negotiate with foreign states as well as serving as an official channel for dealings between the Covenanters and the Parliamentarians. However, to carry out its diplomatic functions effectively and oversee the war-effort by land and sea, not only against the Royalists in England but also against the Catholic Confederation in Ireland, the Committee would have required to operate as a federal British executive: not a step contemplated by the Long Parliament.[47]

For their part, the Covenanting leadership viewed the committee, as a co-ordinating confederal council, the prime – but not the sole – agency for preserving Scottish interests in the management of the affairs of both kingdoms. Its British roots lay with the commission for the Conservators of the Peace that had been established by the Treaty of London in 1641, which evolved into the commission for negotiating the Solemn League and Covenant in Edinburgh on behalf of the English Parliament and the Scottish Estates. English commissioners attached to the Covenanting army of intervention were seemingly not granted consultation within the Committee of Estates equivalent to that accorded to the Scottish Commissioners in London. Commissioners with northern connections, especially Sir William Armyne and Richard Barwis, became the most vociferous critics of the Scottish army's deleterious impact on the English counties where they took free quarter. In time, a vitriolic anti-Scottishness came to characterize the war grouping at Westminster.[48]

The first hint that the Scots were becoming a polarizing influence between the peace and war groupings came after the battle of Marston Moor in July 1644, which Cromwell acclaimed as a triumph for the English forces of godliness. In the short term, any potential fissures between the Parliamentarians and their Scottish allies were covered up when the triumphant generals involved in the battle – Lord Fairfax and his son Sir Thomas Fairfax, the Earl of Manchester, and for the Scots, the Earl of Leven – wrote to the Committee of Both Kingdoms to affirm their continuing commitment to the Solemn League and Covenant. Nevertheless, after further personalized criticism by Cromwell of Scottish officers serving in the parliamentary forces, the reaction of the Scottish Commissioners was not to promote reconciliation but to contemplate, in association with Essex and the peace grouping, the indictment of Cromwell as an 'incendiary' – a source of division between the two nations. However, the Covenanting leadership also shared the concerns of the war grouping about the lack of professionalism among the parliamentary forces: hence the Scottish Commissioners, at the instigation of Argyll, endorsed the Self-Denying Ordinance introduced in the Commons on 9 December 1644, which duly paved the way for the reorganization of the Parliament's armies and the creation of the New Model Army in the spring of 1645.[49]

Here, too, Scottish influence can be discerned. Viewed as a quintessentially English construct,[50] the New Model Army was based on, but without acknowledgement to, the national armies created initially in Sweden then in Scotland as products of the Thirty Years War. Paradoxically, however, under its new commanders Sir Thomas Fairfax and Oliver Cromwell, it was fashioned to attain victory for the English Parliamentarians, not the reconfiguration of Britain envisaged by the Solemn League and Covenant.

Cromwell and the other promoters of the New Model Army manifested their antagonism towards the Scots through the withholding of funding to their forces. Despite the comprehensive vanquishing of the king's armies by early 1646, and the consequent expansion in the Parliament's revenue base, the Covenanting forces were denied ready access to the central government's financial resources throughout 1645 and 1646. This neglect – which the Scots rightly took to be deliberate – became an ever-growing source of friction between themselves and their parliamentary allies. The implications for the English counties in which their forces were quartered were often dire. Reliant as much on supplies from Scotland (raised usually on credit) as from London, or later York, the Scots forces in England felt obliged to take free quarter or impose their own fiscal levies on the counties they occupied. These fiscal demands, which were usually higher than comparable parliamentary exactions, provoked a series of local revolts: in Cumberland and Westmorland; and in the aftermath of Naseby in June 1645, a 'Clubman' uprising in Yorkshire.[51] Yet, anti-Scottish sentiment was not the only motive for these insurrections, nor were the Scots ubiquitously regarded as the villains of the piece. Equally important was a growing aversion to the military, financial and ideological demands of the Parliament-appointed County Committees – the local face of the Westminster administration. Indeed, in parts of Yorkshire and the North, the Covenanters continued to be seen benignly as the kingdom's deliverers from the Royalists and as agents for a godly reconfiguration of Britain.[52]

V   DISSENT BETWEEN THE 'BRETHREN': THE WANING OF COVENANTING INFLUENCE IN ENGLAND, 1645–6

If the Covenanting army fulfilled only a limited role in the campaigning to defeat the king after 1645, it nevertheless remained a powerful reserve force – and one which had major implications for Anglo-Scottish politics as a whole. Even after the creation of the New Model in 1645, the existence of the Covenanter army in England powerfully strengthened the hand of the Scots Commissioners in London in the endless debates on the terms that were to be offered the king. The peace grouping dominating in the Lords became identified with the Presbyterians, while the war grouping, which just held sway in the Commons, became the Independents. The key to these divisions, which emerged before victory over Charles I was assured, was not so much religious affiliations as political attitudes to continued Covenanting intervention in England. In effect, the Presbyterians tended to empathize with the Scots, while the Independents were antagonistic.[53]

The Presbyterians, led by the Earl of Essex, though by no means wholly committed to a religious settlement in accord with Scottish practice, inclined towards the Covenanters to support their conservative desires for an accommodation with Charles I. Accordingly, the Presbyterians ensured that the Parliament passed an order insisting that the Solemn League and Covenant had to be subscribed by all officers in the New Model Army within twenty days of their appointment. The Independents, among whom Cromwell was becoming increasingly prominent, certainly sought a more pluralist, if not wholly tolerant, religious establishment in England. The essence of their radicalism was their political commitment to parliamentary supremacy buttressed by the New Model Army. The Independents were therefore intent on outright victory rather than an accommodation with Charles I. After Naseby in June 1645, as we have seen, the Scots were no longer deemed essential. The Independents were able to insist that ordinary soldiers enlisted in the New Model Army should only 'take the Covenant' at the discretion of both Houses. Nonetheless the Scots, rather than any transient or nebulous middle grouping, had become the third party interest in parliamentary circles in the course of 1645; a position reinforced by their continuing good relations with the city of London.[54]

However, by 1645, the Scots were no longer the political interest of the moment. The resolve of the Scottish Covenanters that the reconfiguration of Britain should encompass an accommodation with the Stuart monarchy suffered critically when Charles's secret correspondence was intercepted and published in the wake of Naseby.[55] At the same time, the Covenanters themselves were compromised by hints of secret negotiations with the regency government of Cardinal Mazarin in France, which involved dealings with prominent Royalists, including Queen Henriette Marie. These negotiations had been in train even before the Uxbridge negotiations of the winter of 1644–5 and were undertaken without reference to the Committee of Both Kingdoms. They led, in July 1645, to the arrival in London of a French embassy led by Jean de Montreuil, who soon recognized that 'the Scots are no longer the master of the settlement of affairs in Great Britain'. Charged to negotiate primarily with the Covenanters and Charles I, the French ambassador met with the Scottish Commissioners in London before progressing to Scotland where he explored the prospects for two eventualities: a tripartite accommodation between the Covenanters, the Presbyterians in the English Parliament, and the king; and secondly, the revival of 'the auld alliance' between France and Scotland as a military pact, should the Scots go to war against the English Parliamentarians. In the context of 1645–6, the latter eventuality seemed the more likely, given the assertiveness of the Independents and the fears the Covenanters shared with the Presbyterians about the rise of a radical element within the New Model Army.[56]

The causes of Covenanters' waning influence were not to be found in England alone. Their army's ability to intervene further in England had been curtailed severely in the course of 1645 by the resurgence of

Royalism in Scotland under James Graham, Marquess of Montrose.
From his initial victory at Tippermuir in Perthshire on 1 September
1644 until his eventual defeat at Philiphaugh in Selkirkshire on 13
September 1645, Montrose, with the assistance of forces from the
Catholic Confederacy in Ireland, had waged a civil war that had
severely destabilized the Covenanting régime in Scotland.[57] In seeking
to prevent any conjunction between the various royalist forces in
England and Scotland, the Covenanting leadership preferred to keep
their forces in England concentrated in the North and to establish
garrisons unilaterally between the Tees and Carlisle (see Map 1).
Thereby, they left themselves open to the charge of breaching the terms
of the Anglo-Scottish treaty of 1643, which had brought them into the
war. When the Scots commanders in England *did* eventually agree to
participate in the siege of Newark-upon-Trent, in November 1645, the
Committee of Estates in Edinburgh insisted that General Leven should
be made supreme commander of both the Covenanting and English
Parliamentarian forces involved in the siege, a blockade that dragged on
until May 1646.

The role of the Scots' forces in Ireland was also problematic. The
Scots Commissioners' accord with the English Presbyterians had
enabled them to secure Scottish representation in the delegation sent by
the Committee of Both Kingdoms to take stock of the war in Ireland in
March 1645. However, political animosity from the Independents led to
Robert Munro being stripped of his overall command of the Scottish
and British forces in Ireland. The Scottish commissioners in London
were effectively removed from executive discussions on Irish affairs by
December that year. And the provocation to Scotland represented by
her exclusion from management of the war in Ireland was paralleled in
the ecclesiastical sphere. The English Parliament's decision in 1646 that
Presbyterianism, once established in the English Church, was not to be
autonomous of Parliament, as in Scotland, was castigated by the Scots as
an 'erastian settlement' and widely regarded in Edinburgh as a betrayal
by the English of their obligations under the Solemn League and
Covenant.[58]

Even more destructive of the erstwhile sense of a common cause
between the Scottish Covenanters and the English Parliamentarians was
their failure to agree on any basis for an agreement with a patently
untrustworthy king. When, over the winter of 1645–6, the English
Parliament embarked on a revision of the peace terms it was prepared
to offer the king, the Scottish Commissioners were at first excluded from

discussions. These were conducted, not in the full Committee of Both Kingdoms, but instead, in an exclusively English-controlled sub-committee: the Scots, by this point, were already regarded as being too protective of the king's interests. These English suspicions were not without justification. By the time the new propositions were ready for presentation to the king, in the summer of 1646, the Scots had achieved a major tactical advantage over their increasingly estranged English 'brethren'. In early May 1646, the king, having finally conceded that the war was lost, surrendered himself to the Scottish army at Newark, regarding the Scots as more likely to take a generous view of his interests than the English Parliament.

The sources of friction were numerous. The Scots remained unconvinced that any meaningful parliamentary pressure was being exerted on Charles to take the Covenant. The Independents had insisted that the English militia as well as the executive and judiciary come under parliamentary control for twenty years, whereas the Scots did not regard control of the militia as solely an English concern. Moreover, the king's exclusion from these key powers, effectively for life, was a further disincentive for him 'to covenant'. Likewise, the issue of control over the forces in Ireland was in danger of going by default if the Parliamentarians took no account of Scottish interests. And while there was little doubt that meaningful Scottish participation on the Committee of Both Kingdoms had run its course, the Covenanting leadership nevertheless remained insistent that the 'making of peace and war' were common issues to be decided jointly by Scotland and England.[59]

There were voices which urged a return to the idealist 'Unionist' agenda of 1643. Argyll, the driving force behind Scotland's ambitions for a British confederation, attempted to transcend divisions within and between Parliamentarians and Covenanters in a celebrated speech to a conference of both Houses of the English Parliament in June 1646. Internal divisions between Presbyterians and Independents were a further complication, especially as the New Model Army inclined towards the latter in terms of restricting royal authority and promoting a controlled measure of religious toleration. On the one side, the Independents' intransigence intensified once the king was in Scottish custody, though the Lords exercised a restraining influence on the Scotophobia then rampant in the Commons (where it was maintained that the disposal of the king was a purely English matter). On the other side, the Scottish Estates were increasingly restless about the continuing cost of their military interventions in England and Ireland. Partly as a result of this, Argyll experienced increasing difficulty in holding together the radical Covenanting mainstream. The marquess steadfastly maintained the imperative of confederal action, while affirming that any move from a purely regal union (three states united under a common Crown) to complete union remained a visionary ideal. But the existing 'Union' implied that the English Parliament should not negotiate unilaterally with Charles I.[60]

The king's outright rejection of the peace propositions presented to him while in the Scots' custody in the summer of 1646 left the Scots Commissioners in London with little alternative but to negotiate an honourable withdrawal from England. Nevertheless, their insistence on continuing to hold the king in their custody until such time as they were satisfactorily recompensed for their past military services increased the anti-Scottish ire of the Independents. It also detached the Presbyterians in the English Parliament from what had hitherto been a firm alliance with the Scottish interest, and led to a marked decline in support from their most steadfast constituency, the City of London. The Covenanting leadership remained adamant that the disposal of the king was to be effected only by joint advice and consent of both kingdoms that 'the Unity between the Kingdomes may be inviolably preserved'.[61]

The initiative in negotiating the final terms for the withdrawal of the Covenanting army from England and the handing over of the king was taken by the English Presbyterians in the autumn of 1646. A satisfactory resolution, without recourse to the war that seemed to be threatened by the Independents, would consolidate the Presbyterians' control over the Long Parliament. Denzell Holles, the leading Scottish protagonist in the Commons, played a key role in securing £400,000 as compensation to the Scots, to be paid in two equal instalments. Lingering hopes that Charles I would take stock of his situation and accept the Newcastle Propositions were dashed by 20 December. Assertively managed by Argyll, the Scottish Estates resolved that an un-Covenanted king should not be brought to Scotland. A vote on 16 January 1647 ensured that Charles was to be left at Newcastle, after the Scots' army withdrew; and it was there, fourteen days later, that he was duly handed over to the English Parliamentarians. That the Covenanters had received no guarantees for his safety or for the future of the Stuart monarchy in England as they departed was confirmation that the 'Scottish moment' had long since passed.[62]

VI CONCLUSION

As was recognized internationally at the time (if not in the subsequent historiography), the Covenanting movement in Scotland provided not only a practical political exemplar but also an ideological framework for revolution throughout the British Isles between 1638 and 1643. It was always a precarious achievement. The extensive territorial commitments of the Covenanting forces from 1642 to 1646 were managed against a backdrop of civil war within Scotland, and divisions within Covenanting ranks on whether to scale down their forces in England, or even to withdraw them entirely. In part, this can be explained by the failure of the English Parliamentarians to honour the spirit, if not the letter, of the Solemn League and Covenant of 1643. But it is also the case that by the mid-1640s, the Scottish alliance with England was no longer the only option on offer. By 1645, an alternative field of engagement beckoned as the Covenanters debated the revival of a confederation with Sweden. Scottish military assistance was sought by the Swedes, their former allies during the Bishops' Wars, in order to wrest the three provinces to the east of the Baltic Sound (Blekinge, Halland and Skåne) from Christian IV of Denmark. In this, Scottish economic interests were also clearly at stake. The acquisition of these provinces by Sweden would eradicate the tolls that had hitherto crippled Scottish trade to and from the Baltic. So, an engagement with Sweden appeared a realistic possibility – at least until 1647, when a power struggle between Argyll and Hamilton in the Scottish Estates negated any prospect of a unified Covenanting response to aid the Presbyterians in England, or of exploiting the growing tensions between the Westminster Parliament and the New Model Army. The Covenanters made only one external commitment: in August 1647, the Kirk called on Scottish mercantile communities in Denmark, Sweden, Poland and Hungary to uphold the religious standards for worship, doctrine and discipline endorsed by the Westminster Assembly in 1645 – one of the few concrete achievements they had to show for their intervention in England.[63]

Civil war within Scotland, recriminations among conservative and radical Covenanters in its aftermath, and divided agendas among them as to British and overseas interventions from 1645 polarized the movement within Scotland. On the one side stood Hamilton, supported principally by the Scottish nobility determined to reassert baronial leadership; and on the other were Argyll and his adherents, drawn mainly from the gentry, burgesses and the Kirk. As Hugh Mowatt, the

Swedish diplomat had clearly realized by the beginning of 1647, the Covenanters were in no position to make a further unified intervention in England – or overseas; still less to reclaim a position of leadership within Britain.[64] When, in the late autumn of 1647, the Hamilton grouping put together their Engagement to defend Charles I and restore his monarchical authority in England – the prelude to the disastrous Scottish invasion of England *against* the Parliamentarians in 1648 – they did so not as a national movement but as a baronial enterprise. Fundamental Covenanting principles were sacrificed. Presbyterianism was no longer an imperative. Confederation was dropped in favour of an incorporating union as had originally been proposed by James I in 1604 (and as had been rejected by the English House of Commons in 1607). As Sir Cheney Culpepper, an English member of the Hartlib circle, diagnosed, this was no more than 'the Scottish Aristocraticall Interese' engaged in a factional and destructive endeavour.[65] Indeed, in relation to the passing of the Scottish moment, this was viewed even by the Scottish Engagers as no more than a 'tragicomediall' epilogue.[66]

6. Centre and Locality in Civil-War England

CLIVE HOLMES

In the late 1640s, Sir John Oglander of Nunwell reflected bleakly on the government of his locality, the Isle of Wight. He had been a most active public servant: a Justice of the Peace for forty years, sheriff of Hampshire, commander of the local militia. Now, after arrest and imprisonment, he had been turned out of all his posts by Parliament. Local authority had fallen to 'a thing called a Committee' consisting, he wrote ironically, of 'brave men' – farmers, an apothecary, a peddler, a baker. Throughout England many of the old gentry families were 'extinct or undone'; the survivors, like himself, were compelled to live 'in submission to the base, unruly multitude'. Oglander's sense of a funda-mental change in the structures of local government and society, of an alien administration displacing natural rulers, has proved attractive to modern-day academic historians – with *their* own professional world in turmoil, *their* masters increasingly unsympathetic. 'Tempora mutantur [the times are changing]', Oglander concluded pathetically: 'O tempora, o mores [What times! What behaviour!]'.[1] The times *had* changed. But the shifts were not so seismic as Oglander insisted or the historians attracted to his viewpoint have believed. Significant continuities in central–local relations survived the experience of war.

In this chapter I will argue three interrelated points. First, that while local responses to the war are diverse – an obvious product of kaleido-scopic experience playing on a multitude of different local structures – such variety is compatible with a considerable measure of uniformity. In particular, the dominant ideological framework within which local concerns (and criticism of central intrusion) are expressed is essentially national. Secondly, that the dominance of a rhetoric of national iden-tity and constitutional probity makes sense, in that the interests of the locality could best be advanced, and its grievances remedied, by co-operating with central authority within the complex, multi-faceted insti-tutions that had been spawned by the circumstances of war. In this respect, national ideology and state structure reinforce each other.

Finally, that understanding of these two points was widely dispersed throughout society: it is not unique to county magistrates or urban patriciates, but is shared by villagers and commoners in relation to highly local grievances. Research in the last twenty years has developed these points, and obliged a serious modification of the older models of central–local relations, which emphasized the distance between Westminster and the local élites, the 'county communities'. The old 'localist' interpretation, for which Oglander is a key text – the characterization of the localities as isolated from the centre, reacting only with suspicion or hostility towards the latter's policy priorities in so far as they understood them – is no longer viable.

These three points have also been affirmed and incorporated in the re-worked edition of a dominant text of the revisionist–localist interpretation, John Morrill's *The Revolt of the Provinces*. In his revised introduction and conclusion to the work – significantly re-titled *Revolt* in *the Provinces* – Professor Morrill recognizes and incorporates the emphases that are at the heart of my essay: indeed, he sometimes seems to be arguing that he *meant* to say that all along. However, as a consequence of its being re-worked, the new volume contains some discordant anomalies, as one would anticipate in any palimpsest construction. To cite but two examples, his view of the neutrality movement in 1642, which insists that 'far from demonstrating the limitations of provincialism, [the neutrality movement] marked its triumph', and his claim that the 1648 revolts sought 'a restoration of local autonomy', seem wholly incommensurable with the new material that Morrill has introduced.[2] More generally, some writing on these themes also seeks (and less accidentally) to have its cake and eat it too: while recognizing the three points stated at the beginning of this essay, authors still try to incorporate them within a framework derived from the localist canon.[3] All this suggests that there may be some value in discussing these issues again. The line of analysis I hope to develop will concentrate on a revised reading of contemporary 1640s texts that are at the heart of the localist interpretation. I hope to show that these works, too, indicate the complex interaction of central and local institutions and the dominance of a national ideology.

Localist historians, led by Alan Everitt in the 1960s, began their discussion from assumptions derived from an analysis of the structures of provincial society. Introversion, they argued, was a product of a number of social patterns, such as endogamous marriage and ancient settlement, and the intense involvement of local men in local government. In consequence, Everitt believed, the English polity was best understood as 'a union of partially independent county states'. Local leaders were 'essentially provincial people', and 'for the most part they were simply not concerned with affairs of state'. The locals only became involved in national affairs, and then only temporarily, 'when the gyrations of politicians became more than usually demented'.[4] This structural analysis, with its *assumptions* about insularity, then dictated the reading of evidence, concerning, say, Charles I's Book of Orders of 1631 or the king's fiscal experiments during the Personal Rule, which in fact sustained more complex or nuanced readings.[5] But the period 1643–8, in particular, seemed to provide grist to the localist mill. A central government that had collapsed into factional conflict (with each of the competing sides making unprecedented demands on the provinces as they sought to fund their war-efforts) might well be thought 'demented'. The localities responded with denunciatory pamphlets and petitions, with riots, and eventually in 1648, with rebellion – an event that is still described as 'the Revolt of the Provinces' in Morrill's re-worked study. These local responses, particularly the tracts and petitions denouncing 'the centre's' intrusions into the localities, are at the heart of the interpretations by Professors Everitt and (in his earlier manifestation) Morrill. It is these tracts that evidence the fierce local resentment at the devolution of provincial government to men from beyond the traditional circles of local government – to parvenus and outsiders. The latter are denounced as acting without regard for local needs and sensitivities: their actions far exceed those warranted by the legislation empowering them; they share the religious and political goals of the Westminster radicals; and they are not averse to feathering their own nests through bribery, graft and peculation. It is this body of evidence that needs further discussion and deconstruction, as a prelude to developing a more nuanced view of the entire question. What I propose to suggest is that we are not being confronted with a visceral response from the localities, as Everitt and the localist school believed, but with a highly politicized and mediated discourse, originating from – not in opposition to – the centre.

I   THE PROBLEMS OF EVIDENCE: HOW 'LOCAL' WAS THE RHETORIC OF LOCALIST COMPLAINT?

The major battleground for these conflicts between 'centre' and 'locality' during the Civil War were the so-called 'county committees' – the executive bodies appointed by Parliament for each English and Welsh county, during the course of the 1640s, to oversee the implementation of Westminster's orders and ordinances (in particular, those concerning the collection of revenue). These tended to supplant the county's traditional, pre-war administrative structures organized around the Justices of the Peace, in which membership of the lay magistracy roughly corresponded with the county's social hierarchy. Perhaps unsurprisingly, from the mid-1640s, evidence for hostility to the committees – whose members often came from outside the county's traditional social élite – is rich and various. By the spring of 1647 everybody was assailing the county committees: the Lords; the Presbyterians; the City fathers; London newspapers; the Reformadoes (or demobilized soldiers); Royalists; even the New Model Army. But in this critical cacophony the dominant note is clearly that of the Peace Party–Presbyterian alliance, culminating in the anti-committee tirades of Clement Walker and Denzell Holles.[6] It is these works that provide the essential core for the localist historical model, and we must therefore address the construction of these texts. This was a gradual, and by no means unilinear, process. There are three major periods of discussion.

The first period is marked by an interplay between the Presbyterian party in Parliament and the London newspaper, the *Scotish Dove*, during the mid-1640s. The *Dove* began a campaign against committee abuse in the winter of 1645–6, and the editors' hostile accounts of the practice of particular local committees led to a more general attack on 'defects in many committees'. These were initially attributed to the venality of the men who staffed the committees, not to the institutions themselves (which the *Dove* recognized as being 'absolutely necessary in these times of distraction').[7] In February 1646, the Commons agreed that 'the Consideration of easing the People from their sufferings under Committees, be taken into Debate'.[8] The *Dove* was quick to praise this initiative[9] – too quick, in fact, for the vote was forgotten, and the *Dove* was reduced to sniping at the deficiencies of particular committees. Then, in the spring and summer of 1646, the Lords took a hand, preparing an ordinance for 'putting down and dissolving the Committees in the several Shires'.[10] The Commons also expressed renewed interest, and again the *Dove* became an enthusiastic proponent of radical surgery:

I (as all the people) hope to see their [committees'] speedy dissolution. . . . I know Committees were usefull and appointed by the Parliament to a good end and use, but [are] now [so] adulterated that nothing but a dissolution can satisfie the people.[11]

Again, however, the Commons dragged its feet, despite reminders from the Lords of their proposed ordinance, and nothing was done. The *Dove* relapsed into silence for the remainder of 1646, except for a hostile reference to the misdeeds of the Committee of Somerset, which was carefully balanced by praise of the Warwickshire Committee.[12]

Reflecting on the events of 1646, Holles blamed 'that faction' – meaning the Independents and the supporters of the New Model Army in the Commons – for the failure of these initiatives. He and his friends, he later claimed, 'got orders ... [and] brought in ordinances' for the suppression of committees, but 'still, by some art or other of theirs, were put by when it was thought in a manner settled'.[13] This is unconvincing. There was generalized antipathy to committees, but no agreement on what would replace them. 'The old form of Government by sheriffs, Justices of Peace, Grand Juries, and other ministers of Justice, in that subordination which law had established', could hardly have dealt with the problems of sequestration and composition; of the vast taxation required to fund the Scots army in England and the New Model; nor could it have coped with repayments of loans, free-quarter debentures, and the arrears of pay due to the soldiers. The *Scotish Dove* intermittently acknowledged this problem, not least because its extreme anti-committee position was challenged by its competitors. The rival newsbook *The Kingdomes Weekly Intelligencer*, for example, rebuked the *Dove* for its over-enthusiastic reporting of parliamentary votes concerning the prospective dissolution of committees, and its consistently negative account of their actions.[14] In response, the *Dove* was obliged to nod grudging approval of some committees whilst insisting on the need for a general reform: 'I wish all had done as well, and that there were none worse, or rather that all were extinct, that all countries might be eased of unnecessary taxes.'[15]

After the silence of the autumn of 1646, the second wave of attack on committees recommenced in Parliament early in 1647, as Holles and his friends pursued the aggressive policy of 'normalization' that was to lead to the fatal dispute over the disbandment of the New Model Army in the spring and early summer of that year. The Commons acted first, by two days, but the Lords again pursued the issue with the greater vigour. The peers were swift to remind the lower House of their proposed ordinance abolishing committees, sent to the Commons in July 1646. And their statements rehearse most of the important themes of the anti-committee case: the 'partiality and injustice' of the committees; the 'great disorders' in some localities associated with their continuance. They emphasize the general enthusiasm 'that those extraordinary Ways of proceeding shall not be continued', and for bringing 'things into the old course and way of government'.[16] The Presbyterian anti-committee lobby received some support from among their allies in London. The City fathers joined the chorus on 3 July 1647. The Reformadoes had already, on 22 March 1647, demanded that the county committees should be suppressed and their officers brought to a 'speedy and strict account'.[17] The latter petition is particularly interesting, in that the Reformadoes had *not* made any such suggestion in their earlier representations to Parliament, nor had they made the equally politically charged demand for the settlement of a Presbyterian system of government in the English Church.[18] Clearly the unemployed officers, lobbying for commands in the projected army to be sent to Ireland, recognized that expressions both of Presbyterian zeal and of anti-committee rhetoric would be well received by Holles and his friends.[19]

Unsurprisingly, the proposed anti-committee legislation of the spring of 1647 made no headway after the Army revolt which followed during that summer, and it is at this time – the third period of the development of the discourse – that Walker and Holles write their defining texts, which give concrete and highly influential form to anti-committee sentiment. They are men embittered by the failure of their general political programme, and they over-emphasize their earlier commitment to a return to normalcy. They see the role of the committees, as the minions of the Independent faction and the acolytes of the New Model Army, with a clarity and consistency that is not apparent in the earlier stages of the discussion of local government.

The localist historiographic tradition neglects the halting and (initially) uncertain and contested development of Presbyterian hostility to committees; it reads the earlier expressions partially, in the light of the formed views, the product of this process, of Walker and Holles. It is appropriate here to return to Walker's text. In his general denunciation of committees he invites his reader to consider detailed evidence of their depravity. Some of this is derived from Somerset, his home county; but in two cases he refers to other printed accounts, as independent confirmation of his analysis. The earlier of the two tracts mentioned by Walker is Edward King's *A Discovery of the Arbitrary, Tyrannical and Illegal Actions of Some of the County of Lincoln*, of February 1647; the second, from July that year, is *The Heads of the Present Greevances of the County of Glamorgan*. These throw more light on the creation of the dominant discourse concerning county committees in later historiography, because neither, if properly contextualized, provides the kind of independent unmediated corroboration that Walker pretends.

The first of Walker's texts – Edward King's *A Discovery of the Arbitrary . . . Actions of Some of the County of Lincoln*, of February 1647 – is an exercise in Presbyterian polemic, not an authentic local voice. In an early article, I interpreted Colonel Edward King's challenge to the Lincolnshire Committee in 1646–7 as a largely local issue, though one that was ultimately adjudicated at Westminster, and which in that process reveals something of the complexity of 'party' formation in Parliament.[20] This local focus is not wholly implausible. King and his tenants *had* been harassed by the Lincolnshire Committee; his stand against the committee's insensitive handling of the raising of tax arrears and the demands of the excise-men in Kesteven (a region only just freed from the depredations of the royalist garrison at Newark and of the Scottish army that had besieged the town) obviously struck a chord with the locals. I am not seeking to deny that there was a powerful local dimension to the dispute. But I did underplay the central context.

The reasons for this are threefold. First, Colonel King is an odd defender of the local community. He had been the 'front man' for the Earl of Manchester – the commander in the adjacent Eastern Association of counties – in the earl's dispute with his follow Parliamentarian commander, Lord Willoughby of Parham, concerning the war-effort in Lincolnshire and the disposal of the resources of the shire back in the autumn of 1643.[21] In this contest, the King–Manchester alliance had triumphed at Westminster, and Lincolnshire (hitherto Willoughby's fiefdom) was duly incorporated into the Eastern Association. The gentry governors of the shire, chastened and humiliated by the public assault on their governance and marginalized by the new centrally imposed arrangements, withdrew in dudgeon. Outmanoeuvred in the locality and in Parliament, Willoughby's frustration burst out in his bleak assessment to his fellow parliamentarian peer, the Earl of Denbigh: 'here we are all hasting to an erlei ruin . . . nobility and gentry are going down apace . . . I thought it a crime to be a nobleman.'[22] In 1644, King, then, had stood in opposition to those seeking to retain a measure of local autonomy, and was a savage critic of the traditional structures of local authority. In the course of this dispute, and its subsequent ramifications, King made contact with the centre and its web of inter-locking committees. He also made some potent friends among Presbyterian activists at Westminster – particularly William Prynne, the Puritan 'martyr' of the 1630s and prolific pamphleteer of the 1640s. Indeed, Prynne was Colonel King's counsel in his defence against Lord Willoughby's attempts to crush his enemy (and King's ally, Manchester) in the House of Lords; later, he was also to advise King on the legal strategy he would pursue in his feud with John Lilburne.[23]

Secondly, in his attack on the Lincolnshire Committee, King emphasized the committeemen's conformity to the developing stereotype: namely, that they were outsiders; 'men of meane qualitie';[24] favourers of subversive sectaries. In so far as this charge is true, it is in part a product of King's earlier attack: the traditional governors of the shire, harried by King acting as Manchester's rottweiler, had stood down from local government. Beyond this, however, King's charge seems wholly exaggerated. King's particular *bête noire*, the lawyer-chairman of the committee, John Archer, was indeed a newcomer to the county, but he was no favourer of sectaries: he refused the Engagement (the oath of allegiance to the new republican Commonwealth established after Charles I's execution in 1649), and would serve as counsel for Christopher Love, a pro-royalist plotter, at his trial in 1651.

King also displayed his concern for the traditional forms of local government (a theme that was a regular part of the anti-committee discourse) not only in his attacks on the Westminster-appointed Lincolnshire governors' illegitimate interference in the traditional procedures of civil litigation and government, but also in his powerfully symbolic choice of forum. The local dimension of his attack on the committee was to come in the form of a charge to the Grand Jury at the Michaelmas (i.e. September–October) Quarter Sessions for 1646 held at Kesteven, Lincolnshire. It was also a highly effective tactic. The Grand Jury responded to his suggestions with alacrity, and a series of indictments was handed down against the excise officers and even against some of the county committee's own agents.

Finally, the date of Edward King's pamphlet – 1 February 1647 – indicates an awareness of the situation at Westminster, not an organic local response. The pamphlet is constructed out of King's charge to the Grand Jury, which had been presented in October 1646, and a personal defence that had been prepared in late December in response to the investigation by the London-based Committee of the Army of the extent of the damage he had caused to local tax collection. In Lincolnshire, at the January 1647 Quarter Sessions, however, King was already moderating his earlier rhetoric and backtracking from the extreme positions he had asserted in the autumn of 1646. But in London his earlier, trenchantly anti-committee statements were published precisely at the time that the second wave of attacks on local committees was being orchestrated by Presbyterians in Parliament (23

January 1647).[25] These considerations of context force us to reassess Colonel King's position as a spokesman for 'localist' concerns. King is not a representative figure of local disillusionment with central interference in the community of the county. Rather, he is a knowing and skilled broker, playing off local and central concerns, deploying and developing the anti-committee rhetoric of the Westminster Presbyterians.

Clement Walker's second piece of required reading on the evils of county committees is a justification of a rising in Glamorgan in 1647. The writers of this Glamorganshire manifesto had stood on their defence 'against all Committees, not', they insisted, 'as being invested with a power from the Parliament, but as abusing that power and trust'. The Glamorgan Committee, they claimed, was stuffed with outsiders to the county; their intention was 'to insult over the gentry' and their abuses were numerous: they were raising money on ordinances (which worked as temporary Acts of Parliament) that had expired; they refused to provide accounts; they were soliciting bribes and embezzling the public revenue so as to enrich themselves.[26] This is the stuff of familiar anti-committee polemic: it is no wonder that Walker refers his readers to it with such enthusiasm.

But the story that underlies this publication is far more complex. The Glamorgan rising had been organized not by enraged locals, but by 'ancient malignants of a deep stain' – that is, by old Royalists. Initially, these Royalists attempted to use the uncertainty created by the revolt of the New Model Army (specifically the army's seizure of the king at Holdenby House in June 1647, and the army's stated concern for liberty of conscience) to challenge the victorious Parliamentarians in South Wales. Warrants were issued by the insurrectionists to levy men 'for the use of the King's Majesty *and* Sir Thomas Fairfax [the army's commander-in-chief]'. The ploy was clever, but, as their claim became increasingly implausible, their propaganda shifted focus and fixed upon the 'unjust and arbitrary disposition of the committees here' as the major justification for their revolt – and this also became the theme of their later published declaration.[27]

Royalists, then, played a major role in fashioning and deploying the developing anti-committee rhetoric. That Royalists loathed the committees is hardly surprising: they were their chief victims. The committees spied out their delinquencies, civil or clerical. To advance their take on sequestration or composition, committees rooted out the minor frauds in the estate surveys and accounts that they were offered. Royalists filled their personal correspondence with complaints against committees of

being 'very hard on the gentry'. In particular, they rejected 'favore and
curtesy to gent[lemen] in matters of sequestration'. Unsurprisingly, their
victims lashed out vituperatively against such 'tradesmen committees',
'base mercenary fellowes', 'men that have neither good blood nor breeding in them'.[28] Gentlemen like Sir John Oglander, who had assumed a
role in local government as a natural right, were sidelined and obliged to
go cap-in-hand to men who refused to play the game according to the
traditional rules: of course they complained bitterly and sardonically of
the 'thing here called a Committee'.[29] This is a language that was
borrowed from its royalist inceptors by jaundiced conservative
'Presbyterian' commentators, as their hopes for a negotiated settlement
and a return to normalcy reeled in the face of the army rebellion in the
summer of 1647.

We have studied the development of an anti-committee discourse
from its beginnings in 1646 to its reaching fruition in the jeremiads of
Walker and Holles. This discourse has determined the perspective of
modern historians, who have employed it, without giving sufficient
consideration to its gradual development and polemical character, to
organize their thinking about the general issues of centre and locality in
the Civil War. The process of construction and appropriation analysed
thus far suggests the limitations of that account. So, too, does another
aspect of the historiography: the *failure* to use another body of anti-
committee rhetoric.

II   THE SILENT WITNESS: THE NEW MODEL ARMY'S
CRITIQUE OF THE COUNTY COMMITTEES

Everybody attacked the committees – and that included the New Model
Army. A number of regiments questioned the personnel and the actions
of the local committees in their statements of regimental grievances
presented on 15 and 16 May 1647. Good men, they claimed, had been
ousted from positions on the local committees and replaced by
'Ambidexters and neuters', who were not slow to employ their power to
delay the payment of the army and to question soldiers for 'offences'
committed under the pressure of military necessity. Colonel Pride's regiment, for example, argued further that the county committees consisted
of 'ungodly men' who were ready to persecute those they viewed as religious deviants.[30] These concerns are then embodied in the army's key
public statements from their *Declaration* of early June 1647, through the

Heads of the Proposals of August that year, to the 'Proposalls' of early October.[31] Even the army's *Humble Representation* of December 1647, a document that concentrates almost exclusively on the soldiers' material grievances, contains a denunciation of the committees, though it requires the purging and replacement of their membership rather than wholesale abolition.[32]

If this strain of army complaint is mentioned in modern studies, it is done so very uneasily. In this respect, historians are neatly caught in the same bind as their major sources. The army *and* the committees are both extensions and cat's-paws of the Independent faction in Parliament, 'the Zanyes and Jack-puddings' of 'the Grandees' who have 'cantonized the Kingdom', in Walker's splendid phrases.[33] How then can we explain the antipathy expressed by the soldiers for the committeemen? Holles, Walker and their allies are obliged to confront this anomaly, and all come to the same conclusion: pure 'spin'. As early as June 1647, a Buckinghamshire commentator hostile to the army questioned the sincerity of the army's anti-committee stance – 'a plausible pretence . . . a device to blinde the people'.[34] Holles, with the benefit of hindsight, made the same point: the army cynically asserted a hostility to committee rule, 'pretending an intention to . . . correct the exorbitancies with which the people had been oppressed and abused', as a ploy to gain support.[35] But the army's rhetoric and (more persuasively) their references, specific or implicit, to committee rule suggest a more subtle and complex account.

Why did the soldiers profess their distrust of the local committees? Their attitude, it seems, was a combination of logic, experience, and of the partisan accounts fed them by radicals in the localities who looked to the New Model for support.

The army had three major reasons for its hostility towards the county committees. First, the army's pay was hugely in arrears, and, in consequence, it was living on free-quarter, 'compelled to grind the faces of the poor'.[36] Yet the army's reluctant hosts were complaining of the vast sums they were paying in taxes, and in the face of these complaints 'many souldiers [declared that they] are ashamed of themselves'.[37] Clearly, money was sticking somewhere, and the army's suspicion focused on the 'neglect or slowness of County Committees, Assessors or Collectors, to do their duties'.[38] This failure might be attributed, the army argued, either to a deliberate attempt to embarrass it and make it the butt of public obloquy, or to a more general backwardness on the part of the committeemen to serve the public.

Secondly, the army's experiences since mid-1646, when they had been quartered in East Anglia and south-eastern England, led them to entertain the deepest suspicions of the local governors of the region. This was nicely indicated in May 1647 when Colonel John Hewson's regiment, in a moment of extreme paranoia, persuaded themselves that they were about to be attacked by the Hertfordshire Trained Bands (the local gentry-officered militia) and barricaded themselves in Much Hadham Church.[39] Local governors, who had given tacit encouragement to violent resistance to the quartering of soldiers from their first arrival,[40] were now suspected of co-operating with Holles and his allies against the army. The anti-army petitions that circulated in Essex emphasizing the poverty of the region as a consequence of excessive demands for free-quarter, and demanding immediate disbandment, were clearly orchestrated by the Presbyterian party at Westminster (particularly the Earl of Warwick, who was hugely influential in the county) and its clerical supporters in London and the locality. But the use of the system of local administration, as well as the parochial network, to circulate copies suggested the complicity of the Essex Committee.[41] The soldiers' suspicions of the governors of the region were fomented by local radicals who looked to the New Model Army for support. A petition from Hertfordshire to Fairfax in mid-June, for example, complained of the influence of malignants (that is, Royalists) and neuters in local government, whereby 'the most cordiall friends of the Parliament are slighted and disregarded', and pressed for the election of men of 'approved fidelity'.[42]

Finally, there was a question of perception. The Army had been informed that the county committees and other offices of local government in more remote areas had been colonized by their (mostly Presbyterian) enemies. In the army's formal charges of treason in July 1647 against the Eleven Members (the Commons-men whom the New Model regarded as the ringleaders of the recent parliamentary attempts to disband it), they accused John Glynne and Sir William Lewes of promoting a gaggle of ex-Royalists – many their close relatives – to committees in Wales, who then sheltered their fellow Royalists from proper investigation.[43]

The earliest indication of concern in the army about the quality and reliability of the local governors is more interesting still. It occurs, also in 1647, in the early propaganda of the Agitators (the elected representatives of the army's officers and rank-and-file, appointed to represent the views of the regiments to the senior commanders).[44] The Agitators' expression of concern about the quality of the local governors in Durham and in Cumberland, for example, indicates that they know of the complaints voiced by the local dissident John Musgrave. And this brings us to another *text* – or, rather (given Musgrave's mania for publishing prolix accounts of his many grievances), to a series of texts.[45] Musgrave claimed that the administration of his native Cumberland had been packed with ex-Royalists and enthusiasts for the old pre-war liturgy, the Book of Common Prayer ('that English masse'),[46] most of them the friends and relations of the local Commons-man Richard Barwis, whose own enthusiasm for the parliamentarian cause had not been over-apparent in the early years of the war.

Musgrave's accusations made little headway in Parliament. The Cumberland Committee's useful opposition to the Scots army of occupation protected them from investigation, and Musgrave's intemperate pertinacity landed him in the Fleet Prison at the order of the Commons. Hence, by 1647, his attempts to find allies who would press his case had led him to the New Model Army. On 8 June 1647, he dedicated his *Fourth Word to the Wise* to Ireton: Cromwell's son-in-law, a senior officer in the New Model, and by then a 'local' Parliament-man.[47] This may have been sardonic: Ireton, a total outsider to the region, had been the nominee of the parliamentarian grandee Lord Wharton – the great patron of Barwis and his faction – to a very rotten borough. Instead, Musgrave's creative connections were with the Agitators. He had earlier read the writings of Lilburne and other Levellers, and he recommended them to his friends. He claimed to be co-operating with the Agitators from early 1647, and attributed his release from the Fleet Prison in July 1647 to the pressure they had exerted on the Council of the Army.[48] They certainly used Musgrave's denunciation of Cumberland's local governors as part of their propaganda against the crypto-Royalists and timeservers on the county committees.

The implications of all this are far-reaching. The 'evidence' of local–central tension conventionally employed by historians shows only that various political actors supposed that an attack on the committees would win or fix support for their respective causes: county committees *were* unpopular, and were subject to attacks phrased in an increasingly consistent language. But this language was developed and deployed by individuals, groups, and entities very much at the heart of the political world. It is not indicative of a visceral local hostility to Westminster, but part of the dialogic process that typifies relationships between centre and localities in this period.

III   THE LANGUAGES OF PROTEST: THE ABSENCE
OF A RHETORIC OF LOCAL PARTICULARISM

This textual analysis brings us to the substantive issues at the heart of this chapter. Further consideration of some of the incidents that we have discussed in relation to the development of this discourse indicates, most obviously, the diversity of local experience. More tellingly, they also demonstrate the complexity of this dialogue between centre and locality and the degree to which it cannot be comprehended within the framework of the old localist model. So, in 1646, Edward King chose to represent himself as the spokesman for a locality subject to the unsympathetic, even corrupt, administration of a committee stuffed with upstarts from beyond the traditional governing classes. Yet he had initially been the avatar of an alien entity, the Eastern Association, locked in conflict with gentlemen from the traditional ruling families of Lincolnshire. The latter – the old local establishment – never forgave him. His stand against the county committee was supported in the Commons by conservatives and traditionalists, allies of Prynne and Holles. But men of precisely the same stamp who represented Lincolnshire in Parliament, and with whom he had feuded in 1644, never accepted King's conversion. Incongruously, they joined with the radicals in their endeavours against King: to censure him and to crush their old enemy.[49]

The development of Musgrave's conflict with Barwis and his nominees to the Cumberland Committee is yet more complicated, producing a pattern of shifting alliances that seem intuitively 'unlikely', even 'bizarre'.[50] Barwis and his entourage of ex-Royalists, neutrals, and Prayer-Book Anglicans had, as Musgrave insisted, the most dubious credentials as enthusiasts for the parliamentarian cause. But there was no doubting their loathing for the Scots, who had occupied Carlisle and were living off the countryside – in part, because the local governors refused to supply them. The Cumberland Committee's subsequent and cynical protests at Scottish rapine and pillage were useful propaganda for the parliamentary Independents in their campaign against the intervention of the Scots in English politics. In consequence, the Independents protected their useful (if suspect) allies in the north from local denunciations. Musgrave's reluctance to accept the cover-up choreographed by the anti-Scots party in Parliament, his determination to secure a proper hearing of the peculation and logrolling of his local enemies – 'to remove oppressors from their seats and gaining justice for poor people' – resulted only in his imprisonment. Despite his being a godly separatist who refused to use the profane months of the year in his correspondence, he was consequently forced into an incongruous and ineffectual alliance with the Scots Commissioners and with High Presbyterians (like William Prynne) as he sought to secure a hearing for his charges and his own release from the Fleet Prison. Only in 1647, as we have seen, did Musgrave's search for allies in his crusade against Barwis lead him to the more congenial environment provided by the New Model Army.

But, amidst divergent experience and complex interaction, there is one essential uniformity. The language in which committees are denounced is common to the sectary Musgrave, the Presbyterian King, and the Glamorgan Royalists. That language is a language of the 'Ancient and fundamentall lawes of the Kingdome';[51] and its lodestones are 'Magna Carta and the Petition of Right'. Defences of local interests are expressed in a language of national identity; often they are published in forums such as Assizes and Quarter Sessions, which emphasize the role of the locality in a legally integrated nation. There is, at least until 1648, no alternative, localist language. I have always thought this the fundamental hurdle to those who wish to assert the quasi-independence of the 'local community'.

The point is reinforced by analysis of other incidents in the Civil War. At the outbreak of war in 1642 and early 1643, for instance, there are plenty of indications of a common desire to avoid the dreadful choice between king and Parliament; John Morrill has found efforts to neutralize the locality in twenty-two counties in this period.[52] They range from proposals to establish local 'third forces' designed to repel the troops of both partisans, as in Lincolnshire;[53] through attempts to negotiate local pacifications or demilitarization pacts, as in Cornwall in August 1642 (when the 'general desire to quiet this county' was noted);[54] to the organization of the county under the nominal control of one of the belligerents, as in Norfolk, while attempting to do as little as possible to mobilize the county's resources for any purpose other than internal defence. The mantra that fills the correspondence of the Norfolk gentry in the summer of 1642, 'the peace of my country [or county]', is typical of a widely held sentiment.[55] For Professor Morrill these kinds of behaviours marked 'the triumph of provincialism'. But this seems a very doubtful reading. They actually marked its *failure*. All these schemes failed. And they failed because, however powerful the fear and disgust roused by the prospect of war, these sentiments could not create an ideology designed to insulate localities from the demands of the state. It was not possible to 'estate ourselves in a civill independency ... to make every countie a free estate'. 'To call the conclusions of England to the bar of Yorkshire', as Sir John Hotham wrote sardonically of an attempt to create a treaty of neutrality in his native county, was simply not feasible within the framework of the dominant national constitutional ideology.[56]

This conclusion is reinforced by consideration of the Clubman movements in 1644 and 1645. The Clubmen were described by Professor Morrill in 1976 as 'the true champions of a fully developed provincialism and conservatism'; twenty years later, he still argued that they were challenging 'national bodies and values'.[57] The claim that they were conservatives is certainly true. But, as in 1642, there is little in their propaganda that suggests a particularist local ideology. Their challenge to the depredations and demands of the belligerents, the essence of their 'provincialism', is expressed almost entirely in the language of national identity, apparent in a constitution legitimized by antiquity and held together by the integument of a common law.

The Clubmen justified their organization and their challenge to the soldiery, by an appeal to the stated ideals of the belligerents enshrined in their propaganda: the values for which *they* were ostensibly fighting. The Dorset and Wiltshire Clubmen, for example, complained that 'our ancient laws and liberties, contrary to Magna Charta and the Petition of Right, are altogether swallowed up in the arbitrary power of the sword'.[58] In Worcestershire, in a statement issued by the king's Commissioners of Array and the Grand Jury (the mechanisms of local government which had been actively employed by Charles in the early stages of the war), a local mobilization was agreed 'to preserve and uphold the ancient privileges of Parliament, and the knowne lawes of the kingdome against all arbitrary government'.[59] As in Yorkshire in 1642, the Clubmen were also vulnerable through their inability to provide a justification for local independence higher than king or Parliament. The demands of the Glamorgan Clubmen, their opponents claimed, were 'that this county should be independent from all England', but they could show no 'authority' to warrant their position.[60]

The same issues are rehearsed again in the local protests that play into the second Civil War, in 1648. Actions and petitions repeatedly indicate the depth of the local revulsion against the demands and personnel of the parliamentarian county committees, an increasingly alien form of local government. The language of denunciation in this respect conformed to the paradigms now available in the tracts by Walker. Committees were stuffed with men 'of weak fortunes', who revelled in the expensive trappings of authority. The Kent Committee was alleged – improbably – to keep 'a seraglio [a harem]', where they upheld 'their state and princely Oeconomie' at the public charge. Their rule was arbitrary, directed to self-enrichment, and only supported by the handful of local 'Seperatists and sectaries'.[61] But, while the depredations of the local committees were emphasized, the standards against which their behaviours were judged, and the demands associated with the ending of their tyranny, were focused on national events and national standards of law and constitutional propriety. This was the case even in Kent, where the initial spark of rebellion was the product (in Brian Lyndon's words) of 'a particularly insensitive local administration'.[62] Across southern England in 1648, Grand Juries and petitioners in their public statements expressed their revulsion against the Vote of No Addresses (Parliament's resolution, passed in January 1648, to break off all further negotiation with the king), requiring that Parliament undertake a personal treaty with Charles, and demanding the disbandment of the army. All sought an immediate return to traditional constitutional norms and legal processes. The Kent petitioners insisted in mid-May

> that According to the Fundamentall Constitution of this Commonwealth, we may for the future be governed and judged by (the English Subjects' undoubted birth-right) the known and established Laws of the Kingdom, and not otherwise.[63]

Lyndon was right to insist that the intention of the local petitioners was not 'to exclude national politics from the shire, but to motivate Parliament to renewed effort'.[64]

But 1648 does provide evidence that some activists had recognized the limitations of a defence of local rights couched in terms of a national legal–ideological system. In Kent, there is an attempt to develop what has been termed a 'local-particularist' conceptual framework. So *The Manifest of the County of Kent* begins: 'We the knights, gentlemen and Franchlins of the county of Kent, the most free people of this late flourishing nation; by the wisdom and valour of our ancestors delivered from the laws of the conqueror . . .'.[65] The archaic usage 'Franchlins' (who later appear as 'Free-yeomen' in the tract) indicates an attempt to use the local legal system's peculiarities, and the mythological origins of these to create a distinct Kentish identity forged in armed struggle against William of Normandy. The same theme is picked up in other petitions, in narrative histories, and in heroic verse. But there is little evidence that these sentiments emerged from a popular culture or indicated a powerful localist sentiment galvanizing the county. Rather, this body of literature is a deliberate royalist ploy, often originating with outsiders like Roger L'Estrange – men who were troubled by the limitations on action imposed by the national constitutionalist language employed in the first Kentish petition, back in 1642, which had been borrowed from the Essex men and was in turn copied by other counties.[66] Its purchase on the cultural identity and actions of those fighting 'a plaine committee-war'[67] is questionable. Its most extreme manifestation is the historicizing poem, *Halesiados*, published in 1648:

> Reteine your pristine prowesse and make good
> That antient-line [of] all-uncorrupted blood . . .
> That Kentishmen were never conquer'd yet.[68]

But this is not a 'ballad' disseminated in the villages for popular consumption, as Everitt suggested.[69] Rather, it is the fantasy of a peculiarly jejune royalist zealot, written after the shattering victory of the New Model Army at Maidstone in the summer of 1648.[70] At best, the attempt to develop an ethos of provincial particularism indicates an awareness of the deficiencies of the existing discursive system as the basis for a violent challenge to central authority. It cannot, however, sustain a view of the intellectual coherence of the county community, even of 'the Community of Kent'. Paradoxically, the advent of royalist outsiders, eager to railroad the local movement on the king's behalf and ready to trumpet the unanimity of Kentishmen to that end, had the effect of splitting the anti-committee movement. Roger L'Estrange later denounced those 'Franklins' – whose pristine virtues he had once apostrophized – as 'thanklesse Peasants.'[71]

IV   CENTRAL POWER AND 'COMMON FOLK': THE DEFENCE OF LOCAL RIGHTS BELOW THE LEVEL OF THE ÉLITES

My final point is that a consciousness of national institutions as the necessary forum in which to advance local aspirations, and an awareness of the dominant discourse, had a wide social dissemination. Earlier studies have tended to view evidence for popular engagement in, say, the choice of sides at the outbreak of the war, or in the Clubman movement, as a matter of social ventriloquism: local élites organized their dependants, and gave them a voice. Recent work, however, has obliged a fundamental modification of such views. In many areas free from gentry dominance, local people made independent decisions, bargained within the complex structures of central authority, and expressed sophisticated views on national politics. Professor John Walter argues, for example, that the clothworkers of Colchester and its hinterland were mobilized for Parliament in 1642, not only by the easy slogans of anti-Popery, but also by the ideas of 'active citizenship' and participation, ideas vigorously promoted in the county by the parliamentary leadership, particularly the Earl of Warwick and his clerical myrmidons like Stephen Marshall.[72] In contrast, a similarly independent community, the lead miners of north-west Derbyshire, committed to the royalist side. These were men whose on-going defence of their property rights had obliged them to 'lobby every possible authority', and in 1642 they chaffered with the king to secure the best deal before providing the military support that he had solicited. We may doubt the wisdom of their choice. They may have done so too, given that it was later employed against them in representations to the Rump Parliament by landowners who sought to erode their customary rights. But their royalist commitment does not make them 'deferential simpletons'; they knew with whom to bargain, and the language in which to frame their negotiations.[73]

Clothworkers and lead miners – whether free from, or suspicious of, élite authority – displayed an independent political consciousness; but so, too, could the inhabitants of agricultural regions dominated by traditional tenurial patterns. The researches of Mark Stoyle on Devon and his survey of the scholarly work on other counties clearly indicate that a resident gentry was not invariably attended by a deferential tenantry. So, in north Devon, the presence of a numerous (if impoverished) group of royalist gentry made little impact in the face of the parliamentarian sympathies of the bulk of the population.[74]

The case of the Derbyshire lead miners does suggest a certain expediency in their attitude to national institutions and national languages of allegiance. They offered support to the side that promised them the fullest assistance in their on-going struggles.

The same could be said of the fenmen.[75] The rhetoric in which they phrased their resistance to drainage projects (which transferred ownership of the fens to the drainage entrepreneurs, thus destroying their livelihoods) indicates an acute sensitivity to the changing configurations of authority and priorities at the centre. The apologetic deference with which the fenmen addressed the king in the 1630s, or the House of Lords in 1640–2, transmuted into aggressive demands for legal and constitutional rights – rights for which they had taken up arms during the Civil War – in their petitions to the Rump Parliament after 1649. 'By the whole current of your declarations, the end of the late wars was to maintain, defend and secure our properties and fundamental legal rights,' they trumpeted in 1650.[76] In 1653, the fenmen changed their tune again, and adapted to the assumed religious priorities of the new (and short-lived) Nominated Parliament, which met that year. Their petitions and pamphlets assailed the now reviled Rump Parliament's corruption, and proclaimed their own status as 'a numerous godly pretious people'. The fenmen of Axholme had got things slightly wrong when, in 1650, they invited the Leveller duo of Lilburne and Wildman to lead their defiance of the fen drainers: for Leveller involvement was unlikely to enhance the Rump's sympathy for their case. But this incident indicates, as do the others, an awareness – however misguided – of the relevance of central politics for local societies, and of the legal and constitutional concerns exercising the national rulers at Westminster.

Even at a level below that of embattled communities like free-miners and fenmen, long used to advancing their claims to central institutions, still humbler men were fully conversant with similar agendas. They recognized the need to employ the complex machinery of the centre to achieve their local ends, and to deploy appropriate languages, whether of zealous religious conviction or of an integrated national law, to that end.

Even countrymen of royalist outlook, who pined for the pre-Civil War political order, proved themselves adept at exploiting the instrumentalities of central, Westminster-derived authority. The experience of the parishioners of Minster, in the Isle of Thanet, Kent, provides a case in point. In 1643, Richard Culmer, a Puritan clergyman, was intruded into the living of Minster by the Committee of Plundered Ministers (the Parliament-approved body that sought to replace royalist clergy throughout the country with 'godly' divines).[77] It was not a happy appointment. Culmer was intemperate and aggressive; a 'choleric man' by his own admission, committed to the High Calvinism of the 1645 *Directory of Public Worship* – Parliament's replacement for the now forbidden Book of Common Prayer. Culmer regarded his new flock as 'savages', traditionalists of the most benighted kind, whose preference was for 'a plum porridge priest'. His parishioners, in turn, complained that there was no communion or prayers during the Christmas holidays, and that Culmer would not read prayers at the graveside (a practice forbidden by the new *Directory*). They retaliated by refusing to demolish monuments of 'idolatry', to repair the church, or to pay their tithes. They covered the footpath from Ramsgate with 'fresh dung' to incommode the godly from that town who sought to attend Culmer's services. Perhaps predictably, they were wholly committed to the 1648 rising in Kent against parliamentarian rule: a godly parliamentarian activist was murdered in the village, while Culmer fled for his life, swimming the Stour in his haste to escape. Before Culmer returned with Fairfax's Army, which put down the Kentish revolt, the parishioners had re-instituted 'Service Book worship [that is, the Book of Common Prayer], Gloria Patri and Dominus Vobiscum'. Culmer sought assistance against his recalcitrant parishioners at Quarter Sessions, before the Kent County Committee (in its various manifestations), before the Committee of Plundered Ministers, and in the courts of Exchequer and Chancery.

But his opponents, the upholders of bucolic village traditionalism, gave as good as they got. They neglected the orders from the authorities, deriding the committees, and mocking even 'Parliament it self' as an impotent scarecrow 'on which every dog pisseth'.[78] But, paradoxically, these parishioners of Thanet, too, appealed to the County Committee of Kent and to the London-based Committee of Plundered Ministers. Moreover, when they heard that 'divers peers' were hawking on the Isle of Thanet with the Earl of Warwick, one of the most powerful parliamentarian grandees, they petitioned the earl against Culmer. Indeed, in their quest to be rid of their hated vicar, they also proffered the living of Minster to two members of the Westminster Assembly of Divines (the Parliament's advisory body of clergy established in 1643), who were tempted by the rich living until dissuaded from it by their censorious colleagues. The men of Minster knew how to make things work – and that even in defence of a measure of local autonomy, this entailed co-operation with agencies and individuals beyond the immediate locality.

V CONCLUSION

This chapter has challenged the localist account of central–local relations in the Civil War, with its emphases on the isolation of the localities and the alienation of local élites from the centre. I have argued for a more integrationist model, akin to that suggested twenty years ago by

Ann Hughes. Then, she insisted that Parliament was better able to extract resources from the provinces during the Civil War, and thus triumph over the king, because it was more successful in incorporating the localities into its war-effort.[79] Her argument had two aspects. First, Parliamentarians were able to locate the public image of governmental authority developed by the Tudors at the heart of their ideology; Royalists, by contrast, were motivated by their individual loyalty to a personal monarch. Her second point seems more paradoxical: she argued that the tensile and resilient strength of the parliamentarian administrative structure was a product of its piecemeal development and complexity. Parliament's provision of a range of inter-layered agencies ensured that disputes among parliamentarian supporters, or within the Parliament-controlled localities, were seldom absolutely determined. The participation of those appealing to the diffuse web of agencies that formed the 'centre' both maintained their engagement with the cause, thus keeping them on-side, and reinforced Parliament's preferred image as the upholder of public responsibility. This essay has argued a similar integrationist line. The war spawned a host of administrative agencies in the localities and at the centre, and those – at all levels of society – who sought to advance personal, sectional or local interests had to play the complex game of politics that was the consequence. Utilizing this system entailed the deployment of the Parliament's preferred rhetorical self-image. Local issues had to be comprehended within a language of national identity and of common law. Paradoxically, opposition to the demands of the centre took place most effectively at Westminster, and affirmed an ideology of national obligation, focused on Parliament as the 'representative of the people' and the bastion of the common law. In the absence of an alternative discourse, a 'Revolt *of* the Provinces' was simply impossible.

7. The Politics of Fairfax's Army, 1645–9

IAN GENTLES

Had there ever been an army like Sir Thomas Fairfax's? Most people in 1649, looking back on the recent purging of Parliament, the trial and execution of the king and the establishment of the English republic – all of which would have been unthinkable but for the interventions of that army – would have answered unhesitatingly: no. Yet the army's beginnings had been unpromising. In the spring of 1645, the Parliament had resolved to consolidate and centralize the three existing armies of the Earl of Essex, the Earl of Manchester and Sir William Waller. The new army's troop strength was set at 22,000, with the addition of another 2,000 or so officers. Like other armies of the time, its numbers would fluctuate wildly during the course of the war. Desertion (especially among the infantry, most of whom were conscripted), sickness, and death were the chronic causes of attrition. After major victories, large numbers of soldiers would creep away with their booty. There would then be frantic new efforts at recruitment to fill the depleted ranks. Called by some the 'New Model', Fairfax's army was derided by its foes in the spring of 1645 as the 'New Noddle'. Its friends fretted over Scottish hostility towards it; over how to pay its wages; and over whether its cavalry would be any match for the king's.

And yet it triumphed. Within two months of its taking the field, Sir Thomas Fairfax's army had delivered a crushing blow to the king at Naseby (14 June 1645); and from then until its invasion of Ireland, a little over four years later, it carried all before it, losing not so much as a skirmish. Reflecting on this unbroken chain of victories, one observer was certain that any honest witness 'will allow this army to be *fulmina belli* [the lightning-bolts of war], the thundering army by the best judges thought to have been sufficient to march all the world over'.[1] People in London also referred to it as 'the praying army'.[2] For, as victory piled upon victory, the soldiers themselves became convinced that they were the instrument of divine providence. Secure in this confidence, they eventually organized themselves politically: petitioning Parliament, electing regimental representatives ('Agitators'), creating an unprecedented General Council, drafting declarations and pamphlets, entering into a Solemn Engagement, and proclaiming to the world that they were 'not a meer mercenary army'.[3] Once politicized, the army invaded London in August 1647, and again in December 1648, to enforce its will on Parliament. In union with a radical minority in Parliament it became the engine that powered the revolutionary momentum of 1648–9, not only bringing the king to trial, but even proposing a new written constitution for the nation.

Almost since the first histories of these upheavals were written in the mid-seventeenth century, the army of Fairfax has been the subject of unflagging attention. The present essay will address four themes that continue to stir debate: the political background of the army's early history; aristocratic involvement in the army's politics; the influence of the Levellers on its membership; and finally, its role in the regicide – the seeming apogee of political radicalism in that turbulent decade. In examining these themes, this essay will also re-pose – and venture to answer – some of the unresolved questions to which the army's political history gives rise, and suggest an agenda for future research. But the starting point must be the army's own: was its creation simply a matter of military business-as-usual – or did it mark a controversial, and bitterly contested, innovation in the Parliament's conduct of its military affairs?

I THE CREATION OF SIR THOMAS FAIRFAX'S ARMY: FACTION AND ITS FORMS

In a pioneering article and subsequent monograph, Mark Kishlansky has argued that the New Model Army was the Long Parliament's 'final achievement of consensus decision-making' before it broke down irretrievably into factionalism and adversary politics. Its formation was 'a rather drab affair' which 'marked no great break with Parliament's past, no ascendancy of a "win-the-war" policy, and no feat of administrative genius'.[4] My reading of the evidence has led me to a very different conclusion: that the New Model was an army born out of irrepressible political conflict.

As early as the summer of 1643, powerful elements in Parliament and in London had become increasingly dissatisfied with the military performance of the Earl of Essex – the Parliamentarians' 'Captain-General' and commander-in-chief since the outbreak of the war in 1642. At first, those in favour of a stronger prosecution of the war had fastened their hopes on Sir William Waller, 'William the Conqueror' as he was popularly known, whose military fortunes during the opening year of the war were notably better than those of Essex, his aristocratic superior. A year later, however, as Waller stumbled and tripped over himself in his attempts to deliver the 'knock-out blow' to the Royalists, the shine had been rubbed off his reputation. Disappointment with the Earl of Manchester – the senior commander in East Anglia – was even keener. In 1643, he had put together the largest and most successful of Parliament's regional forces, the army of the Eastern Association; but after his army's impressive performance at the largest battle of the Civil War, at Marston Moor (2 July 1644), Manchester perplexingly sank into despondency. He brooded over the terrible destructiveness that he and his comrades had unleashed; and, more self-interestedly, reflected that, were the king to win but one major battle, he would be in a position to hang all his opponents for treason.

Manchester's apparent queasiness about the conduct of the war also brought him increasingly into conflict with his able cavalry commander, Oliver Cromwell. In the Eastern Association (the group of East Anglian counties whose forces Manchester commanded), Cromwell became disenchanted as he witnessed his commander-in-chief come under the influence of the army's Major-General, Lawrence Crawford, a Scot and a Presbyterian intent on persecuting officers whom he regarded as religiously sectarian. Manchester, for his part. saw Cromwell as a dangerous social and religious subversive.[5]

Manchester's, Essex's and Waller's poor conduct of the war made the win-the-war coalition in both Houses determined to wipe the slate clean of the old generals. Their most important target was the Earl of Essex, who headed the anti-Scots 'peace interest' at Westminster. As John Adamson has recently pointed out, plans to hobble, if not eliminate, the Earl of Essex as commander-in-chief went back at least to the passage of the ordinance for the Committee of Both Kingdoms in early 1644.[6] A principal purpose of that ordinance had been to remove the direction of the war from the hands of Essex and place it in the hands of an executive committee of the two Houses of Parliament, with representation from Scotland (which had just entered the war on the parliamentarian side), and controlled, for all practical purposes, by a distinct factional leadership.[7] Dominated by the architects and supporters of Parliament's alliance with the Scots – notably the Earl of Northumberland, Viscount Saye and Sele, the younger Sir Henry Vane and Oliver St John, the

committee consistently pursued the policies of the win-the-war party –
the 'fierie', 'hott' or 'violent spirits' as Sir Simonds D'Ewes labelled
them.[8]

But the major opportunity to destroy Essex politically was handed to
the war party by the Captain-General himself when he surrendered his
whole army to the only slightly less incompetent Charles I at Lostwithiel,
in Cornwall, in early September 1644. The radicals seized on Essex's
discomfiture to promote a wholesale restructuring of Parliament's
armies in the aftermath of this catastrophic defeat. Besides launching an
investigation into this debacle (the 'loss of the West'), the Committee of
Both Kingdoms – Parliament's war-party-dominated executive – also set
up a subcommittee 'to draw Instructions for the Armyes of the Lord
Manchester's and Sir William Waller'.[9] As John Adamson has established, the creation of this subcommittee laid the legislative foundation
for the amalgamation of the existing southern parliamentary armies into
a single army under centralized command. The initial form of this
centralization was to be a new council or Committee of War, compris-
ing the delegates of the Committee of Both Kingdoms and the six chief
commanders: Essex, Manchester, Waller, Cromwell, Sir Arthur
Hesilrige, and Lord Robartes. The Lord General was henceforth merely
one voice on this committee, yet he was obliged to promulgate orders
made by the majority as though they were his own. By mid-October
1644, this Committee of War had taken two major decisions: the existing southern forces were to be fused into a single army; and that army
was to have a unified high command, responsible to the Committee of
Both Kingdoms. Essex's inability to resist the corrosion of his power
owed not a little to the continuing investigation of the loss of the West
and the damaging accusations made against his own colonels.[10]

It was against this backdrop of a devastating loss of political and military power that, in the late autumn of 1644, Essex decided to forge an
alliance with the Scots, who now shared his desire for a lenient settlement with the king. This factional realignment was evident by early
December 1644, when the Scots Commissioners in London, and Essex
and his leading supporters in the Commons, Denzell Holles and Sir
Philip Stapilton, held discussions to counter what they saw as 'a high and
mighty plot for the Independent party to have gotten an army for themselves under Cromwell'.[11] Essex wanted to bring down Cromwell by
having him indicted as an 'incendiary' for fomenting conflict between
England and Scotland. But Bulstrode Whitelocke, a Commons lawyer
whom Essex consulted, counselled caution. When it came to political

manoeuvre, Whitelocke emphasized, none was more adroit than Cromwell, 'a gentleman of quick and subtle parts'.[12] Essex and his supporters accordingly drew back. Yet compelling evidence of the Independent 'plot' came to light a few days later, when Zouche Tate, chairman of the Commons Committee for the Reformation of the Army, introduced a resolution for a 'Self-Denying Ordinance' – a bill to deprive members of both Houses of all civilian and military offices obtained since the outbreak of the war. On the surface this was an even-handed proposal to eliminate conflicts of interest and corruption in Parliament's war-effort by requiring all members of both Houses to make a choice: to resign either their parliamentary seats, or their military and civilian commissions. However, the even-handedness of this requirement was vitiated by the fact that while it was a relatively straightforward matter for a member of the Commons to resign his seat in order to keep his offices (though none, in fact, did so), a peer could not renounce his membership of the House of Lords, as there was no mechanism for the renunciation of hereditary titles. In effect, the requirement of Self-Denial excluded the parliamentarian peers from further military participation in the war.

Contemporaries were acutely aware of who stood to gain or lose by the passage of the Self-Denying Ordinance. Of the twenty-four commanders who were required to give up their commissions under this ordinance, only ten were either war-party supporters or of uncertain allegiance; the majority were adherents of the Earl of Essex.[13] The parliamentarian newsbook, *The Kingdomes Weekly Intelligencer*, commented melodramatically that the resolution for Self-Denial was part of a radical scheme to put 'Anabaptists and Brownists' in command of the army.[14] Indeed, Essex's lawyer friend Bulstrode Whitelocke noted that the resolution – far from being the final achievement of 'consensus politics' (as has been claimed by Professor Kishlansky) – 'was set on by that party who contrived the outing of the Lord General, and to bring on their own designs'.[15] It is hardly surprising, then, that the proposal to exempt Essex from the provisions of the Self-Denying Ordinance provoked a six-hour Commons debate, after which it was 'with some difficulty' rejected by a narrow margin of 100 to 93.[16]

But the legislation still had to win the assent of a majority in the House of Lords. Unsurprisingly, when the resolution was sent up to the peers, it was blocked there by the Essexian faction in the upper House. Thanks to their bitter opposition, Self-Denial did not become law for almost another four months.[17] During that time, the Vane–St John-led majority in the Commons (the supporters of the war party) executed an outflanking strategy against the Lords' refusal to sanction a purge of the existing military leadership. They merely went ahead and set up a new southern army, with new commanders. The three existing armies (commanded respectively by Essex, Manchester and Waller) were bled of their officers and men in order to fill up the new one. The three established armies were likewise denied funding, as most of the Parliament's revenues were devoted to the new force. Finally, demoralized and in a state of imminent disintegration, the remnants of the existing armies were transferred to the new force. Essex and his allies had been outmanoeuvred. Having refused to step aside gracefully, the Essexian peers and their Commons supporters found the rug had been unceremoniously pulled from beneath their feet.[18]

By mid-February 1645, the organization and financial framework of the new army were in place.[19] As Adamson has pointed out, the war party then saw to it that this 'newly modelled' force remained firmly under its own control, by setting up a new Committee of the Army under the chairmanship of Robert Scawen, the burgess (or representative in the Commons) for Berwick-upon-Tweed, and a senior member of the household of the Earl of Northumberland – one of the most influential advocates of the recent military reforms.

With this administrative framework in place, the Commons set about the sensitive task of choosing the army's commanders. At least one observer recognized the selection of the commanding officers for the ploy that it was: a means for circumventing the Lords' rejection of the Self-Denying Ordinance. By approving a slate of nominees, none of which was a member of *either* House, the war party would be able to achieve their end 'as well as if the said ordinance were passed'.[20] Indeed, largely for this reason, the nominations – from the commander-in-chief down to the lowliest infantry captain – were hotly contested in both Houses. The vote to appoint Sir Thomas Fairfax as Captain-General – who was then serving as commander of the horse in Parliament's Yorkshire-based northern army – was a straightforward trial of strength between the war and peace parties: the tellers for the ayes (the supporters of the proposal) being Vane junior and Cromwell, while the tellers for the noes (its opponents) were the same men who had earlier tried to exempt Essex from the provisions of the Self-Denying Ordinance: Holles and Stapilton. This time the pro-Essex party could muster only 69 votes, but the number who voted for Fairfax – 101 – was almost identical to the number who had voted against Essex back in December 1644.[21]

Fairfax owed his nomination in part to his achievements in the northern army during 1643–5; but he also owed it to his reputation as a friend and ally of the anti-Essex group in Parliament.[22]

The Commons then proceeded to name the veteran career-soldier Philip Skippon, the Major-General of Essex's army, as commander of the infantry, but left the generalship of the cavalry vacant. Colonels of the twenty-three regiments were approved – men of widely differing political and religious positions, as well as a handful of Scots, but with war-party men in the majority. It was left to Fairfax to bring forward names for the ranks below that of colonel. While Fairfax's nominations were far from uncontested in the Commons, they ran into much heavier weather in the Lords, where they were subjected to microscopic scrutiny for four days. Essex and Manchester took a close interest in the business, and suggested many changes in the regiments drawn from their respective armies.[23] The Scots Commissioners also joined the fray, intervening with a long letter to the Lords that voiced their dissatisfaction at not having been consulted in the Committee of Both Kingdoms over the making of the list.[24] In all, the Essexian peers attempted to alter 57 (or close to a third) of Fairfax's 193 nominations. Overwhelmingly, the officers of whom they disapproved were friends of Cromwell, enemies of Manchester, religious radicals, or Independents – or men who would later publicly show themselves to be such. By contrast, those whom the Essexians wished to promote, or to introduce into the army, were political moderates, religious Presbyterians, or kinsmen or protégés of the Earl of Essex.[25]

Apart perhaps from Sir Simonds D'Ewes, commentators at the time were not gulled by the Lords' claim that the struggle over the officer-list stemmed from their professed concern to improve the calibre of the men selected.[26] It was widely known that there had been 'much strife and contention' – most of it faction-related – over the list.[27] The war-party supporter Peregrine Pelham, for instance, complained that it had been 'much obstructed in the Lords' House'.[28] More explicitly, the acute and well-informed diarist and officer in the London Trained Bands, Thomas Juxon, interpreted the peers' obstructionism as an attempt to put out 'not only Independents, but such as were good, and putting in most vilde [vile] persons of both nations [English and Scots], [by] which [it] appears . . . how little they regard the good of the [English] nation, their peerage [i.e. their status as noblemen] being their great idol'.[29]

Yet Essex's attempts to overthrow Fairfax's nominations were of no effect. To break the deadlock between the Essexian majority in the upper House and the majority in the lower (led by Vane, St John and Cromwell), the Commons-men devised what was termed 'une ruse bien subtile': they prevailed upon the London Common Council to make a loan of £80,000 they had promised to fund the army contingent on there being no tampering with Fairfax's list.[30] Even so, the peers did not give up easily. When the Northumberland–Saye group in the Lords (which had supported Fairfax's proposals from the outset) moved to pass the list as it had been sent up by the Commons, the House was equally divided on the motion. At this point, Viscount Saye pulled a rabbit out of his hat: a proxy from the octogenarian Earl of Mulgrave, who also happened to be Sir Thomas Fairfax's grandfather. The list accordingly passed by the smallest possible margin: twelve votes to eleven (with ten of the defeated eleven bitterly recording their 'dissents' or public protests against the vote).[31] The Scots commissioners were equally discontented. They later complained that 'the officers of the Scottish nation who have been formerly employed in the service of the Parliament are now removed from their respective charges'.[32] Commenting on what was unmistakably a war-party victory, Thomas Juxon relished the fact that 'this very much weakens the Presbyterian and Lord General's and Scots' party'.[33]

The last attempt by the Essexians to impede what was rapidly becoming the unstoppable New Model juggernaut came when Parliament turned to filling the as yet vacant Lieutenant-Generalship of the cavalry (the army's second-in-command). The City magistrates wanted Cromwell, as did the war party in both the Commons and the Lords. However, the Essexian majority in the Lords procrastinated for months; it did not finally relent and give grudging approval for even a limited, three-month appointment, until after Cromwell had performed with distinction on the battlefield at Naseby in June 1645.[34]

To sum up: ever since the summer of 1643 when the first murmurs of discontent had been heard against the Earl of Essex's uninspired leadership, there had been factional conflict in Parliament over who should direct its war-effort – and to what end. Debate centred on the question of whether there should be several armies under separate commands, or one unified army under a centralized command. In the end, the win-the-war faction (under Northumberland and Saye in the Lords, and Vane, St John and Cromwell in the Commons) defeated the Essex–Warwick–Stapilton coalition by their creation of a 'new-modelled', amalgamated force. They achieved this in the teeth of bitter opposition from the Essexians. Far from springing from a desire for 'consensus' and unity, the New Model was a factional project from its outset, and left a legacy of division that lasted well into the late 1640s.

II FACTION AND THE GRANDEES: THE NEW MODEL'S POLITICS AND ADMINISTRATION

Recent historians have argued that both in the beginning stages of the Civil War and later, almost until the time of the king's trial, key members of the nobility made a vital contribution to the parliamentary war-effort.[35] To all appearances, the Self-Denying Ordinance put an end to any aristocratic participation in the parliamentary war-effort. The reality was different, however. In its final version, the ordinance left the way open for those who had been excluded to be reappointed – and Cromwell was not the only individual to benefit from this modification. By 1648, for example, the Earl of Warwick (another of the noblemen forced to resign in 1645) was back as Admiral of the Fleet. More significantly, as recent research has demonstrated, the peers, while they held no actual commands in the New Model, continued to be intimately involved in army politics from the time of its creation at least until late 1647. As we have seen, it was war-party peers who were largely instrumental in securing the appointment of Sir Thomas Fairfax as Captain-General of the new army.[36] In fact, old Lord Fairfax and his son, Sir Thomas, were well connected with both peace- and war-party peers. In late 1644 and early 1645, for example, Lord Fairfax's principal correspondents included, besides Lord Wharton, the Earl of Mulgrave (his father-in-law), the Earls of Manchester and Clare, and Lords Howard of Escrick and Willoughby of Parham – and, perhaps most significantly, Algernon Percy, the tenth Earl of Northumberland, one of the most influential of all the Westminster grandees.[37] This Percy connection was of major importance for the Fairfaxes, providing them with a powerful ally on the Committee of Both Kingdoms, and a parliamentary patron with extensive influence in both Houses.

Crucial to the success of the New Model was the regular infusion of money and supplies that enabled it to stay in the field for the fifteen months it took to defeat the forces of Charles I. Part of this was due to Parliament's success in creating a lucrative market that London merchants were only too happy to supply, as they trailed after the army and sold it the food it required.[38] More importantly, the army's efficient supply was the result of a body whose importance has only recently been recovered, in an article by John Adamson, after generations of archival neglect: the Committee for the Army, a committee of Lords and Commons created on 31 March 1645, contemporaneously with the military reforms.[39] Much of the New Model's extraordinary logistical strength can be regarded as the achievement of this committee. This, too, was a highly partisan body. The committee was dominated by war-party members, of whom Northumberland and Saye were probably the most influential on the Lords' side; of its Commons contingent (who shouldered most of the day-to-day work), by far the most assiduous member was the committee's chairman Robert Scawen, a man who spent most of his adult career in Northumberland's service.

So, too, with the so-called 'Derby House Committee', the Parliament's major executive council of the period 1646–9. It was this committee which provided the cockpit for the struggle for control of military and political affairs after late 1646, when it replaced the Committee of Both Kingdoms as Parliament's chief executive committee. Except for a short period of Presbyterian dominance (from April to June 1647), the Northumberland group and other 'Independent' allies dominated the Committee, and were able to maintain a watching brief for the New Model Army.[40]

Likewise, aristocratic supporters of the army played a key role in promoting the projected settlement known as the Heads of the Proposals in the summer of 1647. As David Scott has suggested, the document was perhaps a reworking of the peace initiative that the Independent and army grandees, in collaboration with a group of royalist Privy Councillors centred on the Duke of Richmond and the Marquess of Hertford, had laid before the king at Newcastle in September 1646.[41] Its terms, the most generous that Charles was ever offered in England, were put before the army's General Council in mid-July 1647. The balance of evidence suggests that the primary draftsman of the Heads – at least in this later recension – was Commissary-General Henry Ireton, Cromwell's son-in-law.[42] Colonel John Lambert also assisted in its preparation, while Cromwell undoubtedly had an input into the document, since, as Sir Lewis Dyve observed, he and 'his Cabbinett Counsell, which are the Lord Say, Saint Jon and Vaine the younger . . . now steer the affaires of the wholl kingdome'.[43] There is clear evidence that the Northumberland–Saye group played an important role in promoting the Proposals once they had been agreed upon. We know, for instance, that Ireton was in daily contact with Lord Wharton, one of the parliamentary commissioners residing at army headquarters; and that Saye seems to have become more engaged with army affairs as time went on. By the autumn of 1647, a royalist newsbook writer could report that Saye often attended meetings of the Council of the Army, where he acted 'as adjutator generall'.[44]

The army grandees' awareness that their most effective friends politically were in the upper House is demonstrated, for instance, by the attempts made by Cromwell to prevail on John Lilburne to cease his public attacks on the Lords' House, and by his refusal to secure Lilburne's release from his imprisonment in the Tower of London in the autumn of 1647. For similar reasons, Cromwell withdrew his support for Colonel Thomas Rainborowe's bid to be appointed Vice-Admiral of the parliamentary fleet.[45] Quietly and behind the scenes, the grandees attempted to mollify the prickly Lilburne by permitting him to leave his cell in the Tower and walk abroad during the day, granting him a small sum from the army's petty cash, paying his arrears, and twice authorizing him to receive large sums of money from the Treasurers-at-War on behalf of his brother's foot regiment.[46] But there was no question of alienating the army's supporters among the nobility.

For the army, this all paid handsome dividends. During the autumn of 1647, Saye and Wharton introduced papers that essentially duplicated the Heads of the Proposals into the Lords' House, where, unsurprisingly, they were accepted.[47] Two weeks later, on 28 October they resumed the debate, now over the Commons' amendments to their legislation.[48] All these steps were taken after careful consultation with the grandees at Putney.[49] This projected settlement, embodied in the Heads of the Proposals, was effectively killed by Charles's flight from military custody at Hampton Court on 15 November, and his subsequent negotiation of a military alliance with the Scots in December. From this point onward, the political objectives of the army leaders increasingly diverged from those of their erstwhile aristocratic supporters.

The fact that it could and *did* diverge attests clearly to the nature of that earlier relationship: it rested principally on a congruency of ideals and objectives, not on some simplistic notion of one group being the string-pullers of the other. That divergence eventually came with Charles's refusal to accept an ultimatum proffered to him by Parliament in December 1647 and the Parliament's decision the following month – under heavy army pressure – to pass the Vote of No Addresses: a drastic measure meant to cut off all further communication between Parliament and the king. Vehemently promoted by Ireton and Cromwell on the floor of the Commons, it passed in the teeth of strenuous opposition. In the

Lords, it proved more controversial still, despite (or because of) its unanimous endorsement by the General Council of the Army. Only after a
regiment of horse and foot, respectively, were stationed in Whitehall and
a guard of 500 thrown around the Houses of Parliament did the House
of Lords agree to ratify the Vote.[50] The Earl of Northumberland spoke
powerfully against it, and from that moment, almost until the regicide,
he remained a steadfast proponent of a negotiated peace with the king.
Throughout the second Civil War, Northumberland's 'interest' maintained close links with Sir Thomas Fairfax, but relations with most of the
other army grandees became increasingly strained.[51]

These vignettes give some impression of the new narrative – and with
it, a new *dramatis personae* – that is beginning to emerge for the 1640s. In
short, the anti-Essex peers of 1645–6, led by Northumberland, Saye and
Wharton, were instrumental in launching the 'new-modelling' of
Parliament's armies; in seeing that the new army enjoyed adequate
financial and logistical support; and in resisting its dismemberment at
the hands of the Hollis–Stapilton group at the end of the first Civil War.
In 1647, collaboration between these peers and the army leadership was
at its most intense, as both groups sought to achieve a rapprochement
with the king based on the Heads of the Proposals. Only after the army
grandees turned against the king – in response to his decision to fight a
new civil war in 1648 – and became his implacable enemies, did their
close alliance with the peers begin to disintegrate.

III   THE LEVELLERS AND THE ARMY'S RADICALIZATION: REALITY OR MIRAGE?

For the past three decades, the question of the degree to which the radical, civilian, London-based movement known as the Levellers infiltrated
and influenced the New Model Army in the spring and summer of 1647
has been strongly contested.[52] In one respect, there is nothing to debate:
no known reference to the Levellers in contemporary sources has been
found before November 1647 when a royalist news-writer (who may well
have been Marchamont Nedham) suggested that the authors of the *Case
of the Armie Truly Stated* 'have given themselves a new name vizt. Levellers
. . .'.[53] A slightly different version of the same story is found in the royalist newsbook *Mercurius Pragmaticus* (which *was* written by Nedham), in
which he gives the credit for christening the radical Agitators as
'Levellers' to no less a personage than the king: 'a most apt title for such

a despicable and desperate knot to be known by, that indeavor to cast downe and level the inclosures of nobility, gentry and propriety, to make us all even: so that every Jack shall vie with a gentleman and every gentleman be made a Jack'.[54] Later, John Lilburne was to assert that it was the army grandees who had 'baptized' the London radicals Levellers.[55] Regardless of who is responsible for the name, an organization that was unknown to contemporaries before November 1647 can hardly be alleged to have influenced the New Model Army (or anyone else) prior to that date.

A more telling argument against Leveller influence on the army has been formulated by John Morrill. He reminds us that the Leveller programme was implicitly anti-army: it deplored Parliament's crushing burden of taxes and the arbitrary methods used to collect them, calling for the radical decentralization of government, if not the withering away altogether of the state. By contrast, the army depended for its very existence on a highly centralized government powerful enough to exact the high levels of taxation required to support it. Its economic interests were utterly incompatible with Leveller objectives. That – so the argument runs – was why ultimately there was no Leveller takeover of the army.[56]

Other historians have been still more dismissive of the suggestion that Levellers may have exercised influence within the New Model. Mark Kishlansky has sweepingly dismissed the work of Woodhouse, Wolfe, Brailsford, Morton, Aylmer and Thomas with the assertion: 'the Levellers and the army were separate and fundamentally divergent movements. Their contact was sporadic and their common causes few.'[57] Finally, John Morrill and Phil Baker have advanced convincing reasons for viewing the October 1647 tract *The Case of the Armie Truly Stated* – a key manifesto in the army's radicalization and one previously supposed to have been a Leveller-inspired work written by John Wildman – as an internally produced army document 'by and for an army'; its most likely primary author was an Agitator from Fairfax's own horse regiment, trooper Edward Sexby.[58]

Cogent though these arguments are, a fresh look at the evidence suggests that two important modifications are necessary. First, from 1646 onward there was a loose grouping of London 'activists' or radical Independents, who sometimes called themselves the 'Godly party' (as, of course, did many such groups), many of whom later became known as Levellers. It was these radical Londoners who, early in 1647 if not before, recognized the potential importance of the New Model Army, now threatened with extinction, and who determined to campaign for its continued existence. Secondly, there is considerable evidence of a receptiveness, between 1647 and 1649, within the army, to Leveller ideas: limitations of space permit only a few quotations from the large number of radical London spokesmen – most of whom can be identified with the group subsequently known as Levellers – who remonstrated in defence of the New Model Army in the spring and summer of 1647.[59]

In May 1647, for example, John Lilburne, the most prominent of the London radicals, described the New Model as 'this innocent army', whose demands were 'rationall, just and equitable'.[60] Around the same time, Lilburne – then imprisoned in the Tower for defaming various Presbyterian peers – decided to try to harness the army's discontent against Parliament to his own cause.[61] He sought both release from prison and compensation for the suffering he had earlier undergone, back in the 1630s, at the hands of the Star Chamber. Another of these London radicals, William Walwyn, also became deeply involved in army affairs at this time – like 'thousands [who] then owned the proceedings of the Army, and ventered their lives for them'. Walwyn visited Cromwell several times at his house in Drury Lane, and persuaded him (he claimed) to abandon Parliament and throw in his lot with the army. Conversely, Walwyn 'was by very eminent persons of the Army, sent for to Reading [in the course of 1647] to be advised withal touching the good of the people'.[62] While Lilburne comes across as a blusterer (did he *really* 'settle the soldiers in a compleat and just posture'?),[63] Walwyn, in almost all his writings, reads like a man whose ego is firmly under control, and whose testimony is sure. A third figure in this group, Richard Overton – another figure who had fallen foul of the Presbyterian-dominated House of Lords – weighed in, in July 1647, with an impassioned appeal to the army to take up his cause against the House of Commons. To the Agitators, his advice was to preserve the power that the rank and file had entrusted to them, and to be 'cautious and wary' towards their officers.[64]

How did the army respond to this extended (if sometimes self-interested) wooing by London radicals? While the soldiers could only have been encouraged by the knowledge that they enjoyed strong civilian support in the capital, they nevertheless remained at all times the managers of their own political agenda. They did not need Lilburne or Walwyn to teach them principles of democratic organization. The well-known examples, such as the mutinous Spanish soldiers in Flanders, who had elected representatives out of every company and organized themselves into a Council, were their probable source of inspiration.[65] Nor did the rank and file allow the appeals of Lilburne and Overton to drive a wedge between them and their officers. Revisionist historians have rightly insisted on the essential unity of purpose between officers and men during the late spring and summer of 1647.[66] Indeed, the account book kept by William Clarke at army headquarters establishes that the Agitators' living, travel and printing expenses were fully covered by the general staff during this critical period.[67]

Yet, despite the strong bond between officers and rank and file, there is evidence that elements in the army were strongly drawn to embrace the broader political programme promoted by the City radicals. Even the officers, in their *Petition and Vindication* of 27 April 1647, told Parliament that it was 'the greatest point of honer to stand by you till the consummation of your worke, the removall of every yoake from the people's necks, and the establishment of those good lawes you shall judge necessary for the Commonwealth'.[68] Among the papers collected by William Clarke, the secretary of the Army's Council, is an unpublished 'Heads of demands made to the parliament', which reflects the unmistakable influence of civilian radicals. Calling for a reform of election abuses, it advocated annual elections, and closed with a ringing assertion of the sovereignty of the people, 'princes and parliaments being but the kingdome's great servants, intrusted for their weale, not for their woe'.[69] There was also considerable and sympathetic interest within the army when the Commons ordered the burning of radical petitions by the common hangman – that ultimate gesture of parliamentary disapproval. One group within the army declared that 'the meanest subject should fully enjoy his right, libertie and proprieties in all things', a demand that contained an implicit threat that a measure of 'levelling' might be required to achieve such a state.[70] Such broad-ranging political concerns also animated individual regiments. Fairfax's own horse regiment, for example, opposed the expedition to Ireland until 'the reall freedome of the free people of England be established'. The foot regiments of Fairfax and Hewson took up the cause of 'those free men of England [Lilburne and Overton] soe much deprived of their libertie . . .'[71] It was also at least in part because of chivvying by City radicals that the rank-and-file Agitators pressured the officers for a march on London in June and July 1647.[72] Revealingly, however, when a committee of senior officers summarized the grievances of the different regiments, they deleted these radical expressions, disingenuously assuring the parliamentary commissioners that the regimental papers had been 'confused and full of tautologies, impertinencies, or weaknesses answerable to soldiers dialect'.[73] The officers, not yet ready for violent political action, confined their summary to 'what pertains unto them as soldiers'.[74]

By the end of the summer of 1647, many soldiers had become disillusioned, not just by such tendentious editing, but by the officer grandees' protracted efforts to reach a settlement with the king. The recruitment of new men to fill the vacancies in many regiments gave some urban radicals the opportunity to enlist for the sole purpose of influencing the army's political agenda. It is perhaps no accident that new Agitators emerged in five cavalry regiments around this time, or that shortly afterwards several other regiments threw up new, still more radical Agitators. In mid-October these 'new Agitators' lobbed a grenade, in the shape of a tract entitled *The Case of the Armie Truly Stated*, into the deliberations of the General Council of the Army at Putney. Anchoring themselves to the principle that 'all power is originally and essentially in the whole body of the people of this nation', they called for a revolution that would include the dissolution of the present Parliament, the holding of biennial elections thereafter, and the extension of voting to 'all the freeborn men of England', as well as the granting of religious liberty and freedom from conscription.

When the tract came before the General Council, it was referred to a committee of field officers and Agitators with instructions to vindicate the army from the aspersions cast upon it. But the day before this committee was to report, Robert Everard, one of the new soldier-Agitators from Cromwell's horse regiment, delivered to headquarters a new and even more disconcerting document entitled *An Agreement of the People*. It had been approved that very day at a meeting of the agents of the five regiments, in addition to other soldiers, plus John Wildman and 'divers country-gentlemen'. Whether its primary author was William Walwyn or John Wildman,[75] its brevity, clarity and sophistication made it a far more arresting document than *The Case of the Armie*. It contained two concepts novel in English political thought. The first was the idea of a written constitution that would attain higher authority than any mere Act of Parliament through being signed by all the freeborn men of England. The second was the concept of powers that were reserved to the people alone and which could not be exercised by any Parliament or governing authority. These included the power of military conscription, the power to legislate on religion, the power to violate the principle of equality before the law, and the power to question or punish anyone for what they had said or done during the Civil War.[76]

At the General Council meeting of 28 October the *Agreement* was strenuously opposed by the officer grandees, who tried to paint its proponents as men who wanted to abolish all government and have all property held in common.[77] Over the several days during which the debate dragged on, however, the officer grandees gradually lost ground to the Levellers and their sympathizers. Clearly, the Leveller influence at Putney was significantly more important than Morrill and Baker have argued. It also had an effect. In the end, the General Council agreed, with only three dissenting votes, that all soldiers should have the vote, as well as anyone else who was not a servant or a beggar.[78] This proved too much for the army's second-in-command, Oliver Cromwell. Frustrated by this turn of events, and worried about the increasingly hostile denunciations of the king emanating from some regiments, Cromwell carried a motion on 8 November to send the Agitators back to their regiments, thereby bringing these alarmingly innovatory deliberations on England's 'constitutions' to a peremptory end.

How did he pull this off? The answer seems to lie in a combination of Fairfax's prestigious support, widespread worries among the officers about army disunity, and the promise that there would be a rendezvous of *all* the regiments, at which the recommendations of the General Council would be heard and put forward for approval.

Unhappy with this move to divert the army from its political concerns, London Levellers and army radicals from two regiments co-operated to stage a mutinous demonstration on behalf of the *Agreement of the People* at the rendezvous near Ware on 15 November. This attempted radical hijacking of the army was ruthlessly put down by the senior officers.[79] A few days later in the Commons, Cromwell explained why he had concluded that the Levellers had to be suppressed: it was, indeed, their 'drive at a levelling and paritye'.[80] What he did not say, but clearly meant his listeners to understand, was that the Levellers had also gained entirely too much influence within the army, to the point where they constituted a challenge to the authority of the high command.

Yet, within less than a year, following the recrudescence of Civil War in 1648 – a second searing experience of fire and sword – the officer grandees found themselves much less hostile to the Levellers. Baffled by the desire of the majority in both Houses to seek, yet again, an accommodation with the king, they again feared destruction at the hands of Holles and his party. Looking about for friends, they gravitated towards the London Levellers, who in their 'Large Petition' of 11 September 1648 called for justice upon 'the capitall authors and promoters of the former or late wars'.[81] Army militants now combined with political radicals to un-dam a torrent of petitions and letters from regiments and garrisons up and down the country calling for justice against the authors of the recent war – a group that obviously included King Charles himself. Many also supported the Levellers' brand of radical social reform.[82]

In this volatile atmosphere Fairfax summoned the Council of Officers to the Abbey Church of St Albans, where Ireton introduced a draft paper shortly to be known as the *Remonstrance of the Army*. In it, Ireton aligned the army with the Levellers by explicitly endorsing the *Agreement of the People*. When, in turn, the *Remonstrance of the Army* was laid before the Commons on 20 November 1648, it called on Parliament to adopt the programme of the Leveller 'Large Petition' of 11 September, and to establish a constitution grounded in a new *Agreement of the People*.[83]

A revised draft of the *Agreement of the People* was debated by the Council of Officers in Whitehall in December 1648 and January 1649. The drafters of the new version of the *Agreement* had taken the measure of political realities. All who had supported the king in any way were to be denied the vote for seven years. Anyone who opposed the *Agreement* was to be permanently excluded.[84] And while most historians have over-looked the restrictive nature of the franchise under this second *Agreement*, this aspect was not missed by its many critics at the time. Even the editor of the friendly newsbook *The Moderate*, conceded that the *Agreement* would initially disenfranchise a large segment of the people.[85]

As Ireton's frequent and lengthy interventions tend to suggest, the *Agreement* was a document that genuinely mattered to him. If the debate had merely been a sop to keep the radicals quiet ('like children with rattles', in Lilburne's sardonic phrase),[86] to distract them while the grandees got on with the real business of cutting off the king's head, it is hard to see why Ireton expended so much time, and made himself so disliked, in his efforts to make the document say what he wanted it to say. On religious toleration, he got his way: freedom, there would be (except for Anglicans and Papists), while Protestant Christianity would remain the public religion of the nation, with a ministry maintained out of public revenue.

But the lower officers rallied to defeat Ireton on two other issues: his attempt to delete the prohibition against *ex post facto* legislation; and secondly, his attempt to give Parliament power over moral questions.[87] The amended version of the second *Agreement*, henceforth known as the 'Officers' Agreement of the People', was laid before the Commons by a high-level delegation of officers on the opening day of the king's trial: 20

January. The Commons ordered this version of the *Agreement* printed, and promised to consider it soon.[88] They never did; and the officers never reminded them of their promise, inevitably raising the possibility that the whole business was a charade, and that the higher officers had no wish for the *Agreement* ever to be implemented. It is true that the *Agreement* had few passionate supporters in Parliament, among the gathered churches (the Independent congregations), or even among the Levellers, who were more worked up about decentralizing authority and promoting economic freedom than about restructuring government. Within the army, the victories of the lower officers against the grandees probably caused the latter to become lukewarm in their support for a document that they had earlier seriously regarded as a projected constitution for England. In any event, the *Agreement* was pushed to the political sidelines, and soon forgotten by almost everyone – everyone, that is, except John Lilburne.

Fury at his betrayal over the *Agreement of the People* led Lilburne, along with other Leveller leaders, to unleash a series of intemperate, reckless attacks on the army grandees in February and March 1649. And by indulging in such unbridled expressions of anger they landed themselves in the Tower on charges of treason, and thus wrote off any further hope of influencing the army. On 1 May, from their place of imprisonment, they issued the movement's last and most radical version of the *Agreement of the People*, in which they gave full vent to their hatred of standing armies and expressed their dream of a decentralized, minimally-governed, libertarian England.[89]

Between March and September 1649 a series of army mutinies at Banbury, Burford, Northampton, Oxford and elsewhere – collectively labelled 'the Leveller rising' – manifested sympathy for the Leveller programme.[90] Yet these risings were quickly put down, thereby terminating the brief and awkward alliance between the Leveller movement and the leadership of the New Model Army.

To recapitulate: in early 1647, when the army's survival was under threat from the Presbyterian faction led by Stapilton and Holles, it was radical Independents in London (some of whom were later to be called Levellers) who rallied to their defence. By patient political spadework over a period of several months they succeeded in building up significant influence among the army's rank and file and even with some officers. The widespread support they garnered at Putney for the first version of the *Agreement of the People* so alarmed the officer grandees that they adjourned the debate and sent the Agitators back to their regiments. An attempted rising in support of the *Agreement* was easily put down. A year later, however, when almost bereft of political support for their demand that the king be put on trial, the army grandees embraced both the Levellers and their *Agreement of the People* – if only as a temporary political marriage of convenience. Had the Leveller leaders played their cards more adroitly, they might well have succeeded in imposing a modified version of their constitution on England. However, their refusal to compromise, as well as their attempts to foment mutiny within the army, brought the alliance to an abrupt end and consigned the Levellers to political oblivion.

IV   THE APOGEE OF ARMY INTERVENTIONISM: THE REGICIDE OF CHARLES I

Just as it was the agency that destroyed political Levellerism, so too it was the army, more than any other body, that engineered the death of the king. When and why did the higher officers determine that Charles I must die? Recent contributors to the debate on this question have argued that it was very late in the day that the officers finally opted for regicide, and that by a timely abdication Charles could have saved his neck almost up to the moment of his execution.[91] Yet it is sometimes overlooked how long the men in the parliamentary armies had been meditating on the king's blood-guilt. As early as 1644, the chaplain Robert Ram wrote that the Royalists were enemies of God who 'maintain the cause of Antichrist', and that 'God now calls upon us to avenge the blood of his saints that hath been shed in the land.'[92] More pointedly, if ambiguously, an unsigned engraving in early 1646 showed Sir Thomas Fairfax with a broken royal sceptre and an axe cleaving through a crown.[93] It was not much longer before the soldiers began to label the king a 'man of blood'.[94] By early 1647, they hardly needed John Lilburne to persuade them that Charles – in Lilburne's words – 'deserves a more severe punishment . . . [than] either of the dethroned kings, Edw. 2 or Rich. 2 . . . he being the greatest delinquent in the 3 kingdoms, and the head of all the rest'.[95] And as almost every one of Lilburne's readership well knew, both Edward II and Richard II had been murdered shortly after their deposition.

However, the divine authority of scripture carried even greater force. In that Bible-saturated century, the phrase 'man of blood' carried a heavy freight of political and theological meaning. Those who heard it would have been reminded of the text from Numbers 35, 33: 'for blood it defileth the land: and the land cannot be cleansed of the blood that is shed therein, but by the blood of him that shed it'. When, at Putney, Lieutenant-Colonel John Jubbes, Captain George Bishop and Colonel Thomas Harrison condemned Charles as a 'man of blood' they were well aware how this phrase would resonate in the ears of their listeners.[96]

The outbreak of the second Civil War in the spring of 1648 forced many in the army to reassess their attitudes towards King Charles. The prospect of renewed bloodshed in a war raised in the king's name and with his certain connivance, greatly increased the soldiers' receptiveness to arguments about their monarch's blood-guilt. With the clouds of war gathering, the officers of the New Model assembled in April 1648 at Windsor, in a grim and fearful mood, before riding off once again to risk their lives in battle. The awareness that some of those present would never meet again welded them together in intense emotion. After searching their hearts under the zealous guidance of Lieutenant-Colonel Goffe, they branded Charles Stuart a man of blood who had defiled the land, which could only be cleansed 'by the blood of him that shed it'.[97]

Five months later, after that second searing experience of war, regiments and garrisons throughout England petitioned army headquarters, enraged that the man who had again dragged the nation through a nightmare of misery and death should be treated as anything less than a murderer.[98] The fury that pervaded the army was eloquently distilled by Ireton in the words of the *Remonstrance* adopted at St Albans on 16 November; Charles was bluntly held guilty of 'the highest treason . . . and . . . of all the innocent blood spilt thereby'. 'Exemplary justice' was required 'in capitall punishment upon the principal author and some prime instruments of our late warres'.[99] There is clear evidence that a significant minority of the Council of Officers doubted the advisability of bringing the king to the scaffold. Indeed, a group of colonels were said to yearn 'to see this kingdome restored . . . in peace and amity, and that the hearts of king and people may be knit together in a threefold cord of love'.[100] Yet, whatever support these colonels may have commanded, their dissent was steamrollered by Ireton and his supporters, who used the volume of army petitions calling for justice against the king to secure adoption of the *Remonstrance* on 16 November. When the army published its *Heads of the Charge against the King* in December, it branded Charles the 'capitall and grand offender and author of our troubles', and spelt out that the crimes he had committed 'have been judged capitall in severall of his Predecessors'.[101]

Yet there were formidable obstacles in the way of exacting justice against the king, not least in the minds of the senior officers themselves. They must have squirmed as City ministers excoriated them again and again for breaking their oath under the Solemn League and Covenant – the oath sworn by all Parliament-men in 1643 – to protect the person of the king.[102] According to the French Resident, the sieur de Grignon, writing on 21 December, the 'abominable proposition' – presumably to try the king – passed by only five votes in the Council of War. Cromwell and Ireton, the two officers who were leading the army politically, were in disagreement, with Ireton wanting to bring the king to trial immediately, while Cromwell favoured the trial of the smaller fry first.[103] Marchamont Nedham, writing in late December, hazarded the guess that only half a dozen of the senior officers were in favour of the king's execution.[104] Even after the army had published its *Heads of the Charge against the King*, those opposed to killing Charles continued to fight a powerful rearguard action. On two separate occasions, at the end of December and in early January, the officers devoted several hours to an audience with the prophetess Elizabeth Poole, who told them that it would be wrong to shed the king's blood.[105] Although Cromwell was not present, her contribution was 'well accepted' by the rest, 'as comeing from an holy and humble spiritt'.

The *Remonstrance* and the *Heads of the Charge* witness to the determination of Ireton and a group of his fellow officers that the king should be condemned to death. It was perhaps this caucus among the officers that the writer of the royalist newsbook *Mercurius Elencticus* had in mind when he commented in mid-December that 'no question . . . what they intend to doe with him . . . their daily practices doe sufficiently evidence a finall destruction both to him and his posterity . . .'.[106] Another Royalist, Thomas Webb (the Duke of Richmond's secretary), wrote a week before the trial opened on 20 January 1649: 'I have very little hopes of the king's life, all seeming to be resolved to the contrary. . . . [T]hey iudge him guilty . . .'[107] But by no means all the officers were committed to regicide as early as Ireton seems to have been. Indeed, Fairfax – the most important officer of all – abhorred both the trial and regicide. While he had backed the army's occupation of London in December 1648 and acquiesced in Pride's Purge, he bent every effort to save the king's life during December and January. As the trial was about to begin, he refused to sit down at the first meeting of the Commissioners for the High Court of Justice,[108] and he completely boycotted the trial itself. Two days before the king was to die, Fairfax hosted a meeting between the Dutch ambassadors and the officers in an endeavour to persuade the latter to spare the king's life; and, on the eve of the execution, he summoned a Council of War at which he again laboured to induce his fellow officers to postpone the execution – all to no avail.[109]

Cromwell's attitude towards the trial and regicide is much harder to read. Stationed in the north since the late summer of 1648, he did not arrive in Whitehall (where he was reported to have taken up occupancy in one of the king's bedrooms) until just after Colonel Pride's purge of the House of Commons on 6 December – the army's *coup d'état* that worked to remove almost all the Commons-men who might otherwise have opposed the trial of the king.[110] During his absence, Cromwell had kept open his lines of communication with the army leadership. At the end of November he had written to Fairfax about his own regiment's 'very great zeal to have impartial justice done upon offenders'; he had also commended the army's *Remonstrance* of 16 November, doubting that any good could be expected from 'this man against whom the Lord hath witnessed'.[111]

John Morrill and Philip Baker have argued that Cromwell wanted the king put on trial and deposed if he would not abdicate; but they have also suggested that he had no wish to see monarchy abolished: while he wanted Charles dead, he dreaded cutting off the king's head, because of all the forces arrayed against, and certain to be provoked by, such an act.[112] That he desired some kind of formal reckoning with the king seems beyond doubt. On 6 November, while mopping up the last remnants of royalist resistance in the north, he had written to the king's gaoler, Colonel Robert Hammond, referring to the Newport treaty (the peace negotiations between Charles and Parliament held at Newport on the Isle of Wight in the autumn of 1648), or perhaps the king himself, as 'an accursed thing', and asking Hammond to consider whether any good could accrue to the People of God 'by this man against whom the Lord hath witnessed'. Acknowledging Hammond's worries, he granted that while a peaceful settlement was desirable, 'peace is only good when we receive it out of our Father's [i.e. God's] hand . . . War is good when led to by our Father.'[113] Nor had he neglected to remind Fairfax of his own regiment's desire to see those guilty of shedding innocent blood brought to justice. Whom could they have had in mind above all others, if not Charles Stuart – 'that man of blood', 'that man against whom the Lord hath witnessed'?[114] It is also significant that there is no evidence that Cromwell dissented from the army's *Heads of the Charge against the King*, with its clear implication that Charles deserved to die for his crimes.

What is less certain is whether Cromwell actually favoured taking the king's life, and if so, at what point he arrived at this momentous decision. Nedham alleged that, on 20 December 1648, Cromwell wrote to Colonel Pride asking him to communicate to the Council of War his opposition to regicide.[115] But what are we to make of Cromwell's repeated time-consuming visits to the Duke of Hamilton – the defeated and captured leader of the Scottish Royalists – in December and January? Hamilton's post-Restoration biographer, Bishop Burnet, informs us that their purpose was to gather evidence against the duke's 'correspondents in England' before and during the second Civil War.[116] This may refer to the leading Royalists against whom Cromwell wished to proceed first, according to the French resident in London.[117] Yet who was the chief of Hamilton's 'correspondents in England' if not the king? Again, it is possible that Cromwell was among the grandees said by Nedham to have been 'bartering with his Ma[jestie]' as late as Christmas Day.

But here Nedham may well be guilty of wishful thinking: he and other Royalists hungered for any crumb of hope to nourish their conviction that the army was divided and that Cromwell was working to save the king's life. It may be that Cromwell supported the idea of deposing rather than killing the king, and continuing the monarchy with Charles's third son, the Duke of Gloucester, on the throne.[118] What may finally have convinced Cromwell of the need for regicide was, as John Adamson has argued, the king's refusal to halt the Marquess of Ormond's mobilization of a royalist army of invasion in Ireland.[119] The hard line that Cromwell took during the trial suggests that he had all but given up on the king by mid-January.[120]

In sum, the army leadership had many reasons to hesitate before executing the king. The Council of Officers, despite the apparent unity expressed in the *Remonstrance* of 16 November 1648, was divided. Fairfax was far from being the only senior commander who balked at condemning Charles to death and abolishing the monarchy. And public opposition was widespread and vociferous. On the other hand, there were powerful elements within the army, the purged House of Commons, and the newly-elected, deeply radical London Common Council (chosen in December 1648, after the army's coup), which kept up a relentless pressure to carry through the indictment of the king for capital crimes against the English people. In the weeks preceding the execution, Cromwell and other grandees engaged in a variety of manoeuvres that are open to more than one construction. They may have been seeking a way out of the impasse with the king, or they may have been staging an elaborate campaign to neutralize opposition and encourage whatever tender shoots of support they could find for regicide. To me, the latter interpretation is more consistent with what we know of the actual unfolding of events.

V CONCLUSION

The four questions dealt with in this essay do not, of course, exhaust the topics of possibly fruitful research on Sir Thomas Fairfax's army. We still have only a shadowy knowledge of how and why the alliance between the radical peers and senior officers broke down during the twelve months between the Vote of No Addresses and the trial of Charles I. Another unresolved question that would repay closer investigation is the nature and significance of the reported political divisions within the Council of Officers during the autumn of 1648. Nevertheless, the last quarter-century has seen more intensive study of the New Model Army – and its role in the drama of the 1640s – than at any point since professional historical research into the Civil War began in the 1870s and 1880s. In those twenty-five years, a variety of controversial reinterpretations has been suggested. In 1979, Mark Kishlansky argued that the creation of the New Model Army was the final act of consensus decision-making by the Long Parliament: when the 'conservative' peers tried to change the names on Fairfax's officer list they were motivated by concern for the principles of merit, seniority and political balance – not political faction. But the overwhelming weight of evidence adduced by more recent scholars does not support this thesis. It points instead to the opposite: that the New Model was a child of the intense political conflict that raged between 1643 and 1645 over the conduct of the war against the king.

Nor, after its founding, did the army function inside a political vacuum. John Adamson has shown that the nobles who acted as midwives at the New Model's birth – the Earl of Northumberland in particular – continued to take a keen interest in its financial and administrative welfare, nursing it through the many vicissitudes of military and political struggle. While the new army was at all times in control of its own political agenda, its leaders – many of whom were themselves Commons-men, kept in close touch with their friends in Westminster. It is also apparent that the political involvement of figures such as Viscount

Saye and Lord Wharton continued to grow through the autumn of
1647, to the point where (as we have noted) one journalist labelled Saye
the 'adjutator generall' of the army – an exaggeration, of course, but one
that nevertheless contains a kernel of truth. While it is doubtful whether
Saye was the chief drafter of the army's Heads of the Proposals, it is
unarguable that he continued to promote a version of the Heads for
several months after they were first submitted to the king. In short, a
dozen or so radical peers played a key role in promoting the interests of
the New Model Army, from its founding at least until the end of 1647.

When it comes to the question of the links between the army and the
radical wing of the Independent party that later came to be called
Levellers, a review of the evidence leads to conclusions that are at odds
with the recent trend of interpretation. Kishlansky, Morrill and Baker
have suggested that the London radicals showed little interest in the New
Model at first, that their interests were in fact deeply contradictory, and
that the army's political agenda was in any case generated from within
its own ranks, with little if any reference to the Levellers. Yet the record
shows numerous expressions of radical civilian support for the New
Model, from February 1647 if not much earlier. Nor were the soldiers'
interests confined to questions of honour, indemnity, pay and pensions.
There are many hints that some had expanded their mental horizons to
take in more abstract issues like political liberty, voting rights, and social
equality. How far this was engendered by Leveller activism or stimulated
by quite separate influences remains an open question. Nevertheless, it
must be conceded that at key moments in 1647 and 1648 the Leveller
leadership enjoyed a critical influence over the army's deliberations. Yet
when the moment of climacteric arrived, the Levellers – John Lilburne
above all – threw away an unrepeatable opportunity to help shape the
post-monarchical polity. Thanks to their hot-headed vilification of the
army grandees, and their ill-considered attempts to stir up mutiny within
the ranks, they consigned themselves to political oblivion.

Finally, our understanding of the regicide has been transformed over
the last decade, though it must be admitted that much of the evidence is
ambiguous and legitimately sustains multiple interpretations. Dr Sean
Kelsey is certain that almost until the last moment the army grandees
were looking for a way to avoid executing the king. John Morrill and Phil
Baker, in a more nuanced interpretation, cautiously support a similar
argument. John Adamson forcefully reminds us of the army's obsession
with the Marquess of Ormond's continuing efforts to organize a royalist
invasion from Ireland. Had Charles been willing unequivocally to order

Ormond to cease and desist he might have saved his own life. These are persuasive arguments, yet there is a powerful body of evidence, dating mostly from the end of the second Civil War, that majority opinion among the senior officers supported inflicting capital punishment on the king as the man against whom God had witnessed for shedding the blood of his own subjects.

There is little doubt that Sir Thomas Fairfax's army and its political interventions will continue to stir up intense debate among students of the 1640s.

8. Rhetoric, Reality and the Varieties of Civil-War Radicalism

PHILIP BAKER

According to popular memory – and much modern historiography – the Civil War was a period characterized not only by military conflict and rebellion but also by a luxuriant variety of various types of social and political radicalism. It was a time, self-evidently, when institutions and values were called into question; when groups of Levellers, Diggers and Ranters roamed the land; when utopian visions and extremist beliefs threatened the very foundations of society. Such is the world that is movingly portrayed in Christopher Hill's classic study, dating from the early 1970s, *The World Turned Upside Down*.[1] More recently, however, the subject of Civil War radicalism has provoked a vexed and tendentious historiography. 'Revisionist' scholars have rejected Hill's influential notion of a popular, demotic phenomenon that heralded the seculariza-tion of society as an anachronistic and overly sympathetic view. For Revisionists, radical belief was a marginal concern in the mid-seven-teenth century and was entirely religious in both its origin and its aims.[2] Yet, arguably, neither perspective provides an adequate approach to the subject. Indeed, the existing conceptualizations of radicalism offer distorted or unnecessarily restricted views of both the impact and the diversity of the radical ideologies that were unleashed by the Civil War. It may be timely, therefore, to rethink our approach to the phenomenon.

This chapter attempts to posit a new definition of what has been regarded as Civil War radicalism, and to suggest new ways of consider-ing the phenomenon. It will suggest that it was actually a much broader and more complex phenomenon, with a far greater impact on contem-poraries, than previous scholars have allowed. Indeed, I hope to demon-strate that at various points during the Civil War, a surprisingly wide spectrum of individuals and groups – and not merely those holding heterodox religious opinions or those outside the ruling élite – funda-mentally challenged contemporary arrangements. At the same time, the chapter will also endeavour to examine the limits of Civil War radicalism, in terms both of its impact and the extent of its innovation.

I 'RADICALISM': THE VIABILITY OF THE TERM

First, however, are we right to talk of radicalism in the context of the Civil War at all? Professor Conal Condren has led the argument for banishing the nineteenth-century labels 'radical', 'conservative' and their associated '-isms' from early modern historical writing altogether, on the grounds of their anachronism and modern political connotations. In projecting modern political dispositions onto earlier periods, he argues, scholars have distorted and refashioned the language and activities of the past to conform to their own political domain.[3] Condren and others were certainly correct in highlighting the anachronism, ubiquity, ambiguity and politically-loaded nature of the sub-field of terms of which 'radical' forms a part. And one outcome is that the concept of radicalism has now largely been divorced from its earlier associations with 'modernity' and 'progress'. Nevertheless, the call to dispense with the word itself has been overwhelmingly rejected by scholars of the period, the vast majority of whom continue to believe in its potential to make the past more intelligible to the present, though certainly many (if by no means all) are now far more circumspect in how and when they use it. Some have constructed functional models of radicalism;[4] others confine it to a particular geographic area;[5] several provide a formal definition of the term.[6] All are agreed, however, that the notion of *fundamental change*, or the pursuit thereof, was central to the phenomenon.[7]

Like this scholarly majority, I too believe that we should continue to use the word 'radicalism' in order to convey the notion of axiomatic political, constitutional, religious, social, economic or cultural change; as a phenomenon, therefore, radicalism was not concerned with the process of superficial reform or amendment.[*] But if we are to avoid restrictive and inherently distorting conceptualizations of Civil War radicalism, we need to recognize that it encompassed a number of ideologies that challenged existing arrangements for different reasons and ends. This should warn us against reifying the phenomenon as a single process with a specific ideological ambition,[8] or approaching it simply as an array of individuals,

---

[*] An axiom was a generally accepted principal or proposition that was sanctioned by experience and tradition.

groups or movements.[9] Rather, we must acknowledge that Civil War radicalism encompassed a variety of ideologies that were radical (relating to the *radix* – the root), in the sense that each of them struck at the foundations of contemporary arrangements by either effecting or visualising axiomatic change – change to the very axioms by which the contemporary world was understood and ordered.

Moreover, it also seems essential to adopt a contextual approach to the phenomenon: for example, the demand for the Root and Branch abolition of episcopacy – the government of the Church of England by bishops – was highly radical in the context of 1640–41, but it lost much of its radical edge during the course of the decade, as the position of the episcopate as a fundamental element of the established Church was gradually undermined.[10] Similarly, contemporaries' fears of radicalism during the 1640s followed an undulating trajectory with two apparent peaks: the first, in the autumn of 1641, coincided with widespread anxieties regarding popular disorder, religious extremism and constitutional radicalism;[11] the second, in late 1647 and early 1648, represented the height of the Leveller 'threat'.[12] Finally, we might achieve a subtler perspective on the whole question of radicalism by paying closer attention to its rhetorical context: the ways in which it was articulated and presented to contemporaries.[13] In an age in which innovation was almost universally abhorred, contemporaries' demands for radical change invariably sought legitimacy through reference to the past – be it to the baronial revolts of their medieval ancestors or, still more distantly, to the biblical paradise of the Garden of Eden.

A second point of academic controversy to which we must refer is the use of evidence in relation to the history of radicalism. There is an obvious political dimension to this debate, with some scholars (primarily of the Left) being accused of having to accept seductive and often intentionally misleading printed accounts if they are to find any evidence of popular, demotic, radical belief. Meanwhile, their predominantly Right-wing, Revisionist critics – who are seen to privilege manuscripts above printed material – are charged with deliberately underestimating, or deliberately ignoring, the level of radicalism in society at large.[14]

All forms of evidence are prone to bias and prejudice, of course, and we cannot simply assume, *a priori*, that a manuscript must inevitably be more accurate and reliable – and as a consequence, more valuable – than a printed work. Indeed, a methodology that deliberately excludes printed polemical sources deprives itself of a range of perceptions of the past, which, whether accurate or not, were a genuine and meaningful element of contemporary opinion.[15] That hostile sources can contribute vital information to a study of radicalism is admirably demonstrated, for example, by Ann Hughes's study of Thomas Edwards's *Gangraena*, his voluminous three-part heresiography (or catalogue of heresies) published in 1646 – and a work of obvious Presbyterian propaganda. In discussing the work's 'accuracy', Hughes maintains that despite Edwards's overall bias, he did not simply fabricate his material. Indeed, *Gangraena* is identified as an essential source for understanding the religious and political debates of the mid-1640s, and one that has much to reveal about contemporary – and modern historians' – perceptions of Civil War radicalism.[16]

II   THE THREAT OF THE 'MANY-HEADED MONSTER'

It is easy to comprehend why numerous contemporaries believed that their world was being 'turned upside down' by the Civil War.[17] The 1640s witnessed the destruction of established structures and institutions – including the Church of England, the House of Lords and the monarchy – that had a fundamental impact upon all three Stuart kingdoms. Moreover, those seismic changes coincided with levels of popular disorder that were unprecedented within living memory. In the countryside, rioters attacked enclosures, gentlemen and their property. In churches and cathedrals, communion rails and images were destroyed; clergymen were harassed or assaulted. Across war-torn counties there were skirmishes between local civilians and marauding and foraging soldiers. And at Westminster, demonstrators surrounded, and at times even invaded, the precincts of Parliament itself.[18] As propertied contemporaries shared a general and ancient anxiety that 'the people' harboured thoughts of social revolution and anarchy, such unrest encouraged a habit of mind that equated the reality of popular disorder with the imminence of fundamental change.[19] And in that sense, the 'many-headed monster' can be identified as an almost generic manifestation of Civil War radicalism. As Sir John Oglander lamented during the early 1640s when fears of a popular rebellion were at their height:

> I believe such times were never before seen in England, when the gentry were made slaves to the commonalty and in their power, not only to abuse but plunder any gentleman. . . . They could call nothing their own and lived in slavery and submission to the unruly, base multitude.[20]

This image of social inversion has proved seductive to many Left-wing historians for whom popular unrest was evidence of a class struggle during the Civil War. 'Class conflict', so scholars such as Brian Manning have argued, was thus a key component of Civil War radicalism.[21]

Yet this contention belies the very limited incidence of social radicalism – in the sense of ideologically-driven conflict between the orders – during the period, and places undue emphasis on source material that is often intentionally misleading.[22] Following the collapse of censorship at the outset of the 1640s, for example, news of the potential threat from the 'many-headed monster' was available in an unprecedented quantity: in thousands of newspapers, pamphlets and books. A great deal of this material, however, was propaganda by either Royalists or Parliamentarians, who, with contemporaries gripped by a 'moral panic', deliberately exaggerated the scale of the threat of social upheaval posed by incidents of crowd action in order to rally support amongst local magistrates and gentry. Ultimately, the possibility of a rising by the 'many-headed monster' during the Civil War was more of a threat in the minds of the propertied than in reality.

Indeed, Revisionists rightly emphasize that the period as a whole saw a continuation, or reopening, of traditional forms of collective unrest – such as attacks on unpopular landlords, and enclosure, grain and tax riots – in which there is very little evidence for the influence of radical ideologies. According to one authority, there were only five rural disturbances in England between 1640 and 1649 in which the destruction of property and rental records may have represented a rejection of the manorial system and landlord power.[23] Popular violence certainly extended beyond traditional targets, however, to acts of iconoclasm and attacks on 'malignants' (Royalists) and 'recusants' (mostly Roman Catholics). But again, for Revisionists, those forms of disorder were not motivated by radical beliefs. Iconoclasts sought to remove the 'Popish' religious innovations of the 1630s, not to destroy organized religion; and attacks on 'malignants' and 'recusants' were attacks on the perceived enemies of Parliament, not on the social and political order.

Nevertheless, this reading of the relationship between popular disorder and fundamental change rests on a limited conceptualization of Civil War radicalism, one that restricts the phenomenon to notions of social inversion and political and economic egalitarianism alongside the religious heterodoxy of the sects. In fact, when we adopt the broader perspective of radicalism outlined above – encompassing those political movements that aimed at the transformation of contemporary institutions from the very roots – then there is one striking example when crowd action contributed to major political and Church-related change: the removal of the bishops from the English House of Lords in February 1642. For hostility to 'prelacy' was not confined to particular members of the élite. It also provoked riots that were among the most notorious instances of popular disorder during the 1640s: the attack on the palace of the Archbishop of Canterbury in May 1640 and the demonstrations around, and mass picketing of, Parliament in December 1641.[24]

This popular opposition to bishops, which was fuelled by fears of Popery and a general animosity towards the policies and personalities of the 1630s, eventually combined with, and gained legitimacy from, the parliamentary and national anti-'prelatical' campaigns. By December 1641, the central demand of the crowds – which contained members of both the 'middling sort of people' and the lower orders[25] – was the removal of the bishops (and thus their votes) from the House of Lords; and popular pressure undoubtedly played a vital role in their exclusion. The contemporary suspicion that Parliament-men and London's civic leaders had orchestrated those demonstrations has found support amongst modern scholars.[26] Thus certain members of the élite were willing to tolerate, and perhaps even sanction, popular disorder as a means to achieving their objectives – as they had previously in May 1641 to secure the execution of the Earl of Strafford. But even if those were 'legitimized' protests, we should not ignore the crucial role of crowd action in the collapse of episcopal authority in the early 1640s.

Overall, however, the Civil War gave rise to surprisingly few significant outbreaks of popular unrest that had subversion of the social order as their goal. The closest thing to the realization of 'a rising of the people' may have been the disorder associated with the infantry of both the Parliamentarian and Royalist armies. The military conflict mobilized tens of thousands of men – many of them conscripts from the lowest ranks of society – and incidents of desertion, plunder, mutiny and even the slaughter of civilians were not uncommon.[27] Nevertheless, such unrest hardly threatened the foundations of society, though some contemporaries depicted it otherwise.[28] Ultimately, the explanation for the relative absence of the 'many-headed monster' from the Civil War may lie in social and economic change. The increasing social mobility of the 'middling sort', together with the dependence of the poor on parish relief, meant that neither was likely to support ideologies that threatened agrarian capitalism and the fundamentals of the social order.[29]

III POLITICAL EXPERIMENTATION

With class-based analyses no longer tenable, Revisionists have over-whelmingly re-characterized Civil War radicalism along religious lines. Indeed, J. C. Davis and Jonathan Scott have gone so far as to argue that the period's religious speculation *was* Civil War radicalism.[30] Nevertheless, this singular emphasis on the religious roots and ends of radical thinking ignores an identifiable secular strand of the phenome-non; and while this obviously did not exist in isolation from the period's rich vein of religious speculation, its aim was fundamentally to alter existing constitutional arrangements; above all, to secure a state of 'liberty' through thorough-going change to the organs of government.

Before the rise of Revisionism, the secular radicalism of the Civil War – which essentially *was* Civil War radicalism for an older generation of scholars – was seen to have evolved from the religious speculations of the second half of the 1640s. A key role was attributed to the Levellers – the authors, as is well known, of a series of draft constitutions between 1647 and 1649 – who, with their background amongst London's religious nonconformist community, were adjudged to have transferred the reli-gious doctrines of the sects to the secular world.[31] More recently, David Wootton has argued that the origins of Leveller ideology – and thus of secular radicalism – can be traced back to 1642–3, when a number of Parliamentarian writers advanced tenets, such as the sovereignty of the people, that clearly struck at the foundations of the existing constitu-tion.[32] This argument is extended still further by Allan Macinnes, who contends that the revolt of the Scottish nobility against Charles I in 1638 – a revolt which, if religious in intent, had by 1641 accomplished a radi-cal restructuring of Scottish civil government through the Scottish Parliament's assumption of the Crown's prerogative powers – served as a 'radical exemplar' for those English peers and gentlemen who were convinced of the necessity for fundamental constitutional change within their own nation.[33]

This latter typology of radicalism, as expounded by Wootton and Macinnes, traces its origins not in the political margins and London's backstreet 'gathered churches', but to powerful dissidents within the governing élite itself. Excluded from power by the king's decision to rule without Parliament from 1629 and aggrieved by what they regarded as the abuses of his reign, a group within the English political élite – a group that ranged from relatively indigent country squires like John Pym at one extreme to wealthy grandees like the Earls of Bedford and

Warwick at the other – had contemplated the reapportionment of the respective powers of Crown and Parliament in order to constrain Charles I's authority and establish a secure and godly 'commonwealth'. Their attempt to realize those ambitions in the 1640s produced a form of secular, constitutional radicalism that was steeped, not only in biblical references to England as suffering Israel, but also in appeals to Roman republican example, and to usages drawn from medieval precedent and the nation's Gothic past.[34] Indeed, within a culture that feared innovation, contemporaries' use of the traditional discourses of mixed monarchy (king-in-Parliament), baronialism and counsel – discourses that were commonly employed by Royalist writers – provided their agenda with a necessary measure of historical legitimization.[35]

If this strand of élite radicalism was largely confined to statements in private during the 1630s, the situation in 1640 – when only a Parliament could provide the necessary money for the king to finance a successful military campaign against the Scots – emboldened these critics of the régime and their allies to express their opinions publicly. For example, in a sermon of September 1640, the clergyman Calybute Downinge – a protégé of the Earl of Warwick – upheld the right of resistance to a prince and stated that the maxim *salus populi* (the welfare of the people) overrode all other laws when a subject's security was threatened – arguments which, as we shall see, were eventually to form the bedrock of the New Model Army's ideological justification for the regicide.[36] Moreover, during the months following the meeting of the new Parliament in November 1640, the Crown was stripped of many of its most important discretionary prerogatives – not least, the power to summon and dismiss Parliament – by Charles's assent to the Triennial Act (February 1641), which obliged him to call the assembly every three years, and to a further Act (in May) that prevented him from dissolving the Parliament without its own consent.[37] In July 1641, the radical legislative programme of Parliament continued with the abolition of the prerogative Courts of Star Chamber and High Commission.[38]

Furthermore, the distinct (and incompatible) agendas of groups of the élites in all three Stuart kingdoms demanded even greater constitutional change. In England, evidence of the king's plotting against Parliament in 1641 convinced the Warwick–Pym group that it was necessary to transfer the majority of the Crown's executive powers to the major officers of state, and to install themselves in those positions. This policy was asserted in explicitly baronial terms in Parliament's Nineteen Propositions of June 1642. These proposed the restoration of the ancient peerage to its dominant role around the monarch, with the revival of a baronial council and the two great medieval offices – the Stewardship and the Constableship – with the full complement of quasi-regal powers attributed to their predecessors. The propositions also envisaged that Charles would consent to a reformation of the Church as advised by Parliament, thus still further undermining the Crown's supremacy over the Church.[39]

In Ireland, fear of subjection to colonial rule by an English Parliament prompted the leaders of the Catholic Rising of October 1641 to uphold the nation's status as a dependency solely of the English Crown. Nevertheless, the desire of some Irish gentry and clergy for the full re-establishment of the Catholic Church in Ireland represented another challenge to the monarch's prerogative in the religious sphere. A similar threat came from Scotland, where many of the king's opponents – the Covenanters – believed that the National Covenant they had subscribed in 1638 had set them upon a divine mission to extirpate Popery and establish a Presbyterian religious uniformity throughout the entire Atlantic archipelago. The Covenanter leadership also regarded the formation of an Anglo-Scottish confederation as the surest means of safeguarding the powers of the Scottish Parliament and the future security of their nation.[40]

In undermining the Crown's prerogative powers and re-conceptualizing the relationships within the regal union, these élite agendas posed a challenge that can properly be designated as 'radical' in the context of the existing constitutional arrangements both within and between the three Stuart kingdoms. It was the course of the Civil War in England, however, that ultimately determined the fate of each agenda. And it was from within England that competing and more extreme ideologies – as we shall see – were eventually to emerge.

Nevertheless, given the need of the Parliamentarian leadership to justify and sustain its opposition to the king, many of the secular ideas that are most readily associated with Civil War radicalism – the association of Charles's monarchy with tyranny, the contractual nature of government, the right of the people to resist an unjust ruler – were discussed in print by members of the political élite during the early stages of the conflict in England.[41] Even before the raising of the royal standard at Nottingham in August 1642, for example, the leading Parliamentarian theorist Henry Parker – the leading polemicist for the cause of the reformist peers – had developed a doctrine of what might be called 'bicameral parliamentary absolutism', albeit couched in the rhetoric of counsel.[42] Parker was also among the contributors to a propaganda campaign over the winter of 1642–3 that discussed far more radical theories – including the right of the people to resist, and resume to themselves the powers of, Parliament – as a means to frustrating a possible peace settlement.[43] However, the act of publishing those theories encouraged their wider dissemination. That they were immediately appropriated by a number of *royalist* commentators – who argued that the people might resume the authority of those representatives who, by resisting the king had betrayed them[44] – is certainly suggestive of their subsequent impact on the development and circulation of such radical notions.

Arguably, the group at Westminster that realized Parker's theoretical ideas most fully during the 1640s was the political Independents: the group principally associated with the parliamentary backers of the New Model Army, and the quest for a hard-line, militarily guaranteed, settlement with the king. In their pursuit of a constitutional arrangement that would render the powers of the monarchy innocuous for all time and thereby safeguard the dominance of Parliament, the Independent grandees eventually set out explicitly to limit the Crown's right to veto legislation through its 'negative voice'.[45] This was evident in the Newcastle Propositions of 1646, the terms of the projected settlement of 1647 (in particular, the Heads of the Proposals), and in the Four Bills presented to Charles at the end of the same year.[46] And despite their diminution of the king's majesty, a number of these schemes, as David Scott has demonstrated, even received a measure of royalist support.[47] Yet each involved a radical reapportionment of the entire basis of sovereignty, and would have created an oligarchic system of government in which a bounded, or 'cypher', monarchy was dominated by an Independent Junto within the two Houses of Parliament – a form of government that might be termed 'monarchical republicanism'.[48] The advocates of that policy, such as the Earl of Northumberland, at times bluntly asserted that their conquest of the king enabled them to 'dispose of the kingdome and affaires as they pleased'.[49] But, as the leading Independent Viscount Saye and Sele demonstrated in his 'political manifesto', *Vindiciae Veritatis* (written about 1646), they also remained capable of articulating their radical vision in the reassuring, superficially traditional language of mixed monarchy.[50]

This account of the secular radicalism of the political élite challenges the characterization of the leading Parliamentarians as 'conservatives' whose sole intention throughout the Civil War was to preserve the existing constitution.[51] Of course, the Independent grandees, along with the overwhelming majority of the population of the Stuart kingdoms, remained committed to a political settlement that included both the monarchy (or at least its outward shell) and the retention of King Charles I (at least as a figurehead king). However, small minorities within all three kingdoms were also contemplating some startling alternative arrangements. For example, when the Highland clan chief the Marquess of Argyll considered abandoning the king to the Long Parliament in 1646, he may have been contemplating the idea of a *de facto* Scottish republic that could preserve its independence in alliance, no longer with England, but with either Sweden or France. Similarly, in Ireland, the Confederates seriously discussed the nomination of a foreign sovereign as their Protector in 1647, with the kings of France and Spain, and even the pope, as potential candidates.[52] It was in England, however, that constitutional axioms were subjected to their most rigorous challenge – perhaps as a consequence of its different social structure, which uniquely contained a prosperous and literate 'middling-sort', and the ingrained reverence in which the English held their native freedoms.[53]

That challenge was evident from the very outset of the 1640s in the striking contemporary interest in the reign of that most tyrannical of English kings, the deposed and murdered Richard II.[54] A tract of January 1643 argued that the deposition of Richard, and of *any* malevolent hereditary ruler, was entirely legitimate.[55] Later that year, the Presbyterian lawyer William Prynne devoted a lengthy appendix to *The Fovrth Part of the Soveraigne Power of Parliaments and Kingdomes* to numerous historical precedents for the censure, deposition and even capital punishment of kings.[56] Moreover, the discussion of such courses of action in relation to Charles I occurred from relatively early on in the Civil War. In August 1643, for example, a pamphlet by the minister John Saltmarsh intimated that strict adherence to parliamentary declarations could, in certain circumstances, necessitate the lawful killing of the king.[57] In the same month, his pamphlet was defended by the Commons-man Henry Marten – who in 1641 had declared, 'I do not think one man wise enough to govern us all'[58] – with the alleged words that 'it was better one family should be destroyed [than] many'.[59] By February 1645, Marchamont Nedham, editor of the parliamentarian newspaper *Mercurius Britanicus*, was proclaiming 'my opinion of [the need for] His *Majesties* death'.[60]

From the mid-1640s, if not earlier, a number of authors openly extolled the virtues of alternative models of government, such as the republican systems of ancient Athens and Rome or contemporary Venice and the United Provinces (the Netherlands).[61] The nature of those systems varied significantly, however, with Venice a model for oligarchic government by elected members of the nobility, while both Athens and Rome were variously adduced as exemplars of government by 'the people' – or, in the case of late republican Rome, as yet another instance of 'aristocracy'. An interest in republican arrangements, which long pre-dated the regicide of 1649, was one outcome of a wider contemporary debate regarding constitutional structures and the relationship between representatives and those they represented. This engaged writers from across the political spectrum and was encouraged by the very uncertainty that surrounded the nature of the political and religious settlements that would eventually be adopted. There was also, by the late 1640s, a growing perception that the tyranny of the king had simply been supplanted by the authoritarian institutions and procedures of a perpetual Parliament – a theme which is explored in the essays by Jason Peacey and Clive Holmes elsewhere in this volume.

This perception was not merely confined to members of the political élite. Amongst some of the 'middling sort' once loyal to Parliament, this revulsion at the reality of parliamentarian rule produced what is perhaps the most widely known of all the strands of 1640s popular political radicalism: the Levellers. Beginning as a petitioner movement in the late 1640s that championed the sovereignty of the people and its inalienable natural rights, the Levellers argued that abuses of power by all existing institutions had vitiated their right to govern and therefore returned the nation to a state of nature. Their core demands, as set out in a series of written constitutions entitled the *Agreements of the People* (envisioned as literal re-formulations of the social contract) and in numerous pamphlets and petitions, included the creation of a new supreme legislature made accountable through frequent elections on an extended franchise; the constitutional guarantee of undeniable individual rights, such as liberty of conscience; and a large-scale decentralization of power.[62]

Despite the Levellers' advocacy of fundamental constitutional change, in many respects they stand as a testimony to the divergence between the rhetoric and the reality of Civil War radicalism. Their very name was a term of abuse created by their opponents that falsely, but effectively, cast them as an attempt by the lower orders to 'level' (and level downwards) the estates and degrees of men. Similarly, although hostile contemporaries – and sympathetic historians – portrayed them as a mass movement, scholars now make very conservative estimates as to the actual number of committed Levellers and their supporters.[63] Such support as they enjoyed came from within London and the army, and – as Ian Gentles describes elsewhere in this volume – it was in tandem with the New Model that, during the Putney debates of 1647 and the final months of 1648, the Levellers were briefly at the political centre-stage. But of almost equal importance with this direct influence was a much more diffuse, but pervasive, influence their existence exerted on contemporary political culture; namely, the fear of social upheaval that they generated among the nation's rulers through their attempts to mobilize mass support outside of the parliamentary arena and the traditional governing élite.

Leveller ideology (in so far as it can be spoken of as a single entity) derived from a number of distinct sources. The writing of one of their leaders, John Lilburne, for example, drew readily on arguments from the common law and from wartime parliamentary declarations;[64] and the Levellers' familiarity with, and use of, these sources serves as a warning against making rigid divisions between 'élite' and 'popular' forms of radicalism. Other Levellers were influenced by the social doctrine of practical Christianity – with its emphasis on charity, community, morality and universal reformation[65] – and the political language of natural law theory. While the latter was also a cornerstone of Parliamentarian resistance theory, its radicalization by the Levellers produced a number of stunning *defences* of innovation, such as that made by Richard Overton in 1646, emphatically casting off all shackles of the past: 'for whatever our Fore-fathers were; or whatever they did or suffered, or were enforced to yeeld unto; we are the men of the present age, and ought to be absolutely free'.[66]

A discourse of fundamental rights and liberties was also a feature of the political manifestos produced by the New Model Army between the summer of 1647 (when it emerged as a political voice in its own right) and the regicide of 1649. The army initially entered the political arena in June 1647 in order to justify its refusal to disband until Parliament addressed the issues of its honour and material grievances. Yet by February 1649, it had overseen a radical redefinition of English government. Nevertheless, in the interim there was a striking consistency of argument and principle in the army's vindication of its conduct. Mark Kishlansky has emphasized its commitment to the advancement of public over private interest, and to the maxim *salus populi suprema lex* (the welfare of the people is the supreme law).[67]

However, he fails to also acknowledge the army's constant adherence to what it interpreted to be the revealed will of God, or providence, as a warrant for action.[68] More attention might also be paid to the actual nature of the army's public declarations, which took the form of rhetorical appeals to the nation at large in support of the 'public weal' (or public interest).

In appealing to the nation on the grounds of abstract principles, and over the heads of the Parliament-men, the army created a public discourse in which the events which came to pass between December 1648 and February 1649 were no longer regarded as unthinkable. In that process, the crucial document is the army's *Remonstrance* of November 1648. The army's seemingly providential victory earlier that year in the second Civil War had almost certainly convinced Cromwell, the New Model's Lieutenant-General, that Charles I was a 'Man against whom the Lord hath witnessed',[69] and in the *Remonstrance*, largely drafted by his son-in-law, Henry Ireton, the army explicitly identified the king with an obstacle to the common good.[70] Thus, when the Commons voted in December that Charles's answer to Parliament's most recent propositions was the basis for a settlement, the army reacted by purging the chamber, leaving a mere rump composed almost exclusively of its own supporters. Similarly, when in January the Lords rejected an ordinance for the king's trial, this 'Rump Parliament' responded with three resolutions that fundamentally altered the basis of English government: that the people were the origin of all just power; that the Commons was the supreme authority in the nation; and that its Acts had the force of law without the concurrence of king or Lords.[71]

Ironically, what the new ruling oligarchy of January 1649 determined was for the public good was, in fact, contrary to the wishes of the overwhelming majority of the nation. A handful of committed republicans apart, there was little genuine desire for the act of regicide, but the king's guilt in having twice caused a war with Parliament – and the fear that if he lived, he would do so again – eventually convinced a tiny minority that the survival of Charles Stuart was incompatible with the freedoms of the English people. Within days of his execution on 30 January 1649, the abolition of the kingship and the House of Lords – on the grounds that both were 'dangerous' to the public interest – completed the destruction of axiomatic elements of England's monarchical system of government.[72] In their absence, the new Commonwealth régime began a decade of experimentation that was to conclude in republican failure and the restoration of the Stuart kings.

IV RELIGIOUS SPECULATION

We have seen that a distinctively secular strand in Civil War radicalism, one which proposed liberation through good government, was influenced by a variety of religious themes and beliefs. Perhaps the most striking characteristic of the period's religious radicalism, however, was an ambition to achieve freedom *from* government. This, in turn, resulted in demands for liberation from all human forms of outward bondage – civil, religious, social and legal – in order to undergo a true Christian subjection.[73]

This 'anti-formalism' was one of the features of a startling outbreak of religious speculation in England during the 1640s. The calling of the Parliament in November 1640 and the collapse of ecclesiastical authority in the early years of the decade saw religious nonconformists and more extreme sectaries grow bolder and more visible than ever before. Indeed, in a climate in which *de facto* licence was granted, at least initially, to all but the most heterodox views, contemporaries were free to voice ideas ranging from the rejection of a compulsory national Church and the demand for complete religious liberty, through to the right of the laity – including women – to preach and prophesy.[74]

For historians such as Christopher Hill, this sudden outburst of religious speculation pointed to the existence of a plebeian, heretical underground stretching back over previous decades, even centuries.[75] Yet as we shall see, the religious radicalism of the Civil War was primarily a phenomenon of the 'middling', not the poorer, sort. Its underlying ideas were not always original, however, and we shall see that a number of them emerged from, and against, orthodox Calvinism and from the spiritualism of the 'Radical Reformation' – the Anabaptist tradition of the 1530s and its continuators.

In a more recent Revisionist account, Jonathan Scott has identified two religious impulses that united the radical speculation of the period: practical Christianity and anti-formalism. In locating the origins of the former, he too looks to the Radical Reformation with its social agenda of community and equality as the wellspring of the developments in the 1640s. Nevertheless, he regards the latter as the more immediate and recent reaction of radical English Protestants confronted with the compulsion of the 1630s Caroline Church.[76]

In spite of their contrasting approaches, however, Hill and Scott provide remarkably similar – and restrictive – overall views of Civil War radicalism. Both focus their attention on the radical 'groups' conventionally associated with the phenomenon: the Levellers, Diggers, Ranters.[77] In their preoccupation with the popular (Hill) and the religious (Scott), the indisputable secular radicalism of the period is, with the exception of the Levellers, simply excluded from their accounts.

This is not to dispute the significance of the Revisionists' general arguments regarding the language and ambitions of religious radicalism, although those are not perhaps as universally applicable as has been suggested. As we shall see, practical Christianity and anti-formalism are not readily compatible with the radicalism of, say, the Fifth Monarchists (the militant movement convinced that the Second Coming of Christ – the 'fifth monarchy' foretold in the Book of Revelation – and the rule of his Saints was imminent). Indeed, the Revisionists' preoccupation with the radical 'groups' and particular individuals (such as Cromwell),[78] as against the genuine Civil War sects, has detracted from the extent to which the ambition to renegotiate the personal relationship with God left many intimately concerned with the formalities of ceremony, doctrine and worship. Members of Baptist congregations, for example, were obsessive formalists. Their discipline, doctrine and ordinances – most obviously that of submission to adult, or believers', baptism (in rejection of infant baptism) – were all founded on the literal interpretation of scripture.[79] And this is doubly significant in that, before the rise of the Quakers, the Baptists were the largest of all the Civil War sects and 'groups'; it has been estimated they numbered 25,000 in 1660.[80] However, that figure represents only one-half of 1 per cent of the total population in 1660,[81] and it has similarly been estimated that no more than 5 per cent of the populace attended religious assemblies outside of the parochial structure between 1643 and 1654.[82] Thus we are clearly discussing tiny minorities within society as a whole. Nevertheless, hostile contemporary accounts abound with swarms of sectaries over-running the country,[83] and this reminds us of the important impact of religious radicalism in terms of the wholly disproportionate fear and anxiety that it generated within society at large.

That fear already existed before 1640, when those who deliberately placed themselves outside of the established Church were an insignificant number. Their visible increase from the early 1640s onwards, however, meant that the threat they were alleged to pose to society was increasingly apparent. The gathering of churches by religious Independents, with their doctrine that the Church consisted in autonomous congregations of the godly, represented a fundamental challenge to the system of a compulsory, organized, state religion. Along with all other religious radicals, Independents rejected the right of any human authority to govern individual conscience or the outward forms of religious worship; their membership of a voluntary association of the godly was founded on a formal covenant that emphasized obedience to God above that of all worldly authorities. Indeed, a number of the sects shunned the notion of a university-educated, ordained and publicly maintained ministry, in favour of preachers who displayed the true gifts of godliness. Moreover, in sects lacking any form of ministerial office, both laymen and women were often free to preach, posing an apparent threat to the patriarchal order. Finally, the common refusal to pay maintenance in support of the established ministry challenged the property rights of the gentry to collect impropriated tithes.[84]

For heresy-spotters like the Presbyterian minister Thomas Edwards, those opinions were nothing less than a 'schismatical abomination' that struck at the very foundations of the social order. From the early 1640s, he responded to the sects and their calls for liberty of conscience in a series of printed polemics that culminated in 1646 with his *Gangraena*.[85] And by that date, the tremendous anxiety engendered by the proliferating varieties and forms of religious radicalism – as catalogued in the writings of Edwards and numerous others – had created a political context in which a disciplinarian Presbyterian Church system seemed attractive, and episcopalian opposition to such a system in Parliament was overcome.

By the mid-1640s, Edwards was also prominent amongst a number of authors who were increasingly alarmed by the apparent prevalence of religious heterodoxy within the New Model Army. From its creation in 1645, the army probably contained many religious Independents and Baptists (though precise numbers are notoriously difficult to determine), and there is even evidence of forms of religious scepticism and unbelief within its ranks. Indeed, the views of a small number of officers, troopers, regimental chaplains and lay preachers clearly mounted a challenge to central tenets of orthodox Christianity, including the authority of scripture, the divinity of Christ and the reality of sin.[86] By the 1650s, the army also included Fifth Monarchists and Quakers, and if the religious radicalism of the Civil War was primarily an English phenomenon – a legacy of its small, but significant, sectarian tradition – the presence in Scotland and Ireland of English armies of occupation led to the founding of nonconformist congregations in both nations.[87]

Once again, this widespread contemporary belief that the army really *was* a seminary of dangerous religious radicalism acquired a life, and hence a reality, of its own. Members of the army were accused of acts of desecration, sacrilege and profanity. They allegedly baptized animals in fonts; stabled their horses in churches; and swore, smoked and drank during religious services and prayers.[88] Moreover, they were charged with acts of iconoclasm that far exceeded anything sanctioned by parliamentary legislation; and there is some evidence that these charges contained a kernel of truth. A small minority of the soldiery attacked tombs and monuments and severely damaged a number of churches and cathedrals. Nevertheless, given that so much of our evidence for Civil War iconoclasm comes from hostile accounts, we must beware of exaggerating its overall impact.[89] In reality, incidents of excessive iconoclastic destruction by the army – and other members of society – were probably exceptionally rare.[90]

The pejorative image of an army of heretics can be juxtaposed with the New Model's perception of itself as an instrument of divine will. This Messianic confidence was founded on the intense religious zeal of numerous officers and troopers, which, in turn, inspired the conviction that God's special dispensation had continually favoured them in battle. Indeed, the language of Providentialism permeates the writings and speeches of many of its men, as in Oliver Cromwell's famous affirmation that the army's military victories were the work of none other 'but the hand of God'.[91] Providentialism was certainly not confined to the New Model, or even to Parliamentarians, as Anthony Milton emphasizes elsewhere in this volume.[92] But amongst a body of men that had been hardened and set apart from the rest of society by their experience of war, it had the capacity to provide an ideological basis for radical change. For if God Himself had witnessed against 'Charles Stuart, that man of blood', Charles's destruction was essential if expectations of the new millennium and Christ's kingdom on earth were to be realized.[93]

A millenarian impulse that drew upon the prophesies in the Books of Daniel and Revelation was perhaps integral to the character of Puritanism, and of English Protestantism more generally. Indeed, both scripture and history were adjudged to have ascribed a special role to England in the realization of God's purpose. Hence, the calling of the Long Parliament, the military conflict and the regicide all contributed to heightened expectations of an imminent kingdom of heaven on earth. Nevertheless, visions of a new godly society took remarkably contrasting forms, as in the case of the Diggers and Fifth Monarchists.[94]

The Diggers, or True Levellers, established a small number of agrarian communes on waste and common land in the Midlands and south of England in 1649–50. Their leader, Gerrard Winstanley, had been inspired by a vision in which God had told him, '*Worke together. Eat bread together*; declare this all abroad.'[95] Winstanley subsequently published a series of pamphlets that envisaged a wholesale restructuring of society: the abolition of private ownership of the land; the community of goods; and the levelling of all differences of rank and position amongst men. The Diggers' vision of a return to the pre-lapsarian condition before the Fall, drew upon a number of contemporary rhetorics, including practical Christianity[96] and the historical myth of the 'Norman Yoke' – the notion that an idealistic state was destroyed by the Conquest of 1066.[97] But in Winstanley, those languages were fused with the concept of the elect nation and a distinctive form of mystical Christianity. The result was a highly radical vision of the earth as a 'Common Treasury' in which *all* men would be free to submit themselves to a second coming within the individual.[98]

On a practical level, however, the Diggers' efforts were a dismal failure. Their digging-up and planting of common land symbolized a rejection of seignorial rights, but it attracted between only a hundred and two hundred followers amongst the labouring poor. [99] The pacifist Diggers had mistakenly believed that the justness of their cause would result in people voluntarily giving up their land to join them. Despite causing brief consternation amongst local landowners and the London press, their colonies were quickly and easily destroyed by countrymen and soldiers. Thus, while Winstanley is rightly credited as a significant figure in Civil War political thought,[100] the attraction of the Diggers to sympathetic, Left-wing historians has far outweighed their actual impact on events. Moreover, those scholars have wrongly characterized the Diggers' ideology as a revolt against the social moderation of the military revolution of 1648–9.[101] In fact, Winstanley's vision represented the final stage in a historic struggle against 'Kingly power' in which the Civil War and regicide had been an integral part.[102]

The downfall of monarchy was also central to the beliefs of the Fifth Monarchists, who emerged during the early 1650s. As the period's most zealous adherents to millennial prophesy, they equated the regicide with the end of the anti-Christian Fourth Monarchy, after which would follow the Fifth: the everlasting 'Kingdom of the Saints'. But this produced a vision of an élitist, hierarchical society in which the Fifth Monarchists, as the 'elect', would establish a theocratic government and impose a godly discipline over the unregenerate masses in preparation

for the return of King Jesus.[103] This form of 'hagiarchic radicalism'* –
with its emphasis on membership of the godly elect, 'the Saints', as the
qualification for rulership – is largely at variance with Revisionist char-
acterizations of Civil War radicalism with their emphasis on the primacy
of practical Christianity. Moreover, the anticipated period of rule by the
Fifth Monarchists themselves in preparation for the Second Coming left
them deeply concerned with the form of secular government.[104] But
although their supporters – who included influential figures in the army
such as Major-General Thomas Harrison – numbered perhaps as many
as ten thousand at their height, neither the Rump nor the Barebones
Parliaments were to meet their demands to transfer power to the saints.
And despite the violence of their language and belief in their right to
destroy the carnal institutions of the old world in preparation for the
next, only a tiny proportion of them were willing to take up arms during
risings in 1657 and 1661, uncertain of whether God had sanctioned such
action.[105]

The ideology of the Fifth Monarchists, like the vast majority of the
beliefs discussed so far, emerged from within theologically orthodox
Calvinist traditions. However, ideologies that repudiated many of the
central tenets of Calvinism – including the doctrine of predestination
(the belief that God, from all eternity, had decreed some to election, and
the reprobate to eternal damnation) and regular preaching and reading
of the Bible – became increasingly prevalent during the course of the
Civil War. This was perhaps most apparent in regard to the issue of
salvation. A number of sects and individuals challenged the notion that
man was incapable himself of doing anything to obtain salvation, by
advocating a *general* atonement: the belief that the death of Christ to save
all men made salvation possible for every individual who voluntarily
exercised their faith in Christ. General (as against Calvinist Particular)
Baptists, whose congregations were visible from the early 1640s, were
the most obvious proponents of that view.[106]

More notoriously, between 1649 and 1651 a small number of individuals known as Ranters promoted the doctrine of antinomianism:
the heresy that believers in Christ lived on earth in a state of grace and
were hence released from the moral law. Influenced by perfectionist
trends that were evident during the Radical Reformation, doctrinal
antinomianism had circulated both before and at earlier points during
the Civil War.[107] But what set the Ranters apart – and what so

* 'Hagiarchy' is literally 'government by the Saints', or the godly elect.

alarmed contemporary society – were the practical consequences of their beliefs. Although they were not an actual sect with a coherent ideology, the Ranters' assurance of their salvation led them to reject all moral constraints and engage in acts of blasphemous swearing, drunkenness and sexual libertinism. Imprisoned by the authorities until they recanted their tenets, the Ranters held a mystical claim to have become one with God, pointing to the development of a more spiritual form of religious speculation that located the divine within the natural world.[108] Laurence Clarkson, for example, denied the authority of scripture and held that God, as the author of all things, could destroy sin within the individual: 'those acts, or what act soever, so far as by thee is esteemed or imagined to be sinful, is not in God, nor from God, yet still . . . all acts that be are from God, yea as pure as God'.[109]

Like the Ranters, the Quakers were also extreme spiritualists who placed the Godhead – in the form of an inner light – within the individual. Recruiting many of their converts from amongst the other religious groups and sects, they emerged in the mid-1650s as the largest of them all (there were perhaps 40,000 Quakers by the early 1660s) and proclaimed salvation for all who embraced the internal spirit.[110] For Quakers, receiving the inner light was a process of judgement and resurrection within the individual, and was perhaps indicative of a gradual (and more widespread) disillusionment with outward notions of the Second Coming.[111] Quakers emphasized the workings of the internal Holy Spirit above any scriptural or worldly authority, and thus rejected the supremacy of the Bible, conventional ideas about the Trinity and the validity of the sacraments, and the Lord's Prayer. They were both aggressive and provocative in asserting their beliefs, launching verbal and printed assaults on 'hireling priests', and withholding tithes from the established ministry. Meanwhile, their physical activities ranged from the disruption of religious services in 'steeple houses' (their term for churches) to, most notoriously, James Nayler's allegedly blasphemous re-enactment in Bristol in 1656 of Christ's entry into Jerusalem. There was also an inherent social radicalism to Quaker ideology. They challenged the norms of social deference by their use of language – rejecting the more respectful 'you' in preference to 'thee' or 'thou' – and in their refusal to recognize titles and thus to bow or to doff hats. Furthermore, some of their writing openly attacked the nobility and gentry as a class for their accumulation of wealth and land at the expense of the common people.[112]

The predictable response of both the government and the nation at large was one of deep alarm, and the authorities rigorously prosecuted the Quakers. Contemporaries were wrong to assume, however, that they intended to invert the social order: they would have enforced some redistribution of wealth and their overall vision was that of a nation of small producers.[113] Like the vast majority of the Civil War sects and religious groups, the Quakers' ambition to create a godly state involved the rejection of numerous axioms of contemporary society, but it did not threaten the private ownership of property or the existing social structure. The writings of Winstanley and the Ranter Abiezer Coppe's outbursts against the rich[114] provide obvious exceptions to that rule, but the Diggers and Ranters were few in number, and their existence – if not the memory of them – was short-lived.

Nevertheless, many contemporary writers identified a generic association between religious radicalism, the lower orders and social inversion.[115] While the Diggers provide obvious support for that perception,[116] research has overwhelmingly demonstrated that the rank-and-file membership of the sects and religious groups was made up of the 'middling sort of people': craftsmen, small traders, yeomen and husbandmen. Some of their leaders were of even higher social status – affluent merchants, wealthy yeomen, the sons of lesser gentry. Many of those derided as 'tub preachers' were, in reality, university-trained ex-ministers of the established Church.[117] All this would point against the religious speculation of the Civil War being the product of a plebeian heretical tradition. A similar conclusion can also be inferred from the economic and political outlook of the larger sects, which reflected the likely interests of the 'middling sort': an attack on tithes, monopolies, excessive taxation, aspects of the legal system and the privileges of the nobility and gentry.[118] For as we have seen, radicalism was not only about religion.

V   CONCLUSION

This chapter has argued that Civil War radicalism was a dynamic and multifarious phenomenon encompassing contemporary demands for fundamental change. Those demands challenged an astonishing array of societal axioms and emanated from across the social strata. Indeed, the outbreak of the Covenanter rebellion in Scotland in 1638 marked the beginnings of a specific climate – a 'radical moment' – which provided contemporaries in all three Stuart kingdoms with the opportunity to call existing arrangements into question.[119] From its origins in the Scots' rejection of a new Prayer Book, that 'moment' spanned the long decade of the 1640s, inspired by an amazing sequence of political, religious and military events which brought about the collapse of numerous traditional institutions, values and assumptions. That destruction was one consequence of Civil War radicalism, the most startling outcome of the 'radical moment', a phenomenon that united the constitutional innovations of the political élite and the mystically-inspired communalism of the Diggers. Indeed, the inability of simple taxonomies to reflect the complexity of Civil War radicalism is entirely the consequence of its unstable quality, its various strands and the often divergent ideas of those who demanded radical change.

Notes

NOTES TO THE INTRODUCTION

Unless otherwise specified, the place of publication for books is London.

1. For Cromwell, see Blair Worden, 'Oliver Cromwell and the Sin of Achan', in D. E. D. Beales and Geoffrey Best (eds), *History, Society and the Churches: Essays in Honour of Owen Chadwick* (Cambridge, 1985), pp. 125–45; Bernard Capp, 'The Fifth Monarchists and Popular Millenarianism', in Barry Reay and J. F. McGregor (eds), *Radical Religion in the English Revolution* (Oxford, 1984), pp. 165–70; Geoffrey Nuttall, 'Millenarianism in the English Commonwealth', *Nederlands Archief voor Kerkgeschiedenis*, 67 (1987), 71–9.

2. This has been one of the major points of interpretation on which something approaching a consensus has emerged since the 1970s.

3. See, *inter alia*, Alan Everitt, *The County Committee of Kent in the Civil War* (Leicester, 1957); C. B. Phillips, 'County Committees and Local Government in Cumberland and Westmorland, 1642–60', *Northern History*, 5 (1970), 34–66; Jean Mather, 'The Parliamentary Committees and the Justices of the Peace, 1642–61', *American Journal of Legal History*, 23 (1979), 120–43; Ann Hughes, *Politics, Society and Civil War in Warwickshire, 1620–60* (Cambridge, 1987).

4. David Underdown, *A Freeborn People: Politics and the Nation in Seventeenth-Century England* (Oxford, 1996), p. 79 (for the quotation).

5. Allan Macinnes and Jane Ohlmeyer (eds), *The Stuart Kingdoms in the Seventeenth Century: Awkward Neighbours* (Dublin, 2002); for a longer perspective, see Hew Strachan, 'Scotland's Military Identity', *Scottish Historical Review*, 85 (2006), 315–32.

6. See the essays in Jane Ohlmeyer (ed.), *Ireland from Independence to Occupation 1641–60* (Cambridge, 1995); Micheál Ó Siochrú, 'The Confederates and the Irish Wars of the 1640s', in Liam Ronayne (ed.), *The Battle of Scariffhollis, 1650* (Letterkenny, 2001), pp. 7–15; Tadhg Ó hAnnracháin, 'Conflicting Loyalties, Conflicted Rebels: Political and Religious Allegiance among the Confederate Catholics of Ireland', *English Historical Review*, 119 (2004), 851–72.

7. Keith Thomas, *Religion and the Decline of Magic: Studies in Popular Beliefs in Sixteenth- and Seventeenth-Century England* (1971), pp. 136–9, 142; Christopher Hill, *Antichrist in Seventeenth-Century England* (London and New York, 1971); Malcolm Gaskill, *Witchfinders: A Seventeenth-Century English Tragedy* (2005), pp. 137–8, and his 'Witchcraft, Politics, and Memory in Seventeenth-Century England', *Historical Journal*, 50 (2007), 289–308.

8. Julie Spraggon, *Puritan Iconoclasm during the English Civil War* (Woodbridge, 2003); Keith Thomas, 'Art and Iconoclasm in Early Modern England', in Kenneth Fincham and Peter Lake (eds), *Religious Politics in Post-Reformation England: Essays in Honour of Nicholas Tyacke* (Woodbridge, 2006), pp. 16–40.

9. Tim Harris, *Restoration: Charles II and his Kingdoms, 1660–85* (2005).

10. In the case of Ireland, while the memory of the Kilkenny Confederation and the subsequent 'Cromwellian' conquest of 1649–51 remained strong in the kingdom, the significance of the events of the 1640s and 1650s was arguably eclipsed by William III's invasion of 1690–1.

11. Tim Harris, *London Crowds in the Reign of Charles II: Propaganda and Politics from the Restoration until the Exclusion Crisis* (Cambridge, 1987).

12. R. C. Richardson, 'Re-fighting the English Revolution: John Nalson (1637–86) and the Frustrations of Late Seventeenth-Century English Historiography', *European Review of History*, 14 (2007), 1–20.

13. See, e.g., Sir William Dugdale, *A Short View of the Late Troubles in England* (1681).

14. Timothy Lang, *The Victorians and the Stuart Heritage: Interpretations of a Discordant Past* (Cambridge, 1995); J. W. Burrow, *A Liberal Descent: Victorian Historians and the English Past* (Cambridge, 1981); J. Hamburger, *Macaulay and the Whig Tradition* (Chicago and London, 1976). For the problems of terminology, see, e.g., G. E. Aylmer, *Rebellion or Revolution? England, 1640–60* (Oxford, 1986). It is noteworthy that Sir Keith Feiling's study of the Tory Party dated its inception to 1640: see his *A History of the Tory Party, 1640–1714* (Oxford, 1924).

15. S. R. Gardiner, *History of the Great Civil War*, first published in three volumes (1886–91); subsequent references are to the four-volume 1893 edition, reprinted in 1987.

16. For a succinct introduction to this theme, see R. C. Richardson, *The Debate on the English Revolution* (3rd edn, Manchester, 1999), pp. 74–99.

17. J. C. D. Clark, *Revolution and Rebellion: State and Society in England in the Seventeenth and Eighteenth Centuries* (Cambridge, 1986).

18. Blair Worden, *Roundhead Reputations: The English Civil War and the Passions of Posterity* (2001).

19. Keith Thomas, 'When the Lid came off England', *New York Review of Books*, 27 May 2004.

20. Cf. George Santayana, *The Life of Reason: The Phases of Human Progress*, 5 vols (New York, 1905–6), I, 284.

21. For the earlier, overtly partisan interpretations against which Gardiner and his contemporaries reacted, see G. P. Gooch, *History and Historians in the Nineteenth Century* (1952) – a work actually completed before the First World War; J. P. Kenyon, *The History Men: The Historical Profession in England since the Renaissance* (1983), pp. 102–8; Richardson, *Debate on the English Revolution*, pp. 74–99.

22. Quoted in A. Dwight Culler, *The Victorian Mirror of History* (New Haven, CT, and London, 1985), p. 281. For the German influence on English historiography, see C. E. McClelland, *The German Historians and England* (Cambridge, 1971), Ch. 6.

23. Among Gardiner's noble Royalists were Lucius Cary, 2nd Viscount Falkland, and William Chillingworth; see Gardiner, *Civil War*, I, 218, 285.

24. Gardiner, *Civil War*, II, 108: '[Laud's] nobler aims were too much in accordance with the needs of his age to be altogether baffled. It is little that every parish church in the land still . . . presents a spectacle which realises his hopes. It is far more that his refusal to submit his mind to the dogmatism of Puritanism, and his appeal to the cultivated intelligence for the solution of religious problems,

has received an ever-increasing response, even in regions in which his memory is devoted to contemptuous obloquy'.

25. Cambridge University Lib., Add. MS 8119/I/W114b (Acton papers): S. R. Gardiner to A. W. Ward, 1 October 1899.

26. See C. S. R. Russell, 'The British Problem and the English Civil War', *History*, 72 (1987), 395–415; and idem, *The Causes of the English Civil War* (Oxford, 1990), Ch. 2: 'The Problem of Multiple Kingdoms'; see also John Adamson, 'The English Context of the British Civil Wars', *History Today*, 48 (1998), 23–9; reprinted in Stanley Carpenter (ed.), *The English Civil War* (2007), pp. 173–80.

27. For one of Conrad Russell's earlier forays into 'British' history, see his 'Why did Charles I call the Long Parliament?', *History*, 69 (1984), 375–83; an approach which received its fullest exposition in his *The Fall of the British Monarchies, 1637–42* (Oxford, 1991).

28. Nicholas Tyacke, 'Archbishop Laud', in Kenneth Fincham (ed.), *The Early Stuart Church, 1603–42* (Basingstoke, 1993), pp. 51–70; and Tyacke's 'Puritanism, Arminianism and Counter-Revolution', in Margo Todd (ed.), *Reformation to Revolution: Politics and Religion in Early Modern England* (London and New York, 1995), pp. 53–70. On the Laudian altar policy, see Kenneth Fincham and Nicholas Tyacke, *Altars Restored: The Changing Face of English Religious Worship, 1547–c.1700* (Oxford, 2007), esp. Chs 5–6.

29. Gardiner, *Civil War*, III, 200.

30. Gardiner, *Civil War*, III, 200.

31. Independently, Nicholas Tyacke reached very similar conclusions and developed them persuasively in his essay 'Puritanism, Arminianism and Counter-Revolution', in Conrad Russell (ed.), *The Origins of the English Civil War* (1973), pp. 119–43.

32. For Marx's influence on the historiography of seventeenth-century England, the most accessible summary is Richardson, *Debate on the English Revolution*, pp. 125–31.

33. For attestations to Weber's influence, see Christopher Hill, *Economic Problems of the Church: From Archbishop Whitgift to the Long Parliament* (Oxford, 1956), p. x; Lawrence Stone, *The Crisis of the Aristocracy, 1558–1641* (Oxford, 1965), p. 6.

34. Max Weber, 'Die protestantische Ethik und der Geist des Kapitalismus', *Archiv für Sozialwissenschaft und Sozialpolitik*, 20 (1904) and 21 (1905); republished, with extensive notes, as *Die protestantische Ethik und der Geist des Kapitalismus* (Berlin, 1920). The first English edition appeared in 1930 as *The Protestant Ethic and the Spirit of Capitalism* in translation by Talcott Parsons, with an introduction by R. H. Tawney.

35. Gardiner, *Civil War*, I, 224; for an admirable recent survey of Irish history, see Toby Barnard, *The Kingdom of Ireland, 1641–1760* (Basingstoke, 2004).

36. Gardiner, *Civil War*, I, 226. His remarks refer, immediately, to the development of Scotland, but he clearly thought they applied to England as well.

37. For the *locus classicus* of this thesis, see Wallace Notestein, 'The Winning of the Initiative by the House of Commons', *Proceedings of the British Academy*, 11 (1924–5), 125–75.

38. John Adamson, 'Eminent Victorians: S. R. Gardiner and the Liberal as Hero', *Historical Journal*, 33 (1990), 641–57, esp. pp. 651–3.

39. Significantly, the one serious academic monograph on the Royalists published in the period between Gardiner and the advent of the Revisionists nearly a century later did not find a British or American publisher; see Paul H. Hardacre, *The Royalists during the Puritan Revolution* (The Hague, 1956). Hardacre notes that 'although amply noticed in martyrologies and other forms of contemporary [i.e. seventeenth-century] writing', the Royalists 'have since been largely neglected'; ibid., p. vii. Royalists also received some attention – though, perhaps significantly, only in defeat – from David Underdown in his book *Royalist Conspiracy in England, 1649–60* (New Haven, CT, 1960).

40. Sir Charles Harding Firth, *The House of Lords during the Civil War* (1910). See B. K. Murray, *The People's Budget, 1909–10: Lloyd George and Liberal Politics* (Oxford, 1980); and Ian Packer, *Lloyd George, Liberalism and the Land: The Land Issue and Party Politics in England, 1906–14* (Woodbridge and Rochester, NY, 2001).

41. Firth, *House of Lords during the Civil War*, p. vi.

42. A rare, and minor, exception was the Marxist historian Brian Manning's 'The Nobles, the People, and the Constitution', *Past & Present*, 9 (1956), 42–64. It was not until the publication of Lawrence Stone's *Crisis of the Aristocracy, 1558–1641* (Oxford, 1965) and Menna Prestwich's *Cranfield: Politics and Profits under the Early Stuarts – the Career of Lionel Cranfield, Earl of Middlesex* (Oxford, 1966) that the issue once again returned to scholarly attention.

43. For contemporary criticism of Gardiner, see also R. G. Usher, *A Critical Study of the Historical Method of S. R. Gardiner* (Washington University Studies, III, Part 2, no. 1, 1915); and P. B. M. Blaas, *Continuity and Anachronism: Parliamentary and Constitutional Development in Whig Historiography and in the Anti-Whig Reaction between 1890 and 1930* (The Hague, 1978).

44. Thomas Ashton, 'Richard Henry Tawney, 1880–1962', *Proceedings of the British Academy*, 48 (1963 for 1962), 461–82; Simon J. D. Green, 'The Tawney–Strauss Connection: on Historicism and Values in the History of Political Ideas', *Journal of Modern History*, 67 (1995), 255–77.

45. R. H. Tawney, *Religion and the Rise of Capitalism: A Historical Study* (1926; rep. Harmondsworth, 1977 edn). Subsequent page references are to this 1977 (Penguin Press) edition. Tawney had first sketched out the project, as one of the works he hoped to write ('if ever I have the chance'), as early as 1914: a work on 'The rise of capitalism, . . . the economic causes for the opposition of the middle classes to the monarchy . . .', and ending with 1688; see J. M. Winter and D. M. Joslin (eds), *R. H. Tawney's Commonplace Book* (Cambridge, 1972), pp. 80–1.

46. Tawney, *Religion and the Rise of Capitalism*, pp. 198–9.

47. Tawney, *Religion and the Rise of Capitalism*, p. 202.

48. Tawney, *Religion and the Rise of Capitalism*, pp. 207, 208. Predictably, Archbishop Laud is condemned not merely because of his religiously-founded hostility to Puritanism, but because he stood in the way of economic progress; he reversed 'the policy of Elizabethan Privy Councils, which characteristically thought diversity of trades more important than unity of religion'; ibid., p. 205.

49. Tawney, *Religion and the Rise of Capitalism*, p. 201.

50. W. C. Sellar and R. J. Yeatman, *1066 and All That* (1930), p. 71.

51. Max Weber, *The Protestant Ethic and the Spirit of Capitalism*, trans. Talcott Parsons, with a foreword by R. H. Tawney (1930). For its impact on Marxist writers, see A. L. Morton, *A People's History of England* (1938), p. 222; and

Christopher Hill, *The English Revolution 1640* (1940), p. 6. Hill wrote that Parliament beat the king because it could appeal to the 'enthusiastic support of the trading and industrial classes in town and countryside, [and] to the yeomen and progressive gentry . . .'.

52. This was a trend that Christopher Hill was too good a historian not to notice, and, in his mature work, not to counsel against: 'Puritanism', he wrote, 'would not have been the historical force it was if it had been a mere economic reflex.' That he felt constrained to make this point at all suggests the existence, then, of historians for whom Puritanism was indeed little more than an 'economic reflex'; see his *Economic Problems of the Church*, p. xiii, and see also his remarks on p. x.

53. For this theme, see Margaret Spufford, 'Puritanism and Social Control', in Anthony Fletcher and John Stevenson (eds), *Order and Disorder in Early Modern England* (Cambridge, 1985), pp. 41–57.

54. See, pp. 21–4, this volume.

55. Where the Church did come in for examination by mainstream historians, it tended to be in its social and juridical guises, rather than its strictly religious (pastoral and theological) dimension. Hill put the point clearly in his *Economic Problems of the Church*, observing that 'the Church was far more than a religious institution: it was a political and economic institution of the greatest power and importance. There might be many reasons, over and above the purely religious, why men should wish to overthrow the ecclesiastical hierarchy in 1640'; Hill, *Economic Problems of the Church*, p. x. It might be argued that, half a century after Hill wrote these words, the historiographical pendulum has swung too far in the other direction, and an insufficiently nuanced emphasis on the social and secular aspects of the Caroline Church has been replaced by an insufficiently nuanced emphasis of another kind, on the devotional and theological.

56. John Burrow, *A History of Histories: Epics, Chronicles, Romances and Inquiries from Herodotus and Thucydides to the Twentieth Century* (2007), p. 486.

57. In this paragraph, I have drawn heavily on Burrow's account of 'Marxism: the Last Grand Narrative?' in his *History of Histories*, pp. 486–7 – even to the point of paraphrasing, at various points, his own.

58. Burrow, *History of Histories*, p. 487.

59. This was published to commemorate the tercentenary of the 'English Revolution *of 1640*' – an event which, significantly, Hill dated to the moment when Charles I was first challenged by the English people, rather than to the outbreak of war in 1642, or the regicide in 1649. It is worthy of note that more recent works on the 1640s have tended (however much they disagree with Hill's explanatory apparatus) to reaffirm the 'revolutionary' aspects of the political crisis in its pre-Civil War phase: e.g., David Cressy, *England on Edge* (Oxford, 2006); and John Adamson, *The Noble Revolt: The Overthrow of Charles I* (2007).

60. Hill, the Marxists' most historically gifted and intellectually nimble representative, was to be one of the moving spirits behind the foundation of the journal *Past & Present* (in 1952), eventually became Master of Balliol (Tawney's own Oxford college), and was later described by E. P. Thompson (another highly influential fellow Marxist) as the 'dean and paragon of English historians'.

61. Hill made much of the fact that the Long Parliament swept away wardships during the 1640s, one of the last of the feudal incidents owed by the

landowning class to the Crown – and one that was not revived at the Restoration.

62. For a discussion of Hill's writings, see David Underdown, 'Puritanism, Revolution, and Christopher Hill', in Geoff Eley and William Hunt (eds), *Reviving the English Revolution: Reflections and Elaborations on the Work of Christopher Hill* (1988), pp. 333–41.

63. Hill's own historical *oeuvre* provides a case in point.

64. Hugh Trevor-Roper was perhaps the most vigorous rower against this tide; Blair Worden, 'Hugh Redwald Trevor-Roper', *Proceedings of the British Academy*, 150 (2007), 246–84, esp. pp. 262–9.

65. For the best survey of this subject, and guide to its voluminous literature, see Felicity Heal and Clive Holmes, *The Gentry in England and Wales, 1500–1700* (1994). J. P. Cooper had objected to counties being taken as the appropriate geographical unit of research as early as 1956, pointing out that it made little sense for affluent families (gentry and noble), which might have multiple holdings, and multiple seats, in a variety of counties: see his *Land, Men and Beliefs: Studies in Early Modern History*, ed. G. E. Aylmer and J. S. Morrill (1983), p. 15. (I owe this observation to Mr Christopher Thompson.)

66. R. H. Tawney, 'The Rise of the Gentry, 1558–1640', *Economic History Review*, 11 (1941), 1–38.

67. H. R. Trevor-Roper, 'The Gentry, 1540–1640', *Economic History Review*, Supplement (1953).

68. Prestwich, *Cranfield*, p. xv.

69. Trevor-Roper, 'The Gentry'.

70. For Trevor-Roper's early interest in Weber, see his *Archbishop Laud, 1573–1645* (1940; 3rd edn, 1988), pp. x, 138n. He later came to castigate the 'German sociologists' for the 'confusion' they had caused; Hugh Trevor-Roper, *Letters from Oxford: Hugh Trevor-Roper to Bernard Berenson*, ed. Richard Davenport-Hines (2006), p. 199. A 'long work . . . on Max Weber's thesis on capitalism and the Reformation' was one of several historical projects that Trevor-Roper began but left unfinished in the 1950s; see Worden, 'Trevor-Roper', p. 263.

71. For the literature, see R. H. Tawney, 'The Rise of the Gentry, 1558–1640', in E. M. Carus-Wilson (ed.), *Essays in Economic History* (1954), pp. 173–214; idem, 'The Rise of the Gentry: A Postscript', *Economic History Review*, 7 (1954), 91–7; Richard Matz, '"The Rise of the Gentry": en debatt om den stora engelska revolutionens sociala bakgrund', *Historisk Tidskrift (Svenska Historiska Föreningen)*, 2nd ser., 78 (1958), 298–322; Perez Zagorin, 'The Social Interpretation of the English Revolution', *Journal of Economic History*, 19 (1959), 376–401; J. H. Hexter, 'Storm over the Gentry', in idem, *Reappraisals in History* (Evanston, IL, 1961), pp. 117–62; G. R. Elton, 'Stuart Government', *Past & Present*, 20 (1961), 76–82; D. C. Coleman, 'The "Gentry" Controversy and the Aristocracy in Crisis', *History*, 51 (1966), 165–78.

72. J. H. Hexter, 'Storm over the Gentry', in his *Reappraisals in History* (London and Evanston, IL, 1961), pp. 117–62.

73. For an introduction, see John Brooke, 'Namier and Namierism', *History and Theory*, 3 (1964), 331–47.

74. As one group of critics has put it, 'a great deal of the most distinguished writing on the political and religious history of the period was centred on questions

about the long-term social and economic causes and nature of the English Revolution. In many ways, what we were seeing here was the fag end, the long death, of the gentry controversy'; Thomas Cogswell, Richard Cust, and Peter Lake, 'Revisionism and its Legacies: the Work of Conrad Russell', in Cogswell , Cust and Lake (eds), *Politics, Religion and Popularity in Early Stuart England: Essays in Honour of Conrad Russell* (Cambridge, 2002), p. 3.

75. David Underdown, *Pride's Purge: Politics in the Puritan Revolution* (Oxford, 1971); Austin Woolrych's *Commonwealth to Protectorate* (Oxford, 1982) was largely researched and written in the 1970s. A subtler and more nuanced model was offered by Blair Worden's *The Rump Parliament, 1648–53* (Cambridge, 1974).

76. So named after one of its more outlandishly named members, Praise-God Barbon.

77. Cogswell, Cust, and Lake, 'Revisionism and its Legacies', p. 2. It is hardly coincidental, given the prevailing *zeitgeist* of their historical moment, that both these fine studies by Underdown and Woolrych focused on moments when gentry influence (indeed, sub-gentry influence) on English politics was at its strongest, and the influence of the titular nobility all but eclipsed.

78. Tawney, *Religion and the Rise of Capitalism*, pp. 207, 208.

79. Perez Zagorin, 'The Court and the Country: a Note on Political Terminology in the Earlier Seventeenth Century', *English Historical Review*, 77 (1962), 306–11; developed in his monograph, *The Court and the Country: The Beginning of the English Revolution* (1969).

80. Lawrence Stone, *The Crisis of the Aristocracy, 1558–1641* (Oxford, 1965).

81. Stone, *Crisis of the Aristocracy*, p. 11.

82. Stone, *Crisis of the Aristocracy*, p. 753.

83. Interestingly, Prestwich was one of the historians who wrote (in 1966) of 'the revolution of 1641'; Prestwich, *Cranfield*, p. xv.

84. Stone, *Crisis of the Aristocracy*, pp. 751–2. Similarly, 'the royalist peers failed to realize that on the Privy Council and in the country they were merely being used by the king as a useful cover for his autocratic pretensions'; ibid.

85. For a fine survey, drawing on this extensive research, see Heal and Holmes, *The Gentry in England and Wales, 1500–1700*.

86. For Stone's admiration for Tawney, see Lawrence Stone, 'R. H. Tawney', *Past & Present*, 21 (1962), 73–7; though it should be noted that this admiration was not uncritical; see Stone's remarks in *Crisis of the Aristocracy*, p. xviii.

87. See also J. C. D. Clark, *Revolution and Rebellion: State and Society in England in the Seventeenth and Eighteenth Centuries* (Cambridge, 1986), pp. 57, 166, where Professor Clark takes a more dismissive view of the usefulness of these county studies than I do.

88. The exception was the work of G. E. Aylmer on the bureaucracies of Charles I and of the English Commonwealth and Protectorate; yet while both these monographs were politically aware, their concern was primarily with the social and economic impact of office-holding. Neither had any significant long-term impact on the received political narratives of the period, nor did either book really strive to do so; see G. E. Aylmer, *The King's Servants: The Civil Service of Charles I, 1625–42* (London and New York, 1961); and his *The State's Servants: The Civil Service of the English Republic, 1649–60* (1973).

89. Some of the finest political history produced in the 1960s and 1970s involved the exploration of the impact of 'localism' on national politics, as, for example, in David Underdown's *Pride's Purge*, and his later work, *A Freeborn People*.

90. Prestwich, *Cranfield*, pp. 10–48, 375–422.

91. Clive Holmes, 'The County Community in Stuart Historiography', *Journal of British Studies*, 19 (1980)', 54, quoting respectively John Morrill, *The Revolt of the Provinces: Conservatives and Radicals in the English Civil War, 1630–50* ([1st edn], 1976), p. 22, and Alan Everitt, *The Local Community and the Great Rebellion* (1969), p. 8. Professor Morrill wrote that the provincialism of the gentry did not exclude 'concern for general or national political and constitutional issues, but rather that such issues took on local colours and were articulated within local contexts'. Accepting Alan Everitt's contention that local identity mattered more to Tudor gentlemen than their national identity, it followed that the proper focus of attention was the county – where national issues were 'articulated' – not the world of Westminster; see Morrill's revised edition, published as *Revolt in the Provinces: the People of England and the Tragedies of War, 1630–48* (2nd edn, 1999), p. 25.

92. Morrill, *The Revolt of the Provinces*. The theme of the largely depoliticized character of the English population is perhaps most strikingly expressed in Professor Underdown's work on Somerset, in which he wrote that 'the war [the Civil War] had been fought between two minorities, struggling in a sea of neutralism and apathy. And the further down the social scale we penetrate, the more neutralism and apathy we encounter'; David Underdown, *Somerset in the Civil War and Interregnum* (Newton Abbot, 1973), pp. 117–18. It is only fair to point out that Underdown's later work substantially revises these conclusions.

93. Holmes, 'County Community', 54–73; and see the untitled review by Anthony Fletcher, in *Historical Journal*, 25 (1982), 259–62.

94. Notably, Ann Hughes, *Politics, Society and Civil War in Warwickshire, 1620–60* (Cambridge, 1987); her *Godly Reformation and its Opponents in Warwickshire, 1640–62* (Dugdale Society, Occasional Papers, 35, Stratford-upon-Avon, 1993); Thomas Cogswell, *Home Divisions: Aristocracy, the State and Provincial Conflict* (Manchester, 1998); John Walter, *Understanding Popular Violence in the English Revolution: The Colchester Plunderers* (Cambridge, 1999); and John Walter, 'Crown and Crowd: Popular Culture and Popular Protest in Early Modern England', in his *Crowds and Popular Politics in Early Modern England* (Manchester, 2006), pp. 14–26.

95. Clive Holmes, 'Centre and Locality in Civil War England', Chapter 6 in this volume, pp. 153–74.

96. Holmes, 'Centre and Locality', p. 173.

97. See Lawrence Stone, 'The Revival of Narrative: Reflections on a New Old History', *Past & Present*, 85 (1979), 3–24; Peter Burke, 'History of Events and the Revival of Narrative', in Peter Burke (ed.), *New Perspectives on Historical Writing* (2nd edn, University Park, PA, 2001), pp. 283–300.

98. Peter Lake, 'Retrospective: Wentworth's Political World in Revisionist and Post-Revisionist Perspective', in J. F. Merritt (ed.), *The Political World of Thomas Wentworth, Earl of Strafford, 1621–41* (Cambridge, 1996), p. 255.

99. C. V. Wedgwood, *The King's Peace, 1637–41* (1955); *The King's War, 1642–7* (1958); *The Trial of Charles I* (1964).

100. Conrad Russell, *The Fall of the British Monarchies, 1637–42* (Oxford, 1991). Kevin Sharpe's fine study of the 1630s, *The Personal Rule of Charles I* (New Haven, CT, and London, 1992), though organized chronologically, retains the broadly analytical and thematic structure favoured by most other historians of the period.

101. Anthony Fletcher, *The Outbreak of the English Civil War* (1981), p. viii. On the longevity of Gardiner's narrative, see also Cogswell, Cust, and Lake, 'Revisionism and its Legacies', p. 1.

102. The *locus classicus* is Christopher Hill's *The World Turned Upside-Down: Radical Ideas during the English Revolution* (London and New York, 1972); discussed above, in Chapter 8, Philip Baker, 'Rhetoric, Reality and the Varieties of Civil War Radicalism'.

103. They might well have been heard earlier had Hugh Trevor-Roper decided to publish the monograph (in 2008 still unpublished) which he prepared at this time on the causes and course of the Civil War; see Blair Worden, 'Godly Mafia', *London Review of Books*, 24 May 2007, pp. 12–13, and Trevor-Roper, *Letters from Oxford*, pp. 241, 244, 249–51. As it was, the first shots were fired by Sir Geoffrey Elton; see his essays from the 1960s and 1970s, 'The Stuart Century', 'A High Road to Civil War?' and 'The Unexplained Revolution', reprinted in G. R. Elton, *Studies in Tudor and Stuart Politics and Government*, 4 vols (Cambridge, 1974–92), II.

104. Conrad Russell, *Parliaments and English Politics, 1621–29* (Oxford, 1979); and see his introduction to the anthology of his own essays, *Unrevolutionary England* (1990), pp. ix–xi. The title of this last book is itself illustrative of how strongly Russell regarded his interpretation of pre-Civil War England negatively – in terms of what it was *not* – rather than in terms of an affirmatory alternative interpretation.

105. One of the earliest and most perceptive accounts of the points rejected by the Revisionists is J. C. D. Clark, *Revolution and Rebellion: State and Society in England in the Seventeenth and Eighteenth Centuries* (Cambridge, 1986).

106. This point is particularly marked in the work of Sharpe, Russell, and Kishlansky: see Conrad Russell, 'Parliamentary History in Perspective, 1604–29', *History*, 61 (1976), 1–27; Kevin Sharpe, 'Introduction: Parliamentary History, 1603–29: In or Out of Perspective?', in Sharpe (ed.), *Faction and Parliament: Essays on Early Stuart History* (Oxford, 1978), pp. 1–42; Sharpe, *Personal Rule*; Mark A. Kishlansky, *Parliamentary Selection: Social and Political Choice in Early Modern England* (Cambridge, 1986).

107. This thesis, first adumbrated in Mark Kishlansky, 'The Emergence of Adversary Politics in the Long Parliament', *Journal of Modern History*, 49 (1977), 617–40, is developed on a much larger scale in his *Parliamentary Selection*.

108. Richard Cust and Ann Hughes (eds), *Conflict in Early Stuart England: Studies in Religion and Politics, 1603–42* (1989); perhaps the most perceptive account of the 'post-revisionist' critique is to be found in Cogswell, Cust, and Lake, 'Revisionism and its Legacies', pp. 1–17.

109. Russell, *Causes of the English Civil War*, p. 213.

110. Russell, *Causes of the English Civil War*, Ch. 8: 'The Man Charles Stuart', and pp. 212–13.

111. Adamson, 'Eminent Victorians', p. 654.

112. See, for example, Glenn Burgess (ed.), *The New British History: Founding a Modern State, 1603–1715* (London and New York, 1999); J. G. A. Pocock, 'The New British History in Atlantic Perspective: an Antipodean Commentary', *American Historical Review*, 104 (1999), 490–500; John Morrill, 'Thinking about the New British History', in David Armitage (ed.), *British Political Thought in History: Literature and Theory, 1500–1800* (Cambridge, 2006), pp. 23–46.

113. Peter Lake, 'Anti-Popery: the Structure of a Prejudice', in Cust and Hughes, *Conflict in Early Stuart England*, p. 72.

114. Jane H. Ohlmeyer, 'Strafford, the "Londonderry Business" and the "New British History"', in Julia F. Merritt (ed.), *The Political World of Thomas Wentworth, Earl of Strafford, 1621–41* (Cambridge, 1996), pp. 209–29; Pocock, 'The New British History in Atlantic Perspective', pp. 490–500; see also the essays in Burgess, *New British History*; for a revisiting of this theme, see Morrill, 'Thinking about the New British History', pp. 23–46.

115. Something of the prevailing attitude towards political history at the beginning of the 1970s is suggested by Geoffrey Elton's remark that 'the writing of political history . . . is at present under something of a cloud. At least some professional historians incline to treat it as a rather old-fashioned and manifestly inadequate – even an uninteresting – form'; G. R. Elton, *Political History: Principles and Practice* (1970), p. 57.

116. Sharpe, 'Introduction: Parliamentary History, 1603–29'.

117. Lake, 'Wentworth's Political World in Revisionist and Post-Revisionist Perspective', p. 260, to which my paragraph is heavily indebted. However, some three decades on from the advent of the Revisionists (in which length of time Gardiner had completed all ten volumes of his *History of England* for 1603–42 and the four sequel volumes on 1642–9), there is still only episodic narrative coverage of the period Gardiner made his own: Russell on 1637–42; Fletcher on 1641–2; Kishlansky on 1644–7; Underdown on 1648–9. There is a fine short synthesis of recent work, by David Scott, *Politics and War in the Three Stuart Kingdoms, 1637–49* (2004).

118. On the lack of a sophisticated post-Gardinerian narrative of the 'Puritan Revolution', see Worden, 'Trevor-Roper', p. 267. Here the author must declare an interest; the first part of his own attempt to provide such a narrative account of the 1640s was published in 2007 as *The Noble Revolt: The Overthrow of Charles I.*

119. See, in particular, Austin Woolrych, *Britain in Revolution, 1625–60* (Oxford, 2002); Michael Braddick, *God's Fury, England's Fire: A New History of the English Civil Wars* (2008). There have also been two 'popular histories': one by a military historian, Trevor Royle, *The Civil War: The War of the Three Kingdoms, 1638–60* (2004); and one by a non-historian: Diane Purkiss, *The English Civil War: A People's History* (2006).

120. Sir Keith Thomas's; see his 'The Man who would be King', *Guardian* [London], 8 March 2008, a review of Braddick, *God's Fury, England's Fire: A New History of the English Civil Wars*.

121. The major publications on this theme began with Nicholas Tyacke's 'Puritanism, Arminianism and Counter-Revolution', in Russell, *The Origins of the English Civil War*, pp. 119–43, and this thesis was more fully developed in Nicholas Tyacke, *Anti-Calvinists: The Rise of English Arminianism c.1590–1640*

(Oxford, 1987). Since Tyacke, the major contributions have come from Anthony Milton and Kenneth Fincham; see Milton's *Catholic and Reformed: Roman and Protestant Churches in English Protestant Thought, 1600–40* (Cambridge, 1995); idem, 'The Creation of Laudianism: a New Approach', in Cogswell, Cust, and Lake, *Politics, Religion and Popularity*, pp. 162–84; Kenneth Fincham and Nicholas Tyacke, *Altars Restored: The Changing Face of English Religious Worship, 1547–c.1700* (Oxford, 2007).

122. P. R. Newman, 'Catholic Royalists of Northern England, 1642–5', *Northern History*, 15 (1979), 88–95; David L. Smith, 'The 4th Earl of Dorset and the Politics of the Sixteen-Twenties', *Historical Research*, 65 (1992), 37–53; idem, *Constitutional Royalism and the Search for Settlement, c.1640–49* (Cambridge, 1994); Geoffrey Smith, *The Cavaliers in Exile, 1640–60* (Basingstoke, 2003); Martin van Gelderen, 'Rebels und Royalists: Gewissen, Kirche und Freiheit in England und Holland (1585–1645)', in Georg Schmidt, Martin van Gelderen, and Christopher Snigula (eds), *Kollektive Freiheitsvorstellungen im frühneuzeitlichen Europa (1400–1800)* (Frankfurt am Main, 2005); and see particularly the important essay by David Scott, 'Counsel and Cabal in the King's Party, 1642–6', in Jason McElligott and David L. Smith (eds), *Royalists and Royalism during the English Civil Wars* (Cambridge, 2007), pp. 112–35.

123. Brian P. Levack, 'The Civil Law, Theories of Absolutism, and Political Conflict in Late Sixteenth- and Early Seventeenth-Century England', in Gordon J. Schochet, P. E. Tatspaugh, and Carol Brobeck (eds), *Law, Literature and the Settlement of Régimes: Papers Presented at the Folger Institute Seminar 'Political Thought in the Elizabethan Age, 1558–1603'* (Washington, DC, 1990), pp. 29–48; Johann Sommerville, 'English and European Political Ideas in the Early Seventeenth Century: Revisionism and the Case of Absolutism', *Journal of British Studies*, 35 (1996), 168–94; Glenn Burgess, *Absolute Monarchy and the Stuart Constitution* (New Haven, CT, and London, 1996); Linda Levy Peck, 'Beyond the Pale: John Cusacke and the Language of Absolutism in Early Stuart Britain', *Historical Journal*, 41 (1998), 121–49; Johann P. Sommerville, *Royalists and Patriots: Politics and Ideology in England 1603–40* (rev. [2nd] edn, 1999); Mark Charles Fissel, 'Early Stuart Absolutism and the Strangers' Consulage', in Buchanan Sharp and Mark C. Fissel (eds), *Law and Authority in Early Modern England: Essays Presented to Thomas Garden Barnes* (Newark, DE, 2007), pp. 186–223.

124. Phil Withington, *The Politics of Commonwealth: Citizens and Freemen in Early Modern England* (Cambridge, 2005).

125. The current generation of writers on the king's party owes much to two scholars who pioneered the exploration of this terrain: Ronald Hutton, whose Oxford DPhil dissertation was published as *The Royalist War Effort, 1642–6*, in 1982; and Ian Roy, whose first contribution to the subject appeared as early as 1962, as 'The Royalist Council of War, 1642–6', *Bulletin of the Institute of Historical Research*, 35 (1962), 150–68; for a more recent contribution, see his 'George Digby, Royalist Intrigue and the Collapse of the Cause', in Ian Gentles, John Morrill, and Blair Worden (eds), *Soldiers, Writers and Statesmen of the English Revolution* (Cambridge, 1998), pp. 68–90.

126. Christopher Hill, 'Parliament and People in Seventeenth-Century England', *Past & Present*, 92 (1981), 100–24; idem, 'Parliament and People in Seventeenth-Century England: a Rejoinder', *Past & Present*, 98 (1983), 155–8.

For a subtler critique of some of the early Revisionists' work, see Derek Hirst, 'Unanimity in the Commons, Aristocratic Intrigues, and the Origins of the English Civil War', *Journal of Modern History*, 50 (1978), 51–71.

127. For an example of the political factionalism underlying the organization of the Parliament's army, following the New-Modelling of 1644–5, see John Adamson, 'Of Armies and Architecture: The Employments of Robert Scawen', in Gentles, Morrill, and Worden, *Soldiers, Writers and Statesmen of the English Revolution*, pp. 36–67; John Adamson, 'The Triumph of Oligarchy: the Management of War and the Committee of Both Kingdoms, 1644–5', in Chris R. Kyle and Jason Peacey (eds), *Parliament at Work: Parliamentary Committees, Political Power, and Public Access in Early Modern England* (Woodbridge, 2002), pp. 101–27.

128. Jason McElligott and David L. Smith, 'Introduction: Rethinking Royalists and Royalism', in McElligott and Smith (eds), *Royalists and Royalism during the English Civil Wars* (Cambridge, 2007), p. 9.

129. Anthony Milton, 'Anglicanism and Royalism in the 1640s', Chapter 2 in this volume, pp. 61–81. For the leading advocate of 'constitutional Royalism', see David L. Smith, *Constitutional Royalism and the Search for Settlement, c.1640–49* (Cambridge, 1994).

130. Henry Hammond, *Considerations of Present Use concerning the Danger resulting from the Change of our Church Government* (1645), pp. 1, 3, 14–15.

131. Alan Cromartie, *The Constitutionalist Revolution: An Essay on the History of England, 1450–1642* (Cambridge, 2006), p. 240.

132. Mervyn James, *English Politics and the Concept of Honour, 1485–1642*, *Past & Present*, Supplement, 3 (1978), reprinted in his *Society, Politics and Culture: Studies in Early Modern England* (Cambridge, 1986); Richard Cust, 'Honour and Politics in Early Stuart England: the Case of *Beaumont* v. *Hastings*', *Past & Present*, 149 (1995), 57–94; Barbara Donagan, 'The Web of Honour: Soldiers, Christians, and Gentlemen in the English Civil War', *Historical Journal*, 44 (2001), 365–89; Ronald G. Asch, '"Honour in All Parts of Europe will be Ever like Itself", Ehre, adlige Standeskultur und Staatsbildung in England und Frankreich im späten 16. und im 17. Jahrhundert: Disziplinierung oder Aushandeln von Statusansprüchen?', in Ronald G. Asch and Dagmar Freist (eds), *Staatsbildung als kultureller Prozess: Strukturwandel und Legitimation von Herrschaft in der Frühen Neuzeit* (Cologne, 2005), pp. 353–79; Andrea Brady, 'Dying with Honour: Literary Propaganda and the Second English Civil War', *Journal of Military History*, 70 (2006), 9–30.

133. A recent study by Roger Manning reveals that the proportion of the English peerage who had actual 'experience of battle, sought military adventure, or pursued military careers' rose steeply in the course of the early seventeenth century: from 36 per cent in 1595 to 69 per cent on the eve of the Civil Wars, reaching a highpoint of 71 per cent in 1645. The figures for Scotland reveal a similar trend, with a rise from 45 per cent in 1595 to a massive 77 per cent in 1645. See Roger B. Manning, *Swordsmen: The Martial Ethos in the Three Kingdoms* (Oxford, 2003), pp. 17–19; quotation at p. 17.

134. Ian Gentles, 'The Politics of Fairfax's Army, 1645–9', this volume, Chapter 7.

135. See Chapter 4, in this volume.

136. John Adamson, 'The Baronial Context of the English Civil War', *Transactions of the Royal Historical Society*, 5th ser., 40 (1990), 93–120. Points in this essay, written when I was in my twenties, might well have been put with greater refinement. There is nevertheless nothing in the essay to justify the claim that it argued 'that the Civil War was most helpfully [*sic*] seen as a baronial revolt', still less that it implied a situation in which Parliament would justify the war 'under the slogan "support your local baron"'. For this *reductio ad absurdum*, see Morrill, *Revolt in the Provinces*, p. 187 and n.

137. For a more extended discussion see Adamson, *Noble Revolt*, pp. 518–19.

138. For the older interpretation, see J. H. Hexter, *The Reign of King Pym* (Cambridge, MA, and London, 1941); Conrad Russell, 'The Parliamentary Career of John Pym, 1621–9', in Peter Clark, A. G. R. Smith, and Nicholas Tyacke (eds), *The English Commonwealth, 1547–1640: Essays in Politics and Society Presented to Joel Hurstfield* (Leicester, 1979), pp. 147–65; for revisions, see John Morrill, 'The Unweariableness of Mr Pym: Influence and Eloquence in the Long Parliament', in Susan Amussen and Mark Kishlansky (eds), *Political Culture and Cultural Politics in Early Modern England: Essays Presented to David Underdown* (Manchester and New York, 1995), pp. 19–54; Adamson, *Noble Revolt*, pp. 54–5, 104–5, 138–9, 310, 387.

139. Not all historians have welcomed the development. One distinguished historian has written, of the 'multiple kingdoms' concept, that '[i]n some respects . . . it is a step backward, as it returns us to the relations between states and kingdoms and élites'; Underdown, *Freeborn People*, p. 5.

140. In particular, see W. P. Kelly, 'Ormond and Strafford, Pupil and Mentor?', *Journal of the Butler Society*, 4 (1997), 88–106; Toby Barnard, 'Aristocratic Values in the Careers of the Dukes of Ormonde', in Toby Barnard and Jane Fenlon (eds), *The Dukes of Ormonde, 1610–1745* (Woodbridge, 2000), pp. 161–75; and Patrick Little, 'The Marquess of Ormond and the English Parliament, 1645–7', in the same volume, pp. 83–99; Michael Perceval-Maxwell, 'Sir Robert Southwell and the Duke of Ormond's Reflections on the 1640s', in Micheál Ó Siochrú (ed.), *Kingdoms in Crisis: Ireland in the 1640s. Essays in Honour of Donal Crógan* (Dublin and Portland, OR, 2001), pp. 229–47; David Edwards, *The Ormond Lordship in County Kilkenny, 1515–1642: The Rise and Fall of the Butler Family* (Dublin, 2003).

141. Archibald Campbell, 8th Earl and 1st Marquess of Argyll, is currently (2008) the subject of a new biography in progress by Allan Macinnes; see also John Scally, 'The Rise and Fall of the Covenanter Parliaments, 1639 to 1651', in Keith Brown and Alastair Mann (eds), *The History of the Scottish Parliament*, II, *Parliament and Politics in Scotland, 1567–1707* (Edinburgh, 2005), pp. 138–62.

142. James Hamilton, 3rd Marquess and 1st Duke of Hamilton, is currently (2008) the subject of a monograph by John Scally; until the appearance of which, see John Scally, 'The Political Career of James Hamilton, 3rd Marquis and 1st Duke of Hamilton, to 1643' (unpublished PhD dissertation, University of Cambridge, 1993), and his 'Counsel in Crisis: James, 3rd Marquis of Hamilton and the Bishops' Wars, 1638–40', in John R. Young (ed.), *Celtic Dimensions of the British Civil Wars: Proceedings of the Second Conference of the Research Centre in Scottish History, University of Strathclyde* (Edinburgh, 1997), pp. 18–34.

143. Chapter 5 in this volume.

144. John Adamson, '"The Frighted Junto": Perceptions of Ireland, and the Last Attempts at Settlement with Charles I', in Jason Peacey (ed.), *Cruel Necessity? The Regicides and the Execution of Charles I* (2001), pp. 36–70. For the trial, see also the important essays by Sean Kelsey: 'The Trial of Charles I', *English Historical Review*, 118 (2003), 583–616; and 'Politics and Procedure in the Trial of Charles I', *Law and History Review*, 22 (2004), 1–26.

145. Adamson, 'Baronial Context', pp. 100–18.

146. Jason Peacey, 'Politics, Accounts and Propaganda in the Long Parliament', in Kyle and Peacey, *Parliament at Work*, pp. 59–78; and Adamson, 'The Triumph of Oligarchy', pp. 59–78, 101–27.

147. Ann Hughes, 'The King, the Parliament, and the Localities during the English Civil War', *Journal of British Studies*, 24 (1985), 236–63; and see David Scott, 'Counsel and Cabal in the King's Party, 1642–6', in McElligott and Smith, *Royalists and Royalism*, pp. 112–35.

148. Scottish grandees, accustomed to referring to their retainers as 'vassals', often reacted with puzzlement that their English brother nobles could not adopt such imperious ways towards, or expect such subservience from, their own tenantry and gentry allies. I am grateful to Dr Peter Donald for a discussion of this point.

149. See Chapter 7.

150. Perhaps the strongest statement of this point is from Russell: 'it appears to be beside the point to try to explain an intention to create a civil war, because it seems that right up to the last moment, little or no such intention existed'; see his *Causes of the English Civil War*, p. 9.

151. Quentin Skinner, 'Classical Liberty and the Coming of the English Civil War', in Martin van Gelderen and Quentin Skinner (eds), *Republicanism: A Shared European Heritage*, 2 vols (Cambridge, 2002), II, 9–28; Alan Cromartie, *The Constitutionalist Revolution: An Essay on the History of England, 1450–1642* (Cambridge, 2006), pp. 234–74; Cressy, *England on Edge*, pp. 8–9.

152. Peter Donald, 'New Light on the Anglo-Scottish Contacts of 1640', *Historical Research*, 62 (1989), 221–9; Adamson, *Noble Revolt*, pp. 53–88, 510–13.

153. Thomas Hobbes, *Leviathan*, ed. Richard Tuck (Cambridger, 1991), pp. 88–9: 'Of the Natural Condition of Mankind as Concerning their Felicity and Misery'; spelling modernized.

154. For the most important statement of this argument, see Mark Kishlansky, 'The Emergence of Adversary Politics in the Long Parliament', *Journal of Modern History*, 49 (1977), 617–40; and his *The Rise of the New Model Army* (Cambridge, 1979), p. 19. Professor Kishlansky's point was also taken up by Conrad Russell, who argued 'we should not exaggerate the extent of revolutionary upheaval even in 1647–9'. Russell also suggested that 'if there were an inherent, as distinct from a contingent, revolutionary potential in the ideas developing before 1637, one would expect it to be much more visible than it appears to be in the very controlled experiment of New England'; Russell, *Causes of the English Civil War*, p. 9.

155. Mark Stoyle, *West Britons: Cornish Identities and the Early Modern British State* (Exeter, 2002), and his *Soldiers and Strangers: An Ethnic History of the English Civil War* (New Haven, CT, and London, 2005).

156. For the Parliamentarians, see John Adamson, 'Strafford's Ghost: The British Context of Viscount Lisle's Lord Lieutenancy of Ireland', in Jane Ohlmeyer (ed.), *Ireland from Independence to Occupation, 1641–60* (Cambridge, 1995), pp. 128–59; for the Royalists, see David Scott, 'Counsel and Cabal', pp. 125–7.

157. On pre-war censorship, see Blair Worden, 'Literature and Political Censorship in Early Modern England', in A. C. Duke and C. A. Tamse (eds), *Too Mighty to be Free: Censorship and the Press in Britain and the Netherlands* (Zutphen, 1987), pp. 45–62; Anthony Milton, 'Licensing, Censorship, and Religious Orthodoxy in Early Stuart England', *Historical Journal*, 41 (1998), 625–51; Cyndia Clegg, 'Censorship and the Courts of Star Chamber and High Commission in England to 1640', *Journal of Modern European History*, 3 (2005), 50–80.

158. The quotation – though, it should be added, not the sentiment – is from Braddick, *God's Fury*, p. 593.

159. Steven Pincus, 'The State and Civil Society in Early Modern England: Capitalism, Causation and Habermas's Bourgeois Public Sphere', in Peter Lake and Steven Pincus (eds), *The Politics of the Public Sphere in Early Modern England* (Manchester, 2007), pp. 213–31. Perhaps the most persuasive and theoretically sophisticated adaptation of Habermas's ideas has been T. C. W. Blanning's *The Culture of Power and the Power of Culture: Old Régime Europe, 1660–1789* (Oxford, 2003).

160. Hobbes, *Leviathan*, p. 230; Withington, *Politics of Commonwealth*, pp. 5–6.

161. Withington, *Politics of Commonwealth*, p. 7.

162. Pincus, 'The State and Civil Society in Early Modern England', pp. 213–31.

163. John Walter, 'Crown and Crowd: Popular Culture and Popular Protest in Early Modern England', in his *Crowds and Popular Politics in Early Modern England* (Manchester, 2006), pp. 14–26; Andy Wood, 'Beyond Post-Revisionism? The Civil War Allegiances of the Miners of the Derbyshire "Peak Country"', *Historical Journal*, 40 (1997), 23–40; idem, *The Politics of Social Conflict: The Peak Country, 1520–1770* (Cambridge, 1999); idem, 'Collective Violence, Social Drama and Rituals of Rebellion in Late Medieval and Early Modern England', in Stuart Carroll (ed.), *Cultures of Violence: Interpersonal Violence in Historical Perspective* (Basingstoke, 2007), pp. 99–116; John Walter, *Understanding Popular Violence in the English Revolution: The Colchester Plunderers* (Cambridge, 1999).

164. Peacey, 'Perceptions of Parliament', this volume, p. 100.

165. In addition to the words by Dr Peacey, already noted, see Michael J. Mendle, *Henry Parker and the English Civil War: The Political Thought of the Public's 'Privado'* (Cambridge, 1995), and see his 'News and the Pamphlet Culture of Mid-Seventeenth-Century England', in Brendan Dooley and Sabrina Baron (eds), *The Politics of Information in Early Modern Europe* (London and New York, 2001), pp. 57–79; and Mendle, 'The "Prints" of the Trials: The Nexus of Politics, Religion, Law and Information in Late Seventeenth-Century England', in Jason McElligott (ed.), *Fear, Exclusion and Revolution: Roger Morrice and Britain in the 1680s* (Aldershot, 2006), pp. 123–37; and David Como, 'Secret Printing, the Crisis of 1640, and the Origins of Civil War Radicalism', in *Past & Present*, 196 (2007), 37–82.

166. Kelsey, 'Trial of Charles I'; Adamson, 'The "Frighted Junto"'.

167. For a succinct and perceptive summary of the general trends in writing on English republicanism, see Blair Worden, 'Republicanism, Regicide and Republic: the English Experience', in van Gelderen and Skinner, *Republicanism: A Shared European Heritage*, I, 315–27.

168. [Peter Heylyn], *Augustus. Or, an Essay of those Meanes and Counsels whereby the Commonwealth of Rome was altered, and reduced, unto a Monarchy* (for Henry Seile, 1632), pp. 2–3 (*STC2* 13268). I have argued elsewhere that this was the position which broadly prevailed in England from the execution of Strafford in May 1641 to early 1642, when Parliament, alarmed at the reaction against this aristocratic 'usurpation', began to deny that it had any intention to marginalize the proper role of the king; see Adamson, *Noble Revolt*, pp. 509, 517. For the importance of Venice in the early-modern political imagination, see David Wootton, 'Ulysses bound? Venice and the Idea of Liberty from Howell to Hume', in David Wootton (ed.), *Republicanism, Liberty, and Commercial Society, 1649–1776* (Stanford, CA, 1994), pp. 341–67.

169. I have attempted to make this argument in *Noble Revolt*, pp. 373–405.

170. In particular, see Quentin Skinner, 'Classical Liberty and the Coming of the English Civil War', in van Gelderen and Skinner, *Republicanism: A Shared European Heritage*, II, 9–28; Johann Sommerville, 'English and European Political Ideas in the Early Seventeenth Century: Revisionism and the Case of Absolutism', *Journal of British Studies*, 35 (1996), 168–94; and his *Royalists and Patriots: Politics and Ideology in England, 1603–40* (1999); Cromartie, *Constitutionalist Revolution*, pp. 234–74.

171. This volume, p. 209.

NOTES TO CHAPTER 1

The author is grateful to John Adamson, Ian Gentles, Sean Kelsey, Sarah Mortimer, Jason Peacey, Ian Roy, Malcolm Smuts, and Blair Worden for reading and commenting on earlier drafts of this essay.

1. Notable examples in this field are Michael Mendle, *Dangerous Positions: Mixed Government, the Estates of the Realm, and the Making of the Answer to the XIX Propositions* (University, AL, 1985); Robert Wilcher, *The Writing of Royalism, 1628–60* (Cambridge, 2001); Jerome de Groot, *Royalist Identities* (Basingstoke, 2004).

2. David Underdown, *Revel, Riot, and Rebellion: Popular Politics and Culture in England 1603–60* (Oxford, 1985); Mark Stoyle, *Loyalty and Locality: Popular Allegiance in Devon during the English Civil War* (Exeter, 1994); idem, *West Britons: Cornish Identities and the Earl Modern British State* (Exeter, 2002), esp. Chs 3–7.

3. The most scholarly examples of this genre being P. R. Newman, *Royalist Officers in England and Wales, 1642–60: A Biographical Dictionary* (New York, 1981); *The Old Service: Royalist Regimental Colonels and the Civil War, 1642–46* (Manchester, 1993).

4. Ronald Hutton, 'The Structure of the Royalist Party, 1642–6', *Historical Journal*, 24 (1981), 553–69; 'Clarendon's History of the Rebellion', *English*

Historical Review, 97 (1982), 70–88; James Daly, 'The Implications of Royalist Politics, 1642–6', *Historical Journal*, 27 (1984), 745–55; Ian Roy, 'The Royalist Council of War, 1642–6', *Bulletin of the Institute of Historical Research*, 35 (1962), 150–68; Roy, '"This Proud and Unthankefull City": a Cavalier View of London in the Civil War', in Stephen Porter (ed.), *London and the Civil War* (Basingstoke, 1996), 149–74; Roy, 'George Digby, Royalist Intrigue and the Collapse of the Cause', in Ian Gentles, John Morrill, and Blair Worden (eds), *Soldiers, Writers and Statesmen of the English Revolution* (Cambridge, 1998), 68–90; David L. Smith, *Constitutional Royalism and the Search for Settlement, c.1640–49* (Cambridge, 1994). The politics of Royalism are also touched upon in Ronald Hutton's book on the king's wartime administration, Peter Newman's essays on 'armed Royalism', and Gerald Aylmer's article on royalist attitudes: Ronald Hutton, *The Royalist War Effort, 1642–6* (1982); P. R. Newman, 'The Royalist Party in Arms: the Peerage and the Army Command, 1642–6', in Colin Jones, Malyn Newitt, and Stephen Roberts (eds), *Politics and People in Revolutionary England* (Oxford, 1986), pp. 81–93; Newman, 'The King's Servants: Conscience, Principle, and Sacrifice in Armed Royalism', in John Morrill, Paul Slack, and Daniel Woolf (eds), *Public Duty and Private Conscience in Seventeenth-Century England* (Oxford, 1993), pp. 225–41; G. E. Aylmer, 'Collective Mentalities in Mid-Seventeenth-Century England, II. Royalist Attitudes', *Transactions of the Royal Historical Society*, 5th ser. 37 (1987), 1–30.

5. See Jason McElligott and David L. Smith, 'Introduction: Rethinking Royalists and Royalism', in McElligott and Smith (eds), *Royalists and Royalism during the English Civil Wars* (Cambridge, 2007), pp. 11–13.

6. David Underdown, *Royalist Conspiracy in England, 1649–60* (New Haven, CT, 1960), pp. 10–11.

7. Hutton, 'Structure of the Royalist Party', p. 553; Paul Seaward, 'Constitutional and Unconstitutional Royalism', *Historical Journal*, 40 (1997), 227.

8. Prince Rupert, the Duke of Richmond, the Marquess of Hertford, the Earls of Bristol, Dorset, Forth, Lindsey, and Southampton, Viscount Falkland, Lords Cottington, Digby, Dunsmore, and Seymour, Sir John Culpeper, Sir Edward Hyde, Sir Edward Nicholas, John Ashburnham, Henry Jermyn, Henry Percy, Henry Wilmot etc.

9. W. C. Sellar and R. J. Yeatman, *1066 And All That* (London, 1930), p. 63. The Roundheads, of course, were 'Right but Repulsive'.

10. For the use of 'character' as a Whig explanatory device, see John Adamson, 'Eminent Victorians: S. R. Gardiner and the Liberal as Hero', *Historical Journal*, 33 (1990), 641–57.

11. For the Oxford Parliament, see David Scott, '"Our Mongrel Parliament": the Oxford Parliament 1644–6', *Parliamentary History* (forthcoming).

12. B. H. G. Wormald, *Clarendon: Politics, History and Religion, 1640–60* (Cambridge, 1951), pp. 3, 81, 122, 150, 154. According to Paul Seaward, Gardiner never used the term, and Firth avoided giving it capital initials: Seaward, 'Constitutional and Unconstitutional Royalism', p. 228.

13. Smith, *Constitutional Royalism*, pp. 4, 5, 255.

14. Smith, *Constitutional Royalism*, p. 220.

15. Put simply, the 'ancient constitution' was 'a loose bundle of customary or conventional practices and principles', defined in large part by the English

common law, that regulated the relations of early Stuart government (the king and his courts, the highest of which was Parliament) and governed. For the various meanings that attached to the term, and its rhetorical uses, see Glenn Burgess, *The Politics of the Ancient Constitution: An Introduction to English Political Thought, 1603–42* (University Park, PA, 1992); Glenn Burgess, *Absolute Monarchy and the Stuart Constitution* (New Haven, CT, 1996), Ch. 5.

16. *The Speeches of the Lord Digby in the High Court of Parliament* (1641), p. 24 (BL, E 196/6, 7). For a presentation copy of this speech in Digby's own hand, see NA, PRO 30/24/2, no. 37.

17. Burgess, *Absolute Monarchy*, pp. 127–36.

18. A point made by the leading parliamentarian polemicist Henry Parker: *Accommodation Cordially Desired and Really Intended* (15 May 1643), p. 8 (BL, E 101/23).

19. Smith, *Constitutional Royalism*, p. 4.

20. Mendle, *Dangerous Positions*, pp. 7–9; Sir Philip Warwick, *Memoires of the Reigne of King Charles I* (1701), pp. 183–4, 197–8.

21. Smith, *Constitutional Royalism*, p. 57.

22. Edward Earl of Clarendon, *The Life of Edward Earl of Clarendon . . . in which is Included a Continuation of his History of the Grand Rebellion*, 2 vols (Oxford, 1857), I, 89.

23. Mendle, *Dangerous Positions*, pp. 20, 184–6.

24. Clarendon, *Life*, I, 85; Wormald, *Clarendon*, pp. 287–8; Seaward, 'Constitutional and Unconstitutional Royalism', 229.

25. Clarendon, *Life*, I, 87; David Scott, unpublished article on Sir John Culpeper, 1640–60 section, History of Parliament Trust, London. The king evidently agreed with Hyde's assessment of Culpeper's religious views: John Bruce (ed.), *Charles I in 1646: Letters of King Charles the First to Henrietta Maria* (Camden Soc. 63, 1856), p. 30; Edward Earl of Clarendon, *History of the Rebellion and Civil Wars in England*, ed. W. D. Macray, 6 vols (Oxford, 1888), IV, 206.

26. Mendle, *Dangerous Positions*, p. 20.

27. Clarendon, *Life*, I, 86–7; Warwick, *Memoires*, pp. 195–6.

28. Clarendon, *Life*, I, 93–5; Wormald, *Clarendon*, p. 62.

29. Warwick conceded that Hyde's language was 'a little too redundant': Warwick, *Memoires*, p. 196. Mendle ascribes to Hyde 'an old man's prissiness': Mendle, *Dangerous Positions*, p. 7.

30. Clarendon, *Life*, I, 145–6, 177.

31. Clarendon, *Life*, I, 173, 198–9; J. L. Sanford, *Studies and Illustrations of the Great Rebellion* (1858), p. 619; T. H. Lister, *Life and Administration of Edward, First Earl of Clarendon*, 3 vols (1837–8), III, 44–6. Hyde seems to have had no liking for Ashburnham, who was Culpeper's close friend (see Clarendon, *Life*, I, 88): Clarendon, *Life*, I, 194–5, 197; *History*, IV, 234, 267–8, 272.

32. Smith, *Constitutional Royalism*, p. 117.

33. *Kingdomes Weekly Intelligencer*, no. 41 (23–30 January 1644), pp. 314–15 (BL, E 30/19); *The Spie, Communicating Intelligence from Oxford*, no. 1 (23–30 January 1644), p. 3 (BL, E 30/20); *Mercurius Etc.*, no. 2 (31 Jan.–6 Feb. 1644), p. 10 (BL, E 31/18).

34. Clarendon, *History*, II, 528.

35. Clarendon, *History*, I, 361.

36. For Richmond and Rupert, see William Ansell Day, *The Pythouse Papers* (1879), pp. 11, 17, 18, 27, 53; BL, Add. MS 18981 (Rupert correspondence), fo. 194; Add. MS 18982 (Rupert correspondence), fo. 79r–v; Eliot Warburton, *Memoirs of Prince Rupert and the Cavaliers*, 3 vols (1849), II, 323, 414–15; III, 149, 151; Staffordshire RO, D(W)1778/I/i/50: Prince Rupert to William Legge, 6 Aug. [1645]. I am grateful to the Earl of Dartmouth for permission to use his family papers. For Lindsey and Rupert, see Bodl. Lib., MS Firth, c. 7 (Rupert letters), fo. 129; Warburton, *Memoirs*, II, 322; NA, SP 16/502/16, fo. 27: BL, Add. MS 30305 (Fairfax correspondence), fos 65–6. I am grateful to Ian Roy for allowing me to see his deciphered texts of these last two references.

37. Clarendon, *Life*, I, 89.

38. Clarendon, *History*, III, 476.

39. Thomas Carte, *The Life of James Duke of Ormond*, 6 vols (Oxford, 1851), VI, 351.

40. Bodl. Lib., MS Clarendon 30, fo. 286. Hyde employed a very similar description – 'the noblest structure, and frame of government, in Church and State, that hath been at any time in the Christian world': [Hyde], *A Full Answer to an Infamous and Trayterous Pamphlet* (28 July 1648), p. 156 (BL, E 455/5).

41. Lord Cottington and Sir John Berkeley are also occasionally located on the unconstitutional wing of the king's party: Smith, *Constitutional Royalism*, pp. 4, 5, 10; Daly, 'Implications of Royalist Politics', p. 745.

42. Smith, *Constitutional Royalism*, pp. 244–50.

43. Warwick, *Memoires*, p. 230.

44. *The Kings Cabinet Opened:* or *Certain Packets of Secret Letters and Papers* (14 July 1645), pp. 7, 12–13 (BL, E 292/27).

45. See above, p. 51.

46. Ann Beatrice Sumner, 'The Political Career of Lord George Digby until the End of the First Civil War' (unpublished PhD dissertation, University of Cambridge, 1985), p. 278. The king consulted Digby, Hyde, and Culpeper before making peace overtures to Essex in June 1644. And if Hyde can be credited, Digby was weighing the possibility of a 'good peace' before the start of the 1645 campaign season: *Calendar of State Papers, Domestic, 1644*, p. 314; Clarendon, *Life*, I, 188.

47. Burgess, *Absolute Monarchy*, Ch. 2.

48. Burgess, *Absolute Monarchy*, pp. 37–8, 210–11, 218–19. Johann Sommerville finds no evidence that Filmer ever argued that kings could and should make law by edict: Sommerville, *Royalists and Patriots: Politics and Ideology in England, 1603–40* (2nd edn, Harlow, 1999), pp. 232–3. On the possible impact of Hobbes's writings on royalist politics, see David Scott, 'Counsel and Cabal in the King's Party, 1642–6', in McElligott and Smith, *Royalists and Royalism*, pp. 131–2.

49. Sommerville, *Royalists and Patriots*, pp. 234–50.

50. J. Digby, *An Apologie of John Earl of Bristol* (24 Dec. 1656), pp. 12–13, 66–8 (BL, E 897/6).

51. The concept of a limited yet absolute monarch is analysed by James Daly and Glenn Burgess: J. W. Daly, 'John Bramhall and the Theoretical Problems of Royalist Moderation', *Journal of British Studies*, 11 (1971), 26–44; idem, 'The Origins and Shaping of English Royalist Thought', *Historical*

Papers/Communications Historiques (Ottawa, 1974), pp. 15–35; idem, 'The Idea of Absolute Monarchy in Seventeenth-Century England', *Historical Journal*, 21 (1978), 227–50; Burgess, *Absolute Monarchy*, Ch. 2.

52. [Hyde], *An Answer to a Pamphlet* (3 May 1648), p. 13 (BL, E 438/3). See also E. Curran, 'A Very Peculiar Royalist: Hobbes in the Context of his Political Contemporaries', *British Journal for the History of Philosophy*, 10 (2002), 182–7.

53. Clarendon, *History*, II, 350–1, 536–7; III, 223–4, 345, 383, 443–4; Warwick, *Memoires*, pp. 227–8; Sir Edward Walker, *Historical Discourses* (1705), p. 239; J. S. Clarke, *The Life of James the Second*, 2 vols (1816), I, 18; J. W. Daly, 'Could Charles I be Trusted? The Royalist Case, 1642–6', *Journal of British Studies*, 6 (1966), 38–9; Smith, *Constitutional Royalism*, pp. 253–4.

54. The martial zeal and foreign background of the king's nephews, Princes Rupert and Maurice, made them natural objects of suspicion for anyone convinced of a royal conspiracy to introduce arbitrary government. But it is revealing that Rupert's correspondence contains very little hint of such sentiments – or indeed political insights of any kind: Daly, 'Implications of Royalist Politics', p. 752.

55. Anthony Milton, 'Anglicanism and Royalism in the 1640s' (this volume, Chapter 2). I am grateful to Anthony Milton for allowing me to read this essay prior to publication.

56. Milton, 'Anglicanism and Royalism'. Digby's failure to have Peter Heylyn's 1644 pamphlet, *The Stumbling-Block of Disobedience and Rebellion*, published was perhaps because he disliked its clericalism: George Vernon, *The Life of . . . Dr Peter Heylyn* (1682), p. 131. Similarly, Falkland's objections to the publication in 1643 of a pamphlet by Gryffith Williams, Bishop of Ossory, *The Discovery of Mysteries*, seems to have owed more to its unabashed clericalism than to any threat it posed to a negotiated settlement: Gryffith Williams, *The Persecution and Oppression . . . of John Bale* (1664), p. 8 [I am grateful to Jason Peacey for this reference]; Smith, *Constitutional Royalism*, p. 245.

57. According to Malcolm Smuts, 'Ireland in the 1630s [under Strafford] provides a classic example of an attempt to erect a civil polity through autocratic government backed by an army': Smuts, 'Force, Love and Authority in Caroline Political Culture', in Ian Atherton and Julie Sanders (eds), *The 1630s: Interdisciplinary Essays on Culture and Politics in the Caroline Era* (Manchester, 2006), p. 31. I am grateful to Professor Smuts for allowing me to read this article prior to publication.

58. Scott, 'Counsel and Cabal', p. 132.

59. Clarendon, *History*, III, 382–3; C. H. Firth (ed.), *The Life of William Cavendish, Duke of Newcastle* (1907), pp. xxii–xxiii, 47, 53, 181–3; Smith, *Constitutional Royalism*, pp. 180, 252–3; Anthony Milton, 'Thomas Wentworth and the Political Thought of the Personal Rule', in J. F. Merritt (ed.), *The Political World of Thomas Wentworth, Earl of Strafford, 1621–41* (Cambridge, 1996), p. 154; *Oxford Dictionary of National Biography* (*ODNB*), William Cavendish, first Duke of Newcastle.

60. For this and similar statements by Newcastle, see S. Arthur Strong (ed.), *A Catalogue of Letters and other Historical Documents Exhibited in the Library at Welbeck* (1903), pp. 176, 177, 192, 201–2; Firth, *Life of Newcastle*, pp. xxii–xxiii, 121, 122, 126.

61. 'Ther hath been a Greate question for kinges', wrote Newcastle, 'wether theye Shoulde Governe, by Love, or feare': Strong, *Catalogue of Letters at Welbeck*, p. 230. For the influence of this 'dialectic' of force and love upon Caroline state-scraft and royalist politics, see Smuts, 'Force, Love and Authority'; Scott, 'Counsel and Cabal', pp. 127–35.

62. Hutton, 'Structure of the Royalist Party', pp. 555–6; Daly, 'Implications of Royalist Politics', pp. 745–50.

63. Ian Roy, 'The Royalist Army in the First Civil War' (unpublished D.Phil. dissertation, University of Oxford, 1963), pp. 79–84. I am grateful to Ian Roy for allowing me to use his personal copy of his thesis.

64. *Most Welcome Newes from York* (23 June 1642), sigg. A2v–A3; *Terrible and True Newes from Beverley and the City of Yorke* (1642), p. 4 (BL, E 154/34); *A Letter sent from a Gentleman to Mr Henry Martin* (1642), p. 5; Vernon F. Snow and Anne Steele Young (eds), *The Private Journals of the Long Parliament, 2 June to 17 September 1642* (New Haven, CT, 1992), p. 233; Arthur Collins (ed.), *Letters and Memorials of State*, 2 vols (1746), II, 667; Clarendon, *History*, II, 181–3, 209–12, 250–1.

65. David L. Smith, '"The More Posed and Wise Advice": the Fourth Earl of Dorset and the English Civil Wars', *Historical Journal*, 34 (1991), 809–14; *A Letter sent from a Gentleman*, p. 5; Centre for Kentish Studies, Sackville MS, U269/C267/13; Collins, *Letters and Memorials of State*, II, 667–8; J. J. Cartwright (ed.), 'Papers Relating to the Delinquency of Lord Savile', in *Camden Miscellany*, VIII (1883), pp. 6–7.

66. Collins, *Letters and Memorials of State*, II, 667–8.

67. W. H. Black (ed.), *Docquets of Letters Patent ... passed under the Great Seal of Charles I, 1642–6* (1837), pp. 30–1; *Calendar of State Papers Venetian, 1642–3*, pp. 274, 279.

68. BL, Add. MS 18980 (Rupert correspondence), fo. 42v.

69. Thomas Carte (ed.), *A Collection of Original Letters and Papers ... Found Among the Duke of Ormond's Papers*, 2 vols (1739), I, 20.

70. Falkland's importance in the king's 'Cabinett-Counsels' is hard to gauge, but it seems to have been declining after the failure of the Oxford Treaty in April 1643. Dorset (Lord Chamberlain to the queen) and Bath were Privy Councillors, and were given additional court offices at the opening of the Oxford Parliament early in 1644. But neither of them was a member of the 'committee for secret affairs', or the 'junto', that Charles created in September 1643 to handle some of his most sensitive affairs (it consisted of Richmond, Cottington, Culpeper, Digby, Hyde, and Nicholas: Clarendon, *Life*, I, 192–4). Similarly, none of the peace faction had a major input in military affairs. Dorset attended 13 of the 54 or so recorded meetings of the royalist Council of War; Savile attended 9; Bath attended 4; Falkland attended 2; and Sunderland attended none, and was prob-ably not a member. According to the Venetian ambassador, Agostini, those at Oxford who urged an accommodation on any conditions were excluded from the Council of War: BL, Harl. MSS 6802, 6804, 6851–2 (Sir Edward Walker's papers); *Calendar of State Papers, Venetian, 1642–3*, p. 274. I agree with Ian Roy's assessment that the 'peace party' lacked leadership, and that those associated with it were 'totally ineffective': Roy, 'The Royalist Army', pp. 83–4.

71. *The Last Newes from Yorke and Hull* (7 July 1642), sig. A4 (BL, E 154/23); *An Answer to the Lord George Digbies Apology* (2 March 1643), p. 70 (BL, E 91/20); *A Letter*

sent from a Gentleman, pp. 3, 5; Clarendon, *History*, II, 106, 253, 351; Roy, 'George Digby', p. 72. The Earl of Newcastle can also be regarded as one of the 'Cavaliers'.

72. Clarendon, *History*, III, 223.

73. Clarendon, *Life*, I, 146; *History*, II, 527. It is interesting to note that Wormald states that Hyde was sworn a Privy Councillor and made Chancellor of the Exchequer 'through the strong advocacy of Falkland', but omits to mention that Digby also 'expostulated very warmly' on his behalf: Wormald, *Clarendon*, p. 123.

74. Hyde often referred approvingly to a 'fair accommodation' or an 'honest accommodation', but clearly regarded the Nineteen Propositions ('these Articles of Deposition'), and every set of parliamentary peace terms thereafter, as entirely unacceptable. His idea of an accommodation would entail a parliamentarian capitulation rather than a negotiated settlement: Bodl. Lib., MS Clarendon 23, fo. 13; Clarendon, *History*, II, 170, 171–2; III, 12, 148, 304; [Hyde], *Full Answer*, pp. 119, 123–4, 129–30, 131–41; R. Scrope and T. Monkhouse (eds), *State Papers Collected by Edward Earl of Clarendon*, 3 vols (Oxford, 1767–86), II, 237, 459; Martin Dzelzainis, '"Undoubted Realities": Clarendon on Sacrilege', *Historical Journal*, 33 (1990), 528–9.

75. The secret deal with Northumberland was based upon the king making him Lord Admiral, which Northumberland believed would satisfy both Houses, and if it did not, then those who *were* satisfied – the Northumberland–Holles interest – would separate themselves from their opponents at Westminster. Hyde thought this offer could do the king no harm, and might well bring him very notable advantages, 'for if the peace did not ensue upon it, such a rupture infallibly would, as might in a little time facilitate the other': Clarendon, *History*, III, 9–11; *Life*, I, 148–59.

76. Clarendon, *History*, III, 9.

77. The rivalry between Hertford and the princes over command of the king's western forces is well known, but it may also have had a political dimension: Clarendon, *History*, III, 67–8, 76, 83, 106, 121–3, 163; *Life*, I, 166; Historical Manuscripts Commission (HMC), *Hatfield Manuscripts*, XXII, 375.

78. Warburton, *Memoirs*, I, 368–9; II, 74; Clarendon, *History*, II, 390; III, 102, 345–6; HMC, *Portland Manuscripts*, I, 124; Roy, 'George Digby', pp. 72, 73–4.

79. *Mercurius Aulicus*, no. 33 (13–19 Aug. 1643), p. 440; Clarendon, *History*, III, 122–3, 141–2, 153–4, 165. There is evidence, though again far from conclusive, that the Earl of Newcastle was sounded out about joining this design: Firth, *Life of Newcastle*, pp. 93–4.

80. David Scott, *Politics and War in the Three Stuart Kingdoms, 1637–49* (Basingstoke, 2004), pp. 63–4.

81. For Hyde's close ties with Hertford, see Clarendon, *History*, II, 529; III, 66, 146, 164; *Life*, I, 169. Hyde was corresponding with the Earl of Holland, a leading figure among the peace party at Westminster, during the summer of 1643: Plas Newydd, Anglesey, MS Box XII, fo. 71. I am grateful to John Adamson for this reference.

82. Scott, *Politics and War*, pp. 64–5; Clarendon, *History*, III, 128, 146; *Life*, I, 168; Warburton, *Memoirs*, II, 268.

83. Clarendon, *History*, III, 141.

84. For the impact of the Cessation and the Covenant upon factional alignments at Westminster, see Scott, *Politics and War*, pp. 68–9.

85. *His Maiesties Gracious Answer to the Proposition of both Houses of Parliament for Ireland* (1642), sig. A3v; Mary Anne Everett Green (ed.), *Letters of Queen Henrietta Maria* (1857), p. 66.

86. *Calendar of State Papers, Domestic, 1641–3*, p. 243.

87. Bodl. Lib., MS Clarendon 21, fo. 25; Green (ed.), *Letters of Queen Henrietta Maria*, p. 66.

88. Joyce Malcolm's estimate that the king received over 22,000 troops from Ireland is almost certainly an exaggeration: Joyce Lee Malcolm, *Caesar's Due: Loyalty and King Charles, 1642–6* (1983), pp. 115–16.

89. Jermyn and Digby, for example: Sheila R. Richards (ed.), *Secret Writing in the Public Records: Henry VIII–George II* (1974), pp. 129–30.

90. *The False and Scandalous Remonstrance of the Inhumane and Bloody Rebells of Ireland* (11 Sept. 1644), p. 120 (BL, E 255/2).

91. Carte, *Life of Ormond*, V, 504; VI, 31–4; Clarendon, *History*, III, 515; Roy, 'George Digby', pp. 75, 78–9. By February 1644, Digby had ensured that grants of Irish office had to be countersigned by himself and Sir Edward Nicholas (the two Secretaries of State); and in July he cut Nicholas out of the loop entirely, by securing the king's agreement that all orders relating to Ireland should pass exclusively through his own hands: Bodl. Lib., MS Carte 15, fos 226r–v; Carte, *Life of Ormond*, VI, 31–4, 173, 175, 176.

92. Bodl. Lib., MS Carte 63, fo. 325; Carte, *Life of Ormond*, VI, 38–40, 125; Roy, 'George Digby', p. 78.

93. Warburton, *Memoirs*, II, 412–13; Carte, *Life of Ormond*, VI, 70; Roy, 'Royalist Army', p. 88. The creation of the Prince's Council benefited Digby in numerous ways – it would remove Richmond, one of Rupert's leading allies, from court; it would put the prince beyond Rupert's immediate influence; it would provide the basis for a rival military powerbase to Rupert's; and it would intrude several of Rupert's leading opponents – notably Hertford and Culpeper – into his brother Maurice's military sphere.

94. Warburton, *Memoirs*, II, 412–13; NA, PC 2/253 (Privy Council registers), pp. 227–8.

95. Carte, *Life of Ormond*, VI, 87; Carte, *Collection of Original Letters*, I, 63; Warburton, *Memoirs*, III, 149, 196.

96. Staffordshire RO, D(W)1778/I/i/34: Lord Digby to William Legge, 1 November 1643; Carte, *Life of Ormond*, VI, 41, 87. Digby attempted to frustrate Rupert's appointment as President of the Council of Wales early in 1644: BL, Add. MS 18981, fos 44, 47, 57–58v, 71v, 76v, 84.

97. For Jermyn's correspondence with Rupert, and his services to the prince at Oxford, which included lobbying the king and the Oxford Parliament for military provisions, see BL, Add. MS 18980, fo. 31; Add. MS 18981, fos 39r–v, 44, 45, 47, 55–6, 57–58v, 59, 63–4, 71v, 86–87v, 92–3, 107r–v, 109, 113; Add. MS 30305 (Fairfax correspondence), fos 88–90; Warburton, *Memoirs*, II, 374–5, 400, 405–6; Carte, *Life of Ormond*, VI, 37–8, 69–70, 87.

98. BL, Add. 18981, fos. 92–3, 107r–v, 109.

99. Carte, *Life of Ormond*, VI, 37–8.

100. Carte, *Life of Ormond*, VI, 152, 167.

101. I owe this insight into Rupert's political vulnerability to John Adamson.

102. Centre for Kentish Studies, U269/C292: Earl of Lindsey to the Earl of Bath, 6 September 1644; Carte, *Life of Ormond*, VI, 206–7; BL, Add. MS 18981, fos 303–4; H. G. Tibbutt (ed.), *The Letters Books of Sir Samuel Luke, 1644–5* (Bedfordshire Historical Record Society, 62, 1963), p. 76.

103. Staffordshire RO, D(W)1778/I/i/39: Prince Rupert to William Legge, 10 October 1644; HMC, *Fourth Report*, p. 297; *Calendar of State Papers, Venetian, 1643–7*, p. 165; C. H. Firth, 'The Journal of Rupert's Marches, 5 September 1642 to 4 July 1646', *English Historical Review*, 13 (1898), 738.

104. Warburton, *Memoirs*, III, 31–2, 52; HMC, *Ormonde Manuscripts*, new series, II, 385; Clarendon, *History*, III, 503. Sir Edward Walker, secretary to the Council of War, clearly believed that 'the old and first Army' was remodelled – or as he saw it 'destroyed' – for political rather than military reasons: Parliamentary Archives [formerly the House of Lords Record Office], WAL/2 (Papers of Sir Edward Walker), fo. 109.

105. BL, Harl. MS 166 (D'Ewes diary), fo. 135. In D'Ewes's transcription of this letter it is dated 12 September, but it is clear from its contents that this is a mistake for 12 December. John Belasyse dated the beginning of Rupert's decline in the king's favour to this period: HMC, *Ormonde Manuscripts*, new series, II, 385.

106. Richmond apparently attempted to persuade the king to go to London to treat in person – an idea that the queen, and subsequently the king himself, equated with disloyalty: Clarendon, *Life*, I, 193–4; *The Kings Cabinet Opened*, pp. 7, 25, 31.

107. Parliamentary Archives, Main Papers, 17/5/45, fo. 233; *Mercurius Civicus*, no. 95 (13–20 March 1645), p. 860 (BL, E 274/8).

108. Among the other Royalists implicated in these negotiations were Goring, the Earl of Newport, and William Legge (the governor of Oxford and Rupert's confidant): Parliamentary Archives, Main Papers, 12/6/45, fos 190–194v, 196v; 16/6/45, fos 219–20, 222.

109. For evidence of this factional divide, see Carte, *Collection of Original Letters*, I, 80, 81; Carte, *Life of Ormond*, VI, 311–12; Warburton, *Memoirs*, III, 149, 151; BL, Add. MS 18982, fos 79r–v; Add. MS 33596 (Misc. letters 1633–56), fo. 11r–v; Staffordshire RO, D(W)1778/I/i/50: Prince Rupert to William Legge, 6 August [1645]; *Calendar of State Papers, Domestic, 1645–7*, pp. 52–3, 58–60, 72–3, 140–1; *Clarendon State Papers*, II, 188–9; J. G. Fotheringham (ed.), *The Diplomatic Correspondence of Jean de Montereul*, 2 vols (Scottish History Society, 29–30), I, 59–60, 73–4.

110. It was reported in January 1646 that the leading Royalists in the West Country were 'violentlie' at odds over whether to transport the Prince of Wales to France, 'soe that there is great difference [*sic*] amongst them: they have the same difference and distractions at Oxford . . .': Derbyshire RO, D803M/Z7 (Gresley of Drakelow MS).

111. Clarendon, *Life*, I, 93.

112. Clarendon, *History*, III, 345, 347; Bodl. Lib., MS Firth c. 7, fos. 139r–v. Digby cultivated Culpeper as his point man in the Prince's Council, and by August 1645 was apparently using Culpeper's contacts with the Duke of Hamilton to forward his secret negotiations with the Covenanters: HMC,

Portland Manuscripts, I, 224, 232, 245–6, 332–3; Carte, *Life of Ormond*, VI, 312–13; *Clarendon State Papers*, II, 188–9, 196–7.

113. BL, Add. MS 33596, fos 7, 11, 15, 17; Bodl. Lib., MS Clarendon 25, fos 145–6; MS Nalson IV, fo. 218; *Clarendon State Papers*, II, 188, 190–2, 196–7, 207, 211, 244–5, 261–4, 268–9; Richards, *Secret Writing*, pp. 128, 129; Sumner, 'Political Career of Lord Digby', pp. 343, 362–3.

114. Bodl. Lib., MS Clarendon 27, fo. 112v; Keith Lindley and David Scott (eds), *The Journal of Thomas Juxon, 1644–7* (Camden Soc. 5th ser. 13, 1999), p. 120; S. Elliott Hoskins, *Charles the Second in the Channel Islands*, 2 vols (1854), I, 425.

115. Bruce, *Charles I in 1646*, pp. 7–8; BL, Add. MS 18982, fo. 104; Fotheringham, *Montereul Correspondence*, I, 23–4.

116. *Clarendon State Papers*, II, 338–9.

117. Bodl. Lib., MS Clarendon 28, fo. 116v. This reference is from Hyde's 'Memorandum concerninge the Prince's remove from Jersey' (Bodl. Lib., MS Clarendon 28, fos 116–118v), most of which has been published in Hoskins, *Charles the Second in the Channel Islands*, I, 429–39. See also Clarendon, *History*, IV, 195–201; HMC, *Beaufort Manuscripts*, pp. 16–17.

118. Bodl. Lib., MS Clarendon 28, fo. 117; Hoskins, *Charles the Second in the Channel Islands*, I, 434–5.

119. Bodl. Lib., MS Clarendon 28, fo. 118; Clarendon, *History*, IV, 200; Hoskins, *Charles the Second in the Channel Islands*, I, 428. Hyde was surprised and dismayed to discover the depth of his disagreement with 'those with whome I have hitherto agreed, and especially with my best friend', i.e. Digby: Carte, *Life of Ormond*, VI, 400. By November 1646, Hyde declared that his and Digby's opinions of 'England, Scotland, France, and Ireland' were 'diametrically contrary': *Clarendon State Papers*, II, 287.

120. Even the politically eccentric Hyde, who would have no truck with either of the two juntos at Westminster, had good hopes of the New Model Army soldiery brokering a settlement: Bodl. Lib., MS Clarendon 29, fo. 238v, 250r–v; MS Clarendon 30, fos 6, 131; *Clarendon State Papers*, II, 379. [Hyde], *Full Answer*, pp. 159–60, 185–7. Not even the regicide caused Hyde to abandon all hope in the army: S. R. Gardiner, 'Draft by Sir Edward Hyde of a Declaration to be issued by Charles II in 1649', *English Historical Review*, 8 (1893), 303–4.

121. *Clarendon State Papers*, II, 242–5, 246–9, 255–6, 260–5, 268–75, 278, 301–13, 312–3, 314, 329–30.

122. They obviously thought in terms of a new war rather than a restoration through a formal political settlement – 'rather a good war than a hopeful treaty': *Clarendon State Papers*, II, 261–4, 274.

123. John Loftis and Paul H. Hardacre (eds), *Colonel Joseph Bampfield's Apology* (Lewisburg, PA, 1993), pp. 48–9, 50; NAS, Hamilton MS, GD 406/1/2044.

124. Richmond's old adversary the Duke of Hamilton was probably behind this order. Argyll, on the other hand, was Richmond's ally: Traquair House, Peebleshire, Stewart of Traquair Papers, 'Fraser Chest' bundle 7 (Correspondence of James Duke of Lennox and Richmond and the Earl of Traquair, 1633–56), no. 14: Thomas Webb to Traquair, 1 Aug. 1646. I am grateful to Patrick Little for this reference.

125. *The Moderate Intelligencer*, no. 82 (24 Sept.–1 Oct. 1646), p. 669 (BL, E 355/23); Fotheringham, *Montereul Correspondence*, I, 276; Loftis and Hardacre,

Colonel Bampfield's Apology, pp. 48–9. For Steward as Clerk of the Closet, see John Bickersteth and Robert W. Dunning, *Clerks of the Closet in the Royal Household* (Stroud, 1991), pp. 21–2. I am grateful to John Adamson for this reference.

126. *Colonel Bampfield's Apology*, pp. 48–9; S. R. Gardiner (ed.), *The Hamilton Papers* (Camden Soc. 2nd ser. 27, 1880), p. 115.

127. Bodl. Lib., MS Tanner 58, fo. 46. As Michael Mendle has highlighted, the rapprochement between non-'Scottified' Royalists and the New Model Army soldiery in 1647 was by no means confined to the grandees of both camps: Michael Mendle, 'Putney's Pronouns: Identity and Indemnity in the Great Debate', in Michael Mendle (ed.), *The Putney Debates of 1647: The Army, the Levellers, and the English State* (Cambridge, 2001), pp. 131–3.

128. Berkeley was sent to army headquarters with the approval of the queen and one at Paris 'that loved him best', which is probably a reference to Culpeper. When Berkeley admitted to Culpeper that he was very little acquainted with the king, Culpeper informed him 'that there was an intention to send Mr John Ashburnham after me', and that Berkeley should procure a pass for him. Sir John Berkeley, *Memoirs of Sir John Berkley* (1698), pp. 4–6.

129. Clarendon, *History*, IV, 232–3, 272. For further evidence of Ashburnham's Scotophobia, see *A Letter Written by John Ashburnham Esquire* (30 Nov. 1647), p. 3 (BL, E 418/4).

130. According to Hyde, Ashburnham, after leaving the king at Newcastle, went to France, but 'having found, upon his address to the queen at Paris upon his first arrival, that his abode in some other place would not be ungrateful to her Majesty', he had removed to Rouen. 'And though the other envoy from Paris [Berkeley] and he did not make their journey into England together, nor had the least communication with each other, being in truth of several parties and purposes, yet they arrived there, and at the army, near the same time': Clarendon, *History*, IV, 232–3; Fotheringham, *Montereul Correspondence*, II, 244.

131. Loftis and Hardacre, *Colonel Bampfield's Apology*, p. 64. Lord Dunsmore, Sir Philip Warwick, and Thomas Webb were also among those allowed to attend the king: Bodl. Lib., MS Clarendon 29, fo. 265r–v; MS Clarendon 30, fos 6, 24; Surrey History Centre, Nicholas papers, G85/5/2/29: Robert Thomson sen. [Nicholas Oudart] to Nicholas, 6/16 August 1647.

132. The Richmond–Hertford grandees were closely involved in drawing up the final draft of the Heads, which were hastened 'with all possible expedition, it being then under the care of some of His Majestie's faithfullest Councell at Law, and some others of eminentest integrity, who were all verie diligent in preparing it, according to the instructions given them by the King, and in pursuite of the Agreement on both parts (the King's negative voice, and some other of the severest points in the Proposalls being struck out)': [George Ashburnham (ed.)], *A Narrative by John Ashburnham*, 2 vols (1830), II, 91–2.

133. Gardiner, *History of the Great Civil War, 1642–9*, 4 vols (1987), III, 310–12; Smith, *Constitutional Royalism*, pp. 117, 145, 152, 212, 292–3; Lindley and Scott, *Journal of Thomas Juxon*, p. 117; Austin Woolrych, *Soldiers and Statesmen: The General Council of the Army and its Debates, 1647–8* (Oxford, 1987), pp. 163–4.

134. The phrase is that of the Independent grandee Oliver St John: BL, Harl. MS 163 (D'Ewes diary), fo. 334.

135. Bodl. Lib., MS Clarendon 29, fo. 92.

136. W. Knowler (ed.), *The Earl of Strafforde's Letters*, 2 vols (1739), II, 185–6.

137. Webb warned Sir John Temple early in 1646 that if 'honest men' at Westminster did not accept the king's offers to treat, the English would become 'vassals to some other people [i.e. the Scots] . . . and in the interim Ireland may be lost'. Cromwell regarded the Engagement as a wicked design 'to vassalise us to a foreign nation [i.e. Scotland]': Bodl. Lib., MS Tanner 60, fo. 409; W. C. Abbott, *The Writings and Speeches of Oliver Cromwell*, 4 vols (Cambridge, MA, 1937–47), I, 691.

138. Bodl. Lib., MS Clarendon 29, fo. 151v; *Clarendon State Papers*, II, 279–80, 291, 319, 342; Clarendon, *History*, IV, 81, 112, 172, 198; HMC, *Beaufort Manuscripts*, p. 17; S. R. Gardiner, *History of the Great Civil War*, III, 116; Albert J. Loomie, 'Alonso de Cárdenas and the Long Parliament, 1640–48', *English Historical Review*, 97 (1982), 299.

139. Notably the Earl of Bristol, Lord Cottington, Sir Arthur Hopton, and Endymion Porter: BL, Add. MS 78268 (Letters to Nicholas), unfol.: Robert Long to Cottington, 6/16 June 1648; BL, Browne Papers, uncat.: Hopton to Browne, 5, 7 October 1646, 11, 17 November 1647; Porter to Browne, 5 February 1648; G. F. Warner (ed.), *The Nicholas Papers, 1641–52* (Camden Soc. 2nd ser. 40, 1886), pp. 70–3. In a letter to Cottington late in 1646, Hyde also referred (somewhat facetiously) to himself and Capel as members of the 'Spanish faction': *Clarendon State Papers*, II, 290–2.

140. *Clarendon State Papers*, II, 330, 346.

141. S. R. Gardiner (ed.), *The Constitutional Documents of the Puritan Revolution* (3rd edn, Oxford, 1906), p. 353. Culpeper had been on friendly terms with Hamilton since at least 1641; and in 1646 the Hamiltonians were considering ways of bringing Culpeper and Jermyn back to England to assist in their negotiations with the king: Henry B. Wheatley (ed.), *The Diary and Correspondence of John Evelyn*, 4 vols (1906), IV, 86; *Clarendon State Papers*, II, 197; HMC, *Portland Manuscripts*, I, 333; NAS, Hamilton MS, GD 406/1/1397; GD 406/1/2108/1.

142. Clarendon, *History*, IV, 296, 302.

143. Sean Kelsey, 'The Death of Charles I', *Historical Journal*, 45 (2002), 740–2. Webb was sounding out leading army officers on the eve of the king's trial, almost certainly on Richmond's instructions: BL, Add. MS 63743 (Craven papers), fo. 1v.

144. NAS, Hamilton MS, GD 406/1/2119.

145. Scott, *Politics and War*, pp. 176–7.

146. Although Cottington and Porter had been involved in initiatives, or had given advice, likely to result in Irish Catholic troops being deployed in the king's cause (HMC, *De L'Isle and Dudley Manuscripts*, VI, 399; *Clarendon State Papers*, II, 202; *False and Scandalous Remonstrance*, pp. 113, 114), they could not stomach a similar policy using the Scottish Covenanters.

147. Clarendon, *History*, V, 233–4; Richard Ollard (ed.), *Clarendon's Four Portraits* (1989), pp. 126–7; Andrew Barclay, unpublished article on Henry Jermyn, 1640–60 section, History of Parliament Trust, London. Ashburnham, who until 1647 was part of the Jermyn–Culpeper circle, was regarded by the king and others as 'a great lover of the church in the right protestant way': Carte, *Life of Ormond*, VI, 147; *Clarendon State Papers*, II, 270; *LJ*, IX, 203.

148. *Clarendon State Papers*, II, 307.

149. *Clarendon State Papers*, II, 231–6, 306–10, 325–6; Wheatley, *Evelyn Diary*, IV, 89–90, 96.

150. *Clarendon State Papers*, II, 365–6. The king himself believed that 'religion is the only firm foundation of all power . . . religion will much sooner regain the militia than the militia will religion'; and that 'if the pulpits teach not obedience, which will never be if Presbiterian government be absolutely setled, the Crowne will have littel [*sic*] comfort of the Militia': *Clarendon State Papers*, II, 248, 296; Dzelzainis, 'Undoubted Realities', p. 516.

151. *Clarendon State Papers*, II, 417–18.

152. *Clarendon State Papers*, II, 264.

153. *Clarendon State Papers*, II, 301.

154. Clarendon, *Life*, I, 94.

155. *Clarendon State Papers*, II, 207.

156. Firth, *Life of Newcastle*, pp. 47, 53; S. R. Gardiner (ed.), *Letters and Papers Illustrating the Relations between Charles the Second and Scotland in 1650* (Scottish History Soc. 57, 1894), pp. 59–60; Warner, *The Nicholas Papers, 1641–52*, p. 173; HMC, *Portland Manuscripts*, II, 137.

157. Hobbes further concluded that 'the Legislative Power (and indeed all Power possible) is contain'd in the Power of the Militia': Thomas Hobbes, *Behemoth: The History of the Civil Wars of England* (1679), pp. 158, 161, 174.

NOTES TO CHAPTER 2

I am grateful to the editor for encouraging me to write this article and for his perceptive comments on it in draft, and to participants at the 'Royalists and Royalism' conference in Cambridge and at the Early Modern Seminar at the University of Reading for their helpful remarks on earlier versions of this paper.

1. John Morrill, 'The Church in England, 1642–9', in John Morrill (ed.), *Reactions to the English Civil War* (1982), pp. 89–114; reprinted in Morrill, *The Nature of the English Revolution* (Harlow, 1993); David Underdown, *Revel, Riot and Rebellion* (Oxford, 1985); Mark Stoyle, *Loyalty and Locality: Popular Allegiance in Devon during the English Civil War* (Exeter, 1994), esp. pp. 204–55.

2. The term 'Anglican' is here used not to imply the existence of a single religious ideology, but rather to distinguish those divines who opposed the Westminster Assembly and its dismantling of the Elizabethan religious settlement from those Presbyterians and Independents who also advocated Royalism. The danger, of course, is that the introduction of a new terminology can imply the emergence of a new body of thought: I hope to deal with problems of 'Anglican' terminology in more detail elsewhere.

3. J. W. Packer, *The Transformation of Anglicanism, 1643–60* (Manchester, 1969); C. F. Allison, *The Rise of Moralism* (1966); David Loewenstein and John Morrill, 'Literature and Religion', in David Loewenstein and J. Mueller (eds), *The Cambridge History of Early Modern English Literature* (Cambridge, 2002), pp. 677–8.

4. David L. Smith, *Constitutional Royalism and the Search for Settlement, c.1640–49* (Cambridge, 1994).

5. *Mercurius Rusticus* (1647), *passim*.

6. C. J. Stranks, *The Life and Writings of Jeremy Taylor* (1952), pp. 67–70; V. D. Sutch, *Gilbert Sheldon: Architect of Anglican Survival, 1640–75* (The Hague, 1973), p. 35; Packer, *Transformation*, pp. 37–8, 188–9; John Spurr, *The Restoration Church of England* (New Haven, CT, 1991), pp. 1–2.

7. Conrad Russell, *The Fall of the British Monarchies, 1637–42* (Oxford, 1991), pp. 246–51, 271–2.

8. Morrill, 'Church in England', p. 158; Russell, *Fall*, pp. 411–12; Anthony Fletcher, *The Outbreak of the English Civil War* (1981), p. 121.

9. *Oxford Dictionary of National Biography* (hereafter *ODNB*), s. n. 'John Prideaux', 'Thomas Westfield', 'Ralph Brownrigg'; Russell, *Fall*, p. 110.

10. Russell, *Fall*, pp. 411–12.

11. NA, LC5/135, Part 5, p. 4. Out of 21 preachers, non-Laudians include John Prideaux, Thomas Winniffe, Thomas Howell, Daniel Featley, John Young, Richard Love, John Hacket and John Bridgeman. Only two of these (Featley and Winniffe) preached the previous year; LC5/134, p. 455.

12. John Adamson, 'Charles I Wins the English Civil War', in Andrew Roberts (ed.), *What Might Have Been* (2004), pp. 40–58; Morrill, *Nature*, p. 158; Russell, *Fall*, pp. 245, 247, 437; J. F. Larkin and P. L. Hughes (eds), *Stuart Royal Proclamations*, 2 vols (Oxford, 1973–83), II, 752–4. Cf. Francis Quarles, *The Loyall Convert* (Oxford, 1644), p. 2. I am grateful to Dr John Adamson for drawing my attention to this event.

13. Russell, *Fall*, pp. 246–7.

14. Smith, *Constitutional Royalism*, pp. 145–7.

15. See below, pp. 73–5.

16. *Basilika: Works of Charles I* (1687), p. 289.

17. Ibid., p. 647.

18. Peter Lake, 'Serving God and the Times: the Calvinist Conformity of Robert Sanderson', *Journal of British Studies*, 27 (1988), 108; George Morley, *A Modest Advertisement concerning the Present Controversie about Church-Government* (1641), pp. 18–19. While Morley's anti-Laudian tone is comprehensive, his specific concern to modify episcopacy may also be linked to the strategy of his patron at the time, the Earl of Pembroke. Pembroke was one of the major backers of a scheme for modified episcopacy as a means of bridging the gulf between the king's position and that of the puritan grandees. I am grateful to John Adamson for this point.

19. Russell, *Fall*, p. 437

20. Adamson, 'Charles I Wins the English Civil War', pp. 56–7.

21. See below, pp. 74–5.

22. On Berkenhead's Laudian credentials see P. W. Thomas, *Sir John Berkenhead, 1617–79* (Oxford, 1969), pp. 15–25.

23. NA, LC5/135, Part 5 p. 10. Among the twenty-one preachers, the following have a clear Laudian pedigree: Bishop Towers, Bishop Warner, Bishop Duppa, Bishop Skinner, Bishop Frewen, Benjamin Laney, Christopher Potter, Richard Baylie, Thomas Laurence, Bishop Walter Curle, John Oliver, Richard Steward, Gilbert Sheldon and Jeremy Taylor. Only Bishop Prideaux and Bishop Westfield have clear non-Laudian credentials.

24. Richard Scrope (ed.), *State Papers Collected by Edward, Earl of Clarendon*, 3 vols (Oxford, 1757), II, 265–8.

25. Stranks, *Jeremy Taylor*, pp. 41–3, 47, 50, 55.

26. For Sheldon as a Laudian see Kenneth Fincham, 'Oxford and the Early Stuart Polity', in Nicholas Tyacke (ed.), *History of the University of Oxford*, IV, *The Seventeenth Century* (Oxford, 1997), 208–9; Kenneth Fincham, 'William Laud and the Exercise of Caroline Ecclesiastical Patronage', *Journal of Ecclesiastical History*, 51 (2000), 82. For Steward's cordial relations with his 'very excellent friend', Laud, see ibid., p. 83. Steward was one of 'my reverend friends' whom Laud appointed in his will to peruse his unpublished sermons after his death (William Scott and J. Bliss (eds), *The Works of the Most Reverend Father in God, William Laud*, 7 vols (Oxford, 1847–60), IV, 449). For Steward's later devotion to Laud's memory, see also *Clarendon State Papers*, II, 328.

27. See my 'The Laudian Moment: Conformist Trajectories in Early Stuart England' (forthcoming).

28. Lake, 'Serving God', pp. 103–4, 108.

29. Laud, *Works*, VI, 589; *ODNB*, s. n. 'William Laud'.

30. I am grateful to John Adamson for this point.

31. Judith Maltby, 'Petitions for Episcopacy and the Book of Common Prayer on the Eve of the Civil War, 1641–2', in Stephen Taylor (ed.), *From Cranmer to Davidson: A Church of England Miscellany* (Church of England Record Society, 7, 1999). See also Peter Lake, 'Puritans, Popularity and Petitions: Local Politics in National Context – Cheshire, 1641', in Thomas Cogswell, Richard Cust and Peter Lake (eds), *Politics, Religion and Popularity* (Cambridge, 2002), esp. pp. 275–7.

32. *A Vindication of Episcopacie* (1644), pp. 31–3. For examples of anti-Laudianism in early royalist verse, see R. Wilcher, *The Writing of English Royalism, 1628–60* (Cambridge, 2001), pp. 46–9, 68, 98. For a very rare allusion to 'abuses, and excesses, and mistakes' in episcopacy in the work of Henry Hammond, see his *Of the Power of the Keyes* (1647), sig. A3r.

33. On anti-Puritanism see, e.g., Wilcher, *Writing*, pp. 37, 104, 109–11, 117–18, 126, 153–4, 234.

34. John Bramhall's *Serpent Salve* (1643) is one of many texts that would gain from such a reading. Despite a moderate rhetoric that has been praised by subsequent historians, the author does not take the opportunity to criticize the policies of the Personal Rule, and manages to avoid endorsing any of the legislation of the constitutional revolution of 1640–41.

35. Wilcher, *Writing*, pp. 193–4; Peter Heylyn, *Memorial of Bishop Waynflete*, ed. J. R. Bloxam (Caxton Society, 1851), p. xxiv. Heylyn's animus may partly relate to Falkland's having singled him out for ridicule in a printed parliamentary speech: see Lucius Cary, Viscount Falkland, *The Lord Faulkland his Learned Speech in Parliament, in the House of Commons, touching the Judges and the late Lord Keeper* (1641), p. 5.

36. Lucius Cary, Viscount Falkland, *A Speech made to the House of Commons concerning Episcopacy* (1641), pp. 3–4, 6–7.

37. Russell, *Fall*, pp. 278, 343, 475; Wilcher, *Writing*, pp. 41–2.

38. John Morrill, 'The Attack on the Church of England in the Long Parliament', in Derek Beales and Geoffrey Best (eds), *History, Society and the Churches* (1985), reprinted in Morrill, *Nature of the English Revolution*.

39. See Michael Mendle, *Dangerous Positions* (University, AL, 1984).

40. *ODNB*, s. n. 'Griffith Williams'; Griffith Williams, *The Persecution and Oppression . . . of John Bale* (1664), p. 5.

41. Ibid., p. 8. I am grateful to Jason Peacey for alerting me to this pamphlet.

42. Griffith Williams, *The Discovery of Mysteries* (1643), p. 2.

43. Ibid., p. 104.

44. John Bramhall, *The Serpent Salve* (1643), pp. 34–5.

45. Peter Heylyn, *The Stumbling-Blocke of Disobedience*, (1657), pp. 207–12; Williams, *Discovery*, p. 26. See also Gerard Langbaine, *Episcopall Inheritance* (1641), pp. 20–1; Peter Heylyn, *Observations on the Historie of the Reign of King Charles* (1656), pp. 61–2. Williams treads more carefully in his *The Grand Rebellion* (Oxford, 1643), pp. 63–4.

46. Heylyn, *Stumbling-Blocke*, pp. 230–2; Williams, *Discovery*, pp. 78–81.

47. Bramhall, *Serpent Salve*, p. 20; John Doughty, *The Kings Cause rationally, briefly and plainly Debated* (1644), p. 27; Henry Ferne, *Episcopacy and Presbytery Considered* (Oxford, 1644), p. 26. For rare examples of clerical supporters of the *Answer*'s reading of the estates, see Quarles, *Loyall Convert*, p. 6, and Ferne's earlier *The Resolving of Conscience* (Cambridge, 1642), pp. 25–6.

48. Ferne, *Episcopacy and Presbytery*, p. 1.

49. Henry Hammond, *Considerations of Present Use concerning the Danger resulting from the Change of our Church Government* (1645), pp. 1, 3, 14–15.

50. Ibid., pp. 1, 15–18.

51. William Chillingworth, *A Sermon Preached before His Majesty at Reading* (Oxford, 1644), p. 16.

52. Spurr, *Restoration Church*, pp. 21–3, 238–40, 281–4, 297.

53. Williams, *Discovery*, pp. 19–20.

54. Andrew Foster, 'The Clerical Estate Revitalised', in Kenneth Fincham (ed.), *The Early Stuart Church, 1603–42* (Basingstoke, 1993); Christopher Haigh and Alison Wall, 'Clergy JPs in England and Wales, 1500–1640', *Historical Journal*, 47 (2004), pp. 233–59.

55. T. P. Slaughter (ed.), *Ideology and Politics on the Eve of the Restoration: Newcastle's Advice to Charles II* (Philadelphia, 1984), pp. 17–18. I am grateful to Dr Lynn Hulse for drawing this passage to my attention.

56. This requires more study, but seems to be one of the findings of the analysis of royalist 'core titles' of the later 1640s studied in G. J. McElligott, 'Propaganda and Censorship: the Underground Royalist Newsbooks, 1647–50' (unpublished PhD dissertation, University of Cambridge, 2001), pp. 121–2.

57. R. S. Bosher, *The Making of the Restoration Settlement* (1951), pp. 39–40; Sutch, *Gilbert Sheldon*, p. 44.

58. *Clarendon State Papers*, II, 267–8; S. R. Gardiner, 'A Scheme of Toleration propounded at Uxbridge in 1645', *English Historical Review*, 2 (1887), pp. 340–2; Sean Kelsey, 'The King's Book: *Eikon Basilike* and the English Revolution of 1649', in Nicholas Tyacke (ed.), *The English Revolution c.1590–1720: Politics, Religion and Communities* (forthcoming). I am grateful to Dr Kelsey for his permission to cite this important article.

59. Compare this with David Scott's warning that constitutional principles cannot be read off straightforwardly from the behaviour of royalist élites in negotiations: David Scott, 'Rethinking Royalist Politics, 1642–9', in this volume.

60. Ussher's scheme for a limited episcopacy was apparently published in 1641 in a pirate version without Ussher's permission, but this does not seem to survive in print (Russell, *Fall*, p. 191). Hammond's *Of the Power of the Keyes* (1647) alludes to schemes for reduced episcopacy in a single brief passage in the preface (sig. A2v), but the main concern of the tract is to oppose *erastian* ideas and to argue for the reintroduction of excommunication. The only royalist divine to have provided a sustained justification of reduced episcopacy seems to have been the singular Herbert Thorndike, in his *Of the Government of Churches* (Cambridge, 1641).

61. Hammond, *Considerations*, p. 14; Ferne, *Episcopacy and Presbytery*, pp. 27, 29.

62. Ferne, *Episcopacy and Presbytery*, pp. 15–16.

63. Bosher, *Making*, p. 47.

64. Thorndike, *Government of Churches*, pp. 88–110; Herbert Thorndike, *A Discourse of the Right of the Church in a Christian State* (1649), pp. 122–8.

65. See Taylor's frank explanation in the 1657 dedication of a collected volume: Jeremy Taylor, *Σίμβολον Εθικοπολεμικον or a Collection of Polemical and Moral Discourses* (1657), sigs. A4v–A5r.

66. S. R. Gardiner (ed.), *The Constitutional Documents of the Puritan Revolution 1625–60* (Oxford, 1947 edn), p. 321.

67. Bodl. Lib., Tanner MS 58, fos 453–6, 460.

68. Ibid., fo. 484 (Bishop Warner of Rochester). Warner rather undermined this careful reservation by appending 'And yet, if I be deemed herein more scrupulous then I neede, I pray informe mee: whom you shall finde willing and ready to retract and conform to better reason and iudgement.'

69. Ibid., fo. 461 (Bishop Morton of Durham).

70. On the Newport negotiations, see especially Kelsey, 'The King's Book'.

71. Loewenstein and Morrill, 'Literature and Religion', p. 664.

72. Anthony Milton, *Catholic and Reformed* (Cambridge, 1995), pp. 491–3; Jeremy Taylor, *Of the Sacred Order and Offices of Episcopacy* (Oxford, 1642), pp. 190–7, and see also pp. 30–2, 99–100, 158–9, 166–70.

73. K. R. Firth, *The Apocalyptic Tradition in Reformation Britain, 1530–1645* (Oxford, 1979), p. 246; B. W. Ball, *A Great Expectation: Eschatological Thought in English Protestantism to 1660* (Leiden, 1975), pp. 72–4; Milton, *Catholic and Reformed*, pp. 118–19.

74. Milton, *Catholic and Reformed*, pp. 336–8, 444; Spurr, *Restoration Church*, pp. 117–21.

75. Thomas Pierce, *The Sinner Impleaded* (1655); Henry Hammond, *Of Fundamentals, Schisme and Heresie* (1654); Laurence Womock, *Arcana Dogmatum* (1659); Peter Heylyn, *Historia Quinqu-Articularis* (1660).

76. Nicholas Tyacke, 'Religious Controversy', in Tyacke, *History*, p. 593.

77. Jeremy Taylor, *Unum Necessarium* (1655); Stranks, *Jeremy Taylor*, pp. 145, 149–57.

78. See above, n. 68.

79. Smith, *Constitutional Royalism*, pp. 245–6; A. Sharp, *Political Ideas of the English Civil Wars, 1641–9* (1983), pp. 30–1. For Williams's Calvinism see his *The Delights of the Saints* (1622), pp. 6–7 and *passim*. Williams still held to the

anti-Arminian tenets of this work in the 1630s: the complete text was republished in his collection *The Best Religion* (1636).

80. Williams, *Persecution and Oppression*, p. 4; Williams, ´Ο Αντιχριστος, *the Great Antichrist revealed* (1660).

81. Michael Hudson, *The Divine Right of Government* (1647), sigs. A2r–A3v, pp. 152–9; Smith, *Constitutional Royalism*, pp. 246–8; Wilcher, *Writing*, p. 251.

82. Loewenstein and Morrill, 'Literature and Religion', p. 647; e.g. Henry Ferne, *A Sermon Preached at the Publique Fast . . . before the Members of the Honourable House of Commons* (Oxford, 1644); Griffith Williams, *A Sermon Preached at the Publique Fast . . . before the Great Assembly of the Members of the Honourable House of Commons* (Oxford, 1644); Henry Leslie, *A Sermon Preached at the Publique fast . . . before the Great Assembly of the Members of the Honourable House of Commons* (Oxford, 1644). On royalist fasts, see Christopher Durston, '"For the Better Humiliation of the People": Public Days of Fasting and Thanksgiving during the English Revolution', *The Seventeenth Century*, 7 (1992), 133, 136.

83. E.g. Chillingworth, *Sermon*, pp. 14, 27–9.

84. Jacqueline Eales, 'Provincial Preaching and Allegiance in the First English Civil War, 1640–46', in Cogswell *et al.*, *Politics*, pp. 194–5, 199, 200, 204.

85. Taylor, *Of the Sacred Order*, pp. 3–4.

86. D. Brady, *The Contribution of British Writers between 1560 and 1830 to the Interpretation of Revelation 13. 16–18* (Tübingen, 1983), p. 128; Williams, *Great Antichrist Revealed*. For a valuable discussion of post-1660 Anglican and royalist apocalyptic writings, see W. Johnston, 'The Anglican Apocalypse in Restoration England', *Journal of Ecclesiastical History*, 55 (2004), 467–501.

87. *Wonderfull Newes: or a True Relation of a Churchwarden in the Towne of Tosceter . . . whose Wife first died wonderfull strangely, and then Himselfe fell Mad, and died. As also his Sister her Hands now rotting the Flesh from the Bones . . . The Causes you shall find in the Ensuing Sad Relation* (1642).

88. E.g., *A Strange and Lamentable Accident that happened lately at Mears Ashby* (1642).

89. Cambridge University Library, MS Mm. I. 45, p. 39.

90. *Mercurius Aulicus*, no. 11 (14 March 1643), pp. 133–4; no. 49 (9 December 1643), p. 703; Quarles, *Loyall Convert*, pp. 18–19.

91. A. Lacey, *The Cult of King Charles the Martyr* (Woodbridge, 2003), pp. 62–4.

92. Ibid., pp. 69–70; Heylyn, *Observations*, pp. 28–30 (cf. pp. 48, 105–6, 109–10). It will be clear that I disagree with Dr Lacey's reading of Heylyn's works. I hope to document my argument in more detail elsewhere.

93. Herbert Thorndike, *A Discourse of the Right of the Church in a Christian State* (1649), pp. 9, 214, cxiii.

94. Ibid., pp. 338–9; Bosher, *Making*, pp. 67–9.

95. Peter Heylyn, *Ecclesia Vindicata* (1657), sigs. a2r–v, d3r–v, e2r.

96. Bodl. Lib., 4o. Rawl. 152; J. H. Walker, 'A Descriptive Bibliography of the Early Printed Works of Peter Heylyn' (unpublished PhD dissertation, University of Birmingham, 1978), pp. xxxvii–xxxix; Heylyn, *Ecclesia Vindicata*, sig. d3v.

97. *ODNB*, s. n. 'Griffith Williams'.

NOTES TO CHAPTER 3

1. John Adamson, 'Politics and the Nobility in Civil War England', *H[istorical] J[ournal]*, 34 (1991); M. Kishlansky, 'Saye What?', *HJ*, 33 (1990); M. Kishlansky, 'Saye No More', *J[ournal of] B[ritish] S[tudies]*, 30 (1991).

2. John Adamson, 'The Peerage in Politics, 1645–9' (unpublished PhD dissertation, University of Cambridge, 1986); John Adamson, 'Parliamentary Management, Men of Business and the House of Lords, 1640–49', in Clive Jones (ed.), *A Pillar of the Constitution* (1989); John Adamson, 'The English Nobility and the Projected Settlement of 1647', *HJ*, 30 (1987); David Underdown, *Pride's Purge* (Oxford, 1971).

3. Mark Kishlansky, 'The Emergence of Adversary Politics in the Long Parliament', *J[ournal of] M[odern] H[istory]*, 49 (1977), p. 619; Kishlansky, 'Saye What?', pp. 918–23; Lotte Glow, 'Political Affiliations in the House of Commons after Pym's Death', *B[ulletin of the] I[nstitute of] H[istorical] R[esearch]*, 38 (1965); Mark Kishlansky, *The Rise of the New Model Army* (Cambridge, 1979).

4. For use of such sources, see Underdown, *Pride's Purge*, p. 54; Adamson, 'Parliamentary Management', pp. 43–9; Adamson, 'English Nobility'; Adamson, 'Politics and the Nobility', pp. 236, 240. For a study which largely ignores them, see David Smith, *The Stuart Parliaments, 1603–89* (1999). For the debate on such sources, see Kishlansky, 'Saye No More', pp. 408–9, 411–14; Adamson, 'Politics and the Nobility'; Kishlansky, 'Saye What?', pp. 924–6, 930.

5. Clement Walker, *Relations and Observations* (1648), sig. B, pp. 15–16, 67–8, 70, 140; J. Harris, *The Antipodes* (1647), sig. A3.

6. John Morrill, *The Revolt of the Provinces* (1980); Robert Ashton, *Counter-Revolution: The Second Civil War and its Origins* (New Haven, CT, 1994), and his 'From Cavalier to Roundhead Tyranny, 1642–9', in John Morrill (ed.), *Reactions to the English Civil War, 1642–9* (1982); Walker, *Relations*, sigs. A2v, A3, B, pp. 18–19.

7. [Robert Chestlin], *Persecutio Undecima* (1648), p. 61; *The Parliamentary or Constitutional History of England*, 24 vols (1761–3), xvi, 80; J. Howldin, *The Lawes Subversion* (1648); John Lilburne, *A Defiance to Tyrants* (1648), p. 2; G. Wither, *Letters of Advice* (1644), pp. 4, 12; J. Musgrave, *Another Word to the Wise* (1646); J. Musgrave, *A Fourth Word to the Wise* (1647), p. 12; William Prynne, *The Machivilian Cromwellist* (1648), p. 3; Walker, *Relations*, pp. 1–3; *Westminster Projects* (1648), p. 2; Keith Lindley and David Scott (eds), *The Journal of Thomas Juxon, 1644–7* (Camden Society, 1999), pp. 24, 49, 70, 95, 103, 106, 113, 116, 135; see, Kishlansky, *Rise of the New Model Army*, p. 226.

8. David Jenkins, *A Discourse Touching the Inconveniences of a Long Continued Parliament* (1647), pp. 2, 4. See also *Certain Queries Lovingly Propounded to Mr William Prynne* (1647), p. 7; Walker, *Relations*, p. 4; Musgrave, *Fourth Word*, p. 7. It was also linked with 'mercenary' and pettifogging lawyers, who sold justice for money, and legislated on the basis of private concern: Chestlin, *Persecutio*, p. 33; Musgrave, *Another Word*.

9. Chestlin, *Persecutio, passim.*

10. Robert Baillie (ed.), *The Letters and Journals of Robert Baillie*, ed. David Laing, 3 vols (Edinburgh, 1841–2), II, 83, 115; *Journal of Thomas Juxon*, pp. 34–5;

see Valerie Pearl, 'Oliver St John and the "Middle Group" in the Long Parliament: August 1643–May 1644', *E[nglish] H[istorical] R[eview]*, 81 (1966); J. H. Hexter, *The Reign of King Pym* (Cambridge, 1941); David Scott, *Politics and War in the Three Stuart Kingdoms, 1637–49* (Basingstoke, 2003).

11. Baillie, *Letters and Journals*, II, 115, 122, 136, 235; Walker, *Relations*, sig. A4–A4v; *Journal of Thomas Juxon*, pp. 35–6, 75; *Mercurius Aulicus* (23 Feb.–2 Mar. 1645), pp. 1392–3.

12. *Mercurius Pragmaticus*, no. 6 (5–9 May 1648), sig. Fv; 'The letters of Sir Cheney Culpeper, 1641–57', ed. M. J. Braddick and M. Greengrass, in *Camden Miscellany XXXIII* (Camden Society, 1996), pp. 297–9; Claydon House, Verney Papers, volume 9, unfol.

13. Prynne, *Machivilian Cromwellist*, p. 3; *Certaine Considerations Touching the Present Factions* (1648), sig. A2; *Journal of Thomas Juxon*, p. 76.

14. Baillie, *Letters and Journals*, II, 83.

15. *The Diplomatic Correspondence of Jean de Montereul*, ed. J. G. Fotheringham, 2 vols (Edinburgh, 1898), I, 15, 22–3; II, 18, 51; Baillie, *Letters and Journals*, II, 319, 512; B[ritish] L[ibrary], Add[itional MS] 21066, fo. 15; 'The letters of Sir Cheney Culpeper', pp. 297–9; J. Wildman, *Putney Projects* (1647), p. 2; Bodl[eian Library], MS Clarendon 30, fo. 233; *Journal of Thomas Juxon*, pp. 76, 94, 104, 135; see, Adamson, 'Peerage in Politics'; Scott, *Politics and War*.

16. Bodl. Lib., MS Clarendon 30, fo. 232; *Certaine Considerations Touching the Present Factions*, sig. A4v; *Westminster Projects*, p. 2; Bodl. Lib., MS Clarendon 31, fo. 67v; Verney Papers, volume 9, unfol.

17. Baillie, *Letters and Journals*, II, 141; *Correspondence of Jean de Montereul*, I, 74, 266; *Journal of Thomas Juxon*, pp. 69, 71; *Mercurius Aulicus*, 7 (11–17 Feb. 1644), p. 828; *Mercurius Aulicus*, no. 41 (8–14 Oct. 1643), p. 580; Adamson, 'Peerage in Politics', pp. 4–5; *A Warning for All the Counties* (1647), p. 7; Bodl. Lib., MS Clarendon 30, fos 256–7; Verney Papers, volume 9, unfol.; *Mercurius Pragmaticus*, no. 19 (1–8 Aug. 1648), sigs. Tv, T3v; *Mercurius Pragmaticus*, no. 21 (15–22 Aug. 1648), sigs. Aav–2.

18. *Mercurius Pragmaticus*, no. 19 (1–8 Aug. 1648), sigs. Tv, T3v; *Mercurius Pragmaticus*, no. 21 (15–22 Aug. 1648), sigs. Aav–2; Bodl. Lib., MS Clarendon 34, fo. 17r–v.

19. *Mercurius Pragmaticus*, no. 7 (9–16 May 1648), sig. Gv; Wildman, *Putney Projects*, pp. 8–9; *Journal of Thomas Juxon*, pp. 116, 147; Bodl. Lib., MS Clarendon 34, fo. 17r–v.

20. *Journal of Thomas Juxon*, pp. 34–5; Underdown, *Pride's Purge*, pp. 69–72; *Correspondence of Jean de Montereul*, II, 109; Prynne, *Machivilian Cromwellist*, p. 3; Verney Papers, volume 8, unfol.; Bodl. Lib., MS Clarendon 34, fo. 17; *Mercurius Pragmaticus*, no. 39 (19–26 Dec. 1648), sig. Eee4.

21. Bodl. Lib., MS Clarendon 34, fo. 72v.

22. *Journal of Thomas Juxon*, pp. 34–5; Adamson, 'Parliamentary Management', p. 49; John Adamson, 'The Triumph of Oligarchy', in Chris Kyle and Jason Peacey (eds), *Parliament at Work: Parliamentary Committees, Political Power and Public Access in Early Modern England* (Woodbridge, 2002), p. 110; Paul Christianson, 'The Peers, the People, and Parliamentary Management in the First Six Months of the Long Parliament', *JMH*, 49 (1977); *Mercurius Aulicus*, 29 (14–20 July 1644), pp. 1088–9. Scholars who have paid least attention to

contemporary comment have often shown least awareness of bicamerality: Pearl, 'Oliver St John', and her 'The "Royal Independents" in the English Civil War', *T[ransactions of the] R[oyal] H[istorical] S[ociety]*, 5th series, 18 (1968), 69–96.

23. *CSPV, 1642–3*, pp. 255, 259.

24. Bodl. Lib., MS Clarendon 30, fo. 233; John Lilburne, *Two Letters* (1647), pp. 4–5; Lilburne, *Additional Plea* (1647), pp. 17–23; *Lieutenant General Cromwell's Last Will and Testament* (1648), pp. 2, 5; *Mercurius Pragmaticus*, no. 17 (18–25 July 1648), sig. R4v; *Mercurius Pragmaticus*, no. 10 (30 May–6 June 1648), sig. K3v; *Mercurius Pragmaticus*, no. 18 (25 July–1 Aug. 1648), sig. S; see, Kishlansky, 'Saye What?', p. 926.

25. Chestlin, *Persecutio*, p. 53; *A Copy of a Letter . . . Touching the Lord Say* (1643); Baillie, *Letters and Journals*, II, 115, 133, 136, 141, 216, 220, 230, 236–7, 240, 279; *Journal of Thomas Juxon*, pp. 53, 75–6; see, Pearl, 'Oliver St John'; Adamson, 'Peerage in Politics', *passim*.

26. Baillie, *Letters and Journals*, II, 136, 141, 187; *Journal of Thomas Juxon*, pp. 34, 52, 75, 84, 104, 131, 154; see, Adamson, 'Peerage in Politics', pp. 115–20.

27. *Correspondence of Jean de Montereul*, I, 23–4, 117; Baillie, *Letters and Journals*, II, 240, 401; III, 16; BL, Add. MS 21066, fo. 15; *Warning for all the Counties*, sig. A4, p. 7; *Westminster Projects*, p. 1; *The Plague at Westminster* (1647); Verney Papers, volume 8, unfol.; Lilburne, *Two Letters*, p. 5; *Mercurius Pragmaticus*, no. 8 (16–23 May 1648), sig. H3; *Mercurius Pragmaticus*, no. 7 (9–16 May 1648), sig. Gv; *Mercurius Pragmaticus*, no. 14 (27 June–4 July 1648), sig. O2v; *Vox Veritatis* (1650), p. 5.

28. *Journal of Thomas Juxon*, p. 157; Bodl. Lib., MS Clarendon 30, fo. 233; *Mercurius Pragmaticus*, no. 11 (23–30 Nov. 1647), sig. L3; Prynne, *Machivilian Cromwellist*, p. 3; *Passes Granted by the Freeborn People of England* (1648), pp. 3–5.

29. Baillie, *Letters and Journals*, II, 141, 216, 335, 401; Adamson, 'Parliamentary Management', p. 34; Pearl, 'Oliver St John', p. 511.

30. *Mercurius Pragmaticus*, no. 19 (1–8 Aug. 1648), sig. Tv; *Mercurius Pragmaticus*, no. 28 (3–10 Sept. 1648), sig. Pp3; *Mercurius Pragmaticus*, no. 21 (15–22 Aug. 1648), sig. Bb2; Walker, *Relations*, p. 23; Lilburne, *Additional Plea*, pp. 17–23; Prynne, *Machivilian Cromwellist*, p. 7.

31. Baillie, *Letters and Journals*, III, 16; Pearl, 'Royal Independents', pp. 87–8; Mercurius Elencticus, *The Second Centurie* (1648), p. 4.

32. *Englands Troublers Troubled* (1648), p. 2; *The Anti-Projector* (Np, nd), p. 4. For discussions of clientage in Parliament, see Adamson, 'Parliamentary Management', pp. 38–42; Adamson, 'Peerage in Politics', p. 159; John Adamson, 'Of Armies and Architecture: the Employments of Robert Scawen', in Ian Gentles, John Morrill and Blair Worden (eds), *Soldiers, Writers and Statesmen of the English Revolution* (Cambridge, 1998). For Oldisworth, see *Newes from Pembroke and Mongomery* (1648); *The Earl of Pembroke's Speech in the House of Peers* (1647); *My Lord of Pembrokes Speech* (1648).

33. Walker, *Relations*, pp. 1–3.

34. Walker identified a third type of MP (whom others occasionally styled 'neutral temporizers'), who could not obviously be linked with any particular faction; those non-aligned members whom Walker considered to be increasingly marginalized, and who were 'principled' in their neutralism: *Westminster Projects*, 5 (1648), p. 4; *Mercurius Elencticus*, no. 55 (5–12 Dec. 1648), sig. Hhh4v; Walker, *Relations*, sig. A4–A4v. This was probably wishful thinking on Walker's part.

35. *Mercurius Pragmaticus*, no. 38 (12–19 Dec. 1648), sig. Ddd; Prynne, *Machivilian Cromwellist*, p. 7.

36. Walker, *Relations*, p. 23; *Mercurius Pragmaticus*, no. 21 (15–22 Aug. 1648), sig. Bb2; Chestlin, *Persecutio*, p. 53.

37. *Mercurius Pragmaticus*, no. 19 (18–25 Jan. 1648), sig. T2r–v.

38. *Mercurius Pragmaticus*, no. 5 (25 Apr.–2 May 1648), sig. E2; *Mercurius Elencticus*, no. 55 (5–12 Dec. 1648), sig. Hhh4v; Mercurius Melancholicus, *The Cuckoo's-Nest at Westminster* (1648), p. 6. For private correspondence, see: Verney Papers, volume 8, unfol.

39. Walker, *Relations*, p. 143; *Mercurius Pragmaticus*, no. 38 (12–19 Dec. 1648), sig. Ddd.

40. *Mercurius Pragmaticus*, no. 19 (18–25 Jan. 1648), sig. T2; *Mercurius Pragmaticus*, no. 5 (25 Apr.–2 May 1648), sig. E; Chestlin, *Persecutio*, p. 33; Adamson, 'Parliamentary Management', p. 46. In being such a client who nevertheless assumed a position of importance in Parliament, Robert Scawen was probably a rare exception to this picture: Adamson, 'Of Armies and Architecture'.

41. *Mercurius Pragmaticus*, no. 21 (15–22 Aug. 1648), sig. Bb2; Baillie, *Letters and Journals*, III, 16.

42. Walker, *Relations*, pp. 1–3. For discussions of ideology and clientage, see Adamson, 'Parliamentary Management', pp. 42, 47. Oldisworth, for example, was regarded as being a more pure Independent than his 'master', the Earl of Pembroke: *A Letter from an Independent* (1645), sig. A2. For the extent of the Earl of Essex's attachment to Presbyterianism, see Adamson, 'Peerage in Politics', p. 125.

43. Walker, *Relations*, pp. 77, 112–13; Sirrahnio [John Harris], *The Royall Quarrell* (1648), p. 5; see, Pearl, 'Royal Independents', p. 74.

44. *Westminster Projects*, 5, pp. 3–4; *The Tell Tale Spirit, or, the Devill of Derby House* (1648); *Journal of Thomas Juxon*, 116; Bodl. Lib., MS Clarendon 34, fo. 17.

45. *Putney Projects*, pp. 10–11, 32; Harris, *Royall Quarrell*, p. 5.

46. Walker, *Relations*, pp. 1–3.

47. Walker, *Relations*, pp. 1–3; *Mercurius Pragmaticus*, no. 5 (12–19 Oct. 1647), p. 37. This certainly helped to explain shifts made between factions by particular grandees: Verney Papers, volume 9, unfol.

48. Kishlansky, *Rise of the New Model Army*, p. 107; Adamson, 'Parliamentary Management', pp. 42, 45; Kishlansky, 'Saye What?', pp. 919–20. For Nedham and 'interest theory', see Blair Worden, ' "Wit in a Roundhead": the Dilemma of Marchamont Nedham', in Susan D. Amussen and Mark A. Kishlansky (eds), *Political Culture and Cultural Politics in Early Modern England* (Manchester, 1995), pp. 317–19.

49. Baillie, *Letters and Journals*, II, 196; *Reasons Why the House of Commons Ought in Justice Forthwith to Suspend the Members* (1647), p. 6; *The Tell Tale Spirit*; David Buchanan, *An Explanation of Some Truths* (1645), p. 56; *Mercurius Aulicus*, no. 32 (6 Aug. 1643), pp. 424–5.

50. *Correspondence of Jean de Montereul*, I, 117; *Westminster Projects*, p. 1; Prynne, *Machivilian Cromwellist*, p. 4; *Mercurius Pragmaticus*, no. 17 (18–25 July 1648), sig. R4v; David Buchanan, *A Short and True Relation* (1645), p. 59.

51. *Mercurius Pragmaticus*, no. 11 (23–30 Nov. 1647), sig. L2v; Bodl. Lib., MS Clarendon 30, fo. 286; Harris, *Antipodes*, sig. B.

52. *A Complaint to the House of Commons* (1643), pp. 11–12; Chestlin, *Persecutio*, pp. 57, 59.

53. *Certain Queries Lovingly Propounded to Mr William Prynne*, p. 7; *Englands Appeale to its own Army* (1647), sigs. A3r–v; Baillie, *Letters and Journals*, II, 316; Tom Tell Troth, *Works of Darkess Brought to Light* (1647), p. 8; *A Key to the Cabinet of the Parliament by their Remembrancer* (1648), p. 2; William Prynne, *A New Magna Charta* (1648), p. 2; Mercurius Elencticus, *A List of the Names of the Members* (1648), p. 8. See also: *Certain Queries Lovingly Propounded to Mr William Prynne*, p. 5; *Englands Troublers Troubled*, p. 2. John Musgrave provided detailed analysis of particular elections, and the characters and connections of those returned: Musgrave, *Fourth Word*, pp. 2, 8, 18.

54. Musgrave, *Another Word*; Musgrave, *Fourth Word*, p. 18; *Parliamentary or Constitutional History*, xvi, 75, 83; *Certain Queries Lovingly Propounded to Mr William Prynne*, p. 3; *Journal of Thomas Juxon*, p. 125. The importance of allegations regarding procedure in the case of the 'Eleven Members' has not always been noted by historians: e.g., Kishlansky, *Rise of the New Model Army*, pp. 243–4

55. *Windsor Projects* (1648), p. 4; Buchanan, *An Explanation*, p. 54; *An Alarum to the House of Lords* (1646), p. 10.

56. *Anti-Projector*, p. 4.

57. *Complaint to the House of Commons*, p. 14; *Mercurius Pragmaticus*, no. 6 (19–26 Oct. 1647), sig. F2v; Chestlin, *Persecutio*, p. 57.

58. *A Warning for all the Counties* (1647), pp. 8–9; Buchanan, *An Explanation*, p. 46; G. S., *A Letter from an Ejected Member* (1648), p. 3; see, Peter Heylyn, *Examen Historicum* (1659), II, 74; *LJ*, IV, 267; Conrad Russell, *The Fall of the British Monarchies* (Oxford, 1991), p. 343.

59. *Reasons Why the House of Commons Ought in Justice Forthwith to Suspend the Members*, p. 7.

60. *A Letter from a Scholler in Oxford-Shire* (1642), p. 15; Chestlin, *Persecutio*, p. 60.

61. Chestlin, *Persecutio*, p. 60.

62. *Parliamentary or Constitutional History*, XVI, 91, 156; *A Brief Justification of the XI Accused Members* (1647), p. 10.

63. Chestlin, *Persecutio*, p. 60.

64. *Complaint to the House of Commons*, p. 12; cf. Kishlansky, *Rise of the New Model Army*, p. 120.

65. *Complaint to the House of Commons*, p. 14.

66. Edward Hyde, Earl of Clarendon, *The History of the Rebellion and Civil Wars in England*, ed. W. D. Macray, 6 vols (Oxford, 1888), I, 363.

67. John Lilburne, *Englands Miserie and Remedie* (1645), p. 3; *Parliamentary or Constitutional History*, xvi, 77–8; Bodl. Lib., MS Clarendon 31, fo. 64; William Prynne, *Ardua Regni* (1648), p. 8; Walker, *Relations*, pp. 73–4; *Mercurius Pragmaticus*, no. 30 (17–24 Oct. 1648), sigs. Ttv–Tt2v; *Journal of Thomas Juxon*, p. 155; see, Kishlansky, *Rise of the New Model Army*, p. 160; Chestlin, *Persecutio*, pp. 59, 60; Jason Peacey, 'Making Parliament Public: Privacy, Print and Political Accountability during the Civil Wars and Interregnum' (paper delivered at the Early Modern History Seminar, Cambridge, October 2000).

68. Prynne, *Machivilian Cromwellist*, p. 6; Chestlin, *Persecutio*, p. 62.

69. Chestlin, *Persecutio*, p. 62; Prynne, *Machivilian Cromwellist*, pp. 5–6; Baillie, *Letters and Journals*, II, 99.

70. *Parliamentary or Constitutional History*, xvi, 75; Walker, *Relations*, pp. 40, 50. See also Prynne, *Machivilian Cromwellist*, p. 6.

71. Bodl. Lib., MS Clarendon 30, fo. 211.

72. Chestlin, *Persecutio*, p. 62; *A Warning for all the Counties*, pp. 2, 3.

73. Walker, *Relations*, sigs, A4–A4v, pp. 36–7, 48–9, 60, 98; Prynne, *Machivilian Cromwellist*, p. 27.

74. *Mercurius Pragmaticus*, no. 38 (12–19 Dec. 1648), sig. Ddd3.

75. *A Letter Without Any Superscription* (1643), p. 4; see, Adamson, 'Peerage in Politics'; Adamson, 'Parliamentary Management'; Lotte Glow, 'The Manipulation of Committees in the Long Parliament, 1641–2', *JBS*, 5 (1965).

76. John Lilburne, *A Defiance to Tyrants* (1648); Prynne, *New Magna Charta*, p. 3.

77. Buchanan, *An Explanation*, p. 52; see, Glow, 'Manipulation', p. 41; *Mercurius Pragmaticus*, no. 22 (22–9 Aug. 1648), sig. Dd; *Mercurius Pragmaticus*, no. 29 (10–17 Oct. 1648), sig. Ssv; *Mercurius Pragmaticus*, no. 20 (8–15 Aug. 1648), sigs. Y3–v.

78. Walker, *Relations*, pp. 4–5.

79. BL, Add. MS 31954, fo. 182; Glow, 'Manipulation', p. 35; Chestlin, *Persecutio*, p. 61.

80. *Mercurius Pragmaticus*, no. 3 (28 Sept.–6 Oct. 1647), sig. C2; *Anti-Projector*, p. 4; *Mercurius Pragmaticus*, no. 38 (12–19 Dec. 1648), sig. Ddd3; *A New Charge Against J.C.* (1647), p. 5; Walker, *Relations*, p. 53.

81. *A Key to the Cabinet of the Parliament* (1648), p. 5.

82. *Westminster Projects* 5, p. 1.

83. *A Complaint to the House of Commons*, pp. 10, 14; *Anti-Projector*, p. 4.

84. G. S., *A Letter from an Ejected Member* (1648), p. 10.

85. *Parliamentary or Constitutional History*, XVI, 75; Walker, *Relations*, pp. 4–5.

86. *Parliamentary or Constitutional History*, XVI, 76, 80; Walker, *Relations*, pp. 4–5; see, Glow, 'Manipulation', p. 37.

87. Chestlin, *Persecutio*, p. 26; John Lilburne, *A Pearle in a Dounghill* (1646), p. 3; Harris, *Antipodes*, sig. B; *Journal of Thomas Juxon*, p. 48; see, Glow, 'Manipulation', p. 37. Walker stressed that 'despatching all affairs privately and in the dark' aided factional 'usurpation', and he claimed that 'justice delights in the light and ought to be as public as the common air'. Ultimately such secrecy heightened concerns regarding corruption which had been fostered by evidence that committee members were 'feasted' by interested parties: Walker, *Relations*, pp. 4–5; *Anti-Projector*, p. 4; Chestlin, *Persecutio*, pp. 60–1.

88. Chestlin, *Persecutio*, pp. 21–2.

89. Musgrave, *Another Word*; John Lilburne, *The Copy of a Letter* (1645); John Lilburne, *Innocency and Truth* (1645), p. 13; John Lilburne, *Just Mans Justification* (2nd edition, 1647), p. 25; see, W. Epstein, 'The Committee for Examinations and Parliamentary Justice, 1642–7', *Journal of Legal History* 7 (1986); Walker, *Relations*, pp. 54, 55–8, 65.

90. Dorothy Gardiner (ed.), *The Oxinden and Peyton Letters, 1642–70* (1937), p. 80; BL, Add. MS 280001, fo. 43; BL, Add. MS 22619, fo. 208; Chestlin, *Persecutio*, p. 60.

91. *Letter from a Scholler in Oxford-shire*, p. 18; Chestlin, *Persecutio*, p. 60; *Journal of Thomas Juxon*, pp. 27, 47; *Mercurius Aulicus*, no. 13 (26 Mar.–2 Apr. 1643), pp. 166–7.

92. Baillie, *Letters and Journals*, II, 141, 178, 187, 236–7, 294, 301; Buchanan, *Short and True Relation*, pp. 51–3, 57; *Journal of Thomas Juxon*, p. 46; see, Adamson, 'Politics and the Nobility', pp. 253–4; Lotte Mulligan, 'Peace Negotiations, Politics and the Committee of Both Kingdoms, 1644–6', *HJ*, 12 (1969); Adamson, 'Triumph of Oligarchy'; Buchanan, *An Explanation*, p. 13.

93. *Certaine Considerations Touching the Present Factions*, sig. A2; *Westminster Projects*, p. 3; *Mercurius Pragmaticus*, no. 23 (29 Aug.–5 Sept. 1648), sig. Eev; no. 19 (1–8 Aug. 1648), sig. Tv; *Mercurius Pragmaticus*, no. 10 (30 May–6 June 1648), sig. K2, K4; no. 32/33 (31 Oct.–14 Nov. 1648), sig. Zz4v; no. 17 (18–25 July 1648), sig. R3–v; no. 28 (3–10 Sept. 1648), sig. Pp4; no. 13 (20–7 June 1648), sig. N; no. 19 (1–8 Aug. 1648), sig. T2v; no. 21 (15–22 Aug. 1648), sig. Bb2; no. 17 (18–25 July 1648), sig. R3–v; no. 9 (23–30 May 1648), sig. I4–v; no. 12 (13–20 June 1648), sigs. Mv–M4.

94. *Mercurius Pragmaticus*, no. 21 (15–22 Aug. 1648), sig. Bb2.

95. Baillie, *Letters and Journals*, II, 141–2, 178, 187; *Journal of Thomas Juxon*, p. 46; *Mercurius Pragmaticus*, no. 18 (11–18 Jan. 1648), sig. Sv. See also: *Mercurius Elencticus*, 7 (5–12 Jan. 1648), p. 47; Walker, *Relations*, pp. 74, 100; *Mercurius Pragmaticus*, no. 9 (23–30 May 1648), sig. I4–v; no. 11 (6–13 June 1648), sigs. Lv–L3; no. 12 (13–20 June 1648), sigs. Mv–M4; *Westminster Projects*, 5, p. 3.

96. Baillie, *Letters and Journals*, II, 236, 236–7, 284, 303, 312–13; Buchanan, *Short and True Relation*, pp. 56–7; see Adamson, 'Triumph of Oligarchy', pp. 116–17.

97. Walker, *Relations*, pp. 45, 77, 115–17, 141, 143, 152. Thomas Juxon claimed that 'there wants nothing now but a dictator', and the existence of such bodies ultimately presaged the dismantling of the three estates, and the promotion of arbitrary government: *Journal of Thomas Juxon*, pp. 46–7.

98. Adamson, 'The Peerage in Politics'.

99. C. Walker, *An Eye-Salve for the Armie* (1647), sig. Av; see Adamson, 'Parliamentary Management', p. 44.

100. Buchanan, *An Explanation*, p. 56.

101. Prynne, *New Magna Charta*, p. 3; Walker, *Eye-Salve for the Armie*, sigs. Av, A3v; Walker, *Relations*, p. 8; *The Grand Account* (Oxford, 1647); *London's Account* (1647); *Moderate Intelligencer*, 100 (28 Jan.–4 Feb. 1647), p. 890.

102. *Turn Apace, Turn Apace: Or, the Money-Mills Must be Kept Going* (1648), pp. 3–4; Walker, *Eye-Salve for the Armie*, sig. A3v.

103. Walker, *Relations*, pp. 5, 141, 145; *Mercurius Pragmaticus*, no. 9 (9–16 Nov. 1647), sig. I4; see Adamson, 'Peerage in Politics', pp. 20–1, 35, 52–4. See also: *Mercurius Aulicus*, no. 57 (28 Jan.–3 Feb. 1644), p. 814; *Mercurius Aulicus*, no. 59 (11–17 Feb. 1644), pp. 827–8.

104. Buchanan, *An Explanation*, pp. 53, 55–6. See also *Parliamentary or Constitutional History*, XVI, 122.

105. Walker, *Relations*, p. 5.

106. *Mercurius Aulicus*, no. 59 (11–17 Feb. 1644), pp. 827–8; Walker, *Relations*, pp. 67, 88; Buchanan, *An Explanation*, pp. 53, 56; see Adamson, 'Peerage in Politics', p. 54; Musgrave, *Another Word*; *Certain Queries Lovingly Propounded to Mr William Prynne*, p. 2.

107. *A Letter from a Scholler in Oxford-Shire*, p. 19; *Complaint to the House of Commons*, pp. 17–18; Buchanan, *An Explanation*, p. 56; Walker, *Relations*, pp. 67, 83, 87, 98, 141.

108. Walker, *Eye-Salve for the Armie,* sig. A4; *Englands Appeale to its Own Army,* sigs. A3r–v; *Windsor Projects,* p. 5; Musgrave, *Another Word;* J. Wildman, *The Lawes Subversion* (1648), p. 4; *Alarum to the House of Lords,* p. 10; *Englands Troublers Troubled,* pp. 2–3; *Westminster Projects,* p. 7; *Mercurius Pragmaticus,* no. 6 (19–26 Oct. 1647), sig. F4v; *Mercurius Pragmaticus,* no. 2 (21–8 Sept. 1647), sig. B3; *Mercurius Pragmaticus,* no. 24 (5–12 Sept. 1648), sig. Gg2v; Mercurius Elencticus, *A List of the Names of the Members of the House of Commons* (1648). See also, *Second Centurie.*

109. *Complaint to the House of Commons,* pp. 17–18.

110. Buchanan, *An Explanation,* p. 53; Musgrave, *Another Word;* Walker, *Relations,* p. 141.

111. *Englands Troublers Troubled,* pp. 2–3; *The Tell Tale Spirit,* sig. A3; Mercurius Elencticus, *A List of the Names of the Members of the House of Commons; Second Centurie; Reasons Why the House of Commons Ought in Justice Forthwith to Suspend the Members,* sig. B2v.

112. *Oxinden and Peyton Letters,* p. 100; BL, Add. MS 28001, fo. 213; *CJ,* IV, 477; Walker, *Relations,* pp. 5–6; *Journal of Thomas Juxon,* p. 96; *CJ,* IV, 362. More common were complaints regarding financial malfeasance, and although financial corruption was considered inevitable in a long parliament, particular criticisms were levelled at practices and procedures in the 1640s, and the 'unmeasureable deceits' and 'fraudulent dealings' which emerged: Walker, *Relations,* p. 17; *Journal of Thomas Juxon,* p. 96; Walker, *Eye-Salve for the Armie,* sig. A2.

113. *CSPV, 1643–7,* pp. 9, 42, 86; *The Case of the Armie,* in W. Haller and G. Davies (eds), *Leveller Tracts, 1647–53* (New York, 1944), p. 79; *Mercurius Aulicus,* no. 13 (26 Mar.–2 Apr. 1643), pp. 162–3; no. 32 (6 Aug. 1643), pp. 424–5. See Jason Peacey, 'Politics, Accounts and Propaganda in the Long Parliament', in Kyle and Peacey, *Parliament at Work.*

114. *Mercurius Aulicus* (20–7 Apr. 1645), p. 1556; Walker, *Relations,* sig. Bv, p. 10.

115. Buchanan, *An Explanation,* p. 56; Musgrave, *Another Word; Mercurius Pragmaticus,* no. 11 (23–30 Nov. 1647), sig. L4; Walker, *Relations,* p. 145; *London's Account,* p. 7.

116. Lilburne, *Innocency and Truth,* pp. 44–6, 68–72; *Reasons Why the House of Commons Ought in Justice Forthwith to Suspend the Members,* sig. B4; *A Vindication of Sir William Lewis* (1647), p. 4. See *The State of the Irish Affairs* (1645), pp. 17–18.

117. *The Scotish Dove,* no. 124 (26 Feb.–4 Mar. 1645/6), p. 583; Musgrave, *Another Word; Mercurius Pragmaticus,* no. 16 (11–18 July 1648, E 453/11), sig. Q4; *Reasons Why the House of Commons Ought in Justice Forthwith to Suspend the Members,* sig. B2v.

118. *Mercurius Elencticus,* no. 47 (11–18 Oct. 1648), pp. 386–7.

119. Adamson, 'Parliamentary Management', p. 48.

120. *Journal of Thomas Juxon,* p. 120.

121. Centre for Kentish Studies, U269/E2/1, and U1475/Z45/2, fo. 121v; *Oxinden and Peyton Letters,* p. 96; BL, Add. MS 28001, fo. 205; David Scott, '"Particular Businesses" in the Long Parliament: the Hull Letters, 1643–8', in Chris Kyle (ed.), *Parliament, Politics and Elections, 1604–48* (Camden Society, 2001), pp. 334, 335, 337, 338, 341.

122. Jason Peacey, ' "The Counterfeit Silly Curr": Money, Politics, and the Forging of Royalist Newspapers in the English Civil War', *Huntington Library Quarterly* (2004); Peacey, 'Addicted to Print: Habits of Purchasing and Reading Newspapers and Polemical Pamphlets, 1640–60' (forthcoming).

123. Peacey, 'Making Parliament Public'; Jason Peacey, *Politicians and Pamphleteers: Propaganda in the Civil Wars and Interregnum* (Aldershot, 2004).

124. Baillie, *Letters and Journals*, II, 190, 202, 215, 252, 278–9, 281–2, 352, 358–9, 367; *Journal of Thomas Juxon*, p. 117; Peacey, 'Politics, Accounts and Propaganda'.

125. Ashton, *Counter-Revolution*, pp. 44–125; Ashton, 'From Cavalier to Roundhead Tyranny'; Morrill, *Revolt of the Provinces*; M. Kishlansky, 'Ideology and Politics in the Parliamentary Armies, 1645–9', in Morrill, *Reactions to the English Civil War*; Kishlansky, *Rise of the New Model Army*, pp. 162, 180.

126. Walker, *Eye-Salve for the Armie*, sigs. Av, A4; Walker, *Relations*, sig. B, pp. 4, 6–7, 9, 12, 16, 17, 50, 58, 115–16.

127. *Parliamentary or Constitutional History*, XVI, 156; Walker, *Relations*, p. 139.

128. *A Publike Declaration and Solemne Protestation* (1648), p. 5.

129. John Lilburne, *A Whip for the Present House of Lords* (1648); *An Alarum to the House of Lords*, p. 9; John Lilburne, *Englands Birthright Justified* (1645), p. 33; *Journal of Thomas Juxon*, p. 104.

130. Wildman, *Putney Projects*, p. 32.

131. *Journal of Thomas Juxon*, p. 103; *Certain Queries Lovingly Propounded to Mr William Prynne*, p. 7. See also: *Englands Troublers Troubled*, p. 3.

132. Buchanan, *An Explanation*, p. 52.

133. Bodl. Lib., MS Clarendon 29, fos. 72r–v.

134. *Warning for all the Counties*, pp. 4–5; *Journal of Thomas Juxon*, p. 149.

135. 'Letters of Sir Cheney Culpeper', p. 231; George Wither, *Justitiarius* (1646), p. 14; Musgrave, *Another Word*; Musgrave, *Fourth Word*, p. 8; *Journal of Thomas Juxon*, pp. 104–5; *Reasons Why the House of Commons Ought in Justice Forthwith to Suspend the Members*, p. 4.

136. *A Moderate Answer to a Late Printed Pamphlet Intituled Nine Queries Upon the Printed Charge of the Army Against the XI Members* (1647), p. 4; *Journal of Thomas Juxon*, pp. 157–8.

137. *Certain Queries Lovingly Propounded to Mr William Prynne*, p. 2.

138. 'Sir Roger Twysden's Journal', *Archaeologia Cantiana*, 2 (1859), p. 188.

139. Wildman, *Putney Projects*, sig. F4v; *Englands Lamentable Slaverie* (1645), pp. 6–7; *A Warning to all the Counties*, pp. 4, 8, 10; T. Harbye, *The Nations Claim of Native Right* (1650), pp. 18–20.

140. Lilburne, *Englands Birthright Justified*, p. 33; Surrey RO, G85/5/2/10a.

141. *A True Relation of the Passages Between the Surrey Petitioners and the Souldiers at Westminster, May the 16. 1648* (1648), p. 2; Harbye, *Nations Claim*, p. 17.

142. Kishlansky, 'Ideology and Politics', p. 176.

143. Musgrave, *Fourth Word*, pp. 11–12; Lilburne, *Englands Birthright Justified*, p. 33; *Independency Stript and Whipt* (1648), p. 14; Harbye, *Nations Claim*, p. 71.

144. Lilburne, *Englands Birthright Justified*, p. 33; *Certain Queries Lovingly Propounded to Mr William Prynne*, p. 3.

145. Kishlansky, *Rise of the New Model Army*, p. 121; Adamson, 'Parliamentary Management', p. 48.

146. W. Waller, *Vindication* (1793), pp. 152, 190; Kishlansky, *Rise of the New Model Army*, p. 223.

NOTES TO CHAPTER 4

I am grateful to the Leverhulme Trust for funding a Fellowship, which facilitated the research for this chapter, and to Dr John Adamson, Professor Hamish Scott and Dr Micheál Ó Siochrú for commenting on an earlier draft of it. In 2004 I gave a version of this chapter as a paper to the Irish and British History Research Seminar at Trinity College, Dublin, and I am indebted to the seminar participants for their constructive comments and suggestions.

1. HMC, *Ormonde Manuscripts*, new ser. (1902), I, 225–6. I am grateful to Dr Ó Siochrú for bringing this reference to my attention.
2. Ibid., I, 226, 228.
3. Ibid., I, 229.
4. There has been healthy discussion of honour by early modern English historians, see particularly Mervyn James, *English Politics and the Concept of Honour, 1485–1642* (first published in 1978); Markku Peltonen, *The Duel in Early Modern England: Civility, Politeness, and Honour* (Cambridge, 2003); Richard Cust, 'Honour and Politics in Early Stuart England', *Past and Present*, 149 (1995), 57–94; and Cynthia Herrup, '"To Pluck Bright Honour from the Pale-Faced Moon": Gender and Honour in the Castlehaven Story', *Transactions of the Royal Historical Society*, 6th ser., 6 (1996), 137–60. The literature on 'honour' in early modern Ireland includes William Palmer, 'That "Insolent Liberty": Honor, Rites of Power, and Persuasion in Sixteenth-Century Ireland', *Renaissance Quarterly*, 46 (1993), 308–27; James Kelly, *That Damn'd Thing called Honour: Duelling in Ireland, 1570–1860* (Cork, 1995); Brendan Kane, 'The Beauty of Virtue: Honor in Early Modern Ireland and England, 1541–1641' (unpublished PhD dissertation, Princeton University, 2004) and Deana Rankin, *Between Spenser and Swift: English Writing in Seventeenth-Century Ireland* (Cambridge, 2005).
5. Barbara Donagan, 'Atrocity, War Crime and Treason in the English Civil War', *American Historical Review*, 99 (1994), 1137–66, and her 'Codes and Conduct in the English Civil War', *Past and Present*, 118 (1988), 65–95.
6. This was a defining characteristic of the upper nobilities in most European states, see for example, Arlette Jouanna, *Le devoir de revolte. La noblesse française et la gestation de l'état moderne, 1559–1661* (Fayard, 1989) and Caroline Hibbard, 'The Theatre of Dynasty', in R. Malcolm Smuts, *The Stuart Court and Europe: Essays in Politics and Political Culture* (Cambridge, 1996). I am grateful to Dr John Adamson for bringing these references to my attention.
7. For an excellent analysis of these honour communities, see Kane, 'The Beauty of Virtue'.
8. He distinguished himself in Spanish service before returning to Ireland in 1642, where he assumed command of the confederate Army of Leinster. Edward Hyde, Earl of Clarendon, *History of the Rebellion*, ed. W. D. Macray, 6 vols (Oxford, 1888; reissued 1992), IV, 419–21, and Pádraig Lenihan, *Confederate*

Catholics at War, 1642–9 (Cork, 2000). For Preston's Continental career, see Brendan Jennings (ed.), *Wild Geese in Spanish Flanders, 1582–1700* (Irish Manuscripts Commission, Dublin, 1964), and Gráinne Henry, *The Irish Military Community in Spanish Flanders, 1586–1621* (Dublin, 1992).

9. John Adamson, 'The Baronial Context of the English Civil War', *Transactions of the Royal Historical Society*, 5th ser., 40 (1990).

10. Ibid., p. 103.

11. Ibid., p. 101.

12. Ibid., p. 109.

13. Barbara Donagan, 'Halcyon Days and the Literature of War: England's Military Education before 1642', *Past and Present*, 147 (1995), 65–100, and Roger Manning, *Swordsmen: The Martial Ethos in the Three Kingdoms* (Oxford, 2003).

14. Manning, *Swordsmen*, pp. 17–18; interestingly, the figures for Scotland are comparable. Also see Keith M. Brown, *Noble Society in Scotland: Wealth, Family and Culture, from Reformation to Revolution* (Edinburgh, 2000). For a Continental perspective see H. M. Scott (ed.), *The European Nobilities in the Seventeenth and Eighteenth Centuries*, I, *Western Europe* (1995); Christopher Storrs and H. M. Scott, 'The Military Revolution and the European Nobility, *c.*1600–1800', *War in History*, 3 (1996), 1–42; Gregory Hanlon, 'The Decline of a Provincial Military Aristocracy: Siena 1560–1740', *Past and Present*, 155 (1997), 64–108.

15. Manning, *Swordsmen*, p. 19.

16. Clarendon, *History of the Rebellion*, IV, 421.

17. Ciaran Brady, *The Chief Governors: The Rise and Fall of Reform Government in Tudor Ireland* (Cambridge, 1994), and S. G. Ellis, *Ireland in the Age of the Tudors, 1447–1603: English Expansion and the End of Gaelic Rule* (1998 edn).

18. For instance, the rebellious Earl of Tyrone and his Ulster allies allegedly mustered 2,000 *buannachts* (or native mercenary soldiers) in 1594, and between 4,000 and 6,000 ordinary swordsmen regularly enlisted for service during the later stages of the Nine Years War. For further details see Ciaran Brady, 'The Captains' Games: Army and Society in Elizabethan Ireland', in Thomas Bartlett and Keith Jeffery (eds), *A Military History of Ireland* (Cambridge, 1996), pp. 144–7. Scottish mercenaries had long since supplemented these native soldiers and between the 1560s and the 1590s some 25,000 Scottish mercenaries found employment in militarized Ulster. These mercenary troops received part of their payment in cattle, Allan I. Macinnes, 'Crown, Clan and Fine: the "Civilising" of Scottish Gaeldom, 1587–1638', *Northern Scotland*, 13 (1993), 33.

19. C. Maxwell (ed.), *Irish History from Contemporary Sources (1509–1610)* (1923), p. 319.

20. Jane Ohlmeyer, ' "Civilizinge of those Rude Partes": Colonization within Britain and Ireland, 1580s–1640s', in Nicholas Canny (ed.), *Oxford History of the British Empire* (Oxford, 1998), I, pp. 124–47 and, 'A Laboratory for Empire? Early Modern Ireland and English Imperialism', in Kevin Kenny (ed.), *Ireland and the British Empire* (Oxford, 2004), pp. 26–60.

21. This happened throughout Western Europe and according to Storrs and Scott represented a temporary threat, especially when compared to the social consequences of the innovations associated with the 'Military Revolution', 'The Military Revolution and the European Nobility', pp. 11–12.

22. For interesting parallels see Gregory Hanlon, 'The Decline of a Provincial Military Aristocracy: Siena, 1560–1740', *Past and Present*, 155 (1997), pp. 64–108.

23. *LJI*, I, 437.

24. These military figures included the Lord Deputy, Sir Arthur Chichester, along with Sir Oliver Lambert (later barons and Earls of Cavan), Sir Edward Blayney (later barons Blayney) and Sir Toby Caulfield (baron of Charlemont): John McCavitt, *Sir Arthur Chichester, Lord Deputy of Ireland 1605–16* (Belfast, 1998), pp. 76–7.

25. *Calendar of State Papers, Ireland [CSPI], 1615–25*, p. 308.

26. Ibid., p. 309.

27. Clodagh Tait, 'Harnessing Corpses: Death, Burial, Disinterment and Commemoration in Ireland, *c.*1550–1655' (unpublished PhD dissertation, National University of Ireland, Cork, 1999), p. 188. Also see *An Elegie on the much Lamented Death of the Right Honorable Sir Arthur Chichester Knight, Lo. Baron of Belfast, Lo. High Treasurer of Ireland, one of the Lords of His Maiesties most Honorable Priuie Counsell, and of the Counsell of Warre* (1643).

28. Ohlmeyer, 'Civilizinge of those Rude Partes'.

29. *CSPI, 1633–47*, pp. 275–6.

30. Manning, *Swordsmen*, p. 18.

31. During the Spanish invasion scares of the 1620s, the lords dominated discussions about how best a government force (of 5,000 foot and 500 horse) could be maintained, and the responsibility for raising the money needed to support this army fell on their shoulders. The commissioners nominated to collect the revenue included virtually every peer eligible to sit in the Irish House of Lords, together with their kinsmen and dependants, *CSPI, 1625–32*, pp. 244, 250. For instance, Randal MacDonnell, first Earl of Antrim, a Catholic of Scottish Gaelic provenance, asked in 1625 that his men (a force of 120 foot plus horse) be suitably attired with his colours (crimson and yellow taffeta) and properly equipped with the latest weapons since he was loath to let them 'go to the field like kernes [native Irish soldiers]', *CSPI, 1625–32*, p. 64.

32. They were Richard, first Earl of Westmeath, Nicholas, sixth Viscount Gormanston, Nicholas, first Viscount Netterville, Nicholas, tenth Baron Howth, and Luke, ninth Baron Killeen, *CSPI, 1647–60*, p. 100.

33. *CSPI, 1625–32*, p. 595.

34. Sheffield City Library, Strafford MS 22, fo. 101: Antrim to Wentworth, 19 September 1632; and *CSPI, 1625–32*, pp. 81, 168, 186, 689.

35. *CSPI, 1625–32*, pp. 81, 398; Jane Ohlmeyer, *Civil War and Restoration in the Three Stuart Kingdoms: The Political Career of Randal MacDonnell First Marquis of Antrim (1609–83)* (Cambridge, 1993), pp. 32, 47–8, 84, 94.

36. NAS, GD 406/1/1154: Antrim to [Hamilton], 17 March 1639.

37. George Hill (ed.), *The Montgomery Manuscripts (1603–1706). Compiled from the Family Papers by William Montgomery of Rosemount* (Belfast, 1869), pp. 91, 94, 151–2, 153 (for the quote), 351–2.

38. Eustace Budgell, *Memoirs of the Lives and Characters of the Illustrious Family of the Boyles: particularly of the Late Eminently Learned Charles, Earl of Orrery . . .* (1737), p. 35.

39. Ibid., p. 57; Patrick Little, 'The Political Career of Roger Boyle, Lord Broghill, 1636–60' (unpublished PhD dissertation, Birkbeck College, University

of London, 2000); John Kerrigan, 'Orrery's Ireland and the British Problem', in David Barker and Willy Maley (eds), *British Identities and English Renaissance Literature* (Cambridge, 2002), pp. 197–225.

40. Henry Hexham, *The Principles of the Art Militarie: Practised in the Warres of the United Netherlands* (1637).

41. Carmel Larkin, 'Principle and Pragmatism: The Early Life and Career of Daniel O'Neill at the Court of Charles I' (unpublished PhD dissertation, National University of Ireland, Maynooth, 2002), Ch. 3.

42. *CSPI, 1625–32*, p. 160. After being imprisoned briefly in 1641 by the Irish insurgents, Blayney garrisoned Monaghan Fort for the king and died in 1646 fighting for the Scots at the battle of Benburb, *CSPI, 1633–47*, p. 475.

43. Aidan Clarke, 'Sir Piers Crosby (1590–1646): Wentworth's "Tawney Ribbon"', *Irish Historical Studies*, 102 (1988).

44. George Hamilton, *A History of the House of Hamilton* (Edinburgh, 1933), p. 1016; Alexia Grosjean and Steve Murdoch, 'Scotland, Scandinavia and Northern Europe 1580–1707' database www.abdn.ac.uk/history/datasets/ssne (Aberdeen, 1998–); and Mary Elizabeth Ailes, *Military Migration and State Formation* (Lincoln, NE, 2002), pp. 31, 52, 62, 65–6, 86–7, 127–8, 146 n. 59. Glenawley returned home in 1662 having secured a Swedish title (and presumably lands as well) and having wed the daughters of high-profile Scots living in Stockholm. Interestingly his daughter by his first wife married a Swede while his two younger daughters by his second spouse wed Irish peers with estates in Ulster.

45. J. T. Gilbert (ed.), *A Contemporary History of Affairs in Ireland, from A.D. 1641 to 1652*, 3 vols (Irish Archaeological Society, Dublin, 1879), II, p. xxxviii; Jennings, *Wild Geese*, and Henry, *The Irish Military Community in Spanish Flanders*.

46. Gilbert, *A Contemporary History*, I, 1–8.

47. Michael Hartnett, *Haicéad* (Oldcastle, County Meath, 1993), pp. 77–8. Butler also appears to have served in Flanders, see Jennings, *Wild Geese*, pp. 258, 263, 270, 287.

48. Manning, *Swordsmen*, pp. 60, 74–7.

49. Donald A. Neill, 'Ancestral Voices: the Influence of the Ancients on the Military Thought of the Seventeenth and Eighteenth Centuries', *Journal of Military History*, 62 (1998), 487–520.

50. Budgell, *Memoirs of the Lives*, pp. 57, 101 (for the quote).

51. *A Discourse of Military Discipline, devided into Three Boockes, declaringe the Partes and Sufficiencie ordained in a Private Souldier* (Brussels, 1634).

52. Rolf Loeber and Geoffrey Parker, 'The Military Revolution in Seventeenth-Century Ireland', in Jane Ohlmeyer (ed.), *Ireland from Independence to Occupation, 1641–60* (Cambridge, 1995), reprinted in Geoffrey Parker, *Empire, War and Faith in Early Modern Europe* (2002); Pádraig Lenihan's introduction to his edited collection, *Conquest and Resistance: War in Seventeenth-Century Ireland* (Leiden, 2001); and Thomas Bartlett, '"The Academy of Warre": Military Affairs in Ireland, 1600 to 1800' (Dublin, 2002).

53. Sir James Turner, *Memoirs of his own Life and Times*, ed. Thomas Thomson (Bannatyne Club, 28, Edinburgh, 1829), p. 26.

54. Also see James Burke, 'The New Model Army and the Problems of Siege Warfare', *Irish Historical Studies*, 27 (1990), 1–29.

55. G. A. Hayes-McCoy, *Irish Battles: A Military History of Ireland* (Belfast, 1989), p. 184.

56. BL, Egerton MS 917, fos 25–7: 'State of the Kingdom of Ireland, 10 December 1646', by [Arthur] Annesley and Sir William Parsons.

57. Manning, *Swordsmen*, p. 18.

58. For example, see *Humble Instructions for the Fetling [sic] of Garrisons in Ireland whereby that Countrey may be sooner reduced, if the War be prosecuted with Effect* (1646).

59. For an excellent evaluation of the military texts dating from the 1640s and the Restoration, including those by Bellings and Castlehaven, see Rankin, *Between Spenser and Swift*.

60. Raymond Gillespie, 'The Social Thought of Richard Bellings', in Micheál Ó Siochrú (ed.), *Kingdoms in Crisis: Ireland in the 1640s* (Dublin, 2001), pp. 212–38. Bellings' history is reprinted in J. T. Gilbert (ed.), *History of the Irish Confederation and War in Ireland*, 7 vols (Dublin, 1882–91). In *Vindiciarum Catholicorum Hiberniae* (Paris, 1650) John Callaghan stressed the honourable conduct of the Old English during the 1640s. I am grateful to Dr Thomas Connors for this observation.

61. [James Touchet,] Earl of Castlehaven, *The Earl of Castlehaven's Review, or, his Memoirs of his Engagement and Carriage in the Irish Wars* (1684).

62. Thomas Carte, *History of the Life of James, First Duke of Ormond*, 6 vols (2nd edn, Oxford, 1851), V, 261, 269. Also see Patrick Little, '"Blood and Friendship": the Earl of Essex's Protection of the Earl of Clanricarde's Interests, 1641–6', *English Historical Review*, 112 (1997), 927–41.

63. This is fully developed in Jane Ohlmeyer, 'The Irish Peers, Political Power and Parliament, 1640–41', in Ciaran Brady and Jane Ohlmeyer (eds), *British Interventions in Early Modern Ireland* (Cambridge, 2004).

64. Contemporaries later debated the wisdom of this decision. Castlehaven argued that it proved disastrous and only served to irritate 'the whole nation', *The Earl of Castlehaven's Review*, p. 34. Sir John Temple maintained that national security depended upon it, *The Irish Rebellion* (1679 edn), p. 244.

65. Gilbert, *History of the Irish Confederation*, I, 20, 24, 26, 28, 31.

66. *The Earl of Castlehaven's Review*, p. 35.

67. Ibid., p. 40.

68. Gilbert, *History of the Irish Confederation*, I, 35, 39, 41; Carte, *Life of Ormond*, V, 280–1. According to Castlehaven, Coote's forces 'frightened the nobility and gentry round about, who seeing the harmless country people, without respect to age, or sex, thus barbarously murdered'; *The Earl of Castlehaven's Review*, p. 36

69. Clarendon, *History of the Rebellion*, V, 419–21.

70. A. B. Grosart (ed.), *The Lismore Papers* 10 vols (new ser, 1886–8), IV, 241.

71. Budgell, *Memoirs of the Lives*, p. 38.

72. Ibid., p. 39.

73. BL, Add MSS 25277, fo. 58.

74. Gilbert, *History of the Irish Confederation*, I, 66; Grosart, *Lismore Papers*, n.s., IV, 259; HMC, *Calendar of the Manuscripts of the Marquess of Ormonde*, n.s., II, 51.

75. Trinity College Dublin (TCD), MS 840, fo. 13.

76. Gilbert (ed.), *History of the Irish Confederation*, II, 29.

77. *A Late and True Relation from Ireland: of the Warlike and Bloody Proceedings of the Rebellious Papists in that Kingdome, from Novemb. 1. to this Present, 1641* (1641), p. 2.

78. Gilbert, *History of the Irish Confederation*, II, 29.

79. Grosart, *Lismore Papers*, second series, IV, 267–8.

80. TCD, MS 813, fos 330v, 331v.

81. *The Last Ioyfull Newes from Ireland . . .* (1642), p. 3.

82. *The English and Scottish Protestants Happy Tryumph over the Rebels in Ireland* (1642), p. 7.

83. Increasingly the most effective Protestant commanders hailed from relatively humble backgrounds. For others – such as Marcus Trevor or the Coote brothers – civil war provided a route to ennoblement. For the Protestant war-effort, see Robert Armstrong, *Protestant War: The 'British' of Ireland and the Wars of the Three Kingdoms* (Manchester, 2005), and Kevin Forkan, 'Scottish-Protestant Ulster and the Crisis of the Three Kingdoms, 1637–52' (unpublished PhD thesis, National University of Ireland, Galway, 2003).

84. *An Exact Relation, of a Battell fought by the Lord Moore, against the Rebels in Ireland; with the Number of them that were slain on Both Sides* (1641), pp. 5–6.

85. The details are in National Library of Ireland, MS 6900.

86. Carte, *Life of Ormond*, V, 272.

87. *A certaine and true relation of a great and glorious victory obtained by the Protestant party in Ireland, under the conduct of the Lord Inchequin* (1642), p. 7.

88. *A great and glorious victory obtained by the Lord Inchequin, Lord President of Munster, over the Irish rebels . . .* ([London], 1647), p. 5.

89. Donough O'Brien, *History of the O'Briens* (1949); Ivar O'Brien, *Murrough the Burner: A Life of Murrough, Sixth Baron and First Earl of Inchiquin, 1614–74* (Whitegate, Co. Clare, 1991); and John A. Murphy, 'Inchiquin's Changes of Religion', *Journal of Cork Historical and Archaeological Society*, 72 (1967), 58–68.

90. Gilbert, *History of the Irish Confederation*, I, 54.

91. Carte, *Life of Ormond*, V, 285, 374–5, 376–80.

92. John Smyth, eleventh Earl of Clanricard, *The Memoirs and Letters of Ulick, Marquis of Clanricarde, and Earl of Saint Albans* (1758), pp. 171, 308.

93. Carte, *Life of Ormond*, V, 314.

94. *Majesty and the kingdome of Ireland, are examined and printed according to order of Parliament* ([London], 1647). In 1648, he then offered his support for the royalist coalition and declared 'on the word and honour of a peer' to fight for Catholicism and the rights, powers and prerogatives of the king, *A Declaration of the Resolutions of His Majesties Forces, published by the Marquisse of Clanrickard against the Parliament of England* (1648), p. 3

95. Fully analysed in Micheál Ó Siochrú, *Confederate Ireland 1642–9: A Constitutional and Political Analysis* (Dublin, 1999) and Tadhg Ó hAnnracháin, *Catholic Reformation in Ireland: The Mission of Rinuccini, 1645–9* (Oxford, 2002).

96. Gilbert, *History of the Irish Confederation*, I, 68.

97. Ibid., I, 257; Clanricard, *Memoirs and Letters*, p. 75; Aidan Clarke, *The Old English in Ireland, 1625–42* (London and Ithaca, NY, 1966; paperback edition, Dublin, 2000), pp. 33, 36, 41–3, 68, 71, 73, 75, 89, 188.

98. Gilbert, *A Contemporary History*, I, 36; *CSPI, 1633–47*, pp. 536–7.

99. Ibid.; Gilbert, *History of the Irish Confederation*, I, 268; HMC, *Ormonde*, NS, II, 4; *CSPI, 1633–47*, p. 310.

100 Ohlmeyer, *Civil War and Restoration*, pp. 210–17.

101. The definitive account of Ormond's career remains to be written. In addition to Carte, *Life of Ormond* see J. C. Beckett, *The Cavalier Duke: A life of James Butler, first Duke of Ormond, 1610–88* (Belfast, 1990); William P. Kelly, 'The Early Career of James Butler, Twelfth Earl, and First Duke of Ormond (1610–88), 1610–43' (unpublished PhD thesis, University of Cambridge, 1994); and T. C. Barnard and Jane Fenlon (eds), *The Dukes of Ormond, 1610–1745* (2000).

102. The standing army was initially a pitiful force of 2,297 foot and 943 horse, which was reinforced by the arrival of 2,600 foot from England over the winter of 1641 to 1642.

103. HMC, *Calendar of the Manuscripts of the Marquis of Ormonde preserved at Kilkenny Castle*, OS (2 vols, 1895), II, 303.

104. Jane Ohlmeyer and Steven Zwicker, 'John Dryden, the House of Ormond, and the Politics of Anglo-Irish Patronage', *Historical Journal*, 49 (2006), 677–706.

105. Clanricard, *The Memoirs and Letters*, p. 250.

106. Frederick FitzGerald, 'Lettice, Baroness of Offaly and the Siege of her Castle of Geashill, 1642', *Journal of the Kildare Archaeological Society*, 3:7 (1902), 418–24, p. 423 (for the quotation).

107. Dionysius Massari, 'My Irish Campaign', *The Catholic Bulletin*, 6–10 (1916–20); 7:4 (1917), p. 246.

108. Carte, *Life of Ormond*, V, 328, 333.

109. Mary Hickson (ed.), *Ireland in the Seventeenth Century*, 2 vols (1884), I, 394; Clanricard, *The Memoirs and Letters*, pp. 72–3.

110. Hickson, *Ireland*, II, p. 192, fo. 204 (for the quote).

111. José Antonio Maravall, *Poder, honor, y élites en el siglo XVII* (Madrid, 1979), pp. 32–41; Harold A. Ellis, 'Genealogy, History, and Aristocratic Reaction in Early Eighteenth-Century France: the Case of Henri de Boulainvilliers', *Journal of Modern History*, 58 (1986), 414–51, and *Boulainvilliers and the French Monarchy: Aristocratic Politics in Early Eighteenth-Century France* (Ithaca, NY, 1988). Pascal Brioist, Hervé Drévillon, and Pierre Serna, *Croiser le Fer: Violence et culture de l' épée dans La France moderne (XVIᵉ–XVIIIᵉ siècle)* (Paris, 2002); and Claude Chauchadis, *La Loi et duel. Le code du point d'honneur dans L'Espagne des XVIe–XVIIe siècles* (Toulouse, 1997). On the duel as being a specifically aristocratic manifestation of that 'moral independence' that went with this community of honour: Micheline Cuénin, *Le Duel sous l'ancien régime* (Paris, 1982); François Billacois, *Le Duel dans la société française des XVIᵉ–XVIIᵉ siècles. Essai de psychosociologie historique* (Paris, 1986), especially pp. 193–219; Ute Frevert, *Ehrenmänner: Das Duell in der bürgerlichen Gesellschaft* (Munich, 1991; English trans. Cambridge, 1995); Peltonen, *The Duel in Early Modern England*, and Kelly, *That Damn'd Thing called Honour*. I am grateful to Dr John Adamson and Professor Hamish Scott for bringing a number of these references to my attention.

112. Discussed further in Rankin, *Between Spenser and Swift*.

113. See, for example, anonymous, *A Brief Compendium of the Birth, Education, Heroick Exploits and Victories of the Truly Valorous and Renowned Gentleman, Thomas Earl of Ossory* . . . ([London?], 1680), p. 3.

NOTES TO CHAPTER 5

1. S[wedish] R[iksarkivet, Stockholm], AOSB ser B. E583; A. Grosjean, *An Unofficial Alliance: Scotland and Sweden, 1569–1654* (Leiden, 2003), pp. 197, 202–5. I would like to thank Dr Alexia Grosjean, University of St Andrews, for providing me with her translation of Hugh Mowatt's letters to Sweden, 1645–7.

2. P. C. Molhugsen, B. L. Meulenbroek, P. P. Witkam, H. J. M. Nellen and C. M. Ridderikhoff (eds), *Briefwisseling van Hugo Grotius (1583–1645)*, 17 vols ('S-Gravenhage and The Hague, 1928–2001), XII, 555, 591–2, 728; XV, *passim* and p. 652; XVI, *passim*.

3. Hartlib Papers, Sheffield, HP9/4/1A–2B. I should like to thank Dr Steve Murdoch, University of St Andrews, for drawing my attention to this source.

4. The British ramifications of the Covenanting movement are covered in more detail in Allan I. Macinnes, *The British Revolution, 1629–60* (Basingstoke, 2004), Chs 4 and 5. For a more Anglocentric take on the movement's British impact, see David Scott, *Politics and War in the Three Stuart Kingdoms, 1637–49* (Basingstoke, 2003), pp. 9–132; and Austin Woolrych, *Britain in Revolution, 1625–60* (Oxford, 2002), pp. 85–332.

5. W. C. Dickinson and G. Donaldson (eds), *A Source Book of Scottish History*, 3 vols (Edinburgh, 1961), III, 95–104; *APS*, V, 272–6; John Leslie, Earl of Rothes, *A Relation of Proceedings Concerning the Affairs of the Kirk of Scotland from August 1637 to July 1638*, ed. J. Nairne (Edinburgh, 1830), pp. 90–2, 96–8, 100–2, 211; Archibald Campbell, Marquess of Argyll, *Instructions to a Son, Containing rules of Conduct in Public and Private Life* (1661), pp. 30–6.

6. J. M. Paul (ed.), *Diary of Sir Archibald Johnston of Wariston, 1632–39* (Edinburgh, 1911), pp. 374–402; John Gordon, *History of Scots Affairs, 1637–41*, ed. J. Robertson and G. Grub, 3 vols (Aberdeen, 1841), II, 3–187.

7. Conrad Russell, *The Causes of the English Civil Wars* (Oxford, 1990), pp. 28–9; Kevin Sharpe, *The Personal Rule of Charles I* (New Haven, CT and London, 1992), pp. 827–31, 895–9.

8. Cf. [Archibald Johnston of Wariston], *Remonstrantie vande edelen, baronnen, state, kercken-dienaers, ende gemeente in het Coningryck van Schotland* (Edinburgh and Amsterdam, 1639); *Informatie, aen alle oprechte christenen in het coningrijcke van Engelandt* (Edinburgh, 1639); [Alexander Henderson], *Vertoog van de vvettelyckheyt van onsen tocht in Engelant* (Edinburgh, 1640); DR, TKUA, A II, no. 14, Akter og Dokumenter nedr. det politiske Forhold til England, 'Korfit Ulfelds or Gregers Krabbes Sendelse til England, 1640'; Steve Murdoch, *Britain, Denmark-Norway and the House of Stuart, 1603–60* (East Linton, 2000), pp. 90–116.

9. Caroline Hibbard, *Charles I and the Popish Plot* (Chapel Hill, NC, 1983), pp. 168–238; Jonathan Scott, *England's Troubles: Seventeenth-century English Political Instability in a European Context* (Cambridge, 2000), pp. 94–7. Paradoxically, the staunchly Protestant Covenanters' build-up of arms during the summer of 1638 and their overtures to France at the outset of the Bishops' Wars laid the basis for suspicions at Charles's Whitehall court that the Scots' betrayal of the king was part of another 'popish plot'. Conversely, the Covenanters' well founded apprehensions that Charles I was attempting to mobilize Spanish Habsburg, as well as Danish, support fuelled rumours of further 'popish plotting' at the

Whitehall court, not only to undermine their movement, but also to obviate the summoning of an English Parliament; Huntington Lib., Bridgewater and Ellesmere MSS, EL 7352, 7815, 7824, 7853, 7857–8; Edinburgh UL, MS Dc. 4. 16 (Instructions of the Committee of Estates of Scotland, 1640–41, pp. 52–3, 92).

10. A. Grosjean, 'General Alexander Leslie, the Scottish Covenanters and the Riksråd Debates, 1638–40', in Allan I. Macinnes, T. Riis and fo. G. Pedersen (eds), *Ships, Guns and Bibles in the North Sea and Baltic States, c.1350–c.1700* (East Linton, 2000), pp. 115–38; DR, TKUA, Skotland, A II, no. 4a, Akter og Dokumenter nedr. det politiske Forhold til Skotland, 1572–1640; E. Marquard (ed.), *Kancelliets Brevbøger: Vedrørende Danmarks Indre Forhold (1637–39)* (Copenhagen, 1944), pp. 171, 213, 348, 672–3, 722.

11. Steve Murdoch, 'Scotland, Scandinavia and the Bishops' Wars, 1638–40', in Allan I. Macinnes and Jane Ohlmeyer (eds), *The Stuart Kingdoms in the Seventeenth Century: Awkward Neighbours* (Dublin, 2002), pp. 113–34; *Kong Christian Den Fjerdes Egenhaendige Breve*, IV (1636–40), pp. 195–6, 272–6, 304–5, 359–60, 364–9, 378–9; DR, TKUA, England A II, no. 14, Akter og Dokumenter til England, 1631–40. This did not stop Charles pressing on with his attempts to procure Danish military aid. But his offer to pawn Orkney and Shetland in return for Danish support in 1640 was unrealistic – not that this stopped him trying again in 1642 (this time with the addition of Newcastle as part of the deal) in a bid for Danish aid against the English Parliamentarians.

12. NLS, Salt and Coal: Events, 1635–62, MS 2263, fos 73–84; NAS, Breadalbane MSS, GD 112/1/510, /514, /520; Allan I. Macinnes, *Charles I and the Making of the Covenanting Movement, 1625–41* (Edinburgh, 1991), pp. 190–2.

13. E. M. Furgol, 'Scotland turned Sweden: the Scottish Covenanters and the Military Revolution, 1638–51', in John Morrill (ed.), *The Scottish National Covenant in its British Context* (Edinburgh, 1990), pp. 134–55; M. C. Fissel, *The Bishops' Wars: Charles I's Campaigns against Scotland, 1638–40* (Cambridge, 1994), pp. 26–9, 39–53, 195–214; Martyn Bennett, *The Civil Wars in Britain and Ireland, 1638–51* (Oxford, 1997), pp. 41–8, 64–8; Huntington Lib., Bridgewater and Ellesmere MSS, EL 7851, 7857. The threatened invasion of the western seaboard by Randal MacDonnell, second Earl (later first Marquess) of Antrim, failed to materialize and Hamilton's naval assault on the east coast proved no more than a fitful stop to trade. However, George Gordon, second Marquess of Huntly, his son James, Lord Aboyne, and those associated with the house of Gordon maintained a five-month resistance in the north-east that was not quashed until the Covenanters concluded the Pacification of Berwick. This truce prevented recourse to bloodshed with the outnumbered and underfunded troops that Charles I had marched to the Anglo-Scottish border in June 1639. During the second campaign, which commenced in the summer of 1640, the Covenanters were obliged to maintain not only an invasion force in England, but also a home guard capable of rapid movement from the north-east to the south-west of Scotland.

14. J. R. Young, 'The Scottish Parliament in the Seventeenth Century: European Perspectives', in Macinnes et al., *Ships, Guns and Bibles in the North Sea and the Baltic States*, pp. 139–72; *APS*, V, pp. 264; 280–2, c. 23–4; 285–90, c. 26–33, 39, 41.

15. Huntington Lib., Bridgewater and Ellesmere MSS, EL 7859, 7810, 7838, 7842–49, 7869, 7872; David Scott, '"Hannibal at our Gates": Loyalists and Fifth-Columnists during the Bishops' Wars: the Case of Yorkshire', *Historical Research*, 70 (1997), 269–93.

16. David Laing (ed.), *The Letters and Journals of Robert Baillie*, 3 vols (Edinburgh, 1841–2), I, 255–61; II, 470–1; *The Intentions of the Army of the Kingdom of Scotland declared to their Brethren in England* (Edinburgh, 1640); Sir John Borough, *Notes on the Treaty carried on at Ripon between King Charles and the Covenanters of Scotland, A.D. 1640*, ed. J. Bruce (Camden Society, 1869), pp. 70–7.

17. Conrad Russell, *The Fall of the British Monarchies, 1637–42* (Oxford, 1991), pp. 27–205, 303–29; Derek Hirst, *England in Conflict, 1603–60: Kingdom, Community, Commonwealth* (1999), pp. 156–90; Woolrych, *Britain in Revolution*, pp. 189–233.

18. Jason Peacey, 'The Outbreak of the Civil Wars in the Three Kingdoms', in Barry Coward (ed.), *The Companion to British History in the Seventeenth Century* (2003), pp. 290–308; Nicholas Canny, 'What Really Happened in Ireland in 1641?', in Jane Ohlmeyer (ed.), *Ireland from Independence to Occupation, 1641–60* (Cambridge, 1995), pp. 24–42.

19. Maija Jannson, *Proceedings in the Opening Session of the Long Parliament, 1640–41*, 3 vols (Rochester, 1999–2000); Thomas Cogswell, *Home Divisions: Aristocracy, the State and Provincial Conflict* (Manchester, 1998), pp. 276–82; Ivan Roots, *The Great Rebellion* (Stroud, 1995), pp. 32–42.

20. Edinburgh UL, MS Dc. 4. 16 (Instructions of the Committee of Estates of Scotland 1640–41), pp. 31–2, 81–3, 94, 98; NAS, Hamilton Papers, GD 406/1/1397. The influence of the Scottish Commissioners is also detectable in the emergence, on 10 May, of a parliamentary bill, albeit with the emphasis more on the replacement than the abolition of episcopacy.

21. John Morrill, *The Nature of the English Revolution* (1993), pp. 45–90.

22. Russell, *The Fall of the British Monarchies*, pp. 83–6, 139–42, 150, 187, 195, 198, 200, 218, 334–5.

23. Edinburgh UL, MS Dc. 4. 16 (Instructions of the Committee of Estates of Scotland 1640–41), pp. 101, 105; Michael Mendle, 'A Machiavellian in the Long Parliament before the Civil War', *Parliamentary History*, 8 (1989), 116–24; William Palmer, 'Oliver St John and the Legal Language of Revolution in England: 1640–42', *Historian*, 51 (1989), 263–82.

24. Edinburgh UL, MS Dc. 4. 16 (Instructions of the Committee of Estates of Scotland 1640–41), pp. 79–83, 86, 94, 100–1, 105–7; Dumfries House, Loudoun Papers, Bundle 1/6; Huntington Lib., Bridgewater and Ellesmere MSS, EL 7755–6; [Archibald Campbell], *An Honourable speech made in the Parlament of Scotland by the Earle of Argile . . . the Thirtieth of September 1641. touching the Prevention of Nationall Dissention, and perpetuating the Happie Peace and Union betwixt The Two Kingdomes, by the frequent holding of Parlaments* (1641); B. P. Levack, *The Formation of the British State: England, Scotland and the Union, 1603–1707* (Oxford, 1987), pp. 110, 130–1. The right of the Irish Parliament to wage war was subsumed within the authority of the English Parliament. In marked contrast to the Irish situation, the sovereign and independent power of the Scottish Estates as a 'free Parliament' was formally recognized by the treaty. The Covenanters were not exclusively concerned with such a bipartisan British approach, however. At the same time

as the Scottish Commissioners were presenting their proposals for union to their English counterparts, the Committee of Estates at Edinburgh was actively, but fruitlessly, promoting a tripartite confederation that would involve the Estates General of the United Provinces. Once the Treaty of London was concluded, the commander of the Scottish forces, General Alexander Leslie, initiated repeated, but unrequited, approaches to Oxenstierna, the Swedish Regent, for an alternative confederation involving Sweden, the Scottish Covenanters and the English Parliamentarians; Edinburgh UL, MS Dc. 4. 16 (Instructions of the Committee of Estates of Scotland 1640–41), pp. 93, 97; *Rikskanseleren Axel Oxenstiernas Skrifter och Brefvexling*, II, 9 (Stockholm, 1898), pp. 486–8; *Kong Christian den Fjerdes Egenhaendige Breve*, V, 142–4).

25. NAS, Hamilton Papers, GD 406/1/1440–1; Anon., *The Truth of the Proceedings in Scotland containing the Discovery of the late Conspiracie* (Edinburgh, 1641); Peter Donald, *An Uncounselled King: Charles I and the Scottish Troubles, 1637–41* (Cambridge, 1990), pp. 313–16. Hamilton's brother William, Earl of Lanark (later second Duke of Hamilton), was also a target.

26. John R. Young, *The Scottish Parliament, 1639–61: A Political and Constitutional Analysis* (Edinburgh, 1996), pp. 30–53; Gilbert Burnet, *The Memoirs of the Lives and Actions of James and William, Dukes of Hamilton and Castleherald* (1838), pp. 46, 184–7. Charles's formal acceptance of the realities of political power in Scotland was manifest in his liberal bestowal of honours and pensions on the Covenanting leadership who had masterminded his defeat, militarily and constitutionally. Argyll was promoted to marquess, General Leslie became Earl of Leven, Wariston was knighted and Henderson was appointed royal chaplain in Scotland.

27. Sir Simon Harcourt, *March 18. A letter sent from Sr Simon Harcourt, to a worthy member of the House of Commons. With a true relation of the proceedings of the English army, under his command to this present March* (1641); Edward Conway, second Viscount Conway, *A Relation from the Right Honourable the Lord Viscount Conway, of the Proceedings of the English Army in Ulster from June 17 to July 30* (1642); David Stevenson, *Scottish Covenanters and Irish Confederates* (Belfast, 1981), pp. 51–65. Although Alexander Leslie, Earl of Leven, was the designated supreme commander of the Scottish forces, he spent only three months in Ireland: between August and November 1642.

28. Henry Parker, *The Danger to England Observed, upon its Deserting the High Court of Parliament* (1642); Dorothy Gardiner (ed.), *The Oxinden Letters, 1607–42* (1933), pp. 311–12; Michael Mendle, 'The Great Council of Parliament and the First Ordinances: the Constitutional Theory of the Civil War', *Journal of British Studies*, 31 (1992), 133–62. In order to revitalize Britannic monarchy, prevent further recourse to war within the British Isles, and resolve the Irish situation through closer association with England, Henry Parker argued subsequently for a confederal executive or 'general junto' drawn equally out of the three kingdoms; see his *The Generall Junto, or the Councell of Union: chosen equally out of England, Scotland and Ireland, for the better compacting of Three Nations into One Monarchy* (1642).

29. John Pym, *A Most Learned and Religious Speech spoken by Mr Pym, at a Conference of both Houses of Parliament the 23 of . . . September* (1642); *The Scots Resolution Declared in a Message Sent from the Privie Councell of the Kingdome of Scotland, to His*

Majestie at Yorke (Edinburgh, 1642); NAS, Hamilton Papers, GD 406/1/1688, 1742–3, 1782, 1808, 1887.

30. NAS, Hamilton Papers, GD 406/1/1828, /1840, /1846; Huntington Lib., Loudoun Scottish Papers, Box 29, LO 10503; *The Proceedings of the Commissioners, appointed by the Kings Maiesty and Parliament of Scotland, for conserving the articles of the Treaty and Peace betwixt the kingdomes of Scotland and England* (1643).

31. Young, *The Scottish Parliament*, pp. 54–70; BL, Egerton MS 2884 (Historical Papers), fo 19; *A Declaration of the Lords of His Majesties Privie-Councell in Scotland and Commissioners for the conserving the Articles of the Treaty: for the Information of His Majesties good Subjects of this Kingdom* (Edinburgh, 1643); Robert Munro, *A Letter of Great Consequence sent . . . out of the Kingdom of Ireland, to the Honorable, the Committee for the Irish Affairs in England, concerning the State of Rebellion there* (1643).

32. *APS*, VI (i), 41–3, 47–9.

33. *The Love and Faithfulnes of the Scottish Nation, the Excellency of the Covenant, the Union between England and Scotland cleared, by Collections, from the Declarations of Parliament and Speeches of severall Independent Brethren* (1646).

34. Huntington Lib., Loudoun Scottish Collection, Box 16, LO 9998. The other politician in whom the Covenanters placed particular trust was Sir Henry Vane junior. He reported to the City that the Scots were so sensible of the dangers to religion if the parliamentary cause should fail that they were ready to circumvent all military and financial difficulties in return for an advance of £100,000. The use of the term 'British', not just 'English', when applied to the forces raised among planters to resist the Irish Confederates, accorded further recognition of the Covenanters' importance to the parliamentarian war effort. The supply of these British forces, as well as that of the distinctive Scottish Covenanting army in Ulster, remained problematic, however; a situation not eased by a further despatch of 10,000 Scottish troops in the summer of 1644 to join the original contingent of 21,000 sent to England; BL, Add. MS 5492 (Ordinances of Parliament 1642–9), fos 11, 54–5, 115–16; *Die Sabbati 30 December 1643. Ordered that the Adventurers of this House for lands in Ireland, and the body of Adventurers in London, doe meete at Grocers-Hall on Thursday in the Afternoon at Two of the Clock* (1643).

35. *The Declaration of the Kingdomes of Scotland and England* (Edinburgh, 1644). All common soldiers who acknowledged past errors in fighting for the Royalists were to be freely accepted into the Covenant. Those of the Scottish nation who had engaged with the royalist cause in England were to be given the opportunity to confess their mistakes and take the Covenant by 1 March, otherwise they were to be treated as 'desperate Malignants' and their estates sequestrated. Those who had deserted the parliamentary cause in England, but were not yet reckoned among the prior authors of civil war, were offered the same timely opportunity to be restored to favour through the Covenant, subject to discretionary fines imposed on their estates. Those who refused pardon were to be forfeited. No indemnity was to be offered to three categories of delinquents, who were to face the summary justice due to traitors: Catholic recusants involved in plotting against Protestantism in Scotland and England and in sustaining civil war to bring both kingdoms 'under the Power and Tyranny of the Pope'; all Irish Rebels, including Protestant Royalists, who had come to England to fight against the parliamentary forces; and principal counsellors, 'who have kindled and

fomented the Fire of Division and Warre' between the king and the Long Parliament. Their moveable and heritable estates were to be forfeited to pay the public debts and common burdens of both kingdoms. The invitation was also made that treason, which had been extended to cover anti-Covenanting activities in Scotland, should now be similarly extended to activities in England which breached the Solemn League and Covenant.

36. Lawrence Kaplan, *Politics and Religion during the English Revolution: The Scots and the Long Parliament, 1643–5* (New York, 1976), *passim*; David Stevenson, *Revolution and Counter-Revolution in Scotland, 1644–51* (1977), pp. 1–81; David L. Smith, *Constitutional Royalism and the Search for Settlement c.1640–49* (Cambridge, 1994), pp. 109–218.

37. Mark Kishlansky, *The Rise of the New Model Army* (Cambridge, 1979), pp. 22–102; Ian Gentles, *The New Model Army in England, Ireland and Scotland, 1645–53* (Oxford, 1992), pp. 1–86; Bennett, *The Civil Wars in Britain and Ireland*, pp. 169–229; J. S. Wheeler, *The Irish and British Wars, 1637–54: Triumph, Tragedy and Failure* (2002), pp. 94–157.

38. David Scott, 'The "Northern Gentlemen", the Parliamentary Independents and Anglo-Scottish Relations in the Long Parliament', *Historical Journal*, 42 (1999), 347–75; Sarah Barber, 'The People of Northern England and Attitudes towards the Scots, 1639–51: "The Lamb and the Dragon cannot be Reconciled"', *Northern History*, 35 (1999), 93–118.

39. *The Journal of Sir Simonds D'Ewes from the Beginning of the Long Parliament to the opening of the Trial of the Earl of Strafford*, ed. Wallace Notestein (New Haven, CT, 1923), p. 9; George Withers, *The British Appeals with Gods Mercifull Replies on the behalfe of the Commonwealth of England* (1650), pp. 12–13; M. Perceval-Maxwell, 'Ireland and Scotland, 1638–48', in Morrill, *The Scottish National Covenant in its British Context*, pp. 193–211.

40. The Scottish Commissioners led by John Campbell, first Earl of Loudoun, were John Maitland, Lord Maitland (later second Earl and first Duke of Lauderdale), Johnston of Wariston and Robert Barclay. Another six commissioners, headed by Argyll, were added in July 1644. They were well aware that an embassy had been sent from the United Provinces to effect a meaningful reconciliation. At the same time, the Covenanting leadership in Edinburgh was intent on reinvigorating the 'auld alliance' with France. William Ker, third Earl of Lothian, was despatched as ambassador in the spring of 1643, and a contingent of troops had earlier been sent to reinforce the Scottish forces (Garde Écossaise) in French service under Argyll's errant half-brother, James, Lord Kintyre (now Earl of Irvine). Although Charles I had been informed officially by the Covenanters of the embassy to France, Lothian was imprisoned at Oxford on his return when calling to pay his respects to the king in November 1643. Scottish forces remained in demand for Swedish service. When Hugh Mowatt was sent to Britain as ambassador to both the Scottish Estates and the English Parliament, he received a warm welcome in Edinburgh as Swedish ambassador, but no promise of troops until the settlement of affairs in England. At the same time, the Covenanting leadership was monitoring the Danish attempts to secure Scottish forces through an embassy despatched under Colonel John Henderson, another expatriate Scot with longstanding ties to the house of Argyll. Although they were not receptive to the raising of forces for Danish

service, other than to decant royalist sympathizers from Scotland, they took umbrage when the Parliamentarians incarcerated Henderson when he was passing through London in June 1645; Grosjean, *An Unofficial Alliance: Scotland and Sweden*, pp. 195–206; BL, Egerton MS 2533 (Nicholas Papers), fo 365; DR, TKUA, Alm. Del I Indtil 1670, 'Latina' vol. 11, fos 272–4, 310–15, 335–7; and TKUA, England, A II, no. 15, Akter og Dokumenter vedr. det politiske Forhold til England, 1641–8.

41. Joad Raymond (ed.), *Making the News: An Anthology of the Newsbooks of Revolutionary England, 1641–60* (Moreton-in-the-Marsh, 1993), pp. 110–12; *A Letter from his Excellency, Robert Earl of Essex, to the Honourable House of Commons concerning the sending of a Commission forthwith to Sir William Waller* (1644).

42. Alexander Henderson, *A Sermon Preached to the Honourable House of Commons, at their Late Solemne Fast, Wednesday, December 27 1643* (1644). The other Scottish clerics attending the Westminster Assembly were Robert Baillie, Robert Douglas, George Gillespie and Samuel Rutherford, all powerful preachers and polemicists.

43. Dumfries House, Loudoun Papers, Bundles 1/26–7, 7/161, and Loudoun Deeds, Bundle 1700/2; H. W. Meikle (ed.), *Correspondence of the Scots Commissioners in London, 1644–6* (Edinburgh, 1907), pp. 6, 10–13, 22–7, 33–4, 45, 50, 53, 57–8. Discrimination against the Irish continued to be a feature of the proposals for reciprocal rights to membership of executive councils of the three kingdoms. The Scots were deemed capable of exercising any office in England and Ireland, but only the English were so qualified in Scotland. Similarly, no mention was made of Irish representation, when the Scots claimed half (but were prepared to settle for a third) of all places of trust in the royal household. The Covenanters were also determined that no Scottish peer should be held to account in England for transgressions in Scotland, in the same way that Strafford had been tried for his malpractices in Ireland. Hamilton, though elevated to a dukedom for his efforts to secure Covenanting support for Charles I in 1642–3, had actually been imprisoned by the king when he reported his incapacity to prevent the Covenanting intervention on the side of the English Parliamentarians in autumn 1643. The Scottish Commissioners in London complained that Hamilton was being kept prisoner in England contrary to Scots law, which required that all subjects who committed wrongs in Scotland should be tried there.

44. Meikle, *Correspondence of the Scots Commissioners*, pp. 9, 29, 59–63; Huntington Lib., Ellesmere and Bridgewater MS, EL 7776; David L. Smith '"The More Posed and Wised Advice": the Fourth Earl of Dorset and the English Civil Wars', *Historical Journal*, 34 (1991), 797–829. The king's principal negotiators were two 'constitutional Royalists', Thomas Wriothesley, fourth Earl of Southampton, and the Anglo-Scot James Stuart, fourth Duke of Lennox and first Duke of Richmond, whose endeavours to play on the sympathy of his Scottish countrymen towards the Stuart monarchy were unproductive; Huntington Lib., Bridgewater and Ellesmere MS, EL 7776; Dumfries House, Loudoun Deeds, Bundle 2/9.

45. *CSPV, 1643–7*, pp. 73–6, 83, 85, 97, 115, 158, 161, 166–7.

46. Cf. DR, TKUA, England, A I, no. 3, Breve, til Vels med Bilag fra Medlemmer af det Engelske Kongehus til medlemmer af det danske, 1613–89.

47. John Adamson, 'The Triumph of Oligarchy: the Management of War and the Committee of Both Kingdoms, 1644–5', in Chris R. Kyle and Jason Peacey (eds), *Parliament at Work: Parliamentary Committees, Political Power and Public Access in Early Modern England* (Woodbridge, 2002), pp. 101–27; Kaplan, *Politics and Religion during the English Revolution*, pp. 33–45; Mark Kishlansky, *A Monarchy Transformed: Britain, 1603–1714* (1996), pp. 155–6, 163–4; NA, SP 21/7 (Committee of Both Kingdoms, Entry Book of Letters Received, 1644–5), pp. 75–9, 112–13, 153, 194–6; and SP 23/1A (Commons' Committee for Scottish Affairs Order Book, October 1643, October–December 1645), pp. 18–21, 48, 50, 58, 63, 71, 77, 102. Developed on the English side from the Committee of Safety, the Committee of Both Kingdoms was obliged to share direction of the war effort, initially with the Committee to Reform the Lord General Essex's Army, which dealt with the compositions of regiments, and then with the Army Committee, which was primarily concerned with supply. Meeting the costs of the Covenanting armies in England and Ireland remained the responsibility of the Committee at Goldsmith's Hall for Scottish Affairs. The number of Scottish Commissioners was raised from four to eleven in July 1644 after five more Parliament-men were added, before Marston Moor, to the original seven members from the Lords and fourteen from the Commons.

48. NA, SP 46/106 (Orders, Warrants and Receipts for Payment of the Scots Army in England 1643–8), fos 150, 255, 257; Meikle, *Correspondence of the Scots Commissioners in London*, pp. 2–4, 39, 46–8, 68–9, 82–3, 88–9, 93, 102, 107, 141, 202; David Scott, 'The Barwis Affair: Political Allegiance and the Scots during the British Civil Wars, *English Historical Review*, 115 (2000), 843–63. Both war and peace groupings had been anxious to involve Scottish expertise in international relations following the establishment of the Committee of Both Kingdoms. In February 1644, the Parliamentarians had taken the initiative in inviting the Covenanters to appoint a Scottish agent to work with Matthew Strickland, their English agent in the United Provinces. Thomas Cunningham, the leading fundraiser and financial facilitator for the Covenanting movement, based at Campvere in Zeeland, was duly nominated the following month. His remit, as prescribed by the Committee of Estates at Edinburgh in May, was not only to promote the joint cause before the States General, but also to extend the Solemn League and Covenant to the Dutch Republic; J. R. Young, 'The Scottish Parliament and European Diplomacy', in Steve Murdoch (ed.), *Scotland and the Thirty Years' War, 1618–48* (Leiden, 2001), pp. 87–92; E. J. Courthope (ed.), *The Journal of Thomas Cunningham of Campvere* (Edinburgh, 1928), pp. 5–7, 14–16, 82–8, 109–17, 251.

49. NA, SP 21/16 (Committee of Both Kingdoms, Entry Book of Letters Received, 1644), pp. 145–7; Huntington Lib., Loudoun Scottish Collection, Box 21, LO 11367; David Mason (ed.), *The Quarrel between the Earl of Manchester and Oliver Cromwell: An Episode of the English Civil Wars* (Camden Society, 1875), pp. 62–70, 78–95; Meikle, *Correspondence of the Scots Commissioners in London*, pp. 50–3; Kaplan, *Politics and Religion during the English Revolution*, pp. 55–96.

50. Mark Kishlansky, 'The Case of the Army Truly Stated: The Creation of the New Model Army', *Past and Present*, 81 (1978), 51–74; Ian Gentles, 'The Choosing of the Officers for the New Model Army', *Historical Research*, 67 (1994), 264–85.

51. Dumfries House, Loudoun Papers, A525/1; Meikle, *Correspondence of the Scots Commissioners in London*, pp. 21, 35–8, 54–7, 72–3, 89–93, 124–30, 144–5, 160–1, 166–7; Bennett, *The Civil Wars in Britain and Ireland*, pp. 182–4.

52. John Shawe, *Brittains Remembrancer: Or, the National Covenant, as it was laid out in a Sermon preached in the Minster at Yorke . . . upon Friday Sept[ember] 20, 1644* (1644), and *The Three Kingdomes Case: or, their Sad Calamities, together with their Causes and Cure, laid down in a Sermon preached at a Publique Fast at Kingston upon Hull* (1646); Keith Lindley and David Scott (eds), *The Journal of Thomas Juxon, 1644–7* (Cambridge, 1999), pp. 27–9, 61–2, 75, 78, 81–7, 114–17; John Morrill, *The Revolt of the Provinces: Conservatives and Radicals in the English Civil War* (1976), pp. 118–22.

53. Huntington Lib., Bridgewater and Ellesmere MS, EL 7778; Dumfries House, Loudoun Papers, A15/4, Bundle 44/1 and Loudoun Deeds, Bundle 1/16; *A Paper delivered in the Lord's House by the Earle of Essex, Lord Generall, at the offering up of his Commission* (1645); David Scott, 'The "Northern Gentlemen", the Parliamentary Independents, and Anglo-Scottish Relations in the Long Parliament', *Historical Journal*, 42 (1999), pp. 347–75.

54. Dumfries House, Loudoun Papers, A15/4, /15; Bulstrode Whitelocke, *Memorials of the English Affairs from the Beginning of the Reign of Charles I to the Happy Restoration of King Charles the Second*, 4 vols (Oxford, 1853), I, 460–7; Lindley and Scott, *Journal of Thomas Juxon*, pp. 94–5, 102–5; William M. Lamont, 'The Puritan Revolution: a Historiographical Essay', in J. G. A. Pocock (ed.), *The Varieties of British Political Thought, 1500–1800* (Cambridge, 1996), pp. 119–45; Woolrych, *Britain in Revolution*, pp. 296–301. The adversarial nature of the divisions between Presbyterians and Independents was laid bare in the summer of 1645, when Thomas, Lord Savile, at the prompting of Saye and Sele, attempted to implicate Denzell Holles and Bulstroke Whitelocke in secret dealings with the Scots to negotiate terms of peace with Charles I; Michael Mahoney, 'The Savile Affair and the Politics of the Long Parliament', *Parliamentary History*, 7 (1988), 212–27.

55. Raymond, *Making the News*, pp. 339–48; Henry Parker, John Sadler and Thomas May, *The King's Cabinet Opened* (1645); Jason Peacey, 'The Exploitation of the Captured Royal Correspondence and Anglo–Scottish Relations in the British Civil Wars, 1645–6', *Scottish Historical Review*, 79 (2000), 213–32.

56. BL, Add. MS 33596 (Historical Letters and Papers 1633–55), fos 7–8; Meikle, *Correspondence of the Scots Commissioners in London*, pp. 150, 153, 160, 163, 19–80; J. G. Fotheringham (ed.), *The Diplomatic Correspondence of Jean de Montereul and the Brothers De Bellièvre, 1645–8*, 2 vols (Edinburgh, 1898–9), I, 5–195; II, 569–83. The principal Covenanting agent in France was Sir Robert Moray, Lieutenant-Colonel of the Scots Guards. Prior to Uxbridge, the Scottish Commissioners in London had been particularly resistant to French suggestions that they unilaterally conclude a peace treaty with Charles I. Indeed, before the arrival of Montreuil, the relationship of the Committee of Estates with the French envoy, M. de Boisivon, sent to Scotland in the wake of the Solemn League and Covenant, had varied from abrasive to outright hostility. The Scots, who the envoy claimed, had contracted to have him assassinated, had him imprisoned in York when he attempted to reach Charles I in the summer of 1644. He subsequently claimed that the existence of the Committee of Both

Kingdoms, which directed the common affairs of England and Scotland from London, made his imprisonment in England a clear violation of international law; ibid., II, 539–68.

57. Stevenson, *Revolution and Counter-Revolution in Scotland*, pp. 19–54; Allan I. Macinnes, *Clanship, Commerce and the House of Stuart, 1603–1788* (East Linton, 1996), pp. 98–110.

58. Dumfries House, Loudoun Papers, A15/5, 7–11, 16 and Bundle 1/25; *Scottish Commissioners in London*, pp. 82–3, 97–8, 109–11, 118–23, 133–4, 137–9, 147; Whitelock, *Memorials of the English Affairs*, pp. 542–3; Wheeler, *The Irish and British Wars*, pp. 148–50; Stevenson, *Revolution and Counter-Revolution in Scotland*, pp. 61–3. The Scottish Commissioners and the Committee of Estates took a more pragmatic approach than the clerical commissioners from the Kirk to the erastian nature of English Presbyterianism as implemented by the Long Parliament in March 1646. In these reforms, all church courts were subordinated to Parliament and their powers of ecclesiastical censure were strictly limited. The National Covenant of 1638 had affirmed that matters of faith, worship and government in Scotland were required to be grounded in parliamentary statutes. The Committees of War established subsequently in the Scottish shires had also not only enforced the civil sanctions required for ecclesiastical transgressions, but determined the ideological soundness of those suspected of being antipathetic to the Covenanting cause; Dumfries House, Loudoun Papers, Green Suitcase, Bundle 1/21, and Loudoun Deeds, Bundles 1/7, 1700/1; Baillie, *Letters*, II, 103, 195, 211, 229–30, 234, 242, 250, 265–6, 270, 286, 299, 317–20, 326, 335–41, 357, 360–2, 485; III, 10–1; Meikle, *Correspondence of the Scots Commissioners in London*, pp. 43, 71, 155; Kaplan, *Politics and Religion during the English Revolution*, pp. 128–44.

59. Dumfries House, Loudoun Papers, A213/4, Bundle 1/23–4 and Green Suitcase, Bundle 1/20; Meikle, *Correspondence of the Scots Commissioners in London*, pp. 104–5, 148–52, 173–7, 181–2, 186–200; Whitelock, *Memorials of the English Affairs*, pp. 548–9, 557, 564, 578; Smith, *Constitutional Royalism and the Search for a Settlement*, pp. 128–31, 149–50, 183–7; Patrick Little, 'The English Parliament and the Irish Constitution', in Micheal Ó Siochrú (ed.), *Kingdoms in Crisis: Ireland in the 1640s* (Dublin, 2000), pp. 106–21.

60. *The Lord Marquess of Argyle's Speech to a Grand Committee of Both Houses of Parliament* (1646); Inverary Castle Archives, Letters, Marquess's Period 1646–9, Bundle 8/192; Raymond, *Making the News*, pp. 349–50; J. R. Young, 'The Scottish Parliament and the Covenanting Revolution: the Emergence of a Scottish Commons', in John R. Young (ed.), *Celtic Dimensions of the British Civil Wars* (Edinburgh, 1997), pp. 164–84; Stevenson, *Revolution and Counter-Revolution in Scotland*, pp. 63–72. Scotophobia was evident in various measures. A relatively innocuous publication by a Scottish writer, David Buchanan, explaining the emerging differences between the Uxbridge and Newcastle propositions was deemed insulting by the Commons and burned by the common hangman. The Lords declined to accept the vote of the Commons on 19 May to dispense with the services of the Covenanting army, having determined twelve days earlier that no move should be made by the New Model Army to interpose itself between the Scottish forces and the Borders. The monthly maintenance for the Scots had been reduced to £15,000 at the outset of 1646.

61. *The Lord Chancellor of Scotland his first Speech: at a Conference in the Painted Chamber with a Committee of Both Houses, Octob[er] 1. 1646* (1646); Dumfries House, Loudoun Deeds, Bundle 1/2; BL, Add. MS 19399 (Royal and Noble Autographs 1646–1768), fo. 4; David Scott, '"Particular Businesses" in the Long Parliament: the Hull Letters, 1644–8', in Chris R. Kyle (ed.), *Parliament, Politics and Elections, 1604–48* (Cambridge, 2001), pp. 321–4, 329–31; [William Prynne], *Scotland's Ancient Obligation to England and Publicke Acknowledgement* (1646).

62. Dumfries House, Loudoun Papers, A213/3 and Loudoun Deeds, Bundle 1/17, /20; Inverary Castle Archives, Letters, Marquess's Period 1646–9, Bundle 8/209; NAS, Hamilton Papers, GD 406/1/2104, 2108, 2114, 2145; *Correspondence of Jean de Montereul*, I, 238–367; II, 583–94; Meikle, *Correspondence of the Scots Commissioners in London*, pp. 201–16; *Papers from the Scottish Quarters, containing the substance of Two Votes made by the Estates at Edinburgh at their General Meeting this present Septemb[er] 1646* (1646). The first instalment of £200,000 was actually paid between 30 January and 3 February 1647, on the surrender of the northern garrisons but prior to the Covenanting forces crossing the Border; the second went by default.

63. Dumfries House, Loudoun Deeds, Bundle 1/1; N. E. Bang (ed.) *Tabeller over Skibsfart og Varetransport gennem Oresund, 1497–60*, 3 vols (Copenhagen, 1906), I, 266–389; [The General Assembly of the Kirk of Scotland], *Unto the Scots Merchants and others our Country-People scattered in Poleland, Swedland, Denmark and Hungary* (Edinburgh, 1647); SR, Stroda Hist. Handlingar, vol. 26, Urstinas tid 1644–54. I am grateful to Dr Steve Murdoch, University of St Andrews, for this last reference.

64. SR, AOSB ser B. E583.

65. Hartlib Papers, HP 13/213A–214B.

66. NAS, Hamilton Papers, GD 406/1/2156; Allan I. Macinnes, 'The First Scottish Tories?', *Scottish Historical Review*, 67 (1988), 56–66.

NOTES TO CHAPTER 6

1. Francis Bamford (ed.), *A Royalist's Notebook: The Commonplace Book of Sir John Oglander, Kt of Nunwell* (1936), pp. 104, 105–6, 109–11.

2. John Morrill, *Revolt in the Provinces: The People of England and the Tragedies of War, 1630–48* (1999), pp. 56, 171.

3. A good example is the excellent section on 'Committee Tyranny' in Robert Ashton, *Counter-Revolution: The Second Civil War and its Origins* (New Haven, CT, 1994), pp. 89–99, where the general model is presented, alongside a good deal of information that would appear to qualify it significantly.

4. Alan Everitt, *The Local Community and the Great Rebellion* (1969), p. 8; Alan Everitt, *Change in the Provinces: The Seventeenth Century* (1969), pp. 46, 47.

5. For my earlier critique of the work of localist historians, see Clive Holmes, 'The County Community in Stuart Historiography', *Journal of British Studies*, 19 (1980), 54–73.

6. Denzell Holles, *Memoirs* (1699). While Holles's work was a private reflection on the events of 1647–8, written in his French exile late in that year,

Clement Walker's tracts were active interventions in the on-going political debate, and have a far more complex publishing history. The key publications are: (1) *The Mystery of the Two Juntoes*, which was first published in the wake of the Army rebellion of June 1647; (2) *The History of Independency*, which appeared in April 1648; and (3) a composite edition of the two tracts, entitled *Relations and Observations Historicall and Politick*, published by Walker in September 1648. His earlier publication, *The Mystery of the Two Juntoes*, was slightly revised for inclusion as Part I of this new work.

7. *Scotish Dove*, no. 108 (7–12 November 1645), pp. 851–3 (BL, E 309/5); no. 110 (19–27 November 1645), p. 866 (BL, E 310/9): see also no. 112 (3–10 December 1645), p. 885 (BL, E 311/19); no. 113 (10–17 December 1645), p. 193 (BL, E 313/1); no. 119 (21–29 January 1646), pp. 942–5 (BL, E 319/17).

8. *CJ*, IV, 435

9. *Scotish Dove*, no. 122 (11–18 February 1646), p. 570 (BL, E 322/38); no. 124 (26 February–4 March 1646), pp. 581–2 (BL, E 325/29).

10. *LJ*, VIII, 287. For the subsequent history of the proposed ordinance, see *LJ*, VIII, 322, 405, 406, 432, 474.

11. *Scotish Dove*, no. 136 ([*recte* 139], 17–25 June 1646), p. 702 (BL, E 341/19). For the Commons' interest in the summer of 1646, see *CJ*, IV, 583.

12. *Scotish Dove*, no. 160 (11–18 November), p. 108 (BL, E 362/14).

13. Holles, *Memoirs*, pp. 130–1.

14. *The Kingdomes Weekly Intelligencer*, no. 148 (5–12 May 1646), p. 99 (BL, E 337/13). See also no. 147 (28 April–5 May 1646), p. 84 (BL, E 336/1); no. 154 (23–30 June 1646), p. 152 (BL, E 342/6).

15. *Scotish Dove*, no. 135 (20–8 May 1646), pp. 667–8 (BL, E 339/4). See also no. 128 (28 March–8 April 1646), p. 614 (BL, E 330/31).

16. *CJ*, V, 60; *LJ*, VIII, 718, 719; IX, 127, 128, 131.

17. *The Humble Petition of the Lord Mayor* (1647), p. 2; *The Petition of the Colonels, Lieutenant-Colonels, Majors and Other Officers* (1647), article 3.

18. [John Saltmarsh], *Perfect Occurences of Both Houses of Parliament*, no. 47 (13–20 November 1646), sig. Yy–[Yy verso] (BL, E 362/23).

19. Juxon believed that the petition was a cynical attempt to curry favour, 'and so render themselves capable of employment': Keith Lindley and David Scott (eds), *The Journal of Thomas Juxon* (Camden Society, 5th ser., 13, 1999), pp. 151–2. I owe this reference to John Adamson.

20. Clive Holmes, 'Colonel King and Lincolnshire Politics, 1642–6', *Historical Journal*, 16 (1973), 451–84.

21. Clive Holmes, *The Eastern Association in the English Civil War* (Cambridge, 1974), pp. 104–5.

22. HMC, *Fourth Report* (1874), Appendix I, p. 268.

23. Holmes, 'Colonel King', p. 460; John Lilburne, *The Iust Mans Iustification* (1646).

24. Edward King, *To the Honourable the House of Commons, the Humble Petition* (1646)

25. Edward King, *A Discovery of the Arbitrary, Tyrannicall and Illegal Actions of Some of the Committee of the County of Lincoln* (1647), title page; *LJ*, VIII, 684; *CJ*, V, 60. In my 'Colonel King' (p. 479), I was in error in dating the pamphlet.

26. *The Heads of the Present Greevances of the County of Glamorgan* ([1 July] 1647), pp. 1, 3, 5 (BL, E 396/3).

27. The development of the rhetoric can be studied in the letters, declarations and warrants published in *A Full Relation of the Whole Proceedings of the Late Rising and Commotion in Wales* (1647), see pp. 5, 9, 10, 11. See also, *A Declaration of the Proceedings of Divers Knights and other Gentlemen in Glamorganshire* (1647). These tracts are reprinted in J. Roland Phillips, *Memoirs of the Civil War in Wales and the Marches*, 2 vols (1874) II, 335–43.

28. Bertram Schofield (ed.), *The Knyvett Letters* (1949), pp. 136, 137; HMC, *Bath Manuscripts*, IV, 279; Clive Holmes (ed.), *The Suffolk Committees for Scandalous Ministers* (Ipswich, 1969), pp. 108, 111, 112.

29. Bamford, *Royalist's Notebook*, pp. 110–11.

30. Worcester College, Oxford: Clarke Papers, XLI, fos 109, 112v, 114, 116, 118v, 123.

31. William Haller and Godfrey Davies (eds), *The Leveller Tracts* (New York, 1944), p. 66; Austin Woolrych, *Soldiers and Statesmen: The General Council of the Army and its Debates, 1647–8* (Oxford, 1987), pp. 164, 200.

32. Woolrych, *Soldiers and Statesmen*, p. 312.

33. Walker, *History of Independency*, sig. A2, pp. 10, 61.

34. *Two Letters Written out of Lancashire and Buckinghamshire* (1647), pp. 5–6.

35. Holles, *Memoirs*, pp. 109–11.

36. *Proposalls from his Excellency, Sir Thomas Fairfax* (1647).

37. The phrase is from the radical *Case of the Army Truly Stated*, printed in D. M. Wolfe (ed.), *Leveller Manifestoes of the Puritan Revolution* (1944), p. 206; but it is very similar to the line taken in the official 7 October 'Proposalls' (for which, see note 36): the soldier obliged to exploit the poor, had become 'an abhorring to himself'.

38. *LJ*, IX, 558.

39. Woolrych, *Soldiers and Statesmen*, p. 65.

40. *The Moderate Intelligencer*, 76 (13–20 August 1646), pp. 601–2 (BL, E 350/21) describes a riot encouraged by the Hampshire Committee against the quartering of Ireton's cavalry in August 1646.

41. *Letters from Saffron Walden* (1647), pp. 3–5, 8.

42. *Four Petitions to his Excellency, Sir Thomas Fairfax* (1647), pp. 15, 15–16.

43. *A Particular Charge or Impeachment* (1647), pp. 23–4.

44. *The Apologie of the Common Souldiers* (1647), p. 6; Woolrych (*Soldiers and Statesmen*, pp. 57–9), provides the best account of the history of this tract.

45. David Scott, 'The Barwis Affair: Political Allegiance and the Scots during the British Civil Wars', *English Historical Review*, 115 (2000), 843–63.

46. Scott, 'The Barwis Affair', p. 847.

47. [John Musgrave], *A Fourth Word to the Wise* (1647), p. 1.

48. John Musgrave, *The Cry of Blood of an Innocent Abel* (1654), p. 9. The Commons finally agreed to take cognizance of Musgrave's complaints on 16 July 1647: this certainly suggests some army pressure.

49. Holmes, 'Colonel King', see particularly pp. 482–3, 484.

50. Scott, 'The Barwis Affair', pp. 844, 852: David Scott's article provides the basis for the bulk of this discussion.

51. Humphrey Willis, *The Power of the Committee of the County of Somerset* (1646), p. 1.

52. Morrill, *Revolt in the Provinces*, p. 54.

53. Clive Holmes, *Seventeenth-Century Lincolnshire* (Lincoln, 1980), pp. 145–50.

54. R. N. Worth (ed.), *The Buller Papers* (Privately printed, 1895), p. 55.

55. Holmes, *Eastern Association*, pp. 56–62.

56. John Hotham, *Reasons why Sir John Hotham cannot in Honour agree to the Treaty of Pacification* (1642), p. 3. Very similar arguments were used to assail the December 1642 attempt in Cheshire to establish neutrality among the local belligerents: see *Neutrality Condemned* (1643).

57. Morrill, *Revolt in the Provinces*, pp. 133, 204.

58. *The Desires and Resolutions of the Clubmen of Dorset and Wilts* (1645), p. 1.

59. *The Kingdomes Weekly Intelligencer*, no. 91 (11–18 March 1645), p. 728 (BL, E 274/2).

60. HMC, *Portland Manuscripts*, I, 349.

61. *A Letter from a Gentleman in Kent* (1648), pp. 1, 2, 13.

62. Brian Lyndon, 'Essex and the King's Cause in 1648', *Historical Journal*, 29 (1986), 19.

63. *To the Right Honourable the Lords and Commons Assembled in Parliament . . . the Humble Petition of the Knights, Gentry, Clergy and Commonalty of the County of Kent* (1648).

64. Lyndon, 'Essex in 1648', p. 37.

65. *The Manifest of the County of Kent* (1648); also in Matthew Carter, *A Most True and Exact Relation of that as Honourable as Unfortunate Expedition of Kent, Essex and Colchester* (1650), pp. 27–9.

66. Roger L'Estrange, *His Vindication from the Calumnies of a Malicious Party in Kent* (1649), sig. [A4].

67. *Letter from a Gentleman in Kent*, p. 8.

68. *Halesiados: A Message from the Normans, to the Generall of the Kentish Forces* (1648), p. 4.

69. Alan Everitt, *The Community of Kent and the Great Rebellion, 1640–60* (Leicester, 1973), p. 243.

70. *Halesiados*, p. 7.

71. L'Estrange, *Vindication*, sig. D3.

72. John Walter, *Understanding Popular Violence in the English Revolution: The Colchester Plunderers* (Cambridge, 1999), particularly Ch. 8; quotation at p. 287.

73. Andy Wood, 'Beyond Post-Revisionism? The Civil War Allegiances of the Miners of the Derbyshire Peak Country', *Historical Journal*, 40 (1997), 23–40.

74. Mark Stoyle, *Loyalty and Locality: Popular Allegiance in Devon during the English Civil War* (Exeter, 1994), particularly Ch. 7.

75. Clive Holmes, 'Drainers and Fenmen: the Problem of Popular Political Consciousness in the Seventeenth Century', in Anthony Fletcher and John Stevenson (eds), *Order and Disorder in Early Modern England* (Cambridge, 1985), pp. 167–71.

76. *Two Petitions Presented to the Supreame Authority of the Nation from . . . Lincolneshire; against the Old-Court Levellers, or Propriety Destroyers, the Prerogative Undertakers* (1650), pp. 6–7.

77. The bulk of this is from Richard Culmer, Junior, *A Parish Looking-Glasse for Persecutors of Ministers* (1657), especially pp. 8–9, 11–12, 13, 14, 16, 19, 27, 29, 30, 31–2.

78. Richard Culmer, *Dean and Chapter News from Canterbury* (2nd edn, 1649), sig. [A3v].

79. Ann Hughes, 'The King, the Parliament and the Localities during the English Civil War', *Journal of British Studies*, 24 (1985), 236–63.

NOTES TO CHAPTER 7

I am extremely grateful to John Adamson, John Morrill and David Scott, for their careful reading of earlier drafts of this essay.

1. *Memoirs of the Life of Mr Ambrose Barnes*, Surtees Society, 50 (1867), p. 109.

2. *England's Remembrancer* (1646), p. 7 (BL, E 515/33).

3. *A Declaration, or, Representation from his Excellencie, Sir Tho. Fairfax and the army*, in the *Army Book of Declarations* (1647), p. 39 (BL, E 409/25).

4. Mark Kishlansky, *The Rise of the New Model Army* (Cambridge, 1979), p. 45; idem, 'The Case of the Army Truly Stated: the Creation of the New Model Army', *Past and Present*, 81 (1979), p. 57. See also his 'The Emergence of Adversary Politics in the Long Parliament', *Journal of Modern History*, 49 (1977), pp. 630, 640, where he states that 'party politics' did not start until the spring of 1646.

5. Bodl. Lib., MS Tanner 61, fos 205v–206.

6. John Adamson, 'The Triumph of Oligarchy: the Management of the War and the Committee of Both Kingdoms, 1644–5', in Chris R. Kyle and Jason Peacey (eds), *Parliament at Work: Parliamentary Committees, Political Power and Public Access in Early Modern England* (Woodbridge, 2002), pp. 107–9.

7. John Adamson, 'Triumph of Oligarchy', pp. 107–10.

8. D'Ewes referred to the win-the-war party as the 'fierie'or 'hott spirits' in 1642 and early 1643; by late 1643 and 1644 he was calling them the 'violent spirits', 'violentados'or 'violenti'; BL Harleian MS 164 (D'Ewes's diary), fos 273, 301v, 308; BL, Harleian MS 164 (D'Ewes's diary), fo. 96v; 166, fos 58v, 77v.

9. NA, SP 21/7, pp. 213–14, quoted in Adamson, 'Triumph of Oligarchy', p. 116.

10. Adamson, 'Triumph of Oligarchy', p. 119.

11. David Lairy (ed.), *The Letters and Journals of Robert Baillie*, 3 vols (Edinburgh, 1841–2), II, 246.

12. Bulstrode Whitelocke, *Memorials of English Affairs*, 4 vols (Oxford, 1853), I, 346; *Diary of Bulstrode Whitelocke, 1605–75*, ed. Ruth Spalding (Oxford, 1990), pp. 160–1.

13. Ian Gentles, *The New Model Army in England, Ireland and Scotland, 1645–53* (Oxford, 1992), p. 8.

14. *Kingdomes Weekly Intelligencer* (10–17 Dec. 1645), pp. 681–2 (BL, E 21/25).

15. Whitelocke, *Memorials*, I, 349; cf. Kishlansky, *Rise of the New Model Army*, p. 45.

16. BL, Sloane MS 1519, fo. 39; *CJ*, III, 726; *Parliament Scout* (12–19 Dec. 1644), p. 626 (BL, E 21/30).

17. It passed the Lords on 3 April 1645; *LJ*, VII, 303. See also Ian Gentles, 'The Choosing of Officers for the New Model Army', *Historical Research*, 67 (1994), pp. 264–5.

18. Gentles, *New Model Army*, pp. 10–14.

19. *LJ*, VII, 204–9.

20. *Mercurius Civicus* (16–23 Jan. 1645), p. 795 (BL, E 25/21).

21. *CJ*, IV, 26.

22. Gentles, *New Model Army*, p. 11.

23. Kishlansky, *Rise of the New Model*, p. 42.

24. *LJ*, VII, 261.

25. Gentles, 'Choosing of Officers', pp. 269–79. The Lords' suggested changes are found in House of Lords Record Office, Main Papers, 10 March 1645, fos 145–8; printed in R. K. G. Temple, 'The Original Officer List of the New Model Army', *Historical Research*, 59 (1986), 50–77.

26. BL, Harl. MS 166 (D'Ewes's diary), fo. 183; cf. Add. MS 31116 (Lawrence Whitacre's diary), fo. 198–v.

27. BL, Sloane MS 1519, fo. 61r–v: Sir Edward Nicholas to 'your highness' [Prince Rupert], 12 March 1645.

28. Hull City RO, BRL 342: Pelham to Nicholas Denman, 18 March 1645.

29. Keith Lindley and David Scott (eds), *The Journal of Thomas Juxon, 1644–47* (Camden Society, 5th ser., 13, 1999), p. 75.

30. NA, PRO 31/3/76, fo. 199v: M. de Sabran to the comte de Brienne, 10/20 March 1645. Sabran went on to note that the Commons radicals had evidently prevailed upon the London magistrates to attach strings to their loan: it was approved 'a condition que tous les chefs et officiers demandez [*sic*] par le dit Fairfax et accordez par la dicte Chambre des Communes, soyent les seuls admis et reçus dans les charges, dont vous jugerez la forte intelligence avec la dite chambre, et la difficulté que les Ecossois et la Chambre Haulte qui sont assez bien ensemble auront de s'opposer à la dite admission et la jalousie qui en naistra'.

31. *LJ*, VII, 276, 277.

32. Bodl. Lib., MS Tanner 60, fo. 93.

33. Lindley and Scott, *Juxon Journal*, p. 76.

34. *CJ*, IV, 176; *LJ*, VII, 433.

35. John Adamson, 'The Baronial Context of the English Civil War', *Transactions of the Royal Historical Society*, 5th ser., 40 (1990), 93–120; David Scott, *Politics and War in the Three Stuart Kingdoms, 1637–49* (2004); John Adamson, *The Noble Revolt: The Overthrow of Charles I* (2007); and see Jane Ohlmeyer, 'The Baronial Context of the Irish Civil Wars', Chapter 4 in this volume.

36. As early as mid-December 1644, Lord Wharton had written admiringly to Ferdinando Lord Fairfax about his son, Sir Thomas, obliquely hinting that he might be a suitable successor to the Earl of Essex; see Robert Bell, *Memorials of the Civil War: Fairfax Correspondence*, 2 vols (1849), I, 142.

37. Bell, *Memorials of the Civil War*, I, 113, 124–36, 142–3, 157, 190. For additional references to the Northumberland–Fairfax connection see Adamson, 'Baronial Context', p. 116, n. 115.

38. Aryeh J. S. Nusbacher, 'The Triple Thread: Supply of Victuals to the Army under Sir Thomas Fairfax, 1645–6' (unpublished DPhil dissertation, University of Oxford, 2001), Ch. 8; Gentles, *New Model Army*, pp. 40–52.

39. The following paragraphs are largely based on John Adamson, 'Of Armies and Architecture: the Employments of Robert Scawen', in Ian Gentles, John Morrill and Blair Worden (eds), *Soldiers, Writers and Statesmen of the English Revolution* (Cambridge, 1998).

40. NA, SP 21/26 (Order Book of the Derby House Committee), pp. 3–123.

41. See David Scott, 'Rethinking Royalist Politics, 1642–9', in this volume, pp. 36–60.

42. C. H. Firth (ed.), *The Clarke Papers*, 4 vols (Camden Society, new ser. 49, 1891–1901), I, 211–13; Bell, *Memorials of the Civil War*, I, 368; John Wildman, *Putney Projects* (1647), p. 5 (BL, E 421/19); *Perfect Summary* (19–26 July 1647), pp. 13–14 (BL, E 518/9); Henry Cary (ed.), *Memorials of the Great Civil War in England*, 2 vols (1842), I, 307–8. See also Gentles, *New Model Army*, pp. 181–2; Austin Woolrych, *Britain in Revolution, 1625–60* (Oxford, 2002), p. 374.

43. H. G. Tibbutt (ed.), *The Tower of London Letterbook of Sir Lewis Dyve, 1646–7* (Bedfordshire Historical Record Society, 38, 1958), p. 84.

44. *Mercurius Elencticus*, no. 3 (12–19 Nov. 1647), p. 18 (BL, E 416/13).

45. Tibbutt, *Dyve Letterbook*, pp. 84, 88.

46. *Perfect Occurrences*, no. 45 (5–12 Nov. 1647), p. 305; (BL, E 520/4), *CJ*, VI, 353. On 7 August 1647, the day after the army occupied London, Lilburne was paid £10 out of the army's contingency fund; Chequers Court, Buckinghamshire, MS 782, fo. 43v. Two days later, Lilburne signed a receipt for £533 15s. for two weeks' pay for his brother Robert's regiment; NA, SP 28/47, fo. 298. Already in June, John Lilburne had signed a receipt for £958 15s. 4d. on behalf of his brother's regiment: NA, SP 28/46, fo. 118.

47. *LJ*, IX, 483–4.

48. *LJ*, IX, 486, 499.

49. John Adamson, 'The English Nobility and the Projected Settlement of 1647', *Historical Journal*, 30 (1987), pp. 597–8.

50. John Rushworth, *Historical Collections*, 8 vols (1721–2), VII, 965; *CJ*, V, 432–3; *LJ*, IX, 661–2; *Kingdomes Weekly Post* (19–26 January 1648), pp. 30–1 (BL, E 423/26); *Perfect Diurnall* (24–31 January 1648), p. 1883 (BL, E 520/31); Clement Walker, *The Compleat History of Independency*, 2 vols (1661), I, 72–3. The authors of *The Earnest and Passionate Petition of Divers Thousands* (1648) alleged that the only purpose of stationing the troops in Whitehall was to intimidate the Lords into supporting ordinances sent to them by the Commons: p. 5 (BL, E 425/10).

51. Adamson, 'Of Armies and Architecture', p. 62.

52. A. S. P. Woodhouse (ed.), *Puritanism and Liberty: Being the Army Debates (1647–9) from the Clarke Manuscripts with Supplementary Documents* (2nd edn, 1950), Introduction, pp. [22]–[23]; D. M. Wolfe, *Leveller Manifestoes of the Puritan Revolution* (New York, 1944), pp. 25, 38; H. N. Brailsford, *The Levellers and the English Revolution* (1961), Chs 8, 10; A. L. Morton, *Freedom in Arms* (New York, 1975); G. E. Aylmer, *The Levellers in the English Revolution* (1975), pp. 22–38; K. V. Thomas, 'The Levellers and the Franchise', in G. E. Aylmer (ed.), *The Interregnum: the Quest for Settlement* (1972); Mark A. Kishlansky, 'The Army and the Levellers: the Roads to Putney', *Historical Journal*, 22 (1979), pp. 795–824; John Morrill, 'The Army Revolt of 1647', in idem, *The Nature of the English Revolution* (Harlow, 1993); Brian Manning, *1649: The Crisis of the English Revolution* (1992),

Ch. 5; Michael Mendle (ed.), *The Putney Debates of 1647: The Army, the Levellers and the English State* (Cambridge, 2001), especially the essays by Austin Woolrych, John Morrill and Philip Baker, and Ian Gentles.

53. Bodl. Lib., MS Clarendon 30, fo. 163v. I owe this reference to the kindness of Dr David Scott.

54. *Mercurius Pragmaticus*, no. 9 (9–16 November 1647), p. 70 (BL, E 414/15).

55. *The Legall Fundamentall Liberties of the People of England* (1649), reprinted in Wolfe, *Leveller Manifestoes*, p. 421.

56. Morrill, 'The Army Revolt of 1647', pp. 321–2.

57. Kishlansky, 'The Army and the Levellers', p. 796. In the same article, however, Kishlansky acknowledges that 'the catalytic effect of the Leveller movement [upon the army] cannot be denied'; ibid., p. 824.

58. John Morrill and Philip Baker, 'The Case of the Armie Truly Restated', in Mendle, *Putney Debates*, pp. 106, 107, 111–19.

59. Those which we can only cite include *The Petition of Many Thousands*, reprinted in Wolfe, *Leveller Manifestoes*, p. 138; a royalist newswriter asserted that this petition had attracted only 400 signatures: Bodl. Lib., MS Clarendon 29, fo. 147. See also *A Warning for All the Counties of England* ([24 Mar.] 1647), p. 9 (BL, E 381/13); *Reall Persecution, or the Foundation of a General Toleration* ([13 Feb.] 1647), BL, 669 f. 10/114, no. 66; *Perfect Diurnall*, no. 188 (1–8 Mar. 1647), p. 1505 (BL, E 515/2); *A New Found Strategem Framed in the Old Forge of Machivilisme* ([18 Apr.] 1647), p. 14 (BL, E 384/11); *The Poore Wise-mans Admonition unto All the Plaine People of London* ([10 June] 1647), pp. 6, 9 (BL, E 392/4); this pamphlet has been attributed to William Walwyn, but the attribution is firmly rejected by J. R. McMichael and Barbara Taft (eds), *The Writings of William Walwyn* (Athens, GA, 1989), p. 530; Derek Massarella, 'The Politics of the Army, 1647–60' (unpublished PhD dissertation, University of York, 1978), pp. 44–5, citing *Several Letters Sent from His Excellency Sir Thomas Fairfax and the Officers of the Army* (1647). See also Barbara Taft, 'From Reading to Whitehall: Henry Ireton's Journey', in Mendle, *Putney Debates*, p. 181.

60. *Rash Oaths Unwarrantable* ([31 May] 1647), p. 53 (BL, E 393/39).

61. John Lilburne, *Ionah's Cry out of the Whales Belly* ([26 July] 1647), p. 9 (BL, E 400/5).

62. *Walwyns Just Defence*, in McMichael and Taft, *The Writings of William Walwyn*, pp. 391–3.

63. Lilburne, *Ionah's Cry*, 9.

64. *An Appeale from the Degenerate Representative Body the Commons of England* ([17 July] 1647), reprinted in Wolfe, *Leveller Manifestoes*, 187.

65. Geoffrey Parker, 'Mutiny and Discontent in the Spanish Army of Flanders, 1572–1607', *Past and Present*, 58 (1973), 40; Edward Grimestone, *A Generall Historie of the Netherlands . . . Continued from the Yeare 1608 till the Yeare of our Lord 1627* (1627), pp. 426, 1159. I am indebted to Sam Glover for this reference.

66. Kishlansky, 'The Army and the Levellers', p. 813.

67. Thoresby Society, Leeds, MS SD IX, unfol., *passim*; this MS is printed (with errors) in the Thoresby Society *Publications*, IX (1902).

68. *Petition and Vindication* ([27 April] 1647), sig. A2r (BL, E 385/19).

69. Worcester College, Oxford, MS 41 (Clarke Papers), fo. 18r–v. This document is undated, but from its position in the volume it evidently originated in early May 1647.

70. *A Second Apologie of All the Private Souldiers* (3 May 1647), pp. 7–8 (BL, E 385/18). Around the same time an untitled soldiers' broadside urged that the liberty of the subject should no longer be enslaved, 'but that justice and judgement may be dealt to the meanest subject of this land according to old law'. Worcester College, Oxford, Pamphlet Collection, BB. 8. 16 (17), cited by Derek Massarella, 'Politics of the Army', p. 27.

71. Worcester College, Oxford, MS 41 (Clarke Papers), fos 106v, 119r–v.

72. Lilburne, *Ionah's Cry out of the Whales Belly*, p. 7.

73. Firth, *Clarke Papers*, I, 97.

74. *Perfect Diurnall*, no. 198 (10–17 May 1647), p. 1588 (BL, E 515/12).

75. Barbara Taft and J. R. McMichael (*The Writings of William Walwyn*, p. 31) and Austin Woolrych (*Soldiers and Statesmen*, p. 215) think it was Walwyn who was the author, as do I; John Morrill and Philip Baker (in Mendle, *Putney Debates*, p. 121) opt for Wildman.

76. Printed in Gardiner, *Constitutional Documents*, pp. 333–4.

77. Firth, *Clarke Papers*, I, 303, 411.

78. This information is drawn, not from William Clarke's minutes, which are silent on how the debate concluded, but from *Perfect Occurrences* (29 Oct.–5 Nov. 1647), p. 306 (BL, E 520/2), and *A Copy of a Letter Sent by the Agents of Severall Regiments . . . to all the Souldiers* (11 Nov. 1647), pp. 1–2 (BL, E 413/18). See also Woolrych, *Soldiers and Statesmen*, pp. 243–4, and Gentles, *New Model Army*, pp. 214 and 502, n. 144.

79. Like Woolrych, I believe that there *was* a mutiny at Ware; see Woolrych, *Soldiers and Statesmen*, p. 285; but for a different view see Mark Kishlansky, 'What Happened at Ware?', *Historical Journal*, 25 (1982), p. 839.

80. David Underdown (ed.), 'The Parliamentary Diary of John Boys, 1647–8', *Bulletin of the Institute of Historical Research*, 39 (1966), p. 153.

81. *To the Right Honourable the Commons of England in Parliament Assembled* (BL, E 464/19 and 669 f. 13/16), printed in Wolfe, *Leveller Manifestoes*, p. 289.

82. For an analysis of the thirty petitions (seventeen of which explicitly endorsed the Leveller programme) that reached army headquarters in the last three months of 1648, see Gentles, *New Model Army*, pp. 267–8.

83. *A Remonstrance of His Excellency Thomas Lord Fairfax . . . and of the Generall Councell of Officers Held at St Albans the 16 of Nov., 1648* (1648), pp. 67, 69 (BL, E 473/11).

84. Worcester College, Oxford, MS 16 (Clarke Papers), fo. 32. I am grateful to Barbara Taft for providing me with a photocopy of fos 31–5 of this MS, which contain the original, and still unpublished text of the Second Agreement, before it was tampered with by John Lilburne and published as *Foundations of Freedom* ([15 Dec.] 1648), BL, E 476/26; reprinted in Wolfe, *Leveller Manifestoes*, pp. 295–7.

85. The *Moderate* (14–21 Nov. 1648), p. 154 (BL, E 473/1). For an admission that the majority 'are not to have any vote', see *A Warning, or a Word of Advice to the City of London* ([30 Nov.] 1648), p. 3 (BL, E 474/6); Ian Gentles, 'The Agreements of the People and their Political Contexts, 1647–9', in Mendle, *Putney Debates*, p. 162.

86. *Legall Fundamentall Liberties* (1649), reprinted in Wolfe, *Leveller Manifestoes*, p. 422.

87. Barbara Taft, 'Voting Lists of the Council of Officers', *Bulletin of the Institute of Historical Research*, 52 (1979), pp. 147–9.

88. *CJ*, VI, 122.

89. Gentles, 'The *Agreements of the People*', pp. 170–1.

90. Some historians have questioned whether the Burford mutiny was in any sense Leveller-inspired. However, in contemporary sources it was commonly referred to as 'the Leveller rising'; see, for example, NA SP 24/25, fo. 12r–v; BL, Add. MS 21417, fo. 134; *Perfect Occurrences*, no. 123 (4–11 May 1649), p. 1031 (BL, E 530/1). See also Massarella, 'Politics of the Army', p. 221.

91. See the essays by John Morrill and Philip Baker, John Adamson, and Sean Kelsey in Jason Peacey (ed.), *The Regicides and the Execution of Charles I* (Basingstoke, 2001).

92. *The Souldiers Catechisme* (1644), pp. 7, 14.

93. A copy of the engraving was bound in with a pamphlet describing the New Model's exploits in Cornwall: *Late Letter from Sir Thomas Fairfax's Army in Truro* (1646), formerly catalogued as Bodl. Lib., Fairfax Deposit, Tracts, 26/1. The Fairfax Deposit has now been unfortunately dispersed, but the engraving is reproduced in Gentles, *New Model Army*, p. 142.

94. Patricia Crawford, '"Charles Stuart, that Man of Blood"', *Journal of British Studies*, 16 (1977), 50–1.

95. *Regall Tyrannie Discovered* ([6 Jan.] 1647), title page (BL, E 370/12).

96. Firth (ed), *Clarke Papers*, I, 373, 383, 417; Crawford, '"Charles Stuart"', pp. 52–3.

97. William Allen, *A Faithful Memorial of that Remarkable Meeting of Many Officers of the Army in England at Windsor Castle, in the Year 1648* ([27 Apr.] 1659), (BL, E 979/3). Even though he published his account more than a decade after the event, I believe that Allen's account is basically reliable.

98. The Thomason pressmarks for these petitions are BL, E 467/34; E 468/18, 32; E 470/23, 32; E 472/6; E 473/1, 23; E 474/5; E 475/4, 13, 24; 669 f. 13/71; E 476/27, E 477/4, 7, 10; E 526/25; E 527/1; E 536/2, 15, 30. A petition is also found in Worcester College, Oxford, MS 114 (Clarke Papers), fos 119–20v. Some of the listed tracts contain more than one petition.

99. *Remonstrance*, pp. 23–4, 64.

100. *The Representations and Consultations of the Generall Councell of the Armie at St. Albans* ([14 Nov.] 1648), p. 3 (BL, E 472/3).

101. *Heads of the Charge against the King* ([24 Dec.] 1648), pp. 4–5 (BL, E 477/25).

102. Elliot Vernon, 'The Quarrel of the Covenant: the London Presbyterians and the Regicide', in Peacey, *Regicides*, pp. 212–19.

103. NA, PRO 31/389 (Paris Archives, Baschet's transcripts), fo. 52.

104. *Mercurius Pragmaticus*, no. 39 (19–26 Dec. 1648), (BL, E 477/30). This report again provokes scepticism, in light of the *Heads of the Charge against the King*, published only three days later. Indeed, writing on 25 December, Nedham had to admit that many of the king's friends in London believed that it was the grandees' intention to execute the king; Bodl. Lib., MS Clarendon 34, fo. 18v. Nedham's grasp of parliamentary politics was much surer than his knowledge of what was happening in the inner councils of the army.

105. Firth, *Clarke Papers*, II, 150–4, 163–9.

106. *Mercurius Elencticus*, no. 56 (12–19 Dec. 1648), p. 535 (BL, E 476/36).

107. Webb, secretary to the Duke of Richmond, was writing to Lord Craven; see BL, Add. MS 63743 (Lord Craven's papers), fo. 1v. I am grateful to Dr David Scott for this reference.

108. Rushworth, *Historical Collections*, VII, 1386.

109. *Moderate Intelligencer*, no. 202 (25 Jan.–1 Feb. 1649), p. 1869 (BL, E 541/4); *The Kingdomes Faithfull and Impartiall Scout* (26 Jan.–1 Feb. 1649), p. 3 (BL, E 541/5); Francois Guizot, *History of the English Revolution of 1640* (1856), Appendix, pp. 460–1.

110. Among the army pay warrants is one bearing Cromwell's signature and dated 2 December; NA, SP 28/251 (Committee for the Eastern Association), unfol.; I am grateful to Dr David Scott for this reference. Does it prove that Oliver was actually in London four days *before* Pride's Purge? His signature is one of several, and comes at the bottom of the warrant. Yet as several newsbooks record his arrival on 6 December, I surmise that he signed this document several days after the date on the warrant. Perhaps significantly, the various sums allocated in the warrant did not begin to be receipted until 15 December 1648.

111. Abbott, *Cromwell*, I, 690, 698–9.

112. John Morrill and Philip Baker, 'Oliver Cromwell, the Regicide and the Sons of Zeruiah', in Peacey, *Regicides*, 29.

113. Abbott, *Cromwell*, I, 676–8.

114. Abbott, *Cromwell*, I, 690, 698–9.

115. Bodl. Lib., MS Clarendon 34, fo. 13–v. The evidence is problematic. Why would Cromwell have *written* when he was on the spot and continually in attendance at the Council of Officers? Why would he have addressed such an important communication to Pride, who was never a key figure in the politics of the army?

116. Gilbert Burnet, *The Memoires of the Lives and Actions of James and William Dukes of Hamilton* (1677), p. 379.

117. S. R. Gardiner, *History of the Great Civil War, 1642–49*, 4 vols (1893), IV, 281–2.

118. David Underdown, *Pride's Purge: Politics in the Puritan Revolution* (Oxford, 1971), p. 183.

119. John Adamson, 'The Frighted Junto: Perceptions of Ireland and the Last Attempts at Settlement with Charles I', in Jason Peacey (ed.), *The Regicides and the Execution of Charles I* (Basingstoke and New York, 2001), pp. 47–51, 60.

120. C. V. Wedgwood, *The Trial of Charles I* (2nd edn, 1968), pp. 157–8, 174–6.

NOTES TO CHAPTER 8

I am extremely grateful to the editor and Dr Ariel Hessayon for their comments on, and criticism of, an earlier draft of this chapter.

1. Christopher Hill, *The World Turned Upside Down: Radical Ideas during the English Revolution* (1972).

2. For example, see Glenn Burgess, 'On Revisionism: An Analysis of Early Stuart Historiography in the 1970s and 1980s', *Historical Journal*, 33 (1990), 609–27, at pp. 626–7; J. C. Davis, 'Religion and the Struggle for Freedom in the English Revolution', *Historical Journal*, 35 (1992), 507–30.

3. Conal Condren, 'Radicals, Conservatives and Moderates in Early Modern Political Thought: A Case of Sandwich Islands Syndrome?', *History of Political Thought*, 10 (1989), 525–42; idem, *The Language of Politics in Seventeenth-Century England* (Basingstoke, 1994), esp. Ch. 5. See also J. C. D. Clark, *Our Shadowed Present: Modernism, Postmodernism and History* (2003), Ch. 4.

4. J. C. Davis, 'Radicalism in a Traditional Society: the Evaluation of Radical Thought in the English Commonwealth, 1649–60', *History of Political Thought*, 3 (1982), 193–213.

5. Gary S. De Krey, 'Radicals, Reformers and Republicans: Academic Language and Political Discourse in Restoration London', in Alan Houston and Steve Pincus (eds), *A Nation Transformed: England after the Restoration* (Cambridge, 2001), pp. 71–99, at p. 74: 'revisionist efforts to ban radicals from the seventeenth century have largely ignored the case of London'.

6. Ibid., p. 80; Jonathan Scott, *England's Troubles: Seventeenth-Century English Political Instability in European Context* (Cambridge, 2000), pp. 33–7, 229–46.

7. Davis, 'Radicalism in a Traditional Society', pp. 202–4; De Krey, 'Radicals, Reformers and Republicans', p. 80; Scott, *England's Troubles*, esp. Ch. 10.

8. Cf. Davis, 'Religion and the Struggle for Freedom', pp. 514–30; Jonathan Scott, 'Radicalism and Restoration: the Shape of the Stuart Experience', *Historical Journal*, 31 (1988), 453–67, at p. 455; idem, *England's Troubles*, pp. 6, 33–7, 229–68.

9. Cf. Hill, *World Turned Upside Down*; idem, *The Experience of Defeat: Milton and Some Contemporaries* (1984).

10. On the need to adopt a contextual approach to the religious radicalism of the period, see Ann Hughes, 'The Meanings of Religious Polemic', in Francis J. Bremer (ed.), *Puritanism: Transatlantic Perspectives on a Seventeenth-Century Anglo-American Faith* (Boston, MA, 1993), pp. 201–29, at p. 221; idem, 'Religion, 1640–60', in Barry Coward (ed.), *A Companion to Stuart Britain* (Oxford, 2003), pp. 350–73, at pp. 362–3.

11. For recent studies stressing the radicalism of the political agenda of 1641, see David Cressy, *England on Edge: Crisis and Revolution, 1640–42* (Oxford, 2006); and John Adamson, *The Noble Revolt: The Overthrow of Charles I* (2007).

12. See Ian Gentles's essay, Chapter 7 in this book, 'The Politics of Fairfax's Army, 1645–9'.

13. This approach is suggested by the work of scholars whose overall view of radicalism is markedly different from that argued here: see Condren, 'Radicals, Conservatives and Moderates'; idem, *Language of Politics*, Ch. 5; Glenn Burgess, 'The Impact on Political Thought: Rhetorics for Troubled Times', in John Morrill (ed.), *The Impact of the English Civil War* (1991), pp. 67–83.

14. For example, see J. C. Davis, *Fear, Myth and History: The Ranters and the Historians* (Cambridge, 1986), esp. Chs 1 and 6; E. P. Thompson, 'On the Rant', repr. in Geoff Eley and William Hunt (eds), *Reviving the English Revolution: Reflections and Elaborations on the Work of Christopher Hill* (1988), pp. 153–60. For

criticism of the Revisionists' attitude to sources, see Richard Cust and Ann Hughes, 'Introduction: After Revisionism', in idem (eds), *Conflict in Early Stuart England: Studies in Religion and Politics, 1603–42* (Harlow, 1989), pp. 1–46, at pp. 12–13.

15. Richard Cust and Ann Hughes, 'Introduction: Continuities and Discontinuities in the English Civil War', in idem (eds), *The English Civil War* (1997), pp. 1–30, at p. 23.

16. Ann Hughes, *Gangraena and the Struggle for the English Revolution* (Oxford, 2004), esp. pp. 432–42; cf. the trenchant remarks of Mark A. Kishlansky in *The Rise of the New Model Army* (Cambridge, 1979), p. ix.

17. For a prominent example of that mentality, see Francis Bamford (ed.), *A Royalist's Notebook: The Commonplace Book of Sir John Oglander, Kt of Nunwell* (1936), pp. 103–33.

18. For vivid accounts of such disorder, see the issues of the Royalist newspaper *Mercurius Rusticus*, printed in Peter Thomas (ed.), *The English Revolution III, Newsbooks 1, Oxford Royalists*, 4 vols (1971), IV, [117]–[302], and Brian Manning, *The English People and the English Revolution* (2nd edn, 1991), Chs 1–7.

19. Christopher Hill, 'The Many-Headed Monster', repr. in his *Change and Continuity in Seventeenth-Century England* (1974), pp. 181–204.

20. Bamford, *Royalist's Notebook*, pp. 104 and 106. For a simultaneous expression of anxiety regarding popular egalitarianism, see the diary of the Parliamentarian Commons-man Sir Simonds D'Ewes, printed in Vernon F. Snow and Anne Steele Young (eds), *The Private Journals of the Long Parliament, 2 June to 17 September 1642* (New Haven, CT, and London, 1992), pp. 44–5. For Oglander, also see Clive Holmes's remarks in his essay in this volume, Chapter 6.

21. Manning, *English People and the English Revolution*.

22. The remainder of this and the following paragraph draws on John Morrill and John Walter, 'Order and Disorder in the English Revolution', repr. in *The Nature of the English Revolution: Essays by John Morrill* (Harlow, 1993), pp. 359–91, at pp. 359–75; John Walter, 'The Impact on Society: a World Turned Upside Down?', in Morrill, *Impact of the English Civil War*, pp. 104–22, at pp. 104–10; John Walter, *Understanding Popular Violence in the English Revolution: The Colchester Plunderers* (Cambridge, 1999), esp. Chs 7 and 8.

23. Andrew Charlesworth (ed.), *An Atlas of Rural Protest in Britain, 1548–1900* (1983), p. 41; see also John Walter, *Crowds and Popular Politics in Early Modern England* (Manchester, 2006).

24. For accounts of those disturbances, see Manning, *English People and the English Revolution*, Ch. 4; Keith Lindley, *Popular Politics and Religion in Civil War London* (Aldershot, 1997), pp. 4–6, 105–13; Cressy, *England on Edge*, Chs 5 and 17.

25. For discussions of the social composition of the crowds, see Manning, *English People and the English Revolution*, pp. 154–5, 157–8; Lindley, *Popular Politics and Religion*, pp. 137–8; Cressy, *England on Edge*, pp. 386–91.

26. Willson Havelock Coates (ed.), *The Journal of Sir Simonds D'Ewes: From the First Recess of the Long Parliament to the Withdrawal of King Charles from London* (New Haven, CT, 1942), pp. 213–16; *CJ*, II, 327, 332, 341; Valerie Pearl, *London and the Outbreak of the Puritan Revolution: City Government and National Politics, 1625–43* (Oxford, 1961), pp. 232–3; Lindley, *Popular Politics and Religion*, pp. 150–3; Adamson, *Noble Revolt*, pp. 468–77.

27. Charles Carlton, *Going to the Wars: The Experience of the British Civil Wars, 1638–51* (1992), esp. Chs 7 and 11; Ian Gentles, *The New Model Army in England, Ireland, and Scotland, 1645–53* (Oxford, 1992), pp. 32–8, 40, 45–7, 53, 60, 88.

28. For example, see *A Relation of the Rare Exployts of the London Souldiers, and Gentlemen Prentizes, Lately Gone Out of the Citie for the Designes of the King and Parliament* (n.p., [26 August] 1642), esp. p. 6 (BL, E 114/13); *The Wicked Resolution of the Cavaliers* ([22 November] 1642) (BL, E 127/42); John Rushworth, *Historical Collections of Private Passages of State*, 8 vols (1721–2), VII, 741.

29. Keith Wrightson, *English Society, 1580–1680* (1982), Chs 6 and 7; Morrill and Walter, 'Order and Disorder', pp. 375–8.

30. Davis, 'Religion and the Struggle for Freedom'; Scott, *England's Troubles*, esp. Chs 10 and 11.

31. For example, see William Haller and Godfrey Davies, 'Introduction', in idem (eds), *The Leveller Tracts, 1647–53* (New York, 1944), pp. 1–50, esp. p. 7; Joseph Frank, *The Levellers, a History of the Writings of Three Seventeenth-Century Social Democrats: John Lilburne, Richard Overton, William Walwyn* (repr. New York, 1969), esp. pp. 2–3, 245–50.

32. David Wootton, 'From Rebellion to Revolution: the Crisis of the Winter of 1642–3 and the Origins of Civil War Radicalism', repr. in Cust and Hughes, *English Civil War*, pp. 340–56.

33. Allan I. Macinnes, *The British Revolution, 1629–60* (Basingstoke, 2005), pp. 125 (for the quotation), 130–1, 133, 136. For an excellent summary of the rebellion and its transformation of Scotland's political structure, see ibid., pp. 112–41.

34. David Scott, *Politics and War in the Three Stuart Kingdoms, 1637–49* (Basingstoke, 2004), pp. 24 and 29; J. S. A. Adamson, 'The Baronial Context of the English Civil War', *Transactions of the Royal Historical Society*, 5th series, 40 (1990), 93–120, esp. pp. 93–109; Macinnes, *British Revolution*, pp. 130–1, 136, 137–8.

35. Jason Peacey, 'The Outbreak of the Civil Wars in the Three Kingdoms', in Coward, *Companion to Stuart Britain*, pp. 290–308, at pp. 292 and 305; J. C. Davis, 'Political Thought During the English Revolution', in Coward, *Companion to Stuart Britain*, pp. 374–96, at pp. 375 and 376.

36. Calybute Downing, *A Sermon Preached to the Renowned Company of the Artillery, 1 September 1640* (1641), pp. 36–8 (corrected pagination) (BL, E 157/4). After delivering the sermon, Downing allegedly retreated to Warwick's house in Essex: see his entry in the *Oxford Dictionary of National Biography* [hereafter *ODNB*] (Oxford, 2004).

37. 'The Triennial Act' and 'The Act Against Dissolving the Long Parliament Without its Own Consent', both printed in Gardiner, *Constitutional Documents*, at pp. 144–55 and 158–9 respectively.

38. 'The Act for the Abolition of the Court of Star Chamber' and 'The Act for the Abolition of the Court of High Commission', both printed in Gardiner, *Constitutional Documents*, pp. 179–86 and 186–9 respectively. The Act abolishing Star Chamber claimed that the court had acted in infringement of Magna Carta and a series of statutes between the reigns of Edward III and Henry VIII.

39. 'The Nineteen Propositions Sent by the Two Houses of Parliament to the King at York', printed in Gardiner, *Constitutional Documents*, pp. 249–54; Adamson, 'Baronial Context', pp. 96–101.

40. Scott, *Politics and War*, pp. 26–7, 29–32, 55–6; Macinnes, *British Revolution*, pp. 126, 139, 143–5.

41. This paragraph draws on a number of David Wootton's arguments in 'Rebellion to Revolution'.

42. Parker's theory was most famously advanced in his anonymous work of June 1642, *Observations Upon Some of his Majesties Late Answers and Expresses*, printed in William Haller (ed.), *Tracts on Liberty in the Puritan Revolution, 1638–47*, 3 vols (repr. New York, 1965), II, 167–213. On the significance of the relationship between Parker and the leading reformist peer, Viscount Saye, see Michael Mendle, *Henry Parker and the English Civil War: The Political Thought of the Public's 'Privado'* (Cambridge, 1995), pp. 5, 18–19, 48, 83.

43. [Henry Parker], *The Contra-Replicant* (n.p., 31 January 1643) (BL, E 87/5); Jeremiah Burroughes, *The Glorious Name of God, the Lord of Hosts* (1643), p. 134 (Wing, B 6075); *Touching the Fundamentall Lawes, or Politique Constitution of this Kingdome* ([24 February] 1643), p. 13 (BL, E 90/21).

44. For example, see *A Present Answer to the Late Complaint unto the House of Commons* (n.p., [11 February] 1643), pp. 3–5 (BL, E 89/6); *A Complaint to the House of Commons* (n.p., [2 January] 1643), p. 23 (BL, E 244/31).

45. John Adamson, 'The *Vindiciae Veritatis* and the Political Creed of Viscount Saye and Sele', *Historical Research*, 60 (1987), 45–63, at pp. 56, 61–2.

46. John Adamson, 'The English Nobility and the Projected Settlement of 1647', *Historical Journal*, 30 (1987), 567–602, at pp. 586–7, 598–9; 'The Four Bills, with the Propositions Accompanying them', printed in Gardiner, *Constitutional Documents*, pp. 335–47.

47. Scott, *Politics and War*, pp. 149–50; idem, 'Rethinking Royalist Politics, 1642–9', in this volume, pp. 36–60.

48. There is, perhaps, surprisingly little discussion of this type of constitutional arrangement in Jonathan Scott's recent study of the republican writing of the Civil War: see his *Commonwealth Principles: Republican Writing of the English Revolution* (Cambridge, 2004), pp. 133–4, 234.

49. National Library of Wales, Wynnstay Manuscripts, 90/16, quoted in Scott, *Politics and War*, p. 127.

50. William Fiennes, Viscount Saye and Sele, *Vindiciae Veritatis* ([12 September] 1654), esp. pp. 6–7, 33–4, 40 (BL, E 811/2); Adamson, '*Vindiciae Veritatis*', pp. 53–6, 63. For the dating of the writing of the *Vindiciae*, see ibid., pp. 51–3.

51. Cf. John Morrill, 'Introduction', in idem (ed.), *Reactions to the English Civil War, 1642–9* (Basingstoke, 1982), pp. 1–27, at pp. 1, 4–5, 7–8; idem, 'The Religious Context of the English Civil War', repr. in his *Nature of the English Revolution*, pp. 45–68, at pp. 50–2.

52. Scott, *Politics and War*, pp. 124, 140, 143.

53. Why England experienced a more radical questioning of the structures of government than either of its immediate neighbours is an intriguing and little studied question, of which the limits of space prevent a more extensive discussion. However, for brief, but interesting, comments on this point, see Wootton, 'Rebellion to Revolution', pp. 342–3, 350–2, and Scott, *Politics and War*, pp. 131–2.

54. For example, see Oliver St John, *Mr S.- John's Speech to the Lords in the Vpper House of Parlament Ianuary 7. 1640* (n.p., 1640), pp. 38–44 (STC, 21589.3); *A Trve Relation of That Memorable Parliament, Which Wrought Wonders* (n.p., [May] 1641) (BL, E 157/12); *The Life and Death of King Richard the Second* ([12 July] 1642) (BL, E 155/15); *A Pious and Learned Speech Delivered in the High Court of Parliament, 1. H[enry]. 4.* ([July] 1642) (BL, E 200/51); *LJ*, v, 76–7. Cf. John Morrill, 'Charles I, Tyranny and the English Civil War', repr. in his *Nature of the English Revolution*, pp. 285–306, at p. 296.

55. [Charles Herle], *An Answer to Mis-led Doctor Ferne* ([10 January] 1643), esp. pp. 14 and 35 (BL, E 245/1).

56. William Prynne, *The Fovrth Part of the Soveraigne Power of Parliaments and Kingdomes* ([28 August] 1643) (BL, E 248/4).

57. John Saltmarsh, *Examinations, or, a Discovery of Some Dangerous Positions Delivered in a Sermon of Reformation* ([12 August] 1643), esp. sigs. A2v–A3v (second pagination) (BL, E 65/5). Saltmarsh's opinion was based on a rigid interpretation of the religious clauses of the *Vow and Covenant*, Parliament's oath of allegiance of 1643.

58. Edward Hyde, Earl of Clarendon, *Selections from 'The History of the Rebellion' and 'The Life by Himself'*, ed. Gertrude Huehns (repr. Oxford, 1978), p. 27.

59. *Mercurius Aulicus*, 33rd week (13–19 August 1643), p. 452, printed in Thomas, *English Revolution III, Newsbooks 1, Oxford Royalists*, I, [463]–[478], quotation at p. [476]; *CJ*, III, 206 n. For his outburst, Marten was briefly imprisoned and banned from the Commons for almost three years.

60. *Mercurius Britanicus*, no. 69 (3–10 February 1645), p. 541 (BL, E 269/6). In May 1646, Nedham implied that the king was a tyrant who might be tried for his prosecution of the war: see ibid., no. 129 (4–11 May 1646), p. 1110 (BL, E 337/9).

61. For example, see *England's Miserie and Remedie* (1645), printed in David Wootton (ed.), *Divine Right and Democracy: An Anthology of Political Writing in Stuart England* (Harmondsworth, 1986), pp. 276–82; *Mercurius Britanicus*, no. 108 (1–8 December 1645), p. 954 (BL, E 311/11); *Vox Plebis* ([19 November] 1646), esp. pp. 3, 58, 66, 68 (BL, E 362/20).

62. A number of the most important Leveller pamphlets – including the *Agreements of the People* – are printed in Haller and Davies, *Leveller Tracts*, and Don M. Wolfe (ed.), *Leveller Manifestoes of the Puritan Revolution* (repr. London and New York, 1967).

63. For example, see F. D. Dow, *Radicalism in the English Revolution, 1640–60* (Oxford, 1985), pp. 31–2; Ann Hughes, 'Gender and Politics in Leveller Literature', in Susan D. Amussen and Mark A. Kishlansky (eds), *Political Culture and Cultural Politics in Early Modern England: Essays Presented to David Underdown* (Manchester, 1995), pp. 162–88, at p. 167.

64. For example, see Diana Parkin-Speer, 'John Lilburne: a Revolutionary Interprets Statutes and Common Law Due Process', *Law and History Review*, 1 (1983), 276–96; Andrew Sharp, 'John Lilburne and the Long Parliament's *Book of Declarations*: a Radical's Exploitation of the Words of Authorities', *History of Political Thought*, 9 (1988), 19–44; idem, 'John Lilburne's Discourse of Law', *Political Science*, 40 (1988), 18–33.

65. For example, see William Walwyn, *A Still and Soft Voice from the Scriptures* (1647), printed in Jack R. McMichael and Barbara Taft (eds), *The Writings of William Walwyn* (Athens, GA, 1989), pp. 265–74, esp. pp. 269–70; [idem], *The Vanitie of the Present Churches* (1649), printed in Haller and Davies, *Leveller Tracts*, pp. 252–75, esp. pp. 263 and 272. See also J. C. Davis, 'The Levellers and Christianity', reprinted in Peter Gaunt (ed.), *The English Civil War: The Essential Readings* (Oxford, 2000), pp. 279–302, esp. pp. 287–9.

66. [Richard Overton], *A Remonstrance of Many Thousand Citizens* (1646), printed in Wolfe, *Leveller Manifestoes*, pp. 113–30, quotation at p. 114. See also Richard A. Gleissner, 'The Levellers and Natural Law Theory: the Putney Debates of 1647', *Journal of British Studies*, 20 (1980), 74–89; Scott, *England's Troubles*, pp. 235, 283–9.

67. Mark Kishlansky, 'Ideology and Politics in the Parliamentary Armies, 1645–9', in Morrill, *Reactions to the English Civil War*, pp. 163–83.

68. For example, see Patricia Crawford, 'Charles Stuart, That Man of Blood', reprinted in Gaunt, *English Civil War*, pp. 303–23; Blair Worden, 'Oliver Cromwell and the Sin of Achan', reprinted in David Smith (ed.), *Cromwell and the Interregnum: The Essential Readings* (Oxford, 2003), pp. 39–59. Cf. Kishlansky, 'Ideology and Politics', p. 182.

69. Abbott, *Cromwell*, I, 699.

70. *A Remonstrance of His Excellency Thomas Lord Fairfax, Lord Generall of the Parliaments Forces, and of the Generall Councell of Officers* (1648), printed in *The Parliamentary or Constitutional History of England*, 24 vols (2nd edn, 1761–3), XVIII, 161–238.

71. *CJ*, VI, 111.

72. 'The Act Abolishing the Office of King' and 'An Act Abolishing the House of Lords', both printed in Gardiner, *Constitutional Documents*, at pp. 384–7 and pp. 387–8 respectively, quotation at pp. 385 and 387.

73. Davis, 'Religion and the Struggle for Freedom'; idem, 'Against Formality: One Aspect of the English Revolution', *Transactions of the Royal Historical Society*, 6th series, 3 (1993), 265–88; Scott, *England's Troubles*, esp. Chs 10 and 11.

74. On this point, see Keith Lindley, 'London and Popular Freedom in the 1640s', in R. C. Richardson and G. M. Ridden (eds), *Freedom and the English Revolution: Essays in History and Literature* (Manchester, 1986), pp. 111–50, at pp. 116–18, 125, 128–31.

75. Christopher Hill, 'From Lollards to Levellers', repr. in *The Collected Essays of Christopher Hill, Volume 2: Religion and Politics in Seventeenth-Century England* (Brighton, 1986), pp. 89–116.

76. Scott, *England's Troubles*, pp. 229–30, 249–53. Scott's approach is, of course, heavily reliant on the earlier work of J. C. Davis.

77. For all his criticism of Hill for accepting the 'sectarianization' of Civil War radicalism – its categorization by hostile contemporaries into specific movements with pejorative titles ('Leveller', 'Digger' etc.) and a fixed membership – Scott's alternative account of a succession of 'moments of radical expectation' revolves around the identical titles: see *England's Troubles*, Chs 10 and 11, esp. pp. 237–9, 253–65.

78. For example, see J. C. Davis, 'Cromwell's Religion', in John Morrill (ed.), *Oliver Cromwell and the English Revolution* (Harlow, 1990), pp. 181–208.

79. For example, see Edward Barber, *A Small Treatise of Baptisme, or, Dipping* (n.p., 1642) (BL, E 143/17); William Kiffin, *A Briefe Remonstrance of the Reasons and Grounds of Those People Commonly Called Anabaptists, for Their Separation, &c.* ([26 July] 1645) (BL, E 293/31); J. F. McGregor, 'The Baptists: Font of All Heresy', in idem and B. Reay (eds), *Radical Religion in the English Revolution* (Oxford, 1984), pp. 23–63, esp. pp. 41, 43, 45, 57, 63; Hughes, 'Religion, 1640–60', p. 365.

80. McGregor, 'Baptists', pp. 29 and 33.

81. Ibid., p. 33.

82. John Morrill, 'The Church in England, 1642–9', reprinted in his *Nature of the English Revolution*, pp. 148–75, at pp. 149–50 and n. 4. Given the growth of the Quakers – who numbered perhaps as many as 40,000 by the early 1660s – that figure is too low for the period after 1654: see Barry Reay, *The Quakers and the English Revolution* (Hounslow, 1985), p. 27.

83. For example, see John Taylor, *A Swarme of Sectaries, and Schismatiques* (n.p., [June] 1641) (BL, E 158/1); *The Discovery of a Swarm of Separatists* ([19 December] 1641) (BL, E 180/25).

84. Dow, *Radicalism in the English Revolution*, pp. 65 and 70; Hughes, 'Religion, 1640–60', pp. 363–4.

85. Thomas Edwards, *Reasons Against the Independant* [*sic*] *Government of Particular Congregations* ([August] 1641) (BL, E 167/16); idem, *Antapologia: or, A Full Answer to the 'Apologeticall Narration'* ([13 July] 1644) (BL, E 1/1); idem, *Gangraena*, 3 Parts (1646; repr. Exeter, 1998).

86. For example, see P[aul] H[obson], *A Discoverie of Truth* (n.p., [17 April] 1645) (BL, E 1176/1); [William Erbery], *Nor Truth, Nor Errour, Nor Day, Nor Night; But in the Evening There shall be Light* ([26 August] 1647) (BL, E 404/20); [John Knowles], *A Friendly Debate on a Weighty Subject* ([16 August] 1650) (BL, E 609/16); Gentles, *New Model Army*, pp. 88–91.

87. Gentles, *New Model Army*, pp. 113–15.

88. For example, see Edwards, *Gangraena*, Part III, 17–18, 253, 266; Gentles, *New Model Army*, p. 109.

89. On the latter point, see also the comments of Stephen Porter in *Destruction in the English Civil Wars* (Stroud, 1994), pp. 130–2. By contrast, although Spraggon's recent study acknowledges the limitations of hostile sources, it draws on them extensively for actual *evidence* of iconoclastic destruction: see Julie Spraggon, *Puritan Iconoclasm during the English Civil War* (Woodbridge, 2003), pp. 200–16.

90. For example, see *Mercurius Aulicus*, 38th week (15–21 September 1644), p. 1168, printed in Thomas, *English Revolution III, Newsbooks 1, Oxford Royalists*, III, [261]–[268], at p. [262]; Gentles, *New Model Army*, pp. 109–10. Various interpretations have been offered for this violence: the over-zealous execution of Parliament's ordinances; the mindless destruction of war; and the vandalism of symbols representative of the enemy. It is perhaps even possible that radical ideologies – such as religious scepticism or the denunciation of the established Church as anti-Christian – provided a source of motivation. For a recent discussion, see Spraggon, *Puritan Iconoclasm*, p. 201.

91. Abbott, *Writings and Speeches*, I, 360 and 638 for the quotation; Gentles, *New Model Army*, pp. 91–4.

92. Anthony Milton, 'Anglicanism and Royalism in the 1640s', pp. 61–81.

93. William Allen, *A Faithful Memorial of that Remarkable Meeting of Many Officers of the Army in England, at Windsor Castle, in the Year 1648* (1659), printed in Sir Walter Scott (ed.), *Somers Tracts*, 13 vols (2nd edn, 1809–15), VI, 498–504, quotation at p. 501; Scott, *England's Troubles*, pp. 153, 155–7.

94. For a more extensive comparison of the Diggers and Fifth Monarchists, which has influenced the following discussion, see Bernard Capp, 'Transplanting the Holy Land: Diggers, Fifth Monarchists and the New Israel', in R. N. Swanson (ed.), *The Holy Land, Holy Lands and Christian History: Studies in Church History*, 36 (2000), 288–98.

95. Gerrard Winstanley, *The New Law of Righteousnes* (1649), printed in George H. Sabine (ed.), *The Works of Gerrard Winstanley: With an Appendix of Documents Relating to the Digger Movement* (New York, 1941), pp. 149–244, quotation at p. 190.

96. For example, see Gerrard Winstanley et al., *The True Levellers Standard Advanced* (1649), printed in Sabine, *Works of Winstanley*, pp. 247–66, at p. 254; Gerrard Winstanley, *A New-Yeers Gift for the Parliament and Armie* (1650), printed in Sabine, *Works of Winstanley*, pp. 353–96, at p. 385.

97. For example, see Winstanley et al., *True Levellers Standard*, in Sabine, *Works of Winstanley*, pp. 259–60; Gerrard Winstanley et al., *An Appeal to the House of Commons* (1649), printed in Sabine, *Works of Winstanley*, pp. 301–12. On the historical myth of the Norman Yoke, see Christopher Hill, 'The Norman Yoke', in his *Puritanism and Revolution: Studies in Interpretation of the English Revolution of the Seventeenth Century* (1958), pp. 50–122.

98. For example, see Winstanley, *New Law of Righteousnes*, in Sabine, *Works of Winstanley*, pp. 160–3; Winstanley et al., *True Levellers Standard*, in Sabine, *Works of Winstanley*, pp. 253 and 257; Winstanley, *New-Yeers Gift*, in Sabine, *Works of Winstanley*, pp. 385–6; Capp, 'Transplanting the Holy Land', pp. 288–9, 292.

99. David W. Mulder, in *The Alchemy of Revolution: Gerrard Winstanley's Occultism and Seventeenth-Century English Communism* (New York, 1990), Appendix A, lists the names of just ninety men that he was able to associate with the Digging experiments.

100. For a recent discussion, see Davis, 'Political Thought', in Coward, *Companion to Stuart Britain*, pp. 380 and 387.

101. For example, see Hill, *World Turned Upside Down*, Chs 1 and 7.

102. For example, see Winstanley, *New-Yeers Gift*, in Sabine, *Works of Winstanley*, pp. 353–74, 384–6; Winstanley et al., *Appeal to the Commons*, in Sabine, *Works of Winstanley*, pp. 303–5.

103. For example, see William Aspinwall, *An Explication and Application of the Seventh Ch. of Daniel* ([20 March] 1654) (BL, E 732/2); John Spittlehouse, *Rome Ruin'd by Whitehall, or, The Papall Crown demolisht* ([31 December] 1649), p. 342 (BL, E 586/2); B. S. Capp, *The Fifth Monarchy Men: A Study in Seventeenth-Century English Millenarianism* (1972), pp. 14, 20, 144.

104. For example, see *Certain Qvaeres Humbly Presented in Way of Petition* ([19 February] 1649) (BL, E 544/5); *A Model of a New Representative, Now Under Consideration* ([15 October] 1651) (BL, E 643/13); John Rogers, *To His Excellency the Lord Generall Cromwell. A Few Proposals, Relating to Civil Government* (n.p., [27 April] 1653) (BL, 669 f. 16/97).

105. Capp, *Fifth Monarchy Men*, pp. 41, 56–75, 81–2, 117–18, 131–2, 199–200.

106. For example, see Francis Cornwell, *Gospel-Repentance Floweth from Faith, and Attendeth a Justified Person all his dayes* ([23 August] 1645) (BL, E 1176/2); James Brown, *Scripture-Redemption Freed From Men's Restrictions* (1653 [wrongly dated 1673]) (Wing, B 5023).

107. For example, see John Traske, *The True Gospel Vindicated, from the Reproach of a New Gospel* (n.p., 1636) (STC, 24178.5); N[icholas] Couling, *The Saints Perfect in This Life, or Never* ([7 November] 1647) (BL, E 1183/7); David R. Como, *Blown by the Spirit: Puritanism and the Emergence of an Antinomian Underground in Pre-Civil War England* (Stanford, CA, 2004); Gertrude Huehns, *Antinomianism in English History: With Special Reference to the Period 1640–60* (1951).

108. For example, see Abiezer Coppe, *A Fiery Flying Roll* and *A Second Fiery Flying Roule* (1650), printed in Nigel Smith (ed.), *A Collection of Ranter Writings from the Seventeenth Century* (1983), pp. 80–116, at pp. 81–3; Nigel Smith, 'The Charge of Atheism and the Language of Radical Speculation, 1640–60', in Michael Hunter and David Wootton (eds), *Atheism from the Reformation to the Enlightenment* (Oxford, 1992), pp. 131–58, at p. 158.

109. Laurence Clarkson, *A Single Eye All Light, No Darkness* (1650), printed in Smith, *Collection of Ranter Writings*, pp. 161–75, quotation at p. 169.

110. Reay, *Quakers and the English Revolution*, p. 27; Norman Penney (ed.), *The Journal of George Fox*, 2 vols (Cambridge, 1911), II, 149.

111. B. Reay, 'Quakerism and Society', in McGregor and Reay, *Radical Religion*, pp. 141–64, at pp. 146 and 147; Smith, 'Charge of Atheism', pp. 136–7, 141; Hughes, 'Religion, 1640–60', p. 350.

112. Reay, 'Quakerism and Society', pp. 146, 149–50, 157, 158–9, 162; Benjamin Nicholson, *A Blast from the Lord* ([12 March] 1653), pp. 5, 7, 10–11 (BL, E 689/19); G[eorge] F[ox], *A Declaration Against all Profession and Professors* ([28 August] 1654), pp. 11–12, 13 (BL, E 809/8).

113. Reay, 'Quakerism and Society', pp. 150 and 151.

114. Coppe, *Fiery Flying Roll* and *Second Fiery Flying Roule*.

115. For example, see Daniel Featley, *The Dippers Dipt* ([7 February] 1645), sigs. C2v–C3v (BL, E 268/11); William Prynne, *A Fresh Discovery of Some Prodigious New Wandering-Blasing-Stars, & Firebrands, Stiling Themselves New-Lights, Firing Our Church and State into New Combustions* ([24 July] 1645), sig. A2v (BL, E 261/5); James Howell, *Instructions and Directions for Forren Travell* ([7 May] 1650), pp. 121–3 (BL, E 1374/2).

116. Although it has been shown that at least one established farmer joined the Digging experiments in Surrey: see John Gurney, 'Gerrard Winstanley and the Digger Movement in Walton and Cobham', *Historical Journal*, 37 (1994), 775–802, at pp. 791 and 793.

117. Barry Reay, 'Radicalism and Religion in the English Revolution: an Introduction', in McGregor and Reay, *Radical Religion*, pp. 1–21, at pp. 18–19. On the degree of formal education experienced by a number of the most notorious sectaries of the Civil War, see Nicholas McDowell, *The English Radical Imagination: Culture, Religion and Revolution, 1630–60* (Oxford, 2003), Ch. 1.

118. Reay, 'Radicalism and Religion', p. 18.

119. Here I am positing a much broader, and chronologically longer, 'radical moment' than that advocated by Jonathan Scott: see his 'Radicalism and Restoration', p. 455. Cf. Anthony Milton's characterization of the 1630s as a 'Laudian moment' within the Caroline Church, in 'The Creation of Laudianism: A New Approach', in Thomas Cogswell, Richard Cust and Peter Lake (eds), *Politics, Religion and Popularity in Early Stuart England: Essays in Honour of Conrad Russell* (Cambridge, 2002), pp. 162–84, esp. p. 183, and 'Anglicanism and Royalism in the 1640s' in this volume, pp. 61–81.

Suggestions for Further Reading

Introduction: High Roads and Blind Alleys – The English Civil War and its Historiography   *John Adamson*

Perhaps the best starting-point for the student of the English Civil War's historiography is Keith Thomas's essay 'When the Lid came off England', published in *The New York Review of Books*, 27 May 2004 (and conveniently available on-line). This is a review of Austin Woolrych's *Britain in Revolution, 1625–60* (Oxford, 2004), itself perhaps the best written and most judicious (at times, overly so) general history of the whole period currently in print. But Thomas's essay also offers a clear-sighted, indeed Olympian, survey of roughly the last hundred years of writing on the 1640s and 1650s, assessing the strengths and weaknesses of the successive waves of historical interpretation. Also helpful in providing a set of intellectual bearings is R. C. Richardson, *The Debate on the English Revolution* (3rd edn, Manchester, 1999), which places modern controversies in a historical context that extends back to the Restoration, and is also alive to the (often unacknowledged) strength of European influences, particularly from the German-speaking world, on the writing of British history.

When it comes to the evaluation of the Revisionists' contribution, both individual and collective, the most illuminating and thought-provoking commentaries have come from Peter Lake. His essay 'Retrospective: Wentworth's Political World in Revisionist and Post-Revisionist Perspective', in J. F. Merritt (ed.), *The Political World of Thomas Wentworth, Earl of Strafford, 1621–41* (Cambridge, 1996), has an intellectual breadth that extends far beyond the promise of its title. It should be read in conjunction with another essay, of equal acuity, which he co-wrote with Richard Cust and Thomas Cogswell, 'Revisionism and its Legacies: the Work of Conrad Russell', in Cogswell, Cust and Lake (eds), *Politics, Religion and Popularity in Early Stuart England: Essays in Honour of Conrad Russell* (Cambridge, 2002). For a view of the limitations inherent in, as well as the virtues of, the 'New British History', see John Adamson, 'The English Context of the British Civil Wars', *History Today*, 48 (1998) no. 11 – reprinted in Stanley Carpenter (ed.), *The English Civil War* (Aldershot and Burlington, VT, 2007). Further insights are to be gained from Ronald Hutton, 'Revisionism in Britain', in Michael Bentley (ed.), *Companion to Historiography* (1997). One of the earliest attempts to place the contribution of the Revisionists in a broader historical context is J. C. D. Clark, *Revolution and Rebellion: State and Society in England in the Seventeenth and Eighteenth Centuries* (Cambridge, 1986), though the effectiveness of its argument is at times compromised by its satirical and overly combative tone. A more immediate sense of how some of the 1970s Revisionists sought to break free from what they rightly saw as the 'determinism' of the past, and to create new methodologies that might effect this, is to be gleaned from the Preface to Mark Kishlansky's *The Rise of the New Model Army* (Cambridge, 1979), pp. ix–xiii.

If the significance and limitations of historiographical developments in recent decades are to be fully appreciated, however, one needs to extend the field of vision back to the advent of 'professional history' in Civil-War studies in the last quarter of the nineteenth century – and to the writings of Samuel Rawson Gardiner in particular. For the broader context, an outstanding general introduction is provided by John Burrow's *A History of Histories* (2007), especially Chapters 25 (on 'The German Influence') and 26 (on 'The Twentieth Century'). There are two distinguished studies of nineteenth and early twentieth-century treatments of the 'Stuart inheritance': Timothy Lang's *The Victorians and the Stuart Heritage: Interpretations of a Discordant Past* (Cambridge, 1995), and, pre-eminently, Blair Worden's *Roundhead Reputations: The English Civil War and the Passions of Posterity* (2001). We still lack a good study of the treatment – or, as it has more often been, non-treatment – of royalist reputations over a similarly expansive period. For Gardiner, who is long overdue a scholarly biography, there is Lang's Chapter 4 ('Samuel Rawson Gardiner and the Search for a National Consensus'), and John Adamson, 'Eminent Victorians: S. R. Gardiner and the Liberal as Hero', *Historical Journal*, 33 (1990), 641–57.

The impact of Jürgen Habermas's theories of the 'public sphere' on Civil-War historiography has yet to receive proper critical scrutiny. In the meantime, however, there are a number of pertinent reflections in the essay by Peter Lake and Steven Pincus, 'Rethinking the Public Sphere in Early Modern England', and in Pincus's essay, 'The State and Civil Society in Early Modern England: Capitalism, Causation and Habermas's Bourgeois Public Sphere', both in Peter Lake and Steven Pincus (eds), *The Politics of the Public Sphere in Early Modern England* (Manchester, 2007).

1　Rethinking Royalist Politics, 1642–9　　*David Scott*

There is still no dedicated volume on the king's party from the Personal Rule to the Restoration. Malcolm Smuts and Barbara Donagan have contributed useful essays on the emergence of the royalist party and the varieties of Royalism respectively, in Jason McElligott and David L. Smith (eds), *Royalists and Royalism during the English Civil Wars* (Cambridge, 2007). For the latest, and the most scholarly, biography of the king, see Richard Cust, *Charles I: A Political Life* (2005). The best study of the queen to date is that of Michelle White, *Henrietta Maria and the English Civil Wars* (Aldershot, 2006). There have been recent biographies of the royalist grandees and rivals, Prince Rupert and George Lord Goring – Charles Spencer, *Prince Rupert, the Last Cavalier* (2007); and Florene S. Memegalos, *George Goring (1608–57): Caroline Courtier and Royalist General* (Aldershot, 2007). The royalist (as well as parliamentarian) experience of war is discussed in Barbara Donagan, *War in England, 1642–9* (Oxford, 2008). And for a royalist take on a key battle of the English Civil War, see Ian Roy and Joyce Macadam, 'Why did Rupert Fight at Marston Moor?', *Journal of the Society for Army Historical Research* (forthcoming). For an insightful account of royalist political and military strategy in 1648–9, see Sean Kelsey, '"A No-King, or a New": Royalists and the Succession, 1648–9', in McElligott and Smith (eds), *Royalists and Royalism*; and '"King of the Sea": the Prince of Wales and the Stuart Monarchy, 1648–9', *History*, 92 (2007), 428–48.

Geoffrey Smith, *The Cavaliers in Exile, 1640–60* (Basingstoke, 2003), examines the royalist exile communities on the Continent, a subject that will also be covered in a collection of essays on Royalism in the 1650s, edited by Jason McElligott (Cambridge, forthcoming). For a stimulating new approach to royalist political thought during the Civil War, see Chapter 4 of Sarah Mortimer's forthcoming book, *Reason and Religion in the English Revolution: The Challenge of Socinianism* (Cambridge, forthcoming). The best treatment of popular Royalism remains that of Mark Stoyle in his *Loyalty and Locality: Popular Allegiance in Devon during the English Civil War* (Exeter, 1994). For the 'ethnic' dimension to Civil-War Royalism, see his *Soldiers and Strangers: An Ethnic History of the English Civil War* (New Haven and London, 2005). Aspects of Irish Royalism and the career of Ireland's greatest Royalist, the Marquess of Ormond, are dealt with in two recent collected editions: Toby Barnard and Jane Fenlon (eds), *The Dukes of Ormonde, 1610–1745* (Woodbridge, 2000); Micheál Ó Siochrú (ed.), *Kingdoms in Crisis: Ireland in the 1640s – Essays in Honour of Dónal Cregan* (Dublin, 2001). There is a dearth of work on the king's supporters in Scotland, although interesting light is thrown on the origins of the Scottish royalist party in John Adamson, *The Noble Revolt: The Overthrow of Charles I* (2007).

2 Anglicanism and Royalism in the 1640s   *Anthony Milton*

While Anglican royalist writings of the 1650s have received some good, if patchy, coverage, those of the 1640s remain virtual *terra incognita* for historians. They feature intermittently in the literary scholar Robert Wilcher's helpful *The Writing of Royalism, 1628–60* (Cambridge, 2001). Useful studies of individual authors are P. W. Thomas, *Sir John Berkenhead, 1617–79* (Oxford, 1969), and Anthony Milton, *Laudian and Royalist Polemic in Seventeenth-Century England: The Career and Writings of Peter Heylyn* (Manchester, 2007). J. W. Packer's study of Henry Hammond – *The Transformation of Anglicanism, 1643–60* (Manchester, 1969) – misses a great deal in its portrait of this central figure, and we still lack up-to-date studies of those royalist clergymen who did not take the trouble to write in verse.

There is some important material on 1640s debates among Royalists on religious matters in Peter King, 'The Episcopate during the Civil Wars, 1642–9', *English Historical Review*, 83 (1968), and Martin Dzelzainis, '"Undoubted Realities": Clarendon on Sacrilege', *Historical Journal* 33 (1990). Some clerical authors, such as Bramhall, Williams and Ferne, find their way into accounts of royalist political writings – e.g. John Sanderson, *'But the People's Creatures': The Philosophical Basis of the English Civil War* (Manchester, 1989); David L. Smith, *Constitutional Royalism and the Search for Settlement, c.1640–49* (Cambridge, 1994), and J. W. Daly, 'John Bramhall and the Theoretical Problems of Royalist Moderation', *Journal of British Studies*, 21 (1971) – but the religious dimensions and agenda of their work are usually passed over. For an alternative reading of 'conformist' anti-Laudianism in the early 1640s to the one presented in this essay, see Judith Maltby, *Prayer Book and People in Elizabethan and Early Stuart England* (Cambridge, 1998). W. A. Shaw, *A History of the English Church during the Civil Wars and under the Commonwealth, 1640–60*, 2 vols (1900), is showing its age, but is still indispensable on institutional religious developments in the 1640s.

On the practicalities of parish Anglicanism in the 1640s, John Morrill, 'The Church in England, 1642–9', in Morrill (ed.), *Reactions to the English Civil War* (1982), is fundamental, although its main emphasis is on forms of non-compliance. See also Mark Stoyle, *Loyalty and Locality: Popular Allegiance in Devon during the English Civil War* (Exeter, 1994), esp. pp. 204–55. There is also important material on the impact of the early 1640s on parish religion and the extent of conservative resistance in David Cressy, *England on Edge: Crisis and Revolution, 1640–42* (Oxford, 2006), which was published after this article was written; see also Julie Spraggon, *Puritan Iconoclasm during the English Civil War* (Woodbridge, 2003), Keith Lindley, *Politics and Religion in Civil War London* (Aldershot, 1997); and Ian Green, 'The Persecution of "Scandalous" and "Malignant" Parish Clergy during the English Civil War', *English Historical Review*, 94 (1979).

3   Perceptions of Parliament: Factions and 'The Public'
Jason Peacey

Historians have long been interested in the impact of the Civil Wars on the working of Parliament, on the emergence and operation of factions, and on the importance of executive committees: see, in particular, Lotte Glow, 'Political Affiliations in the House of Commons after Pym's Death', *Bulletin of the Institute of Historical Research*, 38 (1965); Lotte Glow, 'The Manipulation of Committees in the Long Parliament, 1641–2', *Journal of British Studies*, 5 (1965); Lotte Mulligan (*née* Glow), 'Peace Negotiations, Politics and the Committee of Both Kingdoms, 1644–6', *Historical Journal*, 12 (1969); Valerie Pearl, 'The "Royal Independents" and the English Civil War', *Transactions of the Royal Historical Society*, 5th series, 18 (1968). Such scholarship reached its peak in the work of David Underdown, in particular his *Pride's Purge: Politics in the Puritan Revolution* (Oxford, 1971). For a very long time, however, such studies were preoccupied with the first half of the 1640s, and with the possibility of detecting the existence of a 'middle' group that was distinct from the 'war' and 'peace' parties: see, for example, J. H. Hexter, *The Reign of King Pym* (Cambridge, 1941); Valerie Pearl, 'Oliver St John and the "Middle Group" in the Long Parliament: August 1643–May 1644', *English Historical Review*, 81 (1966). Recent scholarship has persuasively challenged the existence of such a group, especially David Scott, *Politics and War in the Three Stuart Kingdoms, 1637–49* (Basingstoke, 2003).

The most ambitious and challenging recent work, however, has emerged from the contrasting methodologies and interpretations of Mark Kishlansky and John Adamson, and the debate that has ensued: see Mark Kishlansky, 'The Emergence of Adversary Politics in the Long Parliament', *Journal of Modern History*, 49 (1977); Mark Kishlansky, *The Rise of the New Model Army* (Cambridge,

1979); John Adamson, 'The Peerage in Politics, 1645–9' (unpublished PhD dissertation, University of Cambridge, 1986); John Adamson, 'The English Nobility and the Projected Settlement of 1647', *Historical Journal*, 30 (1987); John Adamson, 'Parliamentary Management, Men of Business and the House of Lords, 1640–49', in Clive Jones (ed.), *A Pillar of the Constitution* (1989); Mark Kishlansky, 'Saye What?', *Historical Journal*, 33 (1990); John Adamson, 'Politics and the Nobility in Civil-War England', *Historical Journal*, 34 (1991); Mark Kishlansky, 'Saye No More', *Journal of British Studies*, 30 (1991); John Adamson, 'Of Armies and Architecture: the Employments of Robert Scawen', in Ian Gentles, John Morrill and Blair Worden (eds), *Soldiers, Writers and Statesmen of the English Revolution* (Cambridge, 1998); John Adamson, 'The Triumph of Oligarchy', in Chris Kyle and Jason Peacey (eds), *Parliament at Work: Parliamentary Committees, Political Power and Public Access in Early Modern England* (Woodbridge, 2002). Recent years have also witnessed the attempt to demonstrate the importance of print culture to the political world of parliamentary élites, and to show that contemporary pamphlets and newspapers are much more important for understanding national politics than previous generations of 'revisionist' scholars had been prepared to concede: Jason Peacey, *Politicians and Pamphleteers: Propaganda during the English Civil Wars and Interregnum* (Aldershot, 2004); Jason Peacey, 'Politics, Accounts and Propaganda in the Long Parliament', in Kyle and Peacey (eds), *Parliament at Work*. This present chapter represents part of a broader project to explore the role which print played in changing public perceptions of parliamentary politics and procedures, and in fostering participation in order to exploit Parliament's potential and rectify its 'corruption'. For important evidence regarding the ways in which contemporary observers reflected upon political factionalism, see Keith Lindley and David Scott (eds), *The Journal of Thomas Juxon, 1644–7* (Camden Society, 1999).

4 The Baronial Context of the Irish Civil War   *Jane Ohlmeyer*

For a general introduction, see Jane Ohlmeyer, '"Civilizinge of those Rude Partes": Colonization within Britain and Ireland, 1580s–1640s', in Nicholas Canny (ed.), *Oxford History of the British Empire*, I (Oxford, 1998). Aside from studies of individual powerbrokers, the Irish 'barons' have received little scholarly attention. For the Irish peerage, see G. R. Mayes, 'The Early Stuarts and the Irish Peerage', *English Historical Review*, 73 (1958), and Francis G. James, *The Lords of the Ascendancy: The Irish House of Lords and its Members, 1600–1800* (Dublin, 1995). For studies of individual lords, see Toby Barnard and Jane Fenlon (eds), *The Dukes of Ormond, 1610–1745* (2000); Nicholas Canny, *The Upstart Earl: A Study of the Social and Mental World of Richard Boyle, First Earl of Cork, 1566–1643* (Cambridge, 1982); Patrick Little, *Lord Broghill and the Cromwellian Union with Ireland and Scotland* (Woodbridge, 2004); and Jane Ohlmeyer, *Civil War and Restoration in the Three Stuart Kingdoms: The Political Career of Randal MacDonnell First Marquis of Antrim (1609–83)* (Cambridge, 1993). Also see Patrick Little, 'The Earl of Cork and the Fall of the Earl of Strafford', *Historical Journal*, 39 (1996); and his '"Blood and Friendship": The Earl of Essex's Protection of the Earl of

Clanricarde's Interests, 1641–6', *English Historical Review*, 112 (1997); and 'The Geraldine Ambitions of the First Earl of Cork', *Irish Historical Studies*, 23 (2002).

For a basic overview of Civil-War Ireland, see Jane Ohlmeyer, 'The Wars of Religion, 1603–60', in Thomas Bartlett and Keith Jeffery (eds), *A Military History of Ireland* (Cambridge, 1996). For more detailed studies, see Robert Armstrong, *Protestant War: The 'British' of Ireland and the Wars of the Three Kingdoms* (Manchester, 2005); Pádraig Lenihan, *Confederate Catholics at War, 1642–9* (Cork, 2000); Micheál Ó Siochrú, *Confederate Ireland, 1642–9: A Constitutional and Political Analysis* (Dublin, 1999); and Tadhg Ó hAnnracháin, *Catholic Reformation in Ireland: The Mission of Rinuccini, 1645–9* (Oxford, 2002).

For the wider 'British' context, see John Adamson, 'The Baronial Context of the English Civil War', *Transactions of the Royal Historical Society*, 5th ser., 40 (1990); Keith M. Brown, *Noble Society in Scotland: Wealth, Family and Culture, from Reformation to Revolution* (Edinburgh, 2000); Barbara Donagan, 'Halcyon Days and the Literature of War: England's Military Education before 1642', *Past and Present*, 147 (1995); and her 'Atrocity, War Crime and Treason in the English Civil War', *American Historical Review*, 99 (1994), and also her 'Codes and Conduct in the English Civil War', *Past and Present*, 118 (1988). See also Roger Manning, *Swordsmen: The Martial Ethos in the Three Kingdoms* (Oxford, 2003), and his *An Apprenticeship in Arms: The Origins of the British Army, 1585–1702* (Oxford, 2006). For a continental perspective, see H. M. Scott (ed.), *The European Nobilities in the Seventeenth and Eighteenth Centuries*, I, *Western Europe* (1995).

5   The 'Scottish Moment', 1638–45   *Allan I. Macinnes*

This chapter draws heavily on Allan I. Macinnes, *The British Revolution, 1629–60* (Basingstoke, 2005). There are three highly commended English counterpoints: Austin Woolrych, *Britain in Revolution, 1625–60* (Oxford, 2002), and David Scott, *Politics and War in the Three Stuart Kingdoms, 1637–49* (Basingstoke, 2004), both dealing with the general history of the 1640s; and finally, John Adamson, *The Noble Revolt: The Overthrow of Charles I* (2007), which makes a particularly outstanding contribution to the build-up to civil war. Collectively, they surpass the revisionism of Conrad Russell, *The Fall of the British Monarchies* (Oxford, 1991) and the musings of John Morrill, *The Nature of the English Revolution* (1993). Scottish historians have tended to treat wider British ramifications as incidental rather than integral to their narrative, as is the case in David Stevenson's two works on the Covenanting Movement, *The Scottish Revolution, 1637–44: The Triumph of the Covenanters* (Newton Abbot, 1973), and *Revolution and Counter-Revolution in Scotland, 1644–51* (1977), albeit this tendency is less pronounced, if more peripheral, in his *Scottish Covenanters and Irish Confederates* (Belfast, 1981). However, a new generation of Scottish historians has opened up diplomatic history and international relations in a more thorough and archivally competent manner than their English counterparts, who still tend to rely on State Papers Foreign; see Jonathan Scott, *England's Troubles: Seventeenth-Century English Political Instability in a European Context* (Cambridge, 2000). Although France remains grossly underworked, particularly outstanding work on the Scandinavian connection has been accomplished by

Steve Murdoch in his *Britain, Denmark–Norway and the House of Stuart, 1603–60* (East Linton, 2000) and Alexia Grosjean, *An Unofficial Alliance: Scotland and Sweden, 1569–1654* (Leiden, 2003). John R. Young has dealt incisively and perceptively with Covenanter foreign policy, 'The Scottish Parliament and European Diplomacy 1641–7: The Palatinate, the Dutch Republic and Sweden', in Steve Murdoch (ed.), *Scotland and the Thirty Years' War, 1618–48* (Leiden, 2001). Young has also edited a fine, non-Anglocentric set of essays, *Celtic Dimensions of the British Civil Wars* (Edinburgh, 1997). The most germane and stimulating Irish contributions have been provided by Michael Perceval-Maxwell, *The Outbreak of the Irish Rebellion of 1641* (Montreal, 1994); by Nicholas Canny, *Making Ireland British, 1580–1650* (Oxford, 2001); and especially by Robert Armstrong, 'Ormond, the Confederate Peace Talks and Protestant Royalism', in Micheál Ó Siochrú (ed.), *Kingdoms in Crisis: Ireland in the 1640s* (Dublin, 2000).

6   Centre and Locality in Civil-War England   *Clive Holmes*

Further reading should begin with the study of which this essay has been an extended reflection and critique, John Morrill's *Revolt in the Provinces: The People of England and the Tragedies of War, 1630–48* (1998). Michael Braddick's overview, *God's Fury, England's Fire: A New History of the English Civil Wars* (2008), particularly Chapters 6, 7, and 15, follows his more detailed studies on finance and administration in demonstrating the subtle interweaving of local and national concerns.

The localist interpretation was first advanced by Alan Everitt, *The Community of Kent and the Great Rebellion, 1640–60* (Leicester, 1966). This trail-blazing work inspired a series of local studies of the Civil War; but not all could match its sensitivity and elegant presentation, and some were narrow in focus and antiquarian in their methodology. County-focused studies that display, to a greater or lesser extent, an awareness of the broader issues, and provide lively discussion, include John Morrill, *Cheshire, 1630–60: County Government and Society during the English Revolution* (Oxford, 1977); David Underdown, *Somerset in the Civil War and Interregnum* (Newton Abbot, 1973); Anthony Fletcher, *A County Community in Peace and War: Sussex, 1600–60* (1975); and Ann Hughes, *Politics, Society and Civil War in Warwickshire, 1620–60* (Cambridge, 1987). Hughes's study of Warwickshire and the study of one of the major Parliamentary armies – Clive Holmes, *The Eastern Association in the English Civil War* (Cambridge, 1974) – expressed doubts about the viability of the localist model advanced by Everitt. Both authors then, independently, wrote articles that challenged the conceptual foundations of 'county community' history: Clive Holmes, 'The County Community in Stuart Historiography', *Journal of British Studies*, 19 (1980), 54–73; and Ann Hughes, 'Warwickshire on the Eve of the Civil War: A County Community?', *Midland History*, 7 (1982), 42–72. In a later article, Hughes moved beyond criticism to suggest an important model of the relationships with the localities which were developed by both royalist and parliamentarian administrations: see her 'The King, the Parliament and the Localities during the English Civil War', *Journal of British Studies*, 24 (1985), 236–63.

David Underdown had always been suspicious of the emphasis that 'county community' historians, and their critics, had placed on local élites – to the exclusion of the populace. In *Revel, Riot and Rebellion: Popular Politics and Popular Culture in England* (Oxford, 1985), he insisted on the centrality of popular engagement, and, more daringly, sought to locate popular commitment, royalist or parliamentarian, in particular local ecological patterns and the social structures and cultures dependent on these; his arguments have been questioned and modified by John Morrill in 'The Ecology of Allegiance in the English Civil War' – Chapter 11 of his collection of essays, *The Nature of the English Revolution* (1993) – and in a detailed case study by Mark Stoyle, *Loyalty and Locality: Popular Allegiance in Devon during the English Civil War* (Exeter, 1994). Since Underdown wrote, there have been a series of works that emphasize popular politics and the mobilization of the people for war in a way that emphasizes the dialogic relationship between centre and periphery and between social groups. John Walter's detailed study of Essex, *Understanding Popular Violence in the English Revolution: The Colchester Plunderers* (Cambridge, 1999), though narrow in its specific focus, is very convincing in its account of the power of parliamentary propaganda to mobilize sections of the populace. A. J. Hopper, *'The Readiness of the People': The Formation and Emergence of the Army of the Fairfaxes, 1642–3* (York, 1997), is good on the religious motivations of the Parliamentarians from the Yorkshire clothing towns. David Cressy, *England on Edge: Crisis and Revolution, 1640–42* (Oxford, 2006), focuses on the period immediately before the outbreak of the war; it is particularly strong on the mobilization of opinion through the eruption of printed works, and on disputes over religion at the level of the parish.

The impact of the war in terms of taxation, conscription, and local government in the counties is the theme of Martyn Bennett's rich *The Civil Wars Experienced: Britain and Ireland, 1638–61* (2000), which is at its best on the period of the first Civil War. Philip Tennant's *Edgehill and Beyond: The People's War in the South Midlands, 1642–45* (Stroud, 1992) is an exceptional micro-study of the organization of the war and its costs on a much-disputed area.

Everitt's sympathetic, almost romanticized, account of Kent as a county community has been followed, if with a slightly different spin, by one contemporary scholar. In his *Soldiers and Strangers: An Ethnic History of the Civil War* (New Haven, CT, 2006), Mark Stoyle has argued – not wholly convincingly – for the cultural divergence and isolation of Cornwall as a distinctive *ethnic* community.

7   The Politics of Fairfax's Army, 1645–9   *Ian Gentles*

For a general introduction to the military history of the 1640s, the reader is referred to Ian Gentles, *The English Revolution and the Wars in the Three Kingdoms, 1638–52* (Harlow, 2007), and to the excellent survey by David Scott, *Politics and War in the Three Stuart Kingdoms, 1637–49* (Basingstoke, 2004). The New Model Army's role in the politics of the 1640s has long been a subject of intense debate. The fullest account of its role is Ian Gentles, *The New Model Army in England, Ireland and Scotland, 1645–53* (Oxford, 1992). However, for the first three years of the army's existence, a contrasting account, arguing that its creation was the last instance of 'consensus politics' in the 1640s, is provided in Mark Kishlansky, *The Rise of the New Model Army* (Cambridge, 1979).

Particular episodes in the army's eventful history have been the subject of a series of monographs and articles. The political circumstances which gave rise to the army's creation are treated in Gentles, *The New Model Army*, while an alternative view is provided in John Adamson, 'The Triumph of Oligarchy: The Management of the War and the Committee of Both Kingdoms, 1644–5', in Chris R. Kyle and Jason Peacey (eds), *Parliament at Work: Parliamentary Committees, Political Power and Public Access in Early Modern England* (Woodbridge, 2002). Among the advances of the last decade has been the recovery of the role of the Army Committee, the bicameral body – long overlooked by earlier historians – with responsibility for Parliament's relations (financial, logistical, and political) with the New Model, in John Adamson, 'Of Armies and Architecture: The Employments of Robert Scawen', in Ian Gentles, John Morrill and Blair Worden (eds), *Soldiers, Writers and Statesmen of the English Revolution* (Cambridge, 1998).

Outstanding in its detailed treatment of the politics of the army's officer corps, although possibly intimidating to the non-specialist, is Austin Woolrych's *Soldiers and Statesmen: The General Council of the Army and its Debates, 1647–8* (Oxford, 1987). The extent of Leveller influence within the army – particularly in relation to army-sponsored plans for the post-war settlement of the kingdom – is treated in the series of essays edited by Michael Mendle (ed.), *The Putney Debates of 1647: The Army, the Levellers and the English State* (Cambridge, 2001), especially in the chapters by John Morrill and Philip Baker, 'The Case of the Armie Truly Restated' (with which my chapter in this present volume takes issue), and in Ian Gentles, 'The *Agreements of the People* and their Political Contexts', in the same volume. A contrasting perspective is presented in Mark Kishlansky, 'The Army and the Levellers: the Roads to Putney', *Historical Journal*, 22 (1979). The New Model's codes of conduct (particularly its controversial brutality in the aftermath of the siege of Colchester in 1648) are considered in the latter part of Barbara Donagan's *War in England, 1642–9* (Oxford, 2008), a work which appeared after this essay was in press.

With regard to the king's trial and the regicide, David Underdown's *Pride's Purge: Politics in the Puritan Revolution* (Oxford, 1971), retains an enduring value. The subject has inspired some of the most interesting recent work on the army's role in the king's execution and the 'revolution' of the winter of 1648–9. Some of this work is collected in Jason Peacey (ed.), *The Regicides and the Execution of Charles I* (Basingstoke, 2001), particularly the essays by John Morrill and Philip Baker (on Cromwell), John Adamson (on the major influence on the outcome of the trial exerted by contemporary events in Ireland), and Sean Kelsey (on the trial's staging). These should be supplemented by Kelsey's essays, 'The Trial of Charles I', *English Historical Review*, 118 (2003), and his 'Politics and Procedure in the Trial of Charles I', *Law and History Review*, 22 (2004).

On Cromwell, the outstanding contributions of the last two decades have come from Blair Worden, in particular his 'Oliver Cromwell and the Sin of Achan', in Derek Beales and Geoffrey Best (ed.), *History, Society and the Churches: Essays in Honour of Owen Chadwick* (Cambridge, 1985), which illuminates Cromwell's attitudes towards his involvement in the execution of the king.

8   Rhetoric, Reality and the Varieties of Civil War
   Radicalism   *Philip Baker*

There are surprisingly few studies that aim to provide a comprehensive account of Civil-War radicalism, and, arguably, those that have done so have been too restrictive in their outlook. The classic account remains Christopher Hill's *The World Turned Upside Down: Radical Ideas during the English Revolution* (1972), and his approach may be usefully compared and contrasted with that of Jonathan Scott in *England's Troubles: Seventeenth-Century English Political Instability in European Context* (Cambridge, 2000), Part II. A useful, shorter summary, which adopts a slightly wider perspective, is F. D. Dow, *Radicalism in the English Revolution, 1640–60* (Oxford, 1985).

The question of how historians should approach the subject of radicalism has proved to be a major topic in recent scholarship. For the argument that the category has no validity at all in its application to periods before the nineteenth century, see Conal Condren, *The Language of Politics in Seventeenth-Century England* (Basingstoke, 1994), Chapter 5. By contrast, J. C. Davis's article 'Radicalism in a Traditional Society: The Evaluation of Radical Thought in the English Commonwealth, 1649–60', *History of Political Thought*, 3 (1982), advocates a functional approach to its identification. Since my own chapter was written, Davis has significantly revised his views in 'Reassessing Radicalism in a Traditional Society: Two Questions', in Glenn Burgess and Matthew Festenstein (eds), *English Radicalism, 1550–1850* (Cambridge, 2007); in the same volume, Glenn Burgess's chapter on 'Radicalism and the English Revolution' adopts a perspective that is more squarely in the traditional 'revisionist' mould. Burgess is also among the contributors to the recent Cromohs Virtual Seminar discussion on 'Radicalism and the English Revolution', where methodological concerns are often to the fore: see http://www.cromohs.unifi.it/seminari/index.html

For contrasting perspectives on the origins of Civil-War radicalism, see Christopher Hill, 'From Lollards to Levellers', reprinted in *The Collected Essays of Christopher Hill*, II, *Religion and Politics in Seventeenth-Century England* (Brighton, 1986); Murray Tolmie, *The Triumph of the Saints: The Separate Churches of London, 1616–49* (Cambridge, 1977); David Wootton, 'From Rebellion to Revolution: The Crisis of the Winter of 1642–3 and the Origins of Civil-War Radicalism', reprinted in Richard Cust and Ann Hughes (eds), *The English Civil War* (1997); relevant work that has appeared since this chapter was written includes David R. Como, 'Secret Printing, the Crisis of 1640 and the Origins of Civil-War Radicalism', *Past and Present*, 196 (2007); and John Adamson, *The Noble Revolt: The Overthrow of Charles I* (2007), Chs 1 and 2.

The work of J. C. Davis has been hugely influential in emphasizing the religious ambitions of Civil-War radicalism: see his 'The Levellers and Christianity', reprinted in Peter Gaunt (ed.), *The English Civil War: The Essential Readings* (Oxford, 2000); and David's 'Religion and the Struggle for Freedom in the English Revolution', *Historical Journal*, 35 (1992); and the same author's 'Against Formality: One Aspect of the English Revolution', *Transactions of the Royal Historical Society*, 6th series, 3 (1993). The religious interpretation of radicalism is taken to its apogee in Scott, *England's Troubles*, Part II.

For the political and constitutional radicalism of the early 1640s, see Adamson, *Noble Revolt*, and David Cressy, *England on Edge: Crisis and Revolution, 1640–42* (Oxford, 2006). For the later period, see the contrasting approach of Jonathan Scott in *Commonwealth Principles: Republican Writing of the English Revolution* (Cambridge, 2004). J. C. Davis, 'Reassessing Radicalism', in Burgess and Festenstein, *English Radicalism*, sets out a framework with which future research in this area will have to engage.

Turning to the more traditional radical groups and movements, although there are no up-to-date studies of the Levellers, Joseph Frank, *The Levellers, a History of the Writings of Three Seventeenth-Century Social Democrats: John Lilburne, Richard Overton, William Walwyn* (reprinted New York, 1969) may be usefully compared with H. N. Brailsford, *The Levellers and the English Revolution*, ed. Christopher Hill (2nd edn, Nottingham, 1983). The classic revisionist work in this field is J. C. Davis, *Fear, Myth and History: The Ranters and the Historians* (Cambridge, 1986); the ensuing debate may be followed in J. F. McGregor, Bernard Capp, Nigel Smith, B. J. Gibbons, and J. C. Davis, 'Fear, Myth and Furore: Reappraising the Ranters', *Past and Present*, 140 (1993). Among the recent studies in this area are Kate Peters, *Print Culture and the Early Quakers* (Cambridge, 2005); Stephen Wright, *The Early English Baptists, 1603–49* (Woodbridge, 2006), and John Gurney, *Brave Community: The Digger Movement in the English Revolution* (Manchester and New York, 2007). Finally, the story of one of the most remarkable lives of the Civil-War period is reconstructed by Ariel Hessayon in *Gold Tried in the Fire: The Prophet Theaurajohn Tany and the English Revolution* (Aldershot, 2007).

Index

Note: Peers are indexed by the titles by which they were most commonly known during the 1640s and by which they are most frequently referred to in the text. Later promotions (as, for example, Sir Edward Hyde's to the earldom of Clarendon) are noted in parenthesis. Scottish peerages are indicated thus [S]; Irish peerages [I]; noblemen not otherwise specified are members of the English peerage.